A GUIDE TO
Help Desk Technology, Tools & Techniques

Dione McBride

COURSE TECHNOLOGY

Thomson Learning™

ONE MAIN STREET, CAMBRIDGE, MA 02142

Australia • Canada • Denmark • Japan • Mexico • New Zealand • Philippines
Puerto Rico • Singapore • South Africa • Spain • United Kingdom • United States

A Guide to Help Desk Technology, Tools & Techniques is published by Course Technology.

Associate Publisher:	Kristen Duerr
Product Manager:	Margarita Donovan
Production Editor:	Ellina Beletsky, Anne Valsangiacomo
Development Editor/Project Manager:	Robin Romer
Associate Product Manager:	Tricia Coia
Composition House:	GEX, Inc.
Text Designer:	GEX, Inc.
Cover Designer:	Efrat Reis
Associate Marketing Manager:	Meagan Walsh

Photo Credits: Figure 2-9: 3Com and the 3Com logo are registered trademarks. Palm V™ and the Palm V™ logo are trademarks of Palm Computing, Inc., 3Com Corporation and its subsidiaries. Figure 7-2: CRYPTO-BOX dongles. Courtesy of MARX Software Security. All rights reserved. Figure 8-4: Courtesy of Spectrum Corporation. Figure 8-5: Courtesy of Sensormatic Electronics. Figure 9-2: Courtesy of Siemens Business Communications Systems. Figure 10-2: Courtesy of Mode Office Systems. Figure 10-3: Courtesy of Mode Office Systems. Figure 10-4: Courtesy of Invincible Office Furniture. Figure 10-5: Courtesy of Hello Direct, Inc. Figure 10-6: Courtesy of Plantronics. Figure 10-7: Courtesy of Plantronics. Figure 10-8: Courtesy of Hello Direct, Inc. Figure 10-9: Courtesy of Hello Direct, Inc. Figure 11-2: Courtesy of Hewlett-Packard Company.

Disclaimer

For more information, contact Course Technology, One Main Street, Cambridge, MA 02142; or find us on the World Wide Web at *www.course.com*.

For permission to use material from this text or product, contact us by
- Web: www.thomsonrights.com
- Phone: 1-800-730-2214
- Fax: 1-800-730-2215

ISBN 0-7600-7151-9

Printed in Canada

1 2 3 4 5 WC 02 01 00 99

BRIEF CONTENTS

TABLE OF CONTENTS

Preface

I have worked in Information Technology for many years. In that time, I've been a programmer, trainer, support analyst, technical specialist, system administrator, consultant, and even a support manager. Of all the careers in IT, I believe the hardest working and most underappreciated employees work in support organizations. Support staff have a lot of challenges, yet many seem to really enjoy helping others demystify computers and software. There's no question that support staff work harder than some, but, in the last few years, software vendors have created tools that actually help support staff work smarter rather than harder.

When I began consulting a few years ago, helping service and support groups implement this new technology, I noticed something interesting: A company would evaluate and select a technology, spend weeks setting up the software and training staff members, and begin using it, only to report a few months later that they still could not deliver better customer service! In many cases, the support software actually seemed to get in the way of support staff as they tried to do their jobs. When I investigated further, I realized that the problem wasn't with badly designed software; it was actually a communication gap. There were a lot of books telling managers how to set up help desks, how to hire and train staff, how to evaluate tools, and what managers should measure to demonstrate the help desk's value to the company. At the same time, there were *no* books that explained basic support processes to support staff. Managers frequently assumed staff members understood their full role in the organization and how they were expected to benefit by these tools, while support staff were busy just trying to handle all the calls. Nothing existed to "connect the dots" for support staff so they could understand what they were really expected to do.

This book is designed to give you insight into the business processes behind support and how to apply the appropriate technology to those processes. It's exciting when someone not only enjoys learning a new tool, but also makes the connection between technology and its practical use every day. Technology plays a big part in our business careers and as you learn to apply tools to business processes, these skills will help you—whatever profession you choose.

THE INTENDED AUDIENCE

This book is primarily intended for three kinds of readers:

♦ Readers who are considering career opportunities in a support group and who want a better understanding of some of the available technology that is used in a support environment.

♦ Readers who are interested in gaining hands-on experience with some of the technologies and tools they can reasonably expect to find working in a support group.

♦ Business professionals who want to introduce themselves to the additional terminology and technology specific to the support environment.

THE CUSTOMER SUPPORT CURRICULUM

This book is designed for a customer service course in any Help Desk, Support, or Call Center Curriculum. It is intended for use in community and technical college courses, such as Support Technologies, IT Service Tools, Call Center Technology, and Help Desk Tools. These courses are part of rapidly emerging programs in schools that aim to prepare students for the following degrees or certificates: IT Support Professional; Call Center Support; Computer Help Desk Specialist; Computer Technical Support; Help Desk Support Specialist; Computer User Support; and Computer Support Technician. As the need for and quantity of help desks grows, companies are turning to community and technical colleges to prepare their graduates to fill existing entry-level positions in the technical support industry.

Increasingly, organizations that are committed to providing high-quality technical customer support view their help desks as a strategic asset. Whether the help desk provides support to the customers who use their company's products or the help desk provides technical support to the company's employees, the need for qualified help desk professionals is on the rise.

THE APPROACH

The text is designed to provide an in-depth look at the processes and associated technologies available for customer service and support in a technical or nontechnical environment. The first two chapters are devoted to a discussion about support group processes. Chapters 3 through 7 explore the support tools most commonly used by businesses for internal and external, technical or nontechnical support. The author's goal was to relate specific processes and procedures to specific software features and to explain how readers can directly benefit from these technologies. Chapters 8 and 9 are devoted to generic tools that can be used in any area of business, as well as by support staff. Chapter 10 is devoted to self-management skills, including minimizing stress and maximizing the general work environment. Chapter 11 covers tools typically used by experienced IT support staff. The last two chapters address some of the most recent technologies and trends in support. An understanding of this book provides more than just support skills; many of these technologies are used by IT staff members and other business users.

The end-of-chapter activities are specifically designed to develop the reader's knowledge and help the reader assimilate the chapter concepts. They encourage the reader to expand his or her knowledge through self-study and to practice support skills. The reader can work with classmates in project groups or teams, similar to working in a support environment. Many of the end-of-chapter activities encourage readers to utilize current information resources and solve problems—skills that are essential in the dynamic support industry.

ASSUMED KNOWLEDGE

This book assumes that readers have experience in the following areas, either through course work, work experience, or life experience:

♦ Basic help desk concepts

♦ Basic computer concepts or computer literacy

♦ Internet and World Wide Web concepts

OVERVIEW OF THIS BOOK

The outline of this book takes a detailed look at the technology available for customer support. Each chapter explores in detail a set of processes and a group of related technologies that enforce those processes to deliver better customer support, and includes additional tips and techniques support staff can use to get the most out of those tools.

Chapter 1, Introduction to Help Desk Tools, Technology and Techniques, explores the role technology plays in support, how processes and procedures are used in business, and the types of support tools available to enforce procedures. It also explains how support tools evolve and discusses several reasons why tools won't work in some environments.

Chapter 2, Support Environments and Processes, focuses on basic help desk concepts, internal and external support processes, and core activities all support staff complete. An understanding of support environments and support processes is considered the most basic and important skill that support staff must possess.

Chapter 3, Common Support Software Tools and Features, discusses general support tool features. The chapter begins with a discussion that identifies basic software features, such as user interfaces and required fields. This leads to a review of the types of information collected in support and how support staff use that information as they work with customers.

Chapter 4, Support Performance and Reporting Tools, explains why managers collect and measure support performance. This chapter also reviews the most common support measurements and the tools managers and staff use for reporting. The chapter also discusses commercial software, as well as simple tools that can be used to create reports and graphs.

Chapter 5, Call Management Software, describes the support functions that are common to internal and external support groups. This chapter focuses on identifying some of the most common tools and their vendors. It also explains how to evaluate call management software and how a support group begins using a new support application.

Chapter 6, Problem Resolution Software, presents a methodical approach support providers can use to navigate the problem-solving process and collect knowledge to solve later problems. It discusses how the information support providers capture can be used to prevent problems and minimize their impact. This chapter also includes different approaches to organizing knowledge.

Chapter 7, Asset and Change Management Tools, discusses the fact that internal support groups play an important part in managing a company's assets. This chapter discusses software tools used to track and repair computers and well-known vendors of these software tools. It also explains how technology changes affect a support group directly, by causing more problems.

Chapter 8, Alerts and Notification Tools for Support, deals with establishing service agreements with customers. Special tools help staff and managers make sure that support services are timely. Before customers complain, additional tools notify managers to reassign work or investigate further. This chapter also discusses notification tools that inform customers of support progress.

Chapter 9, Telephone-based Technology, reviews the most commonly used method of communicating with customers and special technologies that can streamline or reduce workload for support staff. This chapter also highlights technologies that many people use now (or will use more frequently in the future) to conduct personal business.

Chapter 10, Office Space in the Support Environment, explains how the office environment affects employee efficiency and health. Some technologies improve shared areas for all employees, while low-tech tools can be used on a personal level. This chapter includes many tips to prevent injury and reduce stress, which eventually helps improve interactions with customers. This information is valuable for everyone who works in a business environment.

Chapter 11, Additional Level Two and Level Three Support Tools, discusses tools frequently used by higher-level support groups, and other IT professionals to manage computer systems for all company users. This chapter explains the performance measurements that are important, as well as specific tools used by this group of support staff.

Chapter 12, Self-Help Tools, describes the benefits of customer self-service for customers as well as support staff. This chapter lists the types of tools available for self-service. Readers will also learn about challenges to implementing self-service tools.

Chapter 13, Service Technology Trends and Career Resources, explains some of the most recently developing changes in IT and support. Some important trends developing include a greater emphasis on professional certification as well as a continuous need for ongoing training and education. This chapter includes many tips on how to enhance both an IT and support career and lists several additional resources for professional development.

Appendix A, Web Site Resources, lists the URLs for many companies and resources related to support. Because of the dynamic nature of the Web, URLs may change frequently. These links are also available on the Course Technology Web site at *www.course.com*, where they will be updated.

FEATURES

To aid you in fully understanding customer service and technical support concepts, there are several features in this book designed to improve its pedagogical value.

- ◆ **Chapter Objectives:** Each chapter in this book begins with a list of the important concepts to be mastered within the chapter. This list provides you with a quick reference to the contents of the chapter as well as a useful study aid.

- ◆ **Illustrations and Tables:** Illustrations help you visualize common components and relationships. Tables list conceptual items and examples in a visual and readable format.

- ◆ **Notes:** Chapters contain Notes designed to expand on the section topic, including resource references, additional examples, and ancillary information.

- ◆ **Tips:** Chapters contain Tips designed to provide you with practical advice and proven strategies related to the concept being discussed.

- ◆ **Bullet Figures:** Selected figures contain bullets that summarize important points to give you an overview of upcoming discussion topics and to help you review material as you skim through the chapter.

- ◆ **Close Ups:** Close Ups provide more in-depth looks at particular topics or present detailed real-life examples. Taken from actual experiences, Close Ups confirm the importance of the topic and often contribute related information to give you additional insight into real-world applications of the topics.

- ◆ **Chapter Summaries:** Each chapter's text is followed by a summary of chapter concepts. These summaries provide a helpful way to recap and revisit the ideas covered in each chapter.

- ◆ **Key Terms:** Each chapter contains a listing of the boldfaced terms introduced in the chapter and their concise definitions. This listing provides a convenient way to review the vocabulary you have learned.

- ◆ **Review Questions:** End-of-chapter assessment begins with a set of 25 to 30 review questions that reinforce the main ideas introduced in each chapter. These questions ensure that you have mastered the concepts and have understood the information you have learned.

 Hands-on Projects: Although it is important to understand the concepts behind help desk topics, no amount of theory can improve on real-world experience. To this end, along with conceptual explanations, each chapter provides Hands-on Projects related to each major topic aimed at providing you with practical experience. Some of these include researching information from people, printed resources, and the Internet, as well as installing and using some of the technologies discussed. Because the Hands-on Projects ask you to go beyond the boundaries of the text itself, they provide you with practice implementing support skills in real-world and help desk situations. The Hands-on Projects were written for Office 2000. However, the instructions for Office 97 can be found at www.course.com.

 Case Projects: There are three Case Projects at the end of each chapter. These cases are designed to help you apply what you have learned to business situations much like those you can expect to encounter in a technical support position. They give you the opportunity to independently synthesize and evaluate information, examine potential solutions, and make recommendations, much as you would in an actual business situation.

TEACHING TOOLS

The following supplemental materials are available when this book is used in a classroom setting. All of the teaching tools available with this book are provided to the instructor on a single CD-ROM.

Electronic Instructor's Manual. The Instructor's Manual that accompanies this textbook includes:

- ◆ Additional instructional material to assist in class preparation, including suggestions for lecture topics.

- ◆ Solutions to all end-of-chapter materials, including the Review Questions, and when applicable, Hands-on Projects, and Case Projects.

Course Test Manager 1.2. Accompanying this book is a powerful assessment tool known as the Course Test Manager. Designed by Course Technology, this cutting-edge Windows-based testing software helps instructors design and administer tests and pre-tests. In addition to being able to generate tests that can be printed and administered, this full-featured program also has an online testing component that allows students to take tests at the computer and have their exams graded automatically.

Data Files. Data files that contain some of the data for the end of chapter exercises are provided on the Instructor's Resource Kit and at www.course.com. Additional files needed to complete some of the end of chapter projects are located on web sites detailed in those projects.

Solution Files. Solution files contain a possible solution to the programs students are asked to create or modify in the end of chapter projects.

PowerPoint presentations. This book comes with Microsoft PowerPoint slides for each chapter. These are included as a teaching aid for classroom presentation, to make available to students on the network for chapter review, or to be printed for classroom distribution. Instructors can feel free to add their own slides for additional topics they introduce to the class.

ACKNOWLEDGMENTS

It's only appropriate in a book about a team-oriented subject such as customer support that I take time to thank the great people I worked with as *we* created this book. I would have continued to find excuses for not writing my first book if I hadn't seen a message Kristen Duerr, Associate Publisher, posted at the SSPA Web page that said, "Want to be an author?…" Thanks Kristen, for taking a chance. Thanks also to Margarita Donovan, Product Manager, who offered time and time again to pick up administrative tasks for me, and to Ellina Beletsky and Anne Valsangiacomo, Production Editors, who monitored my travel itineraries closely and made sure that copyedits and page proofs found me each week, wherever I happened to be working. Additional thanks go to Tricia Coia, Associate Product Manager. Also thanks to Abby Reip, AR Photo Research, for her persistence in tracking down photographs and permissions.

I want to express my sincere appreciation to the professional educators who reviewed the draft manuscript and make great suggestions. They contributed to the completeness and content of the book as a learning tool, and the comments they forwarded when *they* learned something new and useful were very encouraging. The reviewers are: Carol Okolica, Dowling College; John Ross, Fox Valley Technical College; and Michael Walters, Laramie County Community College.

I also want to thank the professionals who made contributions to the Close Up sections that offer "real-world" views of topics in several chapters: John Ragsdale, Clarify, Inc.; Scott Pickard, Norfolk Southern Railroad; Herb Haynes, Cambridge Technology Partners; Francoise Tourniaire, FT Works; Jerome Atchison, Consultant; Mark Thistlewaite, Consultant; Donna Hall, The RightAnswer; and Phil Verghis, Akamai, Inc.

Robin Romer served as developmental editor for this book and her contributions to this effort were invaluable to me. First and foremost, her editorial efforts certainly helped me communicate my thoughts more clearly. I was continuously surprised at how seemingly small questions about technology from Robin resulted in answers that significantly enhanced the text. I also remember several exchanges that started with "I don't know how to explain…" that she managed to sort through and clarify. Robin also served as project manager for the book—while I was running all over the country with my day job, Robin kept track of all the players, all the pieces, and all the deadlines, and helped me prioritize my efforts when time was short. We had many Sunday afternoon and late-night phone calls, and I really appreciate the extra efforts she took to work through these challenges.

Thanks also, to my family, friends, and coworkers who knew just when to ask, "How's the book coming?" Of course, there is a special thanks to my husband, Coy, who spent many weekends and evenings alone while I worked in my office. Even though I bit your head off every time you interrupted me at work, I'm glad you kept coming back! I love you very much and would not have been able to complete this project without your support.

Finally, thanks to the many support professionals I've worked with and learned from over the years. As my customers and my students, you continue to challenge me to stay one step ahead of you, to find new ways to explain things and new ways to apply technology. As we continue to move from a product-oriented to a service-oriented culture, I'm very pleased to see the support profession is finally being recognized as an important contributor to a company's success. I hope that this book will help you find more ways to be successful.

Dione McBride
Forney, Texas

1

INTRODUCTION TO HELP DESK TOOLS, TECHNOLOGY, AND TECHNIQUES

In this chapter you will learn:
- The role automation tools play in support
- How processes and procedures are used in support
- The primary types of support tools available
- How support tools evolve
- The reasons why tools don't work in a particular environment
- How constant change affects support and support technology

Technology includes the development of new materials, equipment, and processes to improve goods and service production. The most common examples of technology in business today are telephone systems and computer hardware and software. As technology continues to grow and change, almost overnight, the role of technical support also changes. In the 1980s, companies established **information centers**, places within companies where employees could receive training and help in using personal computers. These departments evolved and expanded in the 1990s, becoming help desks. A **help desk** is a single point of contact within a company for managing customer problems and requests, and providing solution-oriented support services.

Because only a few people used services from information centers and help desks, these special-purpose departments did not exist in every company. As desktop computers and software replaced typewriters and adding machines, not only were more employees affected by technology, but also they were expected to use the technology to solve specific business problems. No matter what the support groups of the next decade are called, understanding computers and software programs is no longer enough for support staff—they must also know how to apply technology to a growing number of business problems.

Customer support centers and help desks are now important parts of the corporate structure. New companies set up finance departments, marketing departments, and technology support centers because all businesses need those important services to compete in the modern business environment. Just like finance and marketing department managers, support managers need to meet departmental and organizational goals and objectives. At the same time, they must hold down costs as well as hire staff who understand technology and can communicate effectively with both technically- and non-technically-oriented computer users. If successful, their workload increases—as the support group becomes known for providing good services, more people call for support. Support managers turn to technology that is specific to the support industry as a way to meet these challenges. Like other managers, support managers use technology to automate tasks, work more efficiently with fewer staff, and provide higher-quality services.

UNDERSTANDING THE ROLE TECHNOLOGY PLAYS IN SUPPORT

Technology affects support in several ways. First, the increase in the amount of technology has required a corresponding increase in the amount of technical support available. Second, the complexity and interconnection among technology components has increased the need for support. Third, businesses depend on technology to collect and manage information, which enables them to react to trends more quickly. These three aspects all work together.

Today, more technology exists, increasing the need for groups and people to support it. Technology changes have produced better and more complex electronics that are used both at home and in business, including computers, telecommunications systems, network devices, and software. Very specific electronic devices, such as computers and computer software, have many pieces, or components, to understand. A large part of the support business exists just to manage these increasingly complex technical components.

The relationship among technologies makes the support business more difficult. Individual components, such as computers and telephones, work together to form large, interrelated technical systems. These systems produce mountains of information that companies depend upon to compete and grow. The amount of information grows so large that people can no longer manage it without technology. Companies rely on technology to manage information and to identify other data to collect. As illustrated in Figure 1-1, the cycle of technology and information becomes interdependent. More people are involved in using technology to understand business information than there were ten years ago.

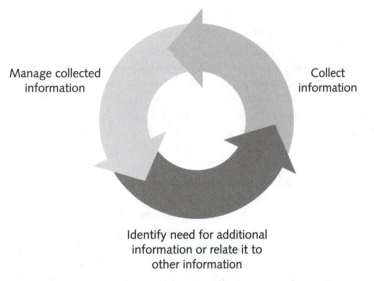

Manage collected
information

Collect
information

Identify need for additional
information or relate it to
other information

Figure 1-1   Information management requires technology

Fortunately, technology can also be used to improve support. Companies use technology to manage specific activities, and specialized technologies exist that enable support groups provide services more efficiently. The support business relies on technology to address two specific challenges: resources and services.

A **support group** is the department within a company that focuses on product support or other support services. Support groups are also known as support organizations, support businesses, call centers, help desks, and contact centers.

Resource Challenges

Support resources are the company employees who provide support services. When hiring new support staff, support managers look for people with good technical, problem-solving, and communication skills. **Technical skills** refers to basic computer literacy and experience with specific hardware or software. Support staff also need good problem-solving skills (although the need for problem-solving skills is not unique to technology issues). Good problem solvers can break down problems into tasks and test solutions based on their knowledge of the problem area. Technical knowledge provides a starting point for solving technology problems and verifying results. Staff members can develop their technical skills through work experience or formal training.

Support resources, the people who deliver support services, are also known as support staff, support employees, support analysts, and support professionals.

Support resources who don't already have enough technical work experience, will need additional technical training. The support manager must balance the cost of training a current staff member against the loss of that staff member's time away from support activities. Fortunately, many technical subjects are closely related. For example, once someone learns how to use Microsoft Office, he or she often finds it easier to learn other Microsoft software applications, which use many of the same or similar features and menu commands. Because computer technologies are closely related, it may be easier or faster to train technical employees than to hire new people who already have these skills but have little experience in the company's environment.

Adult learning theory indicates that adults learn by associating new knowledge to existing knowledge. Thus, unlike business training, it is easier and faster to provide technical training staff. For example, someone who knows Microsoft Word will find it simpler to learn Microsoft Excel because a large part of the application is the same. However, business training frequently includes process and procedure changes, which are problematic because they introduce a change in the environment rather than because they are technically difficult. Companies often find it easier to bring in trained individuals because they have no emotion about the change.

In addition to technical skills, the entire support staff needs good communication skills. **Communication skills** are those skills that enable a person to interact effectively with others by speaking, listening, and writing. They must answer questions in terms everyone understands, translating technical jargon into business terms. Listening skills are important because most support occurs over the telephone. Support staff must interpret callers' needs entirely from their words, without relying on body language, which provides added communication signals. Support staff must also be patient communicators and never appear to talk down to the people they help. Although a technical "know-it-all" may be able to answer any question, the way the answer is delivered determines whether the customer accepts the answer. A **customer** is a person who buys products and services from a company, or an employee within a company who relies upon another group for services.

Customers, the people who receive support services, are also called users, callers, computer users, and business staff.

A fortunate support manager has staff with a good balance of technical and communication skills. Support employees who have that balance are often in short supply, and many support groups have more calls than they can handle. Unfortunately, the challenge of answering telephones, working with upset callers, and trying to stay current on technical skills can cause high levels of stress. There can be a high rate of employee turnover, as members of the support staff leave the support group to take less stressful jobs. Staff members can easily transfer their technical skills to other departments, where working with upset callers on the telephone is not their primary responsibility.

WHAT CAUSED THE IT STAFFING SHORTAGE?

Most business managers know there is a chronic shortage of IT personnel. A government report by the Office of Technology Policy, titled "America's New Deficit: The Shortage of Information Technology Workers," published in October, 1997, estimated that the United States would require more than 1 million IT workers by 2005. There are about 200,000 IT positions that are unfilled in the United States. Studies by market research groups conclude that 25% of all IT executives report they cannot find skilled, trained computer workers and 20% agree that their current IT staff are untrained. What caused this shortage and what are the consequences if the shortage isn't addressed?

The growth of personal computers in the 1980s may have started the shortage. Armed with spreadsheet and database programs such as Lotus 1-2-3 and dBase, computer users discovered they no longer needed to wait for the mainframe programmers to develop or change software for them. They could take mainframe data, manipulate it themselves, and solve their business problems more quickly. As corporate downsizing set in and more computer users were expected to use PC tools, IT organizations reduced programming staff. There were thousands of unemployed programmers and programming looked like a bad profession in the early 1990s. The number of students graduating in the United States with bachelor's degrees in computer science declined by 42% between 1986 and 1995.

While the number of graduates decreased, the demand started to grow again. Client/server technology took off in the early 1990s, requiring professionals who could build and maintain networked and distributed computing systems. Web development is a huge new incentive, as businesses try to enhance their systems to stay ahead of their competitors.

Those students who were learning to program studied COBOL as companies began to identify legacy applications that needed to be changed to handle the year 2000 correctly. (Many COBOL programmers came out of retirement just to handle the Y2K problems.) As the end of the 1900s grew nearer, more IT staff were dedicated to this specific problem area and away from emerging technologies like Web development and eCommerce.

The growth of IT in foreign countries has also affected the U.S. IT labor support. Foreign graduates frequently stayed in this country to gain work experience and because there were more IT jobs in the United States. Now, they are more likely to return home after graduation because countries such as India, Japan, Hong Kong, Indonesia, and Africa are experiencing their own IT growth.

Part of the shortage may result from our own definition of a "technology" worker. Most technology degrees focus on the "sciences" of programming and database design. There are more college programs for a Bachelor of Science degree in computer science than there are degrees for general computer technology. Many IT workers already have degrees in mathematics, physics, and chemistry and find it difficult to return to school once they have family responsibilites. Other IT workers have practical experience from military or clerical work. Despite their lack of computer science training, they are successful IT professionals. They acquired their skills solving real-world problems. However, the practice of requiring computer science degrees ensures that three-fourths of the potential workforce is automatically removed from job consideration.

The expectation of a workforce shortage also increases the impact of the shortage. Specialized talent can easily find jobs with better pay, benefits, and working conditions. Workers also have less commitment to their employers. As a result, companies are looking to non-traditional sources for IT workers. In addition to four-year universities, companies will do more hiring among students from community colleges and third-party IT education companies and will do more in-house training as well as retraining people who are changing careers to enter IT. In other words, companies will have to grow their own IT staff.

Service Challenges

Useful labor that does not result in a physical product, but that helps customers maximize the use of products, is called **professional services**. Companies offer customers more products or services in an attempt to remain competitive. Support groups also add new services to streamline common tasks within the company. For example, many companies have a Facilities Management Department that specializes in assigning and setting up offices for new employees, determining when more office space is needed, and reassigning offices. When a manager hires a new employee, that manager contacts the Facilities Management Department for an office assignment. The manager will also request services from other internal departments, including:

- Asking the Telecommunications Department to deliver a new telephone, make sure telephone wiring is correct, and assign an extension
- Ordering a PC and software through the Purchasing Department
- Requesting that a network administrator assign the new employee a login ID and password on the network

The manager coordinates these activities to ensure that everything is completed in time for the employee's first day of work. Unfortunately, coordinating these tasks may prevent the manager from completing business tasks that only a manager can complete.

An internal support group may eventually handle these requests and other requests. The manager saves time by calling one telephone number to schedule activities with several departments. This leaves the manager more time to concentrate on management tasks.

The support group supervises the outstanding activities for the manager until they are all complete.

Customers who buy products or services outside the company also prefer to call a single telephone number to report problems, request information, or order new products. A single contact number is more convenient, and customers work with a single person, who will act on their behalf within the company to solve the problem.

The greatest service challenge is coordinating people who provide the support to customers. As support groups expand the number of services and problems they address, they must track more tasks and schedule people from different areas of the company. The requirements for each activity and the basic information needed to schedule each task might be very different. The support group can use special software to understand the tasks required, track resources that can solve problems, make sure resources are scheduled, and ensure that all tasks are completed on time.

Importance of Goals, Processes, and Procedures

The support group depends on its resources to deliver services and accomplish its goals. Every company uses a **mission statement**, which is a broad, general written guideline that defines the company's vision and specific goals. For example, if a lot of competition exists in a particular business area, a mission may be to become the best-known company in that area. Mission statements explain why a company exists and help employees work toward shared goals. Technical support groups use mission statements to define how they will help the company achieve its goals. A sample support mission statement is shown in Figure 1-2. When goals are clearly defined, both computer users and support staff understand what services are expected.

> The mission of the support center is to help all company employees make the best use of computer technology to support business activities. We will strive to provide timely response and consistent answers through teamwork and knowledge sharing.

Figure 1-2   Sample support group mission statement

Goals are further refined into different processes and procedures so that the support staff knows how to accomplish the goals. A **process** is a list of the input, the interrelated work activities (or tasks), and the desired output needed to accomplish a goal. A **procedure** is a detailed, step-by-step set of instructions that describes who will perform the tasks in a process, along with how and when those tasks will be performed.

TIP People frequently use the terms *process* and *procedure* interchangeably. However, procedures are actually part of a process, because they describe the actions needed to complete the process.

To better understand the relationship between a goal, processes, and procedures, consider a teenager who wants to drive a car. The teenager's goal is to be able to drive. This goal can be broken down into two processes: (1) getting a driver's license and (2) getting access to a car by borrowing or buying one. The process of getting a driver's license is further broken down into a specific input, a set of procedures, and a specific output.

Input   Teenager needs to drive legally

Process for Getting a Driver's License

Procedures for Getting a Driver's License	
Who	**What (and when)**
Teenager	1. Goes to Dept. of Motor Vehicles 2. Completes eye exam 3. Completes written exam 4. Takes driving test
Driving Official at Dept. of Motor Vehicles	1. Observes driving test 2. Passes or fails the driver

Processing Clerk at Dept. of Motor Vehicles	1. Collects written exam, eye exam, and driving test scores
	2. If all tests are passed
	       2a. Mails driver's license
	       2b. Files exams and information

Output   Driver's license

Each procedure clearly identifies who is expected to complete the steps, what steps are taken, and the order in which they are completed. When procedures are simple and as easy to understand as in this example, it isn't always necessary to write them down.

Business procedures aren't always this simple, yet some support groups rely on employees to follow support procedures without written guidelines. Written procedures identify exactly what is to be delivered, the people or tools required, and the activities to perform. They also make it easier to evaluate whether the support group has met its goals. Formally documented procedures are also easier to automate because they have been tried and verified. Support technology is then applied to the process to automate many procedures and track the progress of each step. Automation enables even a complex process involving many people and dozens of tasks to always result in consistent delivery. **Consistent delivery** means that the output of a process is the same no matter who completes the procedures.

Consistent delivery is important for a support group. If computer users learn that a particular support person is better at solving certain problems, they may be less willing to use whichever resource is available. Many support groups rely on support technology to equalize the difference in skills among support staff.

 Common support processes include call logging, request management, and problem management. A detailed discussion of these processes and their related procedures is covered in Chapter 2.

TYPES OF SUPPORT TOOLS

Just as processes are specific to a particular goal, support tools are specific to the processes and challenges of a particular group. Some tools are designed for support staff, and others are designed for managers of support staff. Computer users can use some support tools to address their own support needs.

Support Staff Tools

The correct technology can help support staff work more efficiently. **Tools** are the equipment, processes, or software that are necessary to perform a task or that assist someone in practicing a profession. Support staff use tools to organize, troubleshoot, and deliver services. For example:

- Logging tools track all questions that the support group receives. It's important to log all questions to make sure that no problem or request is forgotten and that every customer gets an answer. Specialized software can be designed so that each question can be recorded quickly. Information that is usually gathered when logging is discussed in Chapter 3.

- Organizing tools help support staff manage their daily work. If questions need more research, the support staff needs to view these outstanding issues many ways: by customer, by priority, by degree of completeness, and so on. Common ways to organize incomplete work are also discussed in more detail in Chapter 3.

- Troubleshooting tools help equalize the skills of the support staff by providing reference materials the staff can use to quickly and easily find information about a particular problem or topic. For example, there may be some requests that support staff encounter more frequently than others. Reference materials make sure that support staff can complete less frequently encountered tasks well. Support staff can also use troubleshooting tools to learn more about particular subjects. Troubleshooting tools should contain a variety of high-level and detailed information, and should allow staff to add notes or make changes to the reference material to reflect their specific environments. Several troubleshooting tools are discussed in more detail in Chapter 6.

■ Other tools are designed to deliver a particular service. Some applications are designed to enable support staff to complete complex tasks that require more training than they have. For example, some security applications use a series of simple menus and questions that enable a support person to change a password—a sensitive task usually restricted to only a few, highly trained administrators. As the support analyst answers the questions, additional programs update tables and make sure that all steps are completed. Service delivery tools are discussed in Chapter 11.

The activities listed above are very different from each other, so support staff may use separate software programs for each type of activity.

Management Tools

Management-oriented tools enable managers to review all work for the support group and to supervise their resources. The most important tool support managers will use is reporting software. From the reports and graphs generated by this software, managers can prove that the support group meets its goals and contributes to the organization. Managers also regularly run monitoring reports to show how support staff performance improves over time. Not only will managers use such reports to make sure that tasks are completed on time, but they also will use staff reports to make sure that no one is overloaded with work. Prioritizing and reassigning tasks among resources helps managers ensure that the support staff has enough time to deliver services reliably without absorbing undue stress.

Support staff usually capture the additional information management needs for monitoring with the same software they use to organize their daily work. Good support software collects all necessary information in a way that is already part of the staff's work routine—*never requiring extra steps*. For example, it is important for staff members to collect the name of the customer as they log a problem, in case they need to research information specific to that person. The department the customer works in may have nothing to do with solving the problem, but support managers want that information to report on which departments use support services. It would take an extra step for the support person to record the department information, but the software could automatically look up the customer's department as the support staff selects the person from a predefined list of customers.

 Chapters 3 and 4 discuss examples of commonly monitored statistics.

Self-service Tools

Some support groups attempt to minimize the number of easy and repetitive problems by enabling computer users to help themselves. Even a small decrease of 5 to 15% in the total number of calls the support group processes can reduce the support staff's stress. Self-service tools allow customers to find answers to their problems or questions by themselves.

Self-service tools are usually simple to use because they are part of the software that customers use on a regular basis already. One self-service tool is a **list server** (or mailing list server), which is a program that handles subscription requests for a mailing list and distributes new messages, newsletters, or other postings from the list's members to the entire list of subscribers as the messages occur or are scheduled. People subscribe to a list server to receive e-mail messages about a single selected topic.

In many help desks, self-service tools are maintained and supported by the same support staff who handle calls. Support staff have learned the level of detail their customers can understand and are good resources for translating technology into understandable terms.

List servers and additional self-service tools are covered in Chapter 12.

DEVELOPING VERSUS BUYING TOOLS

Once a support group identifies the types of tools it needs, managers must decide whether to use existing technology (such as databases, spreadsheets, or other tracking applications), to purchase new software from software vendors, or to develop their own applications. All support applications begin with a **database**, which is a collection of data organized so that it can be easily accessed, managed, and updated. Databases contain related information, such as sales transactions, product catalogs and inventories, and customer profiles. A small database can be set up with an electronic spreadsheet, such as Microsoft Excel or other software applications, such as Microsoft Access, SQL Server, or Oracle. Figure 1-4 shows a sample database created in Excel.

	A	B	C	D
1	**First Name**	**Last Name**	**Area Code**	**Telephone Number**
2	Mark	Roberts	214	444-2398
3	Mike	Smith	214	330-5913
4	Joseph	Anderson	214	315-3815
5	Mary	Silvers	972	371-3817
6	Ruth	Hendricks	972	482-3815
7	Jay	Martinez	972	472-7730
8	Forest	Culvert	813	238-2744
9	Beatrice	Walker	813	381-4582
10	Marsha	Smith	813	937-2381

Figure 1-4   Sample database records

Common support processes inlcude call logging, request management, and problem management. A detailed discussion of these processes and their related procedures is covered in Chapter 2.

A database field contains a particular item of data. The collection of all fields with data about a single item make up a database record. For example, someone's telephone number would be stored in a field. The collection of fields with telephone number, name, and address for one person would make up one database record. Records are also sometimes called rows in databases in a spreadsheet the record is always called a row. A database column is the set of all instances of a single field from all records.

The sample database has nine records or rows of data. It is very easy to find information in a small database like this sample, but most business databases include thousands of records. By storing the first name and last name in separate fields, and the telephone number in area code and telephone number fields, it will be easy later to sort the data by any of these fields or to retrieve records when you only know one piece of data, such as last name or area code.

Figure 1-5 lists the different types of software applications available to a support organization.

```
        ♦ Homegrown
        ♦ Commercial
        ♦ Shareware
```

Figure 1-5 Types of software applications

Homegrown Software Applications

A **homegrown software application** is a program designed and written by an employee within the company that uses it. Support groups develop their own systems if the support processes for their environment are uniquely different from other support groups. Small support groups frequently use homegrown applications if they don't have the money to purchase software, or if the support group is small and the support processes are simple. The only real cost is someone's time. Most companies already use spreadsheets, databases, and word processing software, all of which are the building blocks for a homegrown application. These applications frequently include simple tools to automate repeated activities and to move data between applications.

Homegrown applications usually have problems if the number of support calls increases or the business needs change. Spreadsheets and Access databases are usually meant for a limited number of people to use at the same time. As the spreadsheet or database gets larger, containing more records, it will begin to take longer to update or retrieve information. The person who designed the tool may be too busy to add new features, or may no longer be with the company. Even if someone is available to add new features, they may need weeks or months to code and test everything.

1

Commercial Software Applications

A **commercial software application** is a program that is written or sold by a company that is in business to develop and sell software. These companies hire programmers who are dedicated to designing and writing the software as well as to regularly adding new features. These software applications are also designed to take advantage of database software that supports hundreds of users and thousands of transactions. Commercial software companies sell to a variety of industries and include special features that match their customers' needs. For example, if several support groups request a feature to measure the number of times people call in with the same problem, that feature may become a standard part of the commercial application.

The disadvantage to using commercial software is the lack of flexibility when matching terms or field labels to existing support processes. In some cases, the support group must redefine some procedures and learn new processes. While the changes are usually more efficient, the changes can add more stress. The support group is also dependent upon the development schedule of the software vendor if there are problems with the software.

Shareware Software Applications

A **shareware software application** is a program written by an independent programmer and distributed free with the understanding that users may need or want to pay for it after a specified trial period. Shareware is a cross between homegrown and commercial software. It usually combines some of the most common support features and is cheaper than a commercial application. Small support groups can benefit by using shareware for the short-term to automate some activities as they define their needs.

Many shareware programmers will add new features to their software, but they provide no commitment to support or enhance the application. Shareware products also use common database tools that are restricted to a limited number of users.

The best support tools are usually commercial applications that the support group can customize to meet their specific needs. The support group can buy an application that will be maintained by the vendor and already includes most of the features it needs. At the same time, they can change some areas of the software to match existing processes and terminology that the support staff already knows.

 Chapters 5 through 7 discuss specific applications.

UNDERSTANDING WHY TOOLS FAIL

Unfortunately, technology does not guarantee that a support group will meet its goals or satisfy its customers. Tools work best when they automate an efficient set of procedures that are part of a well-documented process. This is the most common and frequently hidden reason why a tool fails.

Automation tools also fail when they get in the way of the users. **Human-computer interaction** is the study of how people interact with computers and software and the extent to which computer technologies provide successful interaction with people. All software, including support software, needs to be "user-friendly" or computer users will misunderstand what they should do. Automated teller machines (ATMs) are a good example of computer systems that thousands of people interact with very successfully. The software asks simple "yes" and "no" types of questions, and the choices available are clearly defined and take a minimum amount of effort to select. Whenever possible, support staff should try new tools to make sure that the software features blend with the way they work.

Interactions between support staff and other business departments can also affect the success of support tools. **Workflow** is a flowchart that describes the movement of data and the transfer of control in a business process. Workflow defines criteria that must be met before moving to the next step of a process. Figure 1-6 illustrates the workflow for the driver's license process.

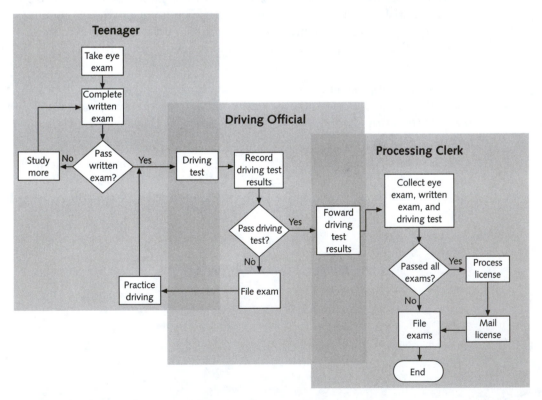

Figure 1-6   Driver's license workflow

1

In this example, the workflow diagram includes triangular decision boxes that ask a "yes" or "no" question. All participants can also see how their tasks relate to everyone else's and what determines a move to the next step.

Some support applications have workflow engines to move outstanding requests or problems to the next step of support. These applications assume that all processes remain within the support group. If many procedures happen outside the support group or are performed by vendors outside the company, support staff may have to take extra steps to complete information that would otherwise be collected automatically. Business needs and the people involved in a process change rapidly. A workflow tool that cannot be changed when people within the process are sick or out of the office fails quickly.

Technology can also fail when people get impatient. Support managers are often tempted to change too many things at once. When they help set up new support software, it is easy to turn on new features. Support staff members are computer users themselves—new support tools should be brought in as slowly as it takes for the support staff to learn how to use the new features. If managers decide to make process changes, they should train support staff on new procedures before they implement them.

CHANGE—THE BIGGEST TREND

The biggest trend in the support industry continues to be change, change, and more change. The technology being supported changes, the tools delivering support services change, and the terminology changes. It is common to find different companies using the same term in different ways. For example, some technical support groups are now called call centers—they provide marketing or other product information as well as answer questions and order products or services for customers. Other companies restrict their call centers exclusively to sales activities. Because the meaning of terms can vary greatly from support group to support group, new staff members should make sure all terminology is defined clearly.

For clarity, this book uses the following terms:
- *Support groups* refers to support organizations, support businesses, call centers, help desks, and contact centers.
- *Support staff* refers to support employees, support analysts, and support professionals.
- *Software* refers to programs, applications, and tools.
- *Customers* refers to users, callers, computer users, and business staff.

A support professional should take advantage of as many outside resources as possible to maintain current technical skills and understand the standard support processes. (Professional organizations and other resources are included in Chapter 13.) The support business changes drastically every three to five years. Successful support groups understand the need to be flexible because technology changes quickly. Support staff who enjoy learning new things not only find it easier to do their daily work, but also enjoy the variety of business problems they help solve.

CHAPTER SUMMARY

❑ Automation tools can be used to address resource and service challenges. Support staff can use technology to organize their work and equalize skills until they can obtain more training or gain experience. Services are delivered more consistently and in a more timely way when tools coordinate all the tasks and resources a support group must manage.

❑ Support groups have common goals, which are defined by processes and procedures. Once the processes and procedures are clearly defined, support technology can automate many procedures. Automation of tasks results in consistent service delivery.

❑ Support staff, managers, and computer users employ different types of tools. Support staff tools organize daily work, assist in troubleshooting activities, and automate complex tasks. Management tools monitor resources and their tasks. Computer user tools may decrease the number of calls a support group receives.

❑ A small support group may start out with very simple support tools. As the support group adds more support staff to handle a larger call volume, it may need to implement technology that is more sophisticated. The best support applications come with standard features, but allow the support group to customize some areas as well.

❑ Automation does not guarantee a support group will meet its goals. Tools that don't consider the human elements of support can interfere with service delivery. Support software must be fast and user-friendly. Support staff need good manual processes that consider their interactions with people in other departments.

❑ Technology continues to change rapidly. Likewise, support concepts, terminology, and tools change every few years. Use outside resources (including publications and professional organizations) to stay abreast of changes and new trends.

KEY TERMS

column — In a database, the set of all instances of a single field from all records.

commercial software application — A program that is written or sold by a company that is in business to develop and sell software.

communication skills — Those skills that enable a person to interact effectively with others by speaking, listening, and writing.

consistent delivery — The output of a process is the same no matter who completes the procedures.

customer — A person who buys products and services from a company, or an employee within a company who relies upon another group for services.

database — A collection of data organized so that it can be easily accessed, managed, and updated.

field — An area in a database that contains a particular item of data.

help desk — A single point of contact within a company for managing customer problems and requests, and providing solution-oriented support services.

homegrown software application — A program designed and written by an employee within the company that uses it.

human-computer interaction — The study of how people interact with computers and software and the extent to which computer technologies provide successful interaction with people.

information center — A place within the company where employees could receive training and help in using personal computers.

list server — A program that handles subscription requests for a mailing list and distributes new messages, newsletters, or other postings from the list's members to the entire list of subscribers as the messages occur or are scheduled; also called a mailing list server.

mission statement — A broad, general written guideline that defines the company's vision and specific goals.

procedure — A detailed, step-by-step set of instructions that describes who will perform the tasks in a process, along with how and when those tasks will be performed.

process — A list of the input, the interrelated work activities (or tasks), and the desired output needed to accomplish a goal.

professional services — Useful labor that does not result in a physical product, but that helps customers maximize the use of products.

record — In a database, the collection of all fields with data about a single item.

rows — *See* **record**.

shareware software application — A program written by an independent programmer and distributed free with the understanding that users may need or want to pay for it after a specified trial period.

support group — The department within a company that focuses on product support or other support services; also known as support organizations, support businesses, call centers, help desks, and contact centers.

support resources — The company employees who provide support services; also known as support staff, support employees, support analysts, and support professionals.

technical skills — Basic computer literacy and experience with specific hardware or software.

technology — The development of new materials, equipment, and processes to improve goods and service production.

tools — The equipment, processes, or software that are necessary to perform a task or that assist someone in practicing a profession.

workflow — A flowchart that describes the movement of data and the transfer of control in a business process.

REVIEW QUESTIONS

1. When managers apply technology to the support business, they attempt to address what challenges?

2. A support manager tries to hire staff with good _____ and _____ skills.

3. List one reason why it may be easier and faster for a company to retrain technically skilled employees than to hire new staff who already have these skills.

4. What is the correct relationship?

   a. Processes are part of procedures.

   b. Procedures are part of processes.

   c. Processes and procedures are the same.

   d. Processes and goals are the same.

5. Why is it important that procedures be written down?

6. Consistent delivery means that:

   a. customers can request their favorite support person.

   b. customers can expect the same service, regardless of who delivers it.

   c. all support staff are equally trained.

   d. a particular support person is better at solving certain problems.

7. List three common support processes.

8. List three ways support staff use tools.

9. The primary tool a support manager uses is _____.

10. How does a manager prove to his or her supervisors that the support group works well?

11. Tools designed to allow customers to find answers to their own problems or questions without calling support staff are called _____.

12. What is a database?

13. List two reasons why commercial software applications are preferable to homegrown applications.

14. What is shareware?

15. The most important and frequently hidden reason a software tool fails is because:

    a. the tool is written poorly.

    b. the tool is difficult to learn.

    c. support staff do not want to change.

    d. the underlying processes and procedures are inefficient or poorly defined.

16. Managers should introduce support tools as quickly and with as many new features as possible. True or False?

17. The interaction between people as they perform tasks and criteria for moving to the next step is covered in _____.

HANDS-ON PROJECTS

Project 1-1

Using self-service tools. Visit the Help Desk FAQ Web site at **http://www.philverghis.com/helpdeskfaq.html**. Review Section 1 – The Basics. Then, answer the following questions:

1. What are some of the common names for help desks?

2. List questions anyone starting or reengineering a help desk should consider when deciding whether to build or buy technology.

3. Marketing customer support is another way of communicating services and deliverables. Identify three activities that support staff can participate in directly.

4. Follow the links on this page to the glossary of common terms at **http://www.incoming.com/resources/glossary2.html**. What is the definition of a call center?

Project 1-2

Comparing definitions. Visit the Call Center Glossary Web site at **http://www.incoming.com/resources/glossary2.html**. Review the definitions provided for each of the key terms in this chapter. Do any conflict with the information provided? How do they differ?

Project 1-3

Exploring mission statements. Many companies publish their mission statements. Search the Web and locate five mission statements. A sample mission statement is available from the

Support Technologies Web site at **http://www.supporttechnologies.com/about.htm**. At least one mission statement you find should be from a support group, and one should be from a software development company. For each mission statement, identify the company vision and goals. How do the goals differ between the support group and the software development company? Did any companies add other parts to the mission statement?

Project 1-4

Finding out about help desk tools. Interview a support staff member or a help desk manager. Ask the following questions:

1. What troubleshooting tools are available for support staff? Describe them.

2. Are there any computer user tools in place? Describe them.

3. Do you use a homegrown or commercial support application? Why?

4. Did you face any special problems when introducing these tools to the support staff?

Write an article with the results of your interview.

Project 1-5

Interacting with computers. Visit the Whatis.com Web site at **http://whatis.com**. Look up the definitions for GUI and HCI. In one or two paragraphs, explain why human learning affects the way people interact with computers, according to this description.

Project 1-6

Building a database. Use Microsoft Excel to build a small database and to generate and use a simple entry form. Use online Help to review other information about these features.

> **TIP** Projects in later chapters will use what you learn from these exercises to manage a database of call tracking information.

Create a simple database in Excel.

1. Start Excel and open a blank workbook, if necessary.

2. Label columns A through D as **First Name**, **Last Name**, **Area Code**, and **Telephone Number**.

3. Enter ten records, using fictitious data for the names, area codes, and telephone numbers. Use several first and last names that begin with the same letters. Use only three area codes for all ten records. Your database should look similar to the one shown in Figure 1-4.

4. Save a copy of the database with the filename **Proj1-6.xls**.

5. Highlight the column names and all the data, cells **A1:D11**.

6. From the menu bar, click **Data**, **Form**.

7. Click the **New** button in the Form window, and then enter fictitious data in each field to create a new record.

8. Click the **Criteria** button, type a letter that matches the first letter of more than one last name in the Last Name text box, and then click the **Find Next** button to scroll the records that match. How many records can you locate? What are the record numbers?

9. Click the **Close** button to close the Form dialog box.

10. From the menu bar, click **File**, **Exit** to close the file Proj1-6, but do not save the changes.

A filter displays only those records in your database that match your selection criteria. Filter the records in your Proj1-6.xls database.

1. Open the **Proj1-6.xls** workbook and display the worksheet with the original ten records.

2. From the menu bar, click **Data**, **Filter**, **AutoFilter**. Each of the first four columns in the worksheet displays a list arrow, indicating it has a pull-down menu of options.

3. Click the list arrow in the **Area Code** column, and then click one of the area codes. What happens?

4. Click the list arrow in the **Area Code** column, and then click **(All)**. What happens?

5. Click the list arrow in the **Area Code** column, and then click one of the area codes that appears more than once in the database.

6. Click the list arrow in the **First Name** column, and then click **(custom...)**. In the upper-left list box, select **equals**. In the upper-right list box, select one of the names from the database. Click the **OK** button. What happens to the spreadsheet display?

7. Click the list arrow in the **First Name** column, and then click **(All)**. What happens?

8. From the menu bar, click **File**, **Exit** to close the file Proj1-6 but do not save the changes.

CASE PROJECTS

1. Help Desk List Servers

Your support staff does not like the homegrown application they use to track customer problems. Join the help desk user newsgroup or a list server for one of the support groups listed in Appendix A. Review the postings about commercial applications that other support groups use and prepare a list of three pros and three cons for the applications mentioned.

2. Prioritizing Skills

You are the support manager for a small software company in a remote area in Colorado. You know it will be difficult to find support staff that have good technical skills, problem-solving skills, and communication skills. You decide to prioritize these skills so you can find qualified candidates more easily. It takes about one month for a new support person to learn how to use the software your company designs and the diagnostic tools that help users install the software correctly. You interview five people and label them as having one of the three primary skills. Which skill is the most important in your situation? Why is it the most important?

3. **Design a Workflow**

The Tornado Company makes hair dryers and wants you to document their repair workflow. If a hair dryer breaks within the first 90 days after purchase, the company will ship a new hair dryer to the customer, free of charge. If the hair dryer breaks after 90 days, the support staff tells the customer that they can repair the hair dryer for a $20 charge, and asks whether the customer wants to repair the hair dryer. If the customer wants the repair, the support staff looks up the address of the closest repair office. Create a workflow diagram that shows the criteria used and actions taken during this process.

2

SUPPORT ENVIRONMENTS AND PROCESSES

In this chapter you will learn:

♦ Basic help desk concepts

♦ Internal support processes

♦ External support processes

♦ What core activities support staff complete in different environments

♦ Special challenges unique to some support organizations

As you learned in Chapter 1, a standard set of instructions or procedures is important when providing support. Once a support group identifies a process, managers and support staff define procedures to support that process. Support staff complete different tasks as they follow procedures, based upon the company's business and the tasks its customers are trying to complete. Business tasks can be simple activities, such as printing a letter or transferring a telephone call from one extension to another. Other tasks, such as printing paychecks for employees, are more complex and require a series of smaller tasks that must be completed in a specific order. Most business tasks are completed using technology that has grown very complex.

The **support environment** is the collection of customers that a support group assists, the tasks customers need or want to complete, the technologies those customers and support staff use to complete tasks, and the experience and skill of the support staff. Support environments vary, depending upon whether the customers work for a profit-making company, a nonprofit company, an educational institution, or a government agency. Because all support environments have common requirements, they use many of the same processes. Over time, companies expand the support group's role to include more activities and processes. Support environments also change as the support role or business goals change.

BASIC HELP DESK CONCEPTS

Before discussing the different types of support environments, it is important to review several important help desk concepts.

A **multilevel support model** defines the role a support person plays in different support processes and the amount of interaction the support person has with a customer. Figure 2-1 illustrates a multilevel support model. Support groups usually have at least two levels of support. The higher support level has staff with more experience or knowledge about a particular subject. Ideally, the lower support level handles the majority of requests or problems.

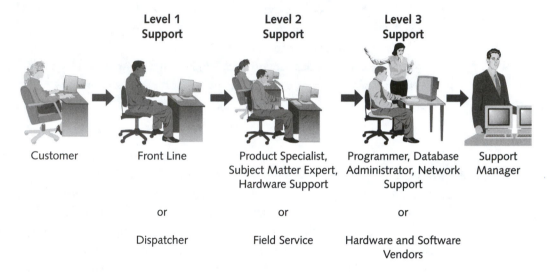

Figure 2-1   Multilevel support model

Front-line support, or **level one support**, is the point of first contact with the customer. Level one support staff answer the telephone, record problem details, and attempt to resolve the problem or answer the question. A **dispatcher** is a front-line support person who answers the telephone but forwards the problem to someone else to solve. Dispatchers pick up overflow calls if all level one support staff are busy or when the problem requires someone to visit a remote location to repair hardware. Otherwise, level one support resolves as many calls as possible, but forwards the calls it cannot resolve to a higher level, namely level two or three support.

Subject matter experts (**SME**) are usually members of level two or level three support, with a greater amount of experience or knowledge about a particular subject than level one support. They have more detailed knowledge about specific products or more experience troubleshooting. Level three support also may include network specialists, database administrators, or programmers. The software or hardware vendors themselves, which support the hardware and software that some companies use, may also be considered part of level three support.

2

Support staff may be organized in teams, with a team leader who helps them with technology-related issues. A support manager supervises multiple teams. The company's support manager, along with other department managers, may report to a director. Some companies consider support an important part of their business, and, as a result, many directors want to be regularly informed about daily support activities.

To **escalate** an issue is to raise the issue to the next level of support or to notify managers. Issues can be escalated in a couple of ways. First, the lower level support staff may already know that a particular problem requires more knowledge or experience to resolve, so they escalate the problem to the next level as soon as they collect the problem details. Second, customers may think that the problem is taking too long to solve and ask that more resources or more experienced staff work on the problem. In this case, support managers are notified as soon as the problem is forwarded to a higher support level.

 Some support tools can be set up to automatically generate special notices after problems remain open too long. These tools are discussed in more detail in Chapter 8.

INTERNAL AND EXTERNAL SUPPORT ENVIRONMENTS

Support environments are divided into two types—internal and external. An **internal support group** is a department within a company that responds to questions, problems, or requests from company employees. Another common name for the internal support group is the **help desk**. Internal support staff answer questions and solve problems about personal computers, printers, telephones, fax machines, and other office equipment. As the internal support group delivers service, it may also:

- Answer questions about software that is purchased or developed within the company
- Troubleshoot software problems and identify hardware problems
- Take requests for network or administrative services (such as giving employees access to network software or changing passwords)
- Refer callers to other support centers or corporate resources
- Distribute information to employees about system availability
- Identify employees who need more attention or training in specific areas
- Install or upgrade new versions of software or hardware

A help desk will continue to add services the longer it exists and as long as it can respond to calls in a timely manner.

 Training users on new hardware or software is not an official responsibility of the help desk. However, if the support staff provide step-by-step instructions on how to complete an activity, training (or retraining) does happen. Most help desk managers will vigorously remind their staff that they should not try to train callers over the telephone because it takes too much time or because the caller can use other resources for training. The correct approach is to refer customers to training and reference manuals or, if possible, enroll them in formal training classes.

In a small company, employees may be able to rely upon a **guru**, a coworker who learns to use new tools quickly and who helps other employees unofficially. This is practical only as long as the guru can still complete his or her own work. Instead, most companies recognize the need to set up a help desk and hire staff that are dedicated to answering technology questions. Frequently, companies set up a help desk as a necessary evil at first, because computer users need a centralized point of contact. The primary purpose of a help desk is to provide technological support services.

Funds for internal help desks usually come from all the departments that use their services, but it is difficult to place a dollar amount on every activity the help desks complete. Budgets for internal help desks are usually tight because it is difficult to show how the help desk aids the company as a whole. As a result, many internal help desks are understaffed and frequently receive more calls than they can handle. The pressure of keeping up with the calls increases stress, which leads to high employee turnover.

Companies that sell products or services to the public may provide external support. An **external support group** addresses questions, problems, or requests from customers who buy their company's products and services. External support groups may be called "customer support," to differentiate them from internal support groups.

 Large companies that sell products usually have both internal and external support groups.

 The help desk support staff does not usually refer to the people who request its services as "customers," because that term is used to describe people external to the company. The term "customer" can also cause confusion if a company has both internal and external support groups. However, some internal support groups may refer to callers as "customers" or "clients" to remind support staff how important these callers are.

External support groups often:

- Troubleshoot computer hardware or software problems and problems with other electronic equipment

- Explain installation or instruction manuals that are difficult to understand (for example, some manuals for electronic equipment, such as televisions, stereos, CD players, and home appliances, are translated from other languages)

- Decide when broken equipment needs to be returned for repair or replacement

- Start or stop services from utility providers, such as water or power companies or local and long-distance telephone companies

- Provide additional information about a product or service

There are two good reasons that a company will set up an external support group. First, if most of a company's competitors provide customer support, then it also must provide some level of support to remain competitive. Second, a company may find it profitable to sell maintenance or repair services for its products. External support groups often charge their customers different rates for different levels of support. As the support group provides good service, customers renew their annual maintenance contracts, providing a source of revenue for the company and funding for the support group.

It is not unusual to find customer support staff working in the same support group for years. External support can be less stressful because it is not always technically challenging. Support staff may answer questions only about household appliances or dispatch service repairs, so support staff do not need as much continuous training. Support groups that generate revenue are also well funded and better staffed than internal support groups. In addition, members of the support staff feel more appreciated because they can affect customer perceptions about their company.

PROCESSES COMMON TO SUPPORT ENVIRONMENTS

All support staff use some of the same processes no matter what support environment they support. Both internal and external support environments use the processes listed in Figure 2-2 to complete the same tasks.

♦ Call logging
♦ Problem management
♦ Problem resolution

Figure 2-2   Processes common to all help desks

Chapter 3 discusses these common help desk processes in more detail.

Call Logging

Call logging is the process of creating records that capture details about problems, requests, and questions as they are reported to the support group. The specific type of information collected for each can vary, depending upon the support environment. A **problem** is an event that prevents someone from completing a task. Some problems take longer to solve than others, requiring support staff to collect additional information. The type of information the support staff collects depends on the problem.

A **request** is a customer order for new hardware, software, or services, or for an enhancement to a product or service a customer already uses. Depending upon the type of request, support staff may need to collect more information from a caller. However, they will collect the same information from two callers who make the same request.

Customers make inquiries about small tasks or subjects they don't understand, which are logged by support staff as **questions**. Unlike problems, the customer may be able to complete a task or work around the question, but the task may take longer than it should because there are too many manual steps. Questions usually begin with standard phrases, such as:

- How do I …?

- Where is the …?

- Who do I call if I need …?

- When will …?

Some questions take only a few minutes to answer. However, questions can become either problems or requests, depending upon the answer. For example, a customer may get a computer error message that doesn't appear to affect anything. When the customer calls the support group to ask what the message means, the customer may learn that the error has caused a problem that will appear when he or she tries to complete a different task.

Problem Management

Problem management is the process of tracking and resolving problems that are reported to a support group. Some problems can be solved quickly while the support staff member is still on the telephone with the caller. Other problems can take days or weeks to resolve, depending on the problem's complexity. The problem management process defines procedures to ensure that staff members collect problem details, work on outstanding problems regularly, assign additional support staff when needed, and provide status updates to the customer. As shown in Figure 2-3, finding the cause of a problem, removing or preventing the cause, and correcting the disruption that the problem caused is part of **problem resolution**.

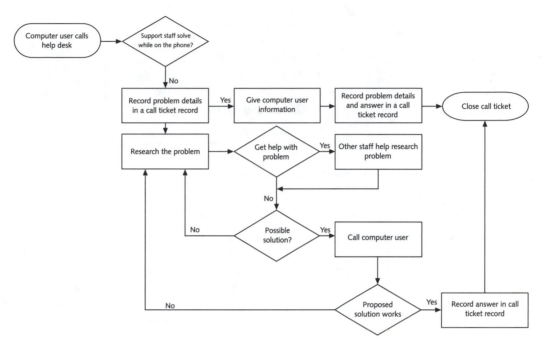

Figure 2-3 Problem resolution process

 The phrase "call management" can refer to problem management, although it also describes managing telephone calls.

In addition to these common processes, internal and external support groups also use specialized processes.

INTERNAL SUPPORT PROCESSES

Computers and software are not just a large part of a company's assets, they are also a source of calls to the help desk. After employees add or change hardware and software, they often refer a problem to the help desk for resolution. The most common internal support processes are listed in Figure 2-4.

> ♦ Asset management
> ♦ Change management
> ♦ Network and system
>   management
> ♦ Request management
> ♦ Hotline support

Figure 2-4 Common internal support processes

Asset Management

Asset management is the process of collecting and maintaining records about technology, such as hardware or software components and other office equipment. Many features of an asset management system relate to financial information, such as tracking inventory levels, purchase prices, cost of repairs, and inventory depreciation. Asset management systems can also contain a list of hardware components and their specifications (hard disk capacity, RAM, network address, etc.), when and where they were purchased, who they are assigned to, where they are physically located, or what software is installed (versions, etc.). This is useful for the help desk when troubleshooting computer problems because customers may not always know the model or speed of the equipment they use. The help desk can then look up the information it needs in the asset management system.

Technology that is used to complete a process is usually labeled with the same name as the process. For example, a business has an asset management process defining why the information is important, what information is collected, how and when it is updated, and who uses and maintains the information. The process and the technology to help a business with this process would be called the asset management system.

If a company doesn't want to perform its own hardware repairs, it may outsource hardware repairs. To **outsource** is to contract a service to an external support group. Some companies use several hardware repair vendors. This information will also be tracked in the asset management system. In case of a hardware failure, it is necessary to know which vendor should be notified for repairs. Once the help desk confirms that the repairs are complete, the asset management system should also contain the repair history.

Hardware repairs aren't the only help desk service a company may outsource. Some companies outsource all their help desk services.

Change Management

Change management is the process of controlling additions, modifications, and deletions of hardware or software in a computerized system. Software or hardware changes can cause a "domino" effect at the help desk, because a change in one area can cause new problems in a related area. To help prevent problems, details of a new hardware purchase or a pending software change can be forwarded by support staff or automatically from the asset management system as part of a change request. A **change request** is a written document that describes a technological change, the reason why the change must be made, the customers potentially affected, and related technologies and tasks required to make the change. To ensure that hardware and software installations for the company are controlled and planned for, technical experts outside the support group review change requests to determine the risk of new problems. Change management systems provide valuable information about the changes that have happened recently to a selected computer or its components. Recent changes may indicate the cause of later problems or demonstrate the true cost of a vendor's product to the company.

Some asset or change management systems include **remote access control**, which is software that allows support staff to temporarily take "control" of a computer from the user and review or install software over the network. Other asset or change management systems may enable **deployment**, the rapid installation of new software or software upgrades on large numbers of desktop computers electronically.

Network and System Management

In many companies, employees share computer resources over a network or intranet; these include network servers, printers, or applications such as accounting programs or e-mail. They expect continuous availability of these resources to complete their jobs. When there is a problem with a computer resource, a quick call to the help desk can confirm whether the problem affects only one person and can be fixed quickly or whether the problem affects many users in multiple areas of the company. The support group may already be working to resolve the problem that affects many people, because someone else has already called.

Network and system management software notifies the support group of problems as they occur, and often before computer users know there is a problem. **Network management software** monitors the "traffic" on a network between PCs, printers, and other shared pieces of hardware. This is helpful when, for example, callers complain of slow retrieval or long wait times between screen changes. **System management software** monitors transactions and errors on a single piece of hardware. This enables support staff to manage the resources of a single, large shared system or application, making sure that file servers have enough storage space and that software running on a device doesn't have any errors that will affect customers. Repeated problems with one device or in the same area of a network can indicate a need for repairs or additional equipment to prevent problems later.

Request Management

Help desk customers may need new hardware, software, or services, or want to enhance something they already use or receive, resulting in a request. Examples of common requests include purchasing and setting up a computer for a new employee, changing login IDs and passwords, delivering office or computer supplies, enrolling students in training classes, or installing new software. **Request management** is the process of collecting information about the customer that will be used to complete the request, identifying the tasks and resources needed to complete the request, and tracking the request until delivery. Requests compose a large percentage of the total calls coming into an internal support group. It is important that requests are not lost, that they be filled within a reasonable amount of time, and that they be completed consistently. Otherwise, customers will find ways to work around the request process.

Hotline Support

Some support questions are answered hundreds or thousands of times with the same answer. **Hotline support** doesn't usually collect information about the caller, it just counts the number of times that a particular question is asked. This kind of support is frequently useful for tracking questions employees have about employment benefits or administrative procedures. Employees call a special telephone number to speak to service representatives or leave questions on voicemail. This information is later used to plan additional employee training or to revise procedure manuals.

 Some external support groups use hotlines to provide a special telephone number for consumer-related questions. For example, the U.S. Department of Agriculture, which lists several hotline numbers, sponsors the National Food Safety Database Web site at **http://www.foodsafety.org**. Many telephone-based services like hotlines, however, are rapidly being replaced by Web pages or fax numbers, as more consumers add PCs and fax machines to their home offices.

EXTERNAL SUPPORT PROCESSES

External support group processes focus on the interaction between a company and its customers. A company's ability to attract and keep customers is based upon the quality of products it sells and how well the company supports what it sells. Figure 2-5 lists common external support processes.

> ◆ Customer management
> ◆ Contract management
> ◆ Relationship management
> ◆ Software change management
> ◆ External information management

Figure 2-5 Common external support processes

2

Customer Management

Customer management is the process of collecting customer information and building a relationship between a company and its customers. Some companies sell their products directly to their customers; others sell their products to other companies to sell to customers. As a result, a company may not always know who might call for support until it receives a telephone call. External support staff collect customer information because companies want to know who owns their products, what options or pieces of the products they use, and the products that cause problems. This information may help companies sell more related products to their customers. In the course of taking calls about customer problems and questions, support staff collect customers' names, addresses, and telephone numbers. Although other departments usually maintain this information in mailing lists for sales campaigns, the help desk needs valid contacts and current telephone numbers so they can warn customers about serious problems related to a specific product.

 TIP Another term for customer management is **account management**.

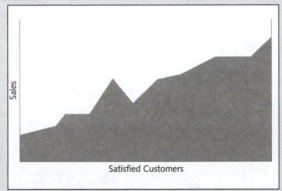

Sales

Satisfied Customers

THE GROWING EMPHASIS ON MANAGING CUSTOMER RELATIONSHIPS

Companies that sell goods or services realize that they need to differentiate themselves from their competition. Mass production has equalized products—there is little differentiation between product features and pricing. Consumers can easily find new suppliers so there is less brand loyalty.

Industry statistics show that 68% of customers who walk away from a vendor do so because of poor customer service. Research also shows that acquiring a new customer costs five to ten times more than retaining an existing one. Customers have become a company's most important asset and competition for new customers is fierce.

In the mid 1990s, companies began to spend more time trying to understand their customers, their customers' habits, and their customers' needs and desires. Companies needed new strategies for delivering customer service to acquire, develop, and retain customers. New technologies make it easier for companies to analyze customer behavior and attributes, in order to develop successful marketing campaigns, strategies, and treatment plans.

The current trends in customer relationship management are actually the next step in the evolution of sales strategies. Salespeople originally sold many products door-to-door and retail stores were small, family-owned businesses. These sales methods allowed a company to develop an understanding about its customer. Service was more personalized and there was a strong sense of customer loyalty and trust. As large-scale production and geographic distribution developed, a variety of affordable goods became available. Door-to-door sales and corner stores grew to be relatively inefficient and gave way to supermarkets and malls. Although consumers gained more products and better cost savings, service became less personalized.

Advertising had to become more efficient in the selling process also. Mass marketing attempted to create brand name recognition. Improvements in television, radio, and printed press allowed companies to send out information, in an attempt to educate consumers about products and acquire new customers.

In the mid-1980s, companies started using information technology to filter masses of data so they could select specific, "targeted" customers by mail or telephone. This first attempt to interact more with customers had a higher potential for receiving a customer response than mass marketing campaigns. Technology enabled companies to sift through massive amounts of data to extract valuable information about customers. Initially, personal computers automated data collection for specific interests. Contact manager software kept track of names and telephone numbers, call center software tracked problems, order entry systems tracked purchases, and accounts receivable software tracked payments and credit limits. Technology is now used to help these separate processes interact to improve workflow and share common repositories of information. Originally, a retailer hired a market research firm to sift through data and perform statistical analysis for trends and buying indicators. Now, companies are doing more of the analysis themselves, to gain control of connecting with their customers.

Customers also are better informed and more demanding than ever before. They demand multiple options for interacting with a company and want to retrieve information or purchase products at any hour of day or night. Vendors must also consider the way in which customers want to be contacted—communication is more often two-way, with customers asking for information and vendors responding to questions. Direct sales forces work with call centers and Web self-service to distribute information and handle requests.

There are also more ways to communicate. These bi-directional contacts are called "touchpoints" or "channels," and include the Internet and call centers. Each form of communication appeals to different types of customers. Each form also has different costs associated with its deployment and use—marketing managers must evaluate when different methods are appropriate and which are more profitable.

Some customers are a better investment than others. Companies track and analyze their marketing efforts in an attempt to identify those customers they want to keep. The top

2

20% of customers represent 80% of a company's profits, and companies want to treat their best customers especially well. They may create special customer treatment programs, such as "gold" or "platinum" levels of service, with corresponding privileges beyond those of regular customers. These customers may receive special discounts, increased credit lines, flexible payment plans, and other incentives to develop further customer loyalty.

The extra attention seems to be paying off. Companies that are identified as "service" leaders have several important characteristics:

- They grow twice as fast as their low-service competitors.

- They experience a 6% annual market share growth versus a 1 percent share loss, because they take customers away from their competition.

- They have the same number of customers as their competition, but they sell more to each customer.

- They charge 10% more for their products than low-service competitors and still gain new customers.

The emphasis on customer satisfaction will continue to grow as more businesses deliver services rather than physical products. Companies already evaluate the service they receive from their business partners along the same standards they have for their own customers; companies that don't deliver consistent, superior service will not be in business long.

Contract Management

Customers may purchase support contracts when they buy products. Depending upon the type of product or service, a support contract includes several elements, which are outlined in the service level agreement.

A **service level agreement (SLA)** is a formal, written definition of the services the support group will deliver, when and how they will deliver those services, the customer's role in providing information about problems, and how service is measured. Different levels of support determine how quickly the support group will respond. **Entitlements** define the number of calls a customer can make to the help desk for a set fee or the office hours when they can reach someone in customer support. Services delivered outside the customer's entitlement are categorized and tied to a financial code, or **charge code**, that an accounting or billing application uses to generate an invoice for the customer.

Support staff play an active role in contract management because they deliver services according to the service level agreement and because they determine when services fall outside the entitlements. Service level agreements are negotiated between support managers and their customers. Good service level agreements include details about:

- Hours of operation
- Services provided
- Ways to contact the support group

- Customer responsibilities
- Priorities and targeted response times
- Escalation procedures

To organize problems so that important issues are handled first, a service level agreement usually defines a problem's severity and appropriate performance targets. Figure 2-6 is an example of service response and resolution times for a single service level. A customer with a different service level would see different response times, update frequencies, and resolution times.

Call Severities and Target Resolution Times				
Severity	Definition	Response Time	Update Frequency	Resolution Time
1	Issues preventing your ability to conduct day-to-day business, an inaccessible or inoperable production system, data corruption, or data unavailability. Total system failure that affects more than one computer user.	15 minutes	1 hour	4 hours
2	A major component of an application or product is inaccessible, preventing day-to-day business. A single computer user is affected.	30 minutes	2 hours	6 hours
3	Important problems that delay completion of a daily task or activity. This is the default level.	1 hour	4 hours	8 hours
4	Minor issues that are inconvenient, but have available workarounds and can be addressed as time allows. Includes enhancements or requests for new services.	4 hours	2 days	5 days

Figure 2-6   Sample service responses

Some products that customers purchase come with a short- or long-term warranty. During the warranty period, the customer may return the product for repair, replacement, or refund. To save time and shipping costs, customer support groups may require customers to speak to a support person before they return the item. The support person records the details of the problem and the desired corrective action, and assigns a special code or number to the product, called a **return merchandise authorization (RMA)**. RMAs are usually used when the product is relatively expensive or when the company receives a high volume of returned merchandise. For example, companies frequently use an RMA process when customers return computers they purchased through mail order, computer components (such as hard drives, printers, or monitors), and other electronic equipment that is under warranty from the manufacturer. The customer must include the assigned RMA with the returned item. When the product and its RMA arrive, the support group can make sure that the correct person processes the returned item, the reason it was returned is clearly understood, and the planned correction is completed.

Relationship Management

Because it is less expensive to keep customers than to find new ones, companies spend time trying to keep their customers happy, satisfied, and loyal. **Relationship management** is the process of collecting and managing customer information to improve customer loyalty. A customer's attitude about the quality of a product or service is important to building a good customer relationship. **Customer surveys** are a tool to collect feedback about products or services.

Support groups frequently survey their customers, either randomly or regularly, to determine the customers' level of satisfaction with support group services. Random surveys are frequently based upon customers' problem history. For example, if customers have an unusually large number of calls to the help desk within a few weeks, it can be useful to survey the customers to find out whether increases in calls have changed their perception of the overall quality of the product or service. Some surveys are also automatically scheduled for very severe types of problems. At other times, collecting formal feedback from all customers once or twice a year may help a company understand what services it should add. Figure 2-7 shows a sample customer survey that would be distributed by the support group after a problem is solved.

Customer Satisfaction Survey

The help desk is interested in your evaluation of our computer support. Please take a few minutes to complete this survey and return it to the help desk manager.

Thank you!

1. Is this the first time you called the help desk? (PLEASE CIRCLE ONE) Yes   No

2. How long has it been since you had to call the help desk? _____ Weeks _____ Months

3. In general, how satisfied are you with the support you received from the help desk? (PLEASE CIRCLE ONE RESPONSE)

Very Dissatisfied						Very Satisfied		
1	2	3	4	5	6	7	8	9	10

4. Please rate the service you received from the support analyst and other support staff who helped you. (PLEASE CIRCLE ONE RESPONSE FOR EACH QUESTION)

Question	Very Dissatisfied						Very Satisfied		
About the Support Analyst									
Was polite	1	2	3	4	5	6	7	8	9	10
Was knowledgeable	1	2	3	4	5	6	7	8	9	10
Communicated clearly	1	2	3	4	5	6	7	8	9	10
Helpful at all times	1	2	3	4	5	6	7	8	9	10
Provided accurate answers	1	2	3	4	5	6	7	8	9	10
Worked until the problem was solved	1	2	3	4	5	6	7	8	9	10
Met your expectations	1	2	3	4	5	6	7	8	9	10
About the Help Desk									
Connected to a support analyst quickly	1	2	3	4	5	6	7	8	9	10
Person who routed the call was polite	1	2	3	4	5	6	7	8	9	10

5. Please include below any specific comments about the particular problem you encountered, and how your support analyst assisted you.

Figure 2-7   Sample customer survey

Software Change Management

Companies that develop and sell software packages track features that don't work properly or consistently and customer enhancement requests for additional features in the software. Similar to change management, **software change management** is the process computer software developers use to prioritize, manage, and control software changes, especially when many programmers are working on many computer programs.

Programmers are included in the multilevel support model as a higher level of support. Support staff collect problem details during problem management. They turn this information into a software change request and forward it to a programming group. Unfortunately, software changes may take even longer to research and resolve than other technological problems, because programmers are often already involved in other development projects and are not always available for support. As a result, customers may call back several times to check on requests or problems they reported, just to make sure that someone will work on them. This increases the number of calls to the support group.

External Information Management

External support groups have an additional challenge to managing customer technology problems because much of the information about the problem is outside the support environment. Customers using complex software or hardware may have a difficult time helping the support staff troubleshoot their problems over the telephone—for example, there is too much information to relate over the telephone or they don't know how to describe the problem correctly. This is complicated when a company sells products across a large region or even worldwide. In the event the support staff need to "see" what is happening, they may use dial-up software (similar to remote access control software used by internal support groups) to access customers' systems. They may collect files and error messages from the customer's system to help troubleshoot problems or to forward to higher levels of support. An **attachment** is an additional file appended to a call record that provides detailed information for troubleshooting. Attachments save the support group time as the problem is escalated, because the people troubleshooting the customer problem have all the supporting materials in one place.

SUPPORT PROCESS CHALLENGES

Some internal support groups use processes similar to the processes in place for external support groups, and vice versa. The term **chargeback** refers to the accounting activity of allocating the expenses of an internal support group back to the departments that use its services, based upon the number of services they use (similar to entitlements for external customers). Many internal help desks also initiate customer surveys and establish service level agreements for their customers.

External customer support groups for companies that sell hardware find it handy to keep an inventory of customer purchases, using asset management processes. For example, a company may sell software it develops and resell hardware from a vendor such as Hewlett-Packard. Customers can call the support group to report any type of problem, but if they have a hardware problem, the support group contacts Hewlett-Packard to fix the hardware problem, and the support group manages the outstanding issue until it is fixed. The support group will use customer asset management to determine whether the hardware is covered under a maintenance contract. Some support groups may also use remote access control software to explore their customers' computer systems during troubleshooting.

There are additional support challenges that blur the distinction between internal and external support processes. Figure 2–8 lists specific challenges that require additional, specialized processes.

◆ High call volume

◆ Company mergers

◆ Retail support

◆ Field service and repairs

◆ Enterprise support

◆ Global or international support

◆ Educational organizations

Figure 2-8 Special support challenges

High Call Volume

The number of calls directed to a single telephone number will determine not only the number of staff required to handle the calls, but the need for special technologies as well. Many average-sized support groups have twenty to thirty people answering the phone with another ten to twenty more experienced staff available to handle complex problems. Depending upon the complexity of the problem and the length of the telephone call, an average-sized help desk may handle 200 to 600 calls per day! Large help desks may receive 1000 or more telephone calls per day and may have a support staff of 100 to 200 people. High-volume support groups almost always have an **automatic call distribution (ACD) system**, special telephone equipment that manages incoming calls by answering calls to route them quickly to staff who are not already on the telephone.

In addition to the number of telephone calls support staff must handle, the number of times they update call records affects how they document their work. One help desk may record 1000 calls in a day, each of which were handled in a few minutes, entered once in the database, and never updated. Another help desk may receive only 400 calls in a day, but because of the complexity of the problems, the call record could be updated five to ten times before the problem is solved. Call logging technology must be fast when adding call records and must be able to process multiple updates.

Company Mergers

When one company buys another, the merger complicates the support challenges. If the acquiring company takes over support from the purchased company, the acquiring company's support staff must quickly support many new types of hardware and software. As a result, support staff must be able to troubleshoot a larger variety of problems. Companies that merge will try to standardize on the best technology for the new, combined companies to save money on repairs and support. It can take years to standardize all the computer systems as business grows and, in some cases, the expense of changing may be so great that the business cannot standardize. Over time, old systems break and are replaced, leaving newer equipment to be supported. As the old equipment disappears, new support staff have less incentive to learn to support the old equipment. At the same time, experienced support staff leave or lose their expertise with older equipment because they use it infrequently. It becomes harder to support nonstandard equipment the longer it works.

The two companies may have also offered different products and services to their customers. Customers may expect different service level agreements. In addition, it will take time before customers are comfortable with the new support staff. At the same time, support staff need to learn new contact names and must help customers understand new procedures for reporting problems.

Retail Support

Retail support usually includes high call volume challenges, nonstandardized equipment to support, and technically unsophisticated customers (namely, the store employees). Store managers and sales staff are skilled in waiting on customers in a restaurant, selling gas in a service station, or selling goods in a department store. Although the support staff may under-stand the computer systems used in the retail location, they frequently work with store employees who are uncomfortable with technology and do not understand a lot of jargon. To make matters worse, retail customers trying to purchase goods at a store won't wait long to pay for their selections. Support staff must troubleshoot quickly, communicate well with store employees, and talk the employees through technology corrections they may not understand.

Retail computer systems are also frequently interrelated to financial systems. Cash registers have evolved from mechanical devices to complex, electronic models. **Point of sale systems** are modern versions of cash registers that print receipts, validate charge cards, record sales, transmit sales nightly to a centralized computer system, count the number of items sold, request stock replacements, and track customer demographics. Several processes and pieces of software address each of these activities. Problems that aren't fixed quickly can result in more problems with later activities. Many companies network their point of sale systems so that price changes can be controlled and updated electronically from a single location. The potential problems from errors in any part of a point of sale system can generate hundreds of new problem reports with the support group.

Field Service and Repairs

Companies that sell hardware frequently have support staff who travel to the physical location of the hardware problem. Depending upon the size of the company, travel may be between offices within a single building, between offices in a single city, or to offices in different parts of the country. These staff may be employees or hired technicians if the business outsources hard-ware repairs. Field staff are **dispatched**, or sent, to the site where they diagnose problems and then install replacement parts or new equipment. Routing support calls directly to these people to take problem details is impractical because they are usually between locations. However, field support must be alerted when they are assigned new problems. A **pager** is a small, wireless telecommunications receiver, generally used by people who are continually changing their location or who are not necessarily able to answer a telephone call immediately.

TIP

A pager is also sometimes called a "beeper." Pagers have become almost as familiar as telephones over the years as hardware prices have fallen. Mobile telephones are popular, but services are still more expensive than pager services. Many parents have learned that pagers are a handy way for their children to contact them quickly in case of emergency. Other parents give their children pagers to carry, which has become a "cool" way to let kids know it's time to check in at home.

Any small mobile handheld device that provides computing and information storage and retrieval capabilities is called a **personal digital assistant** (**PDA**), or **handheld computer**. These devices are usually small enough to store in a pocket, as shown in Figure 2-9. These devices allow field service representatives to download call records, keep notes about what they have done, collect telephone numbers, and return updates to the call tracking database at the end of the day. This information then becomes part of the asset repair history and may be used for later troubleshooting.

Figure 2-9   Personal digital assistant

Enterprise Support

Enterprise support is provided by a company that has multiple support groups located in different regions of the country to enable better support coverage over different time zones. After companies merge, they may keep multiple help desks to provide better support to their customers. Each help desk has staff who support different products. In an effort to establish process consistency, the company attempts to use a single call logging and problem management software application for all the help desks. It can be difficult to set up the call logging or problem resolution software, which will be used by support to handle all the different needs, if procedures and terminology are different between groups. For example, different support groups may escalate outstanding problems differently or use different severity codes to prioritize outstanding problems. The support staff are affected when the business decides it must standardize the way support is measured, because someone will have to change procedures.

Global or International Support

Supporting customers internationally in an enterprise support environment has two additional challenges: language and world time zones. While English *is* the language of business in most parts of the world, international help desks quickly discover that there are differences between spoken and written English. Most European and Asian businesspeople can communicate in conversational English, but many problems can quickly advance and require a thorough understanding of both the language and culture. Even when support staff work indirectly on a problem, helping front-line support staff who must communicate directly with the customer behind the scenes, troubleshooting may be slower because support staff tend to think about problems in their native language. Mental translation of problem details is time-consuming and mentally taxing, which prevents staff from working on other problems. Translation errors can delay problem resolution as well.

Help desks that support American versions of English and United Kingdom English quickly discover small variations in the languages. For example, "color" is spelled "colour" in the UK. "Checks" and "schedule" are both pronounced in the UK with a soft, "sh" sound at the beginning. Some common adjectives used in the United States are considered extremely vulgar in the United Kingdom. Fortunately, since the United States established an early domination in producing computers and software, computer programming languages and most computer jargon is the same worldwide.

Time zone differences are even more pronounced in international support. Many countries, such as Australia and Japan, range from twelve to fourteen hours ahead of U.S. Pacific Coast time zones. Unless the support group provides twenty-four-hour support, five or seven days a week, there is no time when parties to a problem from these different time zones are at their offices at the same time! A support group that is available via telephone twenty-four hours a day, seven days a week is called **24x7 support** or 24 by 7 support. For example, a Bangkok customer discovers a problem and decides to call a support group during local, Bangkok, business hours. Front-line support staff in the United States are working during a third shift of support. If support staff are multilingual, they may be able to communicate with the customer, but higher level staff are hired for their technical expertise, rather than for their foreign language skills.

2

One approach to providing global support is to establish regionally located help desks (part of enterprise support) to meet the language and time zone challenges. However, if the help desks support the same products over all the regions, it makes sense to try to share the expertise of all support staff. Although call tracking software may be customized regionally for the preferred language of support staff, a **knowledge base** (a centralized collection of accumulated knowledge about questions, issues, procedures, or problems) is usually stored in English. Regional support staff may need to translate written documents before customers can use them, which creates a delay in solving problems.

As the sun works its way across the face of the planet, many support groups would like to see problems seamlessly handed off at the end of the workday to another support group in a different time zone, in a concept called **follow the sun support**. If a customer in one time zone reports a problem that isn't resolved before the end of the business day in that time zone, the support person hands off the problem to someone who is still working in another time zone. The goal is to make sure that serious problems are continuously worked on, so that service levels are the same for all customers, regardless of geographic location. The simplest technology approach for this level of support is to use a single (possibly very large) database for all users, so everyone has access to the same information. For this to work, support staff need fast and reliable network response.

Educational Organizations

Help desks for universities, colleges, and even public school systems usually consider the people they support as "internal" to the organization. They face the challenge of volume, but in a slightly different way.

The staff providing the services is usually a small handful of permanent employees and a few student volunteers or computer science interns. **Frequently asked questions** (**FAQs**) are written collections of common customer queries and their answers. While the staff may handle software problems directly, they usually support their customers by maintaining FAQs and troubleshooting tips.

TIP   The Internet News service is an excellent example of the use of FAQs. When readers "subscribe" to the mailing list on a particular subject, they often have questions about the format of material, what should be sent to the list, and even how to discontinue receiving the mail. The FAQs are distributed to all new people joining mailing lists.

An educational community can be made up of several thousand students and full- or part-time faculty members. The students may only be part of the university for a short time, because they may attend for a single semester. Not only must student login accounts be added at the beginning of a semester, but they also must be terminated at the end of each semester. Software problems with packages such as e-mail and Internet browsers are very repetitive but because there is a constant flow of new students, the volume of questions as well as the administrative functions remain very high.

CHAPTER SUMMARY

❐ Support groups define processes specific to the goals of their business. The majority of support groups use processes that are specific to supporting either internal or external customers. Processes for these groups either focus on technology issues or on the relationship between a company and its customers. There are also special environments that require a blending of traditionally internal and external processes.

❐ Internal support groups, or help desks, support the company's employees. Questions and problems focus on technologies used to complete business tasks. It is difficult to show how an internal support group aids the company, so funding may be short and many help desks are understaffed.

❐ External support groups take questions and solve problems for people outside of the company who buy their company's products and services. External support groups focus on the relationship between a company and its customers. Questions and problems may not necessarily be technically challenging, unless the business sells electronics, computers, or computer software. These groups often generate revenue directly and may be better funded and staffed than internal support groups.

❐ Call logging, problem management, and problem resolution are support processes common to all support groups. Other processes are specific to the type of environment, but many businesses have both internal and external support groups.

❐ Some very special environments challenge both internal and external support groups. These challenges include handling large numbers of calls daily, supporting companies that merge and may support different products, dispatching information for field service and repairs, and providing support internationally across time zones and in multiple languages. Additional technologies are used by the support group to address specialized needs.

KEY TERMS

24x7 support — The support group is available via telephone twenty-four hours a day, seven days a week.

account management — *See* customer management.

asset management — The process of collecting and maintaining records about technology, such as hardware or software components and other office equipment.

attachment — An additional file appended to a call record that provides detailed information for troubleshooting.

automatic call distribution (ACD) system — Special telephone equipment that manages incoming calls by answering calls to route them quickly to staff who are not already on the telephone.

call logging — The process of creating records that capture details about problems, requests, and questions as they are reported to the support group.

change management — The process of controlling additions, modifications, and deletions of hardware or software in a computerized system.

2

change request — A written document that describes a technological change, the reason why the change must be made, the customers potentially affected, and the related technologies and tasks required to make the change.

charge code — A financial code used by an accounting or billing application to generate an invoice for a customer.

chargeback — The accounting activity of allocating expenses of an internal support group back to the departments that use its services, based upon the number of services they use.

customer management — The process of collecting customer information and building a relationship between a company and its customers.

customer surveys — A tool to collect feedback from customers about products or services.

deployment — The rapid installation of new software or software upgrades on large numbers of desktop computers electronically.

dispatch — To send.

dispatcher — A front-line support person who answers telephone calls but forwards problems to someone else to solve.

enterprise support — Multiple support groups located in different regions of the country to allow better support coverage over different time zones.

entitlements — The number of calls a customer can make to the help desk for a set fee or the office hours when they can reach someone in customer support.

escalate — To raise an issue to the next level of support or to notify managers.

external support group — A support group that addresses questions, problems, or requests from customers who buy their company's products and services.

follow the sun support — A support concept whereby problems are seamlessly handed off at the end of the workday to another support group in a different time zone.

frequently asked questions (FAQs) — Written collections of common customer queries and their answers.

front-line support — The point of first contact with the customer.

guru — A coworker who learns to use new tools quickly and who helps other employees unofficially.

handheld computer — *See* personal digital assistant.

help desk — A common name for an internal support group. *See also* internal support group.

hotline support — A support group that doesn't usually collect information about the caller; it just counts the number of times a particular question is asked.

internal support group — A department within a company that responds to questions, problems, or requests from company employees.

knowledge base — A centralized collection of accumulated knowledge about questions, issues, procedures, or problems.

level one support — *See* front-line support.

multilevel support model — Defines the role a support person plays in different support processes and the amount of interaction the support person has with a customer.

network management software — Software that monitors the "traffic" on a network between PCs, printers, and other shared pieces of hardware.

outsource — To contract a service to an external support group.

pager — A small, wireless telecommunications receiver, generally used by people who are continually changing their location or who are not necessarily able to answer a telephone call immediately.

personal digital assistant (PDA) — Any small mobile handheld device that provides computing and information storage, and retrieval capabilities.

point of sale systems — The modern versions of cash registers that print receipts, validate charge cards, record sales, transmit sales nightly to a centralized computer system, count the number of items sold, request stock replacements, and track customer demographics.

problem — An event that prevents someone from completing a task.

problem management — The process of tracking and resolving problems that are reported to a support group.

problem resolution — Finding the cause of a problem, removing or preventing the cause, and correcting the disruption the problem caused.

questions — Inquiries customers make about small tasks or subjects they don't understand.

relationship management — The process of collecting and managing customer information to improve customer loyalty.

remote access control — Software that allows support staff to temporarily take "control" of the computer from the user and review or install software over the network.

request — A customer order for new hardware, software, or services, or for an enhancement to a product or service a customer already uses.

request management — The process of collecting information about the customer that will be used to complete the request, identifying the tasks and resources needed to complete the request, and tracking the request until delivery.

return merchandise authorization (RMA) — A special code or number assigned to a product being returned that is used to record details of the problem and the desired corrective action.

service level agreement (SLA) — A formal, written definition of the services a support group will deliver, when and how they will deliver those services, the customer's role in providing information about problems, and how service is measured.

software change management — The process computer software developers use to prioritize, manage, and control software changes, especially when many programmers are working on many computer programs.

subject matter expert (SME) — Members of level two or level three support with a greater amount of experience or knowledge about a particular subject than level one support.

support environment — The collection of customers that a support group assists, the tasks customers need or want to complete, the technologies those customers and support staff use to complete tasks, and the experience and skill of the support staff.

system management software — Software that monitors transactions and errors on a single piece of hardware.

REVIEW QUESTIONS

2

1. Identify at least three technologies used by company employees to complete their business tasks.

2. The primary purpose or service of an internal help desk is to answer questions and solve problems for _____.

3. In addition to answering questions and solving problems, what are four other types of services that may be available from an internal help desk?

4. Identify two sources of stress for staff of an internal help desk.

5. What types of products or services might require an external support group?

6. List two reasons why a company may set up an external support group.

7. What three processes are common to both internal and external support groups?

8. A(n) _____ is an event that prevents someone from completing a task.

9. What three steps are completed as part of problem resolution?

10. _____ is another phrase for problem management.

11. The information from an asset management system that would be most useful to support staff trying to resolve a software problem is the:

   a. location of the equipment.

   b. purchase price of the equipment.

   c. list of installed software and their versions.

   d. person who approved the purchase of the equipment.

12. _____ is the process that attempts to prevent problems by monitoring additions, modifications, and deletions made to a PC.

13. _____ software monitors transactions and errors on a single piece of hardware. _____ software monitors transactions or traffic between multiple pieces of hardware.

14. What are the main steps in request management?

15. What is the difference between the information collected for a request and the information collected from a hotline?

16. When would a company not know who its customers are before they call?

17. A service level agreement does not include:

   a. how services are delivered.

   b. the hours of operation for the support group and contact numbers.

   c. the customer's role in providing information.

   d. the names of support staff members and their telephone numbers.

18. List three products that might require an RMA.

19. What do customer surveys attempt to measure?

20. _____ , a process similar to change management, is used by software developers to prioritize, manage, and control customer requests for enhancements.

21. What technology is used to automatically route telephone calls to support staff?

22. How can company mergers add to stress on support staff?

23. What type of business could result in high call volume challenges, nonstandardized equipment to support, and technically unsophisticated customers to support?

24. What differentiates a point of sale system from a cash register?

25. What piece of support technology has become common enough that even a child understands how to use it?

26. _____ consists of multiple support groups located in different regions of the country.

27. Name two challenges an international support group faces.

28. What is a knowledge base?

29. What is follow the sun support?

30. Is a university support group considered internal or external?

HANDS-ON PROJECTS

Project 2-1

Categorizing internal help desk calls. The following summaries are examples of the types of telephone calls a help desk might receive. Categorize each item as a question, request, or problem.

1. How do I get access to the accounting database?

2. When I try to log in, it says my password has expired.

3. I need to set up a login and password on the network for a new employee.

4. All my printed pages have black smudge marks on them.

5. It's taking more than an hour to get my three-page document printed.

6. When I click on a hypertext link on our Web page, I get a "404" error.

7. I can't see other PCs under Network Neighborhood.

8. Netscape was unable to locate the server **home.netscape.com**.

9. When I select WordPerfect from the Programs menu, I get a message that says "can't locate."

10. What are the help desk hours?

11. Is there another printer on the network I can print to?

12. Please install a new color printer.

13. How do I add a column in an Excel spreadsheet?

14. I need to print the report titles at the top of all my spreadsheet pages.

15. When I try to retrieve a Word document, it says it is already locked by another user.

16. How do I order an upgrade to my project management software?

17. My mouse doesn't move smoothly across the screen.

18. Is there a way to insert a graph into a Word document?

19. I spilled coffee on my keyboard, and the keys stick.

20. I'm not getting any telephone calls since last week.

21. My voice mail box is full; how do I clean it out?

22. I can't save any more files because the disk is full.

23. The toner cartridge in the third-floor printer needs to be changed.

24. They worked on my PC yesterday, and now I can't log in.

25. My CRT is smoking, and I smell something burning.

26. How do I turn the sound off?

27. How do I turn off headers in Word for just the first page?

28. There is a strange file on my home directory, and I can't delete it.

29. How do I access our Web page from my home computer?

30. I think there is a virus on my PC. Can someone look at it?

Project 2-2

Categorizing external help desk calls. The following items are examples of the types of telephone calls customer support might receive. Categorize each item as a question, request, or problem.

1. Where is the nearest service center?

2. How long is my computer under warranty?

3. My trial period has expired; how do I get a permanent serial number?

4. Do I have to place orders through my sales representative?

5. How do I find out who my sales representative is?

6. What are your support hours?

7. Can I get extended support for weekends and holidays?

8. When are your next training classes?

9. Do you have a list of consultants who are trained to work with your software?

10. I need to return my monitor. It was broken during shipping.

11. What is the location of your Web page?

12. How long will release 5 be supported?

13. Do I need to worry about any date or time problems with your product?

14. What UNIX platforms will your software run on?

15. I get an error when I try to install this under Linux.

16. After installing your software, my screen has gone blue and a lot of numbers appear.

17. I can't get your sound card to work with Dune.

18. What microphones work with your software?

19. I can't get my microphone to record anything.

20. Can I run the software on a database other than Microsoft Access?

21. Has anyone had a problem trying to set up the Outlook group scheduler with your resource application?

22. How do I set up e-mail in your software?

23. When I try to log in, it says my serial number has expired.

24. I need to export data from your database to Excel.

25. The install program asks for disks, but I have only a CD-ROM.

26. I'm stumped at the gates. Where should I have found the golden key to unlock the gate?

27. Every day I get a reminder to register my software, but I already have.

28. Your modem can't find my COM port.

29. Do I have to ship back everything or just the broken mouse?

30. Where can I buy accessories for the laptop computer I bought from your company?

Project 2-3

Collecting real-world information about support. Interview a classmate, coworker, or business person who has worked in support, or arrange a visit to your educational organization's support group. Identify any special support challenges for this support group and summarize them in a one-page report. Use the following questions to help collect information for the report:

1. What was the support environment (internal or external)?

2. How many telephone calls were received a day?

3. What processes were part of this environment?

Project 2-4

Locating hotlines. There are many consumer-oriented hotlines. Go to the kitchen, bathroom, garage, or a grocery store and review packages of food, toiletries, or household items, looking for at least two hotline numbers for consumer questions. If you cannot find a product, complete a Web search for "hotline." Answer the following questions based on your search:

1. Was the hotline established to support a product or was it a general, consumer information number?

2. Call the hotline. Did you speak with a person, or was it a recorded message? If you spoke with a person, what questions were they prepared to answer?

3. Would you recommend this hotline to other consumers? Explain your answer.

4. If you used a Web search to find this hotline and if a consumer did not have access to the Web, what other ways could they use to find information about this product?

Project 2-5

Analyzing FAQs. Visit a university or college home page on the Web, or a news group. Find an FAQ list and print the list of questions (it is not necessary to print the individual questions and answers, just the index or a summary of the questions). Answer the following questions:

1. Who is the intended user of this FAQ?

2. How many questions are included?

3. Are there any questions that should be added?

Project 2-6

Comparing SLAs. Complete a Web search, looking for examples of service level agreements. Collect one example from a university and one from a business help desk. (*Hint*: Use the phrase "service level agreement" for your Web search to find these examples. Be sure to check the search engine's online Help for how to enter the text to search for a phrase instead of the individual words. Many search engines do phrase searching when the phrase is in quotation marks.) Answer the following questions for each SLA, and then summarize the differences between them in a few paragraphs:

1. What elements are included in the SLA (e.g., hours of operation, priorities, escalation procedures, etc.)?

2. What are the emergency procedures?

3. Are there any additional items documented in the SLA?

Project 2-7

Locating hardware repair services. Using your local Yellow Pages or the Yellow Pages for a large city, locate at least two vendors who provide computer hardware repairs. Answer the following questions for each vendor:

1. Are these local companies or do they have offices nationwide?

2. Visit the Web sites of these companies if they are listed. Identify companies who provide services for companies, rather than for single individuals.

3. What are their service hours?

4. Do they dispatch field repair workers?

5. Are there any special services they offer that you might not expect, such as loaner equipment, free pickup and delivery, or preventive maintenance checkups?

Project 2-8

Evaluating PDAs. Visit the 3Com Web site at **http://www.3com.com** and the Hewlett-Packard Web site at **http://www.hp.com** and follow the links to their PDA products. Answer the following questions about both vendors' products:

1. How many different models are available?
2. What is the memory capacity of these devices? How does this compare to a PC?
3. What are the physical dimensions?
4. What are the operating systems used?
5. What types of software are available for these devices?

Project 2-9

Reviewing different service levels. Visit the Netscape support Web page at **http://home.netscape.com/support** and follow the links until you find a list of support services that are available. Prepare a short report describing three different levels of support available and the intended customer for those service levels.

CASE PROJECTS

1. Managing Outsourced Hardware Repairs

You are the manager for an internal support group. Your company buys computers from three different resellers and buys an extended service program for hardware repairs from each company. They will not dispatch a field service repairperson without a valid serial number for each device. Your company uses an asset management system, and all new equipment is tracked with its serial number in this system. As new equipment arrives, the hardware setup team schedules the installation of equipment with each customer. The hardware setup team also moves equipment as people move their offices. Design a process with written procedures to make sure that serial number information and the location of each computer is recorded and updated. Be sure to include situations in which the hardware vendor replaces equipment, as well as those in which your own staff do so.

2. Using Surveys to Monitor Customer Loyalty

Your company develops accounting software and the vice president of product development wants to determine if the software's quality affects your customers' satisfaction. The vice president wants to begin by focusing on the most severe problems reported. Design a customer survey that will be automatically mailed when each "critical" problem is reported and that focuses on questions about the product. Include a short summary paragraph that explains why you want your customers to complete this information. Be sure to collect enough information to determine how you can prevent the problem from happening again and to determine whether you are likely to lose this customer to a competitor.

3. **Set Up a Lab Support Group**

Work with three to five classmates and set up a "help desk" to provide support for questions and problems you experience within your computer lab environment. Decide on and document the information needed to address problems. Assign different people to track and manage questions and problems. Another person should create and maintain FAQs as you discover questions that you think other classmates may also experience. Write a procedural guide for submitting questions, managing problems, and publishing the FAQs. Include an escalation procedure for problems or questions the students cannot resolve, and escalate these issues to your instructor.

2

3

COMMON SUPPORT SOFTWARE TOOLS AND FEATURES

In this chapter you will learn:

♦ The basic characteristics of all support software

♦ The primary features of call logging software

♦ The key features of problem management software

♦ How problem resolution software relates to problem management

♦ Additional support tools that assist with specific support processes

---

As companies use and rely on more technologies, the demand to support the companies' business users increases as well. It is no longer possible to track problems or requests with pen and paper systems. Instead, support groups depend on support software, which automates the processes of logging questions and problems and tracking the history of interactions with callers. Support managers also will use the software to determine why business users are calling and what the support staff are doing about the calls. Without automated assistance, it is difficult to measure a support group's performance and even harder to prove that a support group is meeting its goals.

Newly established support groups begin in **reactive mode**, in which support staff respond to problems that computer users report. Effective software helps the support group move to a **proactive mode**, in which support staff use tools to detect problems early and prevent more serious problems, rather than waiting for computer users to report problems. The support staff use software to be more productive while they help computer users be more productive in their own tasks.

When selecting new software, a support manager must review the software's features carefully to ensure that it will work well in the support environment and enable the support group to add new services. The software must enable support staff to work more efficiently and must collect statistics as staff complete their daily activities. These statistics make it possible for managers to quantify support activities by tracking how many calls the support group receives, how long it takes to complete tasks, and how many problems require more than one resource.

BASIC CHARACTERISTICS OF ALL SUPPORT SOFTWARE

Support software varies in look and feel and may emphasize different processes, but it includes two core activities: putting data in and getting information out. **Data** is raw numbers or facts collected in a database. **Information** is data that is organized into something meaningful. As the business of support and support software development matures, new features continue to increase support productivity. These features can be grouped into the categories listed in Figure 3-1.

> ◆ Multiuser access
>
> ◆ Data entry
>
> ◆ Information retrieval

Figure 3-1   Support software feature categories

Multiuser Access

Groupware is software that enables multiple people to work together electronically. Groupware, such as Lotus Notes and Microsoft Exchange, enables people to share different types of information, such as schedules, task lists, or word processing files, even when they don't work in the same office or building. Administrators set up the software so workgroups can view the same information. People within a group can also define the kinds of information they are interested in and when they should receive notifications. Groupware users can also decide whether to allow others to change data once it is entered, or if only the owner can make changes.

Support software is a specialized form of groupware that enables support staff to share details of problems or requests. Support groups are usually made up of teams. Teams can be divided into support levels, or multiple teams can exist within each level, depending upon the support group's needs. Team members work together, and a team regularly routes or escalates calls to other teams. If a customer wants an update on an outstanding problem, a level one resource can easily retrieve a call record that was escalated to another team and review the problem history. At the same time, any team member can collect additional information, update the call record, or electronically ask the person who originally spoke with the customer to call the customer back with an update.

Data Entry

Software with a high degree of user friendliness or ease of use enables speedy data entry. The combination of the user interface, required fields, auto-fill fields, pull-down lists, shortcut keys, and tab order defines a software application's **ease of use**. The faster that support staff can record problem details, the faster they can begin resolving the problem.

User Interface

A **user interface** is the portion of the software with which the user interacts. The support staff add records to the database with a text or graphical user interface. A **graphical user interface (GUI)** is a picture-oriented way to interact with a computer, using a mouse or joystick to select commands instead of typing them. Microsoft Windows has been the standard GUI for business computer users for many years. Over time, GUIs replaced text-entry interfaces because they required minimal typing skills.

The way that data is organized under a GUI allows it to be manipulated quickly.

Required Entry Fields

In some support environments, there are certain fields that support staff must complete for every call record. **Required entry fields** are data entry fields that must be completed correctly before the record can be saved in the database. They cannot be left blank. For example, the problem summary is usually a required field because it does not make sense to save a call record without a synopsis of the problem. If the support analyst forgets to record data, a pop-up message warns that the call record cannot be saved. Over time, collecting the required data becomes a regular habit.

A required entry field is the fastest way to ensure that all support staff remember to collect needed information. However, too many required entry fields slow down data entry and frustrate both the support staff and customers. As a result, staff members may take shortcuts by selecting the first available value or entering nonsense data. When that happens, managers can no longer rely upon the data as a valid measure of performance. Most support software can be customized to add or remove required fields as needed. A well-designed data entry form limits required fields to those that contribute information to solving the problem or request (support staff would not be able to troubleshoot without the information).

Of course, support staff must still type in details about a support problem, but some software features help to minimize the amount of typing required and to standardize terminology. These features include auto-fill, pull-down menus, shortcut keys, and tab order.

Auto-Fill Fields

With **auto-fill**, as the user begins to type a word or phrase, the complete word or phrase that matches the typed letters is pulled in from a list of stored words. For example, a user might type "prob" and the word "problem" appears. Another form of auto-fill occurs when a user types an abbreviation, which is then expanded to a full word or phrase. Support staff can learn a standard set of abbreviations, which can dramatically increase their speed when recording call details. For example, support staff can type "esc" and the auto-fill feature expands it to "ticket escalated to level two."

TIP

Microsoft Word has auto-fill features called AutoCorrect, AutoText, and AutoComplete. On the menu bar, click Tools, AutoCorrect, and then on the AutoCorrect or AutoText tab, enter words or abbreviations you want to replace automatically with the full text.

A third type of auto-fill is information that the software enters without any user input, such as a date or time. For example, most support software records the dates and times when a call record is created, updated, and closed. A support person may forget to record the date and time or enter the incorrect date and time. To ensure accuracy, the software automatically records the date and time when certain fields change and when the record is saved.

Auto-fill is also called **canned text** or **predefined phrases**.

Pull-down Lists

A **pull-down list** is a predefined list of acceptable values from which only one value can be selected. Figure 3-2 shows a pull-down list in a call logging software program. In Windows-based applications, pressing the first letter of the desired value usually scrolls the pull-down list to the first value for that letter.

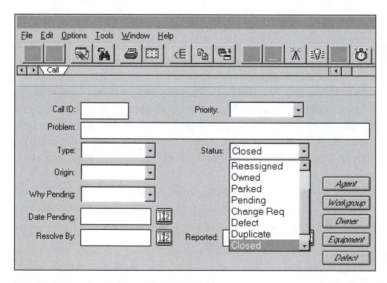

Figure 3-2 Sample pull-down list

Pull-down lists are also called **picklists**.

3

In addition to speeding up data entry by eliminating typing, pull-down lists ensure that data is entered consistently. For example, if the Windows version associated with a problem is stored in a character entry field, support staff can enter the Windows version in a variety of formats or abbreviations that can be interpreted roughly the same way:

Win98
Windows 98
Windows98 (without a space)
MS Windows
Windows

A pull-down list forces support staff to select the one and only acceptable format for this value.

Shortcut Keys

Some support staff type very well and prefer to keep their hands on the keyboard. For them, shortcut keys speed up data entry. A **shortcut key** or **accelerator key** is a key or combination of keys that replaces several separate steps to automate a task. Windows-based software usually allows the use of shortcut keys. For example, computer users can save a file in any Microsoft application by using the mouse to click the File menu, and then click the Save command. The shortcut key for saving a file is holding down the Ctrl key while pressing the letter "S." Common tasks within an application should be assigned shortcut keys to save time.

Tab Order

Another technique to keep the support staff's hands on the keyboard is to arrange entry fields in a logical order and to have the staff press the Tab key to move from one field to the next. **Tab order** is the sequence in which the cursor advances from field to field when the Tab key is pressed. If the entry fields are not arranged in the order in which information is given and the cursor does not move correctly between entry fields, the staff members will have to lift their hands from the keyboard and use the mouse to position the cursor.

Information Retrieval

Well-designed software should have a variety of ways to find and remove data from the database. (Some methods are used by managers and administrators, rather than support staff.) Like data entry, retrieval should be simple and fast. The support staff should be able to quickly search for one record, or a group of records that matches a set of conditions. **Query by example (QBE)** is a search technique that uses queries or questions to find records that match specific conditions. An example of a simple query is:

Find all call records created before March 12, 2002.

Depending on the size of the database, this simple query can return hundreds of records. Adding comparison operators to contrast a specific characteristic between two expressions can reduce the records found by this search. For example, "is greater than" and "is equal to" or the corresponding symbols ">" and "=" allow you to compare two numbers or strings of letters and words. **Comparison operators**, words such as AND, OR, or NOT, evaluate comparisons to determine if they are true or false.

Find all calls created before March 12, 2002 AND where the caller's name is Harry Smith.

Limiting a search with comparison operators results in fewer found records, which makes it easier to find a specific piece of information. Support staff repeatedly use many of the same queries as they work. To help them work more efficiently, most support software includes a basic set of predefined queries. Other software allows the support staff to define and save additional, custom queries.

Comparison operatiors are also called **logical operators**.

In addition to finding specific records, support software should make it simple for support staff to print the details of one or more selected records. Some support software also works with a network fax application to allow staff to "print" records to a fax machine. This is very useful when, for example, a company outsources hardware repairs to another company. The fax feature brings up an electronic fax cover sheet, auto-fills the summary of the problem, and then sends the fax. Without this timesaving feature, support staff would have to print the record, prepare a fax cover sheet, and then manually fax the information.

Most support software works with e-mail. An e-mail option or icon opens an e-mail message composition window. This feature may auto-fill the e-mail address based upon the caller information for that record, as well as place the problem summary or the call record number in the subject field. When support staff complete the message, the support software passes the e-mail to the company's standard e-mail system for routing.

Reports are another type of output that is critical for support software to create; otherwise management cannot measure and analyze a support group's performance against its goals. To create reports, managers use queries to select the appropriate data. They can then print the report results on paper, send the results by fax or e-mail, or store them as a file on the network.

Chapter 4 covers support performance measurements and reporting in detail.

FEATURES OF CALL LOGGING SOFTWARE

As support groups become more common, there are certain processes that all companies put in place. Support staff learn quickly how to adapt software features for their particular support environments, but all call logging software has the fields and features listed in Figure 3-3.

> ♦ Reference number
>
> ♦ Caller information
>
> ♦ Problem or request details
>
> ♦ Type of call
>
> ♦ Resolution

3

Figure 3-3   Call logging software features

Reference Number

Almost all support software automatically generates a **reference number**, a unique code that identifies a specific record in a database, for each call logged. A help desk receives many calls, some with very similar descriptions. Also, one caller may experience the same problem several times. As long as a problem is resolved while the caller is still on the telephone, it is not necessary to know the call record's reference number. However, problems that take days or weeks to resolve are assigned a unique reference number to ensure that the customer and support staff are discussing the same problem during each conversation. One of the fastest ways for support staff to find a caller's record is to create a query for the reference number.

 Electronic records have many names, including calls, tickets, incidents, events, and problems. Some support groups create new acronyms to represent a record, such as Customer Action Request (CAR), Development Action Request (DAR), Call Record (CR), or Problem Report (PR).

Many support groups ask their customers to remember the reference number assigned to their problems so support staff can retrieve the records quickly in subsequent contact with the caller. Be aware that support staff cannot rely upon callers to have their reference number available each time they call back about a problem. It is too easy for people to write down the wrong reference number or misplace it. As long as support staff can quickly query for open calls by customer, and there are a limited number of open calls per customer, they should not need a reference number to retrieve the problem details.

 Software that requires support staff to know the call reference number to retrieve the record is inefficient. Support staff should be able to find any call record based on a search for the caller's name and a description of the problem.

Caller Information

Customers who call a support group often get annoyed if they have to repeat too much information every time they call or are transferred to another support person. When the support group collects information about customers, the support software should store it. Support staff should be able to quickly retrieve the existing information and verify that the most important items are still accurate for each new call.

Caller information includes facts about the customer at the time a problem or question is reported. The types and amount of caller information a support group maintains within the support software depend upon the type of problem and whether the customer has a question, problem, or request. If the problem or question cannot be answered while the caller is on the telephone, then the support staff must collect the caller's name and telephone number so they can contact the caller if they need more information or when they have a solution. Depending upon the customer's availability, support staff may also collect a pager number, e-mail address, or the customer's preferred contact method (voice message, page, or e-mail).

 Customers appreciate it when support staff ask for a preferred notification method and use it for follow-up calls.

Figure 3-4 lists caller information that might be collected about customers.

Useful Caller Information	
Basic Information	First Name
	Last Name
	Preferred Name or Nickname
	Title
	Department
	Telephone Number or Extension
	E-mail Address
	Fax Number
	Pager Number and PIN
	Work Shift/Time Zone
	Second Telephone Number
	Preferred Notification Method
	Location
Additional Internal Customer Information	Login ID
	Employee Number
	Manager's Name
	Building
	Floor
	Cost Center
	VIP Status
Additional External Customer Information	Home Telephone Number
	Personal Web Page
	Mailing Address
	Account Number
	Sales Representative

Figure 3-4   Caller information that support groups may collect

Sometimes, it is also important to know the physical location of the customer. If a support person must go onsite to make repairs or to install new software, the support staff need to know the customer's location. In addition, support staff also need to be able to identify a physical piece of equipment, and to identify it on the network. Telephone jacks are sometimes numbered on the wall plate, so the support staff can troubleshoot network or telephone problems. The support staff might also find out in which department an employee works, so that management can determine which departments use (or abuse) support services based on the number of support calls they make.

Some internal support groups track calls from "special" employees or company VIPs. A **VIP**, or **very important person**, is a person who performs a special role in the company, such as the secretary to the company president. For example, if the president's secretary cannot complete daily tasks, this may have a greater effect on the company than problems in other departments. Support software may display a special indicator on VIP caller records to alert support staff that this caller needs or expects a special level of service.

Internal support groups may also associate caller information in the call logging system with equipment or software. Computer users don't always know the hardware or software information when they have a problem. After support staff discover hardware and software versions installed at a customer's location, the information can be used to troubleshoot later problems faster.

External support groups need similar information. Instead of VIP status, they need to know the type of support contract or services the customer should receive and what products he or she owns. They collect mailing addresses instead of location, building, and floor. They may also notify the customer's account manager, in case issues need to be forwarded directly to that person. An **account manager** is a company representative assigned to manage the interactions between a company and its customers.

 Account managers may also be called "client partners" or "sales representatives." These people play a key role in customer management. See the Chapter 2 Close Up, "The Growing Emphasis on Managing Customer Relationships," for more information.

Problem or Request Details

A **call summary** is a concise description of the problem or request that is a few sentences in length. Some software allows short summaries (forty to eighty characters); others allow a short paragraph (240 characters). The summary usually appears in the user interface along with the reference number to identify the specific problem. If support staff need more information, there may also be another field (possibly on another screen, or one that opens a separate window) to record more details, such as problem symptoms or troubleshooting activities. This second field is usually a **free format** or text type of field, which means that the data is not stored in a specific structure. A word processing document is an example of free format—the number and length of paragraphs and sentences can vary, depending on the purpose.

Free format text is also referred to as **free text**.

Types of Calls

Another call logging feature provides a way to categorize and organize different call records. This is done with one or more fields in the GUI. A **category** is a classification of problems or requests. The category field is usually required when the call record is created and is often a pull-down list of predefined values. Support groups may categorize calls by software application or by feature, depending upon their reporting needs. Some sample categories include:

- Mainframe software
- PC software
- Login problems
- Printer problems
- Telephone problems
- New user requests

Support staff can use categories as part of a QBE condition to narrow search results. For example, a support person may need to find all printer problems reported during a certain day or by a department. If the support staff resolve the caller's problem, request, or question during the initial call, categories can be linked to automated displays in another section of the GUI that list the more frequently occurring questions or problems for that subject area. Support managers also use categories when creating performance reports to help identify problem trends.

 Using too specific categories slows down the call logging process because support staff may need more time to scroll through a long pull-down list to decide which category should be used. On the other hand, using too general categories does not adequately limit the number of records retrieved during searches. For example, the PC software category can be broken into the specific software applications, such as Word and Excel. Then, an increase in Excel questions after a new release will be more apparent.

Resolution

It is important in the call logging process to document how problems were solved, in case the problem returns or the customer is not satisfied with the solution. Separate fields or other database records may be used to record the solution to or the cause of the problem. A **resolution** field contains information on how a problem is solved or can be prevented. Support staff can use the resolution when responding to calls by other computer users with the same problem.

Some support staff take shortcuts when recording resolutions. Instead of explaining what was done to fix the problem, they enter "fixed" in the resolution field or leave it blank. This wastes time with future calls because support staff must solve the same problem every time it is reported. When the call record includes an explanation of the specific steps that actually resolved the problem (and excludes blind alleys that delayed a solution), support staff can assist other callers with the same problem. Documenting resolutions allows staff to share their experiences and skills.

3

software toolbox

JOHN RAGSDALE
SENIOR PRODUCT MARKETING MANAGER
CLARIFY, INC. (SOFTWARE PUBLISHER)
SAN JOSE, CALIFORNIA
THE EVOLVING USER INTERFACE FOR SUPPORT

As support groups evolve and standardize processes, most companies look to the leading software vendors to provide software that supports and enforces core support processes and procedures (also called "best practices"), workflow, and data management. Companies use this "out-of-the-box functionality" as a guideline for implementation and ongoing management. The people who implement support software tools not only have to develop a technical implementation plan (determining hardware and software required, identifying installation requirements, defining basic table information, and loading initial customer information), but they also have to improve processes for support, problem management, escalation, and customer management.

Although research analysts still evaluate applications based on out-of-the-box functionality, software developers are moving away from trying to fit more and more features into the applications, because it is growing increasingly difficult to find a set of enhancements that meets the needs of a majority of the customer base. A single version of data entry forms no longer satisfies the needs of all support staff in a single company either. As companies consolidate their support and customer management operations, support staff may support many different products, and they need to track specific data for historical and reporting purposes.

Resource-based configurations support these different workflows. Administrators build customized forms and fields, based upon the role support staff play and the products they work with. Application pull-down lists can be customized in the same way, so a PC support staff member and a telecommunications subject matter expert can track different information, with different workflows, while using the same database.

Being able to control how support staff interact with the system on such a granular level means that productivity is increased, and the system helps collect the information that is truly needed by the support group. It also allows companies to support worldwide support operations using a single server instance, which has obvious benefits for not only budgets, but combined reporting as well.

The latest trend for software developers is toward a toolkit approach—providing a core framework with tools to support easy customizations. These customizations include custom menus, such as drop-in controls, colorful chart and graph options, and simpler code bases, such as XML, which make creating new flows and features simpler and faster to implement. In years to come, instead of full-featured, deep functionality in a single, out-of-the-box workflow, expect to see applications shipped with multiple, optional workflows, allowing the company to design a completely site-specific application. The key here is to provide upgradeable software that enables companies to preserve their customizations, so that neither database nor user interface changes are lost in future releases.

FEATURES OF PROBLEM MANAGEMENT SOFTWARE

Not all support calls can be resolved while the caller is still on the telephone with the support group. This may occur because:

- The volume of calls exceeds what the support staff can handle on a given day.
- The support group is understaffed.
- Level one support cannot resolve some problems because they don't have the necessary skills or security permissions.
- The caller doesn't provide enough information or can't reproduce the problem while talking to the support staff.

Outstanding calls are managed with a problem management process. **Problem management** is the process of collecting problem details, working on outstanding problems, assigning additional support staff as needed, and providing status updates to customers. Support software usually includes features to help support staff manage outstanding problems. Problem management requires the fields and features that are listed in Figure 3-5.

```
♦ Ownership
♦ Workgroup assignment
♦ Current state
♦ Priority
♦ Escalation
♦ Problem history and
   troubleshooting log
♦ Pending work
```

Figure 3-5 Problem management software features

Ownership

Customers want to make sure the problems they report will be addressed quickly and by a person who clearly understands the problem and its history. An essential factor in providing service is ownership of an outstanding issue. Once a call is logged, one person should be the **owner**, the support staff employee who is responsible for moving the call to a resolution and for updating the customer. Ownership can be transferred at any time to another staff member. Problem management software should record the name of the support staff member who created the call record as well as the current owner.

The call record originator is not always the first owner, especially in dispatch support groups. First, a dispatcher collects the problem details and the required caller information. The dispatcher's login or name is tracked as the creator of the call record. Then, the field service representative who is assigned the problem becomes the problem owner until the hardware is repaired. Support managers track outstanding repair call records by owner to see how unresolved work is distributed.

Workgroup Assignments

A **workgroup** is a team of people who work together on a project. Problem management is usually implemented with workgroups. Larger support groups organize front-line and level two support staff into teams. Teams specialize in specific categories of problems, such as mainframe software issues or PC installation requests. Subject matter experts (SME), who are members of level two or level three support, may work on large projects as well as assist with problems that the front-line staff cannot address. They may also work in physically remote areas, so front-line staff cannot always tell who is in the office and available to take ownership of a call.

A **queue** is a line of things to be processed in sequential order. New call records that cannot be closed immediately may be routed to a workgroup using a team queue in the problem management software. Multiple staff members with the correct subject matter skills are assigned as owners of the queue. When calls are assigned to the queue, all queue owners receive an electronic notification that there is a new call to review. As support staff become available, they remove the oldest call records from the queue. Records remain "in the queue" until someone can work on them.

Moving a call record to a queue is half a step toward ownership—the number of support staff who can become responsible for this problem is narrowed to a specific team. A team leader or manager makes sure someone from the team accepts ownership in a short amount of time.

 The order of call records in the queue may change, if outstanding problems are solved in order of severity, rather than in "first in first out" order. The Priority section below also discusses this issue.

Routing outstanding work to queues is also easier for dispatchers (who only log calls and route them to subject matter specialists). Rather than having to know the names of support staff members on the network troubleshooting team, the front-line staff can route a call to the network queue. All the people on the network troubleshooting team are alerted to each new call record. When members of the network troubleshooting team are sick or on vacation, they don't see the alerts, which remain in the problem management software. The network team manager can assign a different person each day to monitor the network queue or can assign owners to calls according to staff availability.

 Some applications automatically route different problem categories to the appropriate workgroup or queue.

The amount of time an item stays in the queue waiting for ownership is an important performance measurement for many support groups and is discussed in more detail in Chapter 4.

Current State

An individual's outstanding call records can be in different stages of the problem management process. Support staff may be able to track the progress of a handful of outstanding problems easily. However, some support groups manage twenty to fifty open problems per person at a time, and they need a better way to group their work by stage. **Status** is the condition or state of a call record as it progresses through the problem management process. When managers and support staff review the list of outstanding problems, they can tell at a glance where each call record is in the problem management process.

For example, when a dispatcher routes call records to a workgroup, records start in a "New" or "Unassigned" status. Once support staff members remove them from the queue, the calls move to an "Assigned" status. When support is researching the problem, it could be in an "Investigating" status. Ultimately, all calls move to a "Closed" status. If the computer user calls in within a day of the call being closed, because the problem has reappeared, the call may move to a "Reopened" status and begin the cycle again.

 Calls can always move immediately to a closed status if the call is solved while the caller is still on the telephone.

Status fields are usually pull-down lists and can have multiple open or multiple closed statuses. Some support software automatically sets the status when a particular activity occurs. For example, as soon as a support engineer enters his or her name as the call owner, the software changes the status to "Assigned." When resolution text is entered, the software changes the status to "Closed."

Multiple statuses are helpful for managing outstanding problems and for developing service level agreements with customers. For example, managers can calculate the average amount of time a call record spends in "Investigating" status. Then, they can set up an automatic notification if a call record exceeds the average. As a result, it is important for all support staff to use each status the same way.

Automatic alerts and notifications are discussed in more detail in Chapter 8.

Call Priority

3

Call priority is the order in which call records are handled, according to the business impact of the problem or request. Most service level agreements define call priorities and specify their target resolution times. A common method of measuring call priority is with a numerical scale with values that range from 1 to 3 or 1 to 5, where 1 is the highest priority. Some support groups use words such as Serious, Moderate, and Minor, to define call priority, because words identify the problems' relative importance more clearly.

As more support groups enable callers to track their own call records over the Web, they have moved away from classifying any problem as "minor", because callers can be sensitive to this word. As far as customers are concerned, all their problems or questions are important and should be treated that way.

Support software usually allows the support group to define its priorities. A call record can be created with one priority. Then, as troubleshooting progresses, or as the result of more information, support staff can change the priority.

Escalation

Another way time and record age are used to manage call records is through escalation. To escalate an issue is to raise it to the next level of support or to notify someone that an important milestone has passed. For example, if the time a call record stays in a queue pending ownership exceeds a predefined value, such as four hours, the support software can send an electronic message to the queue owners or support manager. The software generates a second escalation notice before the call record reaches the maximum open time, and hopefully the support staff will resolve the problem before it exceeds the target resolution time. The software continues to generate more escalation notices after the maximum open time, until the call record is closed. In most cases, software sends warnings to the queue owners (if the call is still in the queue), to the call owner, to other team members, and eventually to managers.

Escalation notices ensure that outstanding problems move through the problem management process according to preestablished timeframes. This helps support groups control the total age of a call record, which is also used to measure support performance.

Problem History and Troubleshooting Log

A **problem history** is the chronological sequence of activities that have occurred since the call record was created. For example, the date and time a call record moved from "Assigned" to "Investigating" status, as well as the name of the call owner, would be recorded automatically by the problem management software in a special history field. Status changes, owner changes, workgroup changes, the number of times a record was updated, and automated escalation notices are all part of the problem history. In contrast, a **troubleshooting log** is a chronological sequence of the activities the support staff performed to solve the problem. In this case, support staff record each attempted solution and the results in a field or screen. They record unsuccessful solutions to share with subject matter experts until they find the final solution. New troubleshooting entries are added to the top or bottom of the file. Once they are saved, entries will be protected so they can't be accidentally changed or erased during later editing sessions.

If support staff record troubleshooting activities in a free format text field, it can be difficult to tell when each action was taken. Timing and activity sequence can be important troubleshooting aids because other actions may be taking place at the same time. Some support software automatically dates and time stamps new troubleshooting log entries. Figure 3-6 shows a troubleshooting log.

3/20/2002 2:03 PM User dmcbranna ********************************
        Marty can't get Word to correctly display Word document. Every time she tries to apply the
        network formatting to text at the bottom of the document, the screen starts to flash and roll and she
        can no longer read it.
3/21/2002 2:15 PM User dmcbranna ********************************
        I need to know which version of Word she is using and where she got the formatting template.
        Called but got her voice mail. Asked Marty to call back on ticket number 34582 with the
        information.
3/21/2002 4:15 PM User hwilson   ********************************
        Marty called but doesn't know how to find the version of Word. Walked her through using the
        Help, About Word menu. She is using Word 97 SR-1. She got the formatting template from
        someone on the Web.

        I e-mailed a new version of the formatting template for her version of Word. Call is now closed.

Figure 3-6   Sample troubleshooting log

The three date/time stamps in the log indicate that the problem log was updated three times. The first time, the support person with the login ID "dmcbranna" recorded the basic information, but did not have a resolution. Then dmcbranna tried to call the computer user back, but had to leave a message. The support person recorded the information needed and the fact that the computer user did not answer when called. The last entry shows that another support person with a login ID of "hwilson" picked up the customer's return call, collected and recorded the missing information, and solved the problem. Later, if the customer or support manager has any questions about what happened and/or when it happened, he or she can refer to the troubleshooting log for the details.

It is important that all information be recorded in a troubleshooting log because, as in the above example, the original support person may not be available when the customer calls back. The troubleshooting log ensures that any support person can retrieve the call, review the history, and assist the caller. The customer doesn't have to wait until the original support person is available.

A team can deliver support more efficiently and quickly than staff working as individuals. Each staff member records troubleshooting actions to assist the team in the event that he or she cannot complete the work.

3

Pending Work

The support staff may carry dozens of open call records at any time. They may answer the telephones and create new calls themselves, pick up call records from the queue and accept ownership, and then manage their open work through various statuses. One of the most important features support software should have is a way to organize and view work in progress, or **pending work**. This is usually done with a special, predefined query, which is available from a pull-down list because it will be used many times everyday.

Most "Pending" or "To Do" lists arrange work so that items without owners or in queue are separated from owned items. That is because most support groups place unowned call records at a higher priority than work in progress, to ensure that someone takes the responsibility for moving call records through the problem management process. It is also important to review all new problems as they come in, to identify those that can be resolved quickly. If the problem will take some time to resolve, the first information the customer should have is the name of the support analyst who accepted ownership of the problem. At the same time, support staff can set the customer's expectations of the earliest time when someone will start working on the problem.

Another way to organize pending work is by the date the record was created or last modified. Sorting records by creation date quickly identifies items that may be overdue. Sorting records by last modified date identifies records that haven't been worked on in some time, and whose troubleshooting logs therefore haven't been updated. Some applications keep an extra field to record a follow-up date or a desired close date. Some support staff organize similar calls by category, others by the caller information. Closed call records can be grouped by date closed or by customer name. The primary purpose of a pending work list is to enable the support staff to manage work and to quickly find records they have updated.

PROBLEM RESOLUTION ELEMENTS

Some support software applications provide call logging and problem management features. More sophisticated support applications include problem resolution features as well. **Problem resolution** is the process of finding the cause of a problem, removing or preventing the cause, and correcting the disruption. Problem resolution software has special features to facilitate the problem resolution process.

As explained earlier, raw data is organized into information. Eventually, information becomes knowledge, when another person can apply it to a particular problem. This knowledge is stored in a knowledge base, a centralized collection of accumulated knowledge about questions, issues, procedures, or problems. Figure 3-7 shows how data becomes knowledge.

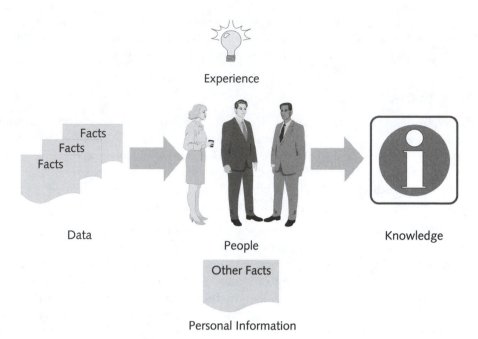

Figure 3-7   The development of knowledge

For example, programmers use a 404 code when a Web URL cannot be found. The code "404" is just a piece of data, but because most Web programmers use 404 codes for missing Web URLs, this code is now part of information about a particular error. The support analyst takes this information and begins some troubleshooting steps to determine the cause of the problem. (For example, was the page deleted? Was the Web server down?) The final cause of the problem and the steps taken to determine the cause are entered in the knowledge base when the problem is resolved. The next time someone reports a similar problem, the new knowledge—understanding what the error code means, the possible causes, and the ways to eliminate the possible causes to find a solution—can be applied to the new situation.

A support group may begin to develop a knowledge base by using information they already have. Old call records are one way to begin building knowledge, and most support applications allow support staff to search historical records. As long as there is a resolution for each call, support staff can search the summaries and categories of previous calls, review the troubleshooting steps taken for each situation, and try those same steps.

Unfortunately, there are disadvantages to using old call records:

- Hundreds of records may have the same or similar summaries. The support staff must read the details of each record, determine if that situation is the same, and then begin troubleshooting.

- Solutions may change over time. A solution for one release of software may no longer work with a later release. It is easy to waste time attempting solutions that are no longer relevant.

■ Reading old call records is inefficient, especially if the help desk handles hundreds of calls a day. Unless the records can be sorted by category and date, the volume of data will be too big to be useful.

Good problem resolution software handles different kinds of data and organizes information in multiple ways, because knowledge may exist in text or graphical forms.

Chapter 6 discusses in detail more effective and efficient problem resolution methods than using old call records.

INTEGRATION OF OTHER SUPPORT TOOLS

Call logging, problem management, and problem resolution are the core processes for every support group. Other support processes, such as asset management and change management, may be equally important to some support groups. Advanced support software may have features to support these processes. An **integrated feature** is a software feature that enables support staff to handle these other support processes, using the same application. For example, logging calls and tracking related PC information (such as company assets) can be done with the same GUI and similar menus. A **programming interface** is a set of program instructions that passes data between two different software applications. In this case, customer information may be provided by an interface to the company human resources software. Human resources staff maintain employee names, telephone numbers, and cost center information, and the interface passes the new information to the call logging system for support staff to use. The two applications have different GUIs and menus and may be used by different groups of people.

An integration or an interface affects how quickly a support staff can complete the different processes. For example, the problem resolution tool may be integrated with the problem management system. If it is integrated, the support staff can select a call record in problem management and select a menu option or button to pass the category and summary of the call to the problem resolution module. The query results may be presented in another window with a GUI that looks like the call logging screens.

Later chapters discuss specific tools for several related support processes that are frequently integrated into a single application, including:

■ Asset management

■ Change management

■ Automatic call distribution, or ACD

■ Network and system management

■ User self-service

The more tightly these tools are integrated with call logging and problem management software, the less time it takes for support staff to move from one process to another.

CHAPTER SUMMARY

❏ Support software is groupware, which enables support staff and teams to work together. With groupware, even if the responsible support analyst is unavailable, anyone else in the support group can review the call record details and inform the caller of the status of a problem or question.

❏ Graphical user interfaces (GUIs) provide a rapid format in which users can enter data. They may support ease of use features, including auto-fill fields, pull-down lists, and accelerator keys, to minimize typing. Ease of use doesn't mean that the software is simple—it means that data can be entered quickly.

❏ All data output begins with a query. Comparison operators, such as AND, OR, and NOT, link several conditions to limit the number of records returned from a search.

❏ Call logging activities require some specific information for every record. Reference numbers allow staff to quickly retrieve call records, and are usually used when calls are not resolved while the customer is still on the telephone. A caller's name, telephone number, and other information may help support staff deliver services correctly. Call records are also categorized to allow quick record retrieval and to allow managers to identify problem trends. The call resolution field is a quick way to isolate the steps to take to solve later problems.

❏ When calls aren't closed while the customer is still on the telephone, they are sometimes routed in a queue to a support team. A call owner manages open calls until they are resolved. Statuses provide a quick way to see a call's progress through the problem management process. If the call record is not addressed regularly, then the software generates automatic escalation notices. As the owner completes troubleshooting, the activities and the date and time are recorded in the problem history. "To do" lists arrange outstanding calls in a variety of ways until outstanding calls are closed.

❏ Historical call records provide a simple source of knowledge, provided that the resolution fields are updated. Searching call records, however, is inefficient, compared to using other problem resolution tools.

❏ The more closely other support applications are integrated with the problem management system, the faster support staff can move from one process to another as they provide service.

3

KEY TERMS

accelerator key — *See* shortcut key.

account manager — A company representative assigned to manage the interactions between a company and its customers.

auto-fill — As the user begins to type a word or phrase, the complete word or phrase that matches the typed letters is pulled in from a list of stored words.

call priority — The order in which call records are handled, according to the business impact of the problem or request.

call summary — A concise description of the problem or request that is a few sentences in length.

caller information — Facts about the customer at the time a problem or question is reported.

canned text — *See* auto-fill.

category — A classification of problems or requests.

comparison operators — Words, such as AND, OR, or NOT, that evaluate comparisons to determine if they are true or false.

data — Raw numbers or facts collected in a database.

ease of use — The user friendliness of software, as defined by the combination of the user interface, required fields, auto-fill fields, pull-down lists, shortcut keys, and tab order.

free format — A text type of field in which data is not stored in a specific structure.

free text — *See* free format.

graphical user interface (GUI) — A picture-oriented way to interact with a computer, using a mouse or joystick to select commands instead of typing them.

groupware — Software that enables multiple people to work together electronically.

information — Data that is organized into something meaningful.

integrated feature — A software feature that enables support staff to complete other support processes within the same application.

logical operators — *See* comparison operators.

owner — The support staff employee who is responsible for moving a call to a resolution and for updating the customer.

pending work — Work in progress.

picklist — *See* pull-down list.

predefined phrases — *See* auto-fill.

proactive mode — When the support staff uses tools to detect problems early and prevent more serious problems, rather than waiting for computer users to report problems.

problem history — The chronological sequence of activities that has occurred since a call record was created.

problem management — The process of collecting problem details, working on outstanding problems, assigning additional support staff as needed, and providing status updates to customers.

problem resolution — The process of finding the cause of a problem, removing or preventing the cause, and correcting the disruption.

programming interface — A set of program instructions that passes data between two different software applications.

pull-down list — A predefined list of acceptable values from which only one value can be selected.

query by example (QBE) — A search technique that uses queries or questions to find records that match specified conditions.

queue — A line of things to be processed in sequential order.

reactive mode — When the support staff only respond to problems that computer users report.

reference number — A unique code that identifies a specific record in a database.

required entry fields — Data entry fields that must be completed correctly before a record can be saved in the database.

resolution — Information on how a problem is solved or can be prevented.

shortcut key — A key or combination of keys that replaces several separate steps to automate a task.

status — The condition or state of a call record as it progresses through the problem management process.

tab order — The sequence in which the cursor advances from field to field when the Tab key is pressed.

troubleshooting log — The chronological sequence of the activities the support staff performed to solve the problem.

user interface — The portion of the software with which the user interacts.

very important person (VIP) — Someone who performs a special role in the company.

workgroup — A team of people who work together on a project.

REVIEW QUESTIONS

1. When a support group attempts to prevent problems, it is said to be in _____ mode. _____ mode means that the support group waits for customers to report problems.

2. _____ software is designed to allow different people to work together on an issue.

3. Support staff add records to a database with a (n) _____ or _____ interface.

3

4. GUIs have advantages over text entry because they:

   a. require minimal typing skills.

   b. are more fun to use.

   c. are newer technology.

   d. are standard parts of all software.

5. List two examples of data that might be defined as required entry fields.

6. What can happen if there are too many required entry fields during data entry?

7. Which of the following is not an example of an auto-fill field?

   a. The date the record was created

   b. A predefined phrase

   c. The call record summary

   d. The customer name

8. What are two benefits of using a pull-down list for a field?

9. Describe two features that provide benefits for computer users who are skilled typists.

10. Ease of use does not include:

    a. menus.

    b. graphical elements.

    c. price.

    d. required entry fields.

11. _____ is a search technique that uses questions to find records.

12. Describe three forms of information output.

13. Why are unique call record reference numbers important?

14. List five pieces of information that a support group might collect about customers.

15. The call summary is a brief description of a problem. If more information is needed, there may be a (n) _____ field, which allows an unlimited amount of information.

16. The primary users of call categories are:

    a. support managers and computer users.

    b. computer users and support staff.

    c. support staff and support managers.

    d. workgroup leaders and support staff.

17. Why is it important to describe the actions taken to solve a problem?

18. Who is responsible to the caller to make sure that the call record moves to a resolution?

   a. The dispatcher

   b. The support manager

   c. The owner

   d. The creator of the call record

19. What does "in the queue" mean?

20. What is the purpose of assigning statuses to call records?

21. When support groups use numbered priorities, what is usually the highest priority?

   a. 1

   b. 5

   c. 10

   d. 0

22. An escalation notice would be sent in all of the following cases except:

   a. before the call exceeds the maximum open time.

   b. after the call exceeds the maximum open time.

   c. when a call record is not assigned an owner by the predefined time.

   d. when a call record is assigned an owner.

23. When troubleshooting activities are recorded in a free form text field, _____ help identify who accomplished each activity and when.

24. List five ways outstanding work can be organized in a support staff "Pending" list.

25. What are three disadvantages to using old call records as a knowledge base?

26. Which approach to making two software applications work together is usually better for support staff: an integrated feature or a programming interface? Why?

HANDS-ON PROJECTS

Project 3-1

Categorizing call records. The following categories are defined in the support software:

   General Procedures

   Hardware — Mouse

   Hardware — Other

   Hardware — Printers

   Hardware — Setup

Password Problems

Security

Spreadsheets

Telephone

Web Browsers

Windows Desktop

Word Processing

The following summaries are examples of the types of telephone calls a help desk might receive. Select the best category from the list above for each question or problem.

1. How do I get access to the accounting database?

2. When I try to log in, it says my password has expired.

3. I need to set up a login and password on the network for a new employee.

4. All my printed pages have black smudge marks on them.

5. It's taking more than an hour to get my three-page document printed.

6. When I click on a hypertext link on our Web page, I get a "404" error.

7. I can't see other PCs under Network Neighborhood.

8. Netscape was unable to locate the server home.netscape.com.

9. When I select WordPerfect from the Programs menu, I get a message that says "can't locate."

10. What are the help desk hours?

11. Is there another printer on the network I can print to?

12. Please install a new color printer.

13. How do I add a column in an Excel spreadsheet?

14. I need to print the report titles at the top of all my spreadsheet pages.

15. When I try to retrieve a Word document, it says it is already locked by another user.

16. How do I order an upgrade to my project management software?

17. My mouse cursor doesn't move smoothly across the screen.

18. Is there a way to insert a graph into a Word document?

19. I spilled coffee on my keyboard and the keys stick.

20. I'm not getting any telephone calls since last week.

21. My voicemail box is full, how do I clean it out?

22. I can't save any more files because the disk is full.

23. The toner cartridge in the third-floor printer needs to be changed.

24. They worked on my PC yesterday, and now I can't log in.

25. My CRT is smoking and I smell something burning.

26. How do I turn the sound off?

27. How do I turn off headers in Word for just the first page?

28. There is a strange file on my home directory, and I can't delete it.

29. How do I access our Web page from my home computer?

30. I think there is a virus on my PC—can someone look at it?

Project 3-2

Working with auto-fill features. Use the AutoText feature of Word to create some standard help desk phrases.

1. On the Word menu bar, click **Tools**, then **AutoCorrect**. Click the **AutoText** tab.

2. Type each of the following phrases into the "Enter AutoText entries here" field, and click the **Add** button after each entry:

   Called back but had to leave a voicemail message.

   Returned call and left a status update.

   Please call customer and leave an update.

3. Click **OK** to close the AutoCorrect dialog box.

4. Practice using the AutoText or auto-fill phrases in a word processing document by creating a troubleshooting log, similar to the one in Figure 3-6.

Project 3-3

Understanding workflow processes. Every support group has its own processes and procedures for problem management and resolution. Figures 3-8 and 3-9 show the workflow for two different help desks.

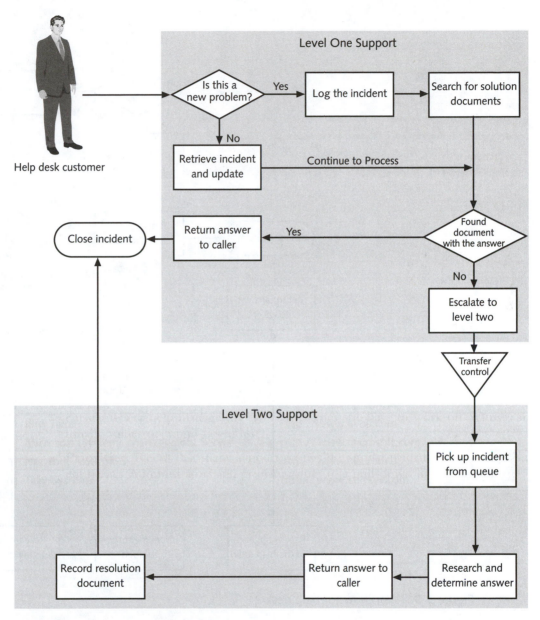

Figure 3-8 Workflow for help desk 1

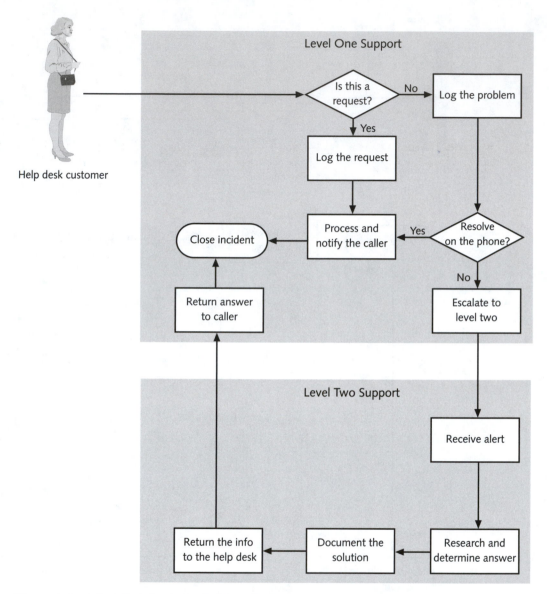

Figure 3-9   Workflow for help desk 2

Review the workflow documents and then answer the following questions:

1. Which help desk uses a knowledge base?
2. Which help desk escalates all calls to level two if they cannot be answered while the caller is on the telephone?
3. Which help desk handles both requests and problems?
4. Which help desk does not transfer ownership of call records?

5. Which help desk seems to indicate that customers have to call in for status updates regularly?

6. Who contacts the customer in Figure 3-8?

7. Who contacts the customer in Figure 3-9?

Project 3-4

Understanding troubleshooting logs. The Word file **Project0304.doc** contains the history and troubleshooting log for a call record. This example is relatively simple because there are only a few entries, but troubleshooting logs can be very long and involve a lot of different steps. There may also be some solutions that are attempted but that fail before a real solution is found. Read the entries and answer the following questions:

1. How many support staff worked on the call?

2. How many times did the customer call in for an update?

3. How many owners did the call record have?

4. How many different actions were tried to resolve the problem?

5. How long was the call "in queue" and without an owner?

6. How many days did it take to get the problem resolved?

Project 3-5

Experiencing user interface features. Visit two Web pages of your choice that allow you to sign up for e-mail information or an information service that you are interested in. Record both URLs to compare with your classmates' choices. Answer the following questions:

1. How are required entry fields marked? Do the number and kinds of required entry fields make sense? Is there any information collected that doesn't appear to be useful to the objective of providing you with your requested information? If so, can you suggest how or why the Web page owner will be using this information?

2. What happens if you do not complete required entry fields?

3. How do pull-down lists appear on the Web page? Can you navigate the pull-down lists with the mouse, or can you use the Page Up and Page Down keys from the keyboard? Can you navigate the pull-down lists by pressing a letter?

4. Is there a tab order defined for this Web page, or are you required to move between fields with the mouse?

Discuss your experiences with classmates. Based on your collective experiences, rate the Web pages on ease of use.

Project 3-6

Using common navigation features. Write down the name and version of the Web browser you use. Then answer the following questions:

1. What are some common actions you take when you are on the Web and using your browser? For example, do you download files, follow hyperlinks, or scroll through e-mail messages?

2. Are any of these activities available with a shortcut key? If so, what shortcuts are supported?

Project 3-7

Providing support information and using knowledge bases. Many Web pages allow anyone to send questions to the support group. Visit the Web page for Microsoft, Oracle, Symantec, or any other well-known software vendor, and go to the support area. Write down the URL to compare your findings with those of other students. Answer the following questions:

1. Does the vendor allow you to search a knowledge base? If so, how do you access the information (FAQs, search engine, or pull-down list of categories and a predefined list of hot topics)?

2. If you don't find the answer to your question and need to contact support, what information must you supply with your request?

3. Do you have any choice about how they contact you? What is your preferred method for the support group to use to contact you?

Discuss your experiences with classmates. Based on your collective experiences, rate the Web pages on the quality of their knowledge bases and on their sensitivity to the needs of their customers.

Project 3-8

Applying statuses to track progress. Review the procedural document in the Word file **Project0308.doc** and answer the following questions:

1. How many people are required to complete this procedure?

2. How many levels of approval are necessary?

3. What communication method is used to place the order with the vendor?

4. Given the way this procedural document is written, are there any improvements you can suggest that would make the document less confusing and would reduce the amount of maintenance if one of the employees leaves the workgroup?

5. How many statuses would you recommend for this process? What statuses would you use to track service requests as they move through this process?

Project 3-9

Addressing ownership issues and knowledge bases. Review the procedural document in Word file **Project0309.doc** and answer the following questions:

1. How many support levels currently exist?
2. How does the support group propose to address the issue of ownership?
3. Does the support group plan to use a knowledge base?

Project 3-10

Understanding software requirements. Open the Excel workbook in file **Project0310.xls**, and answer the following questions:

1. How many support staff will use the software application, according to this requirement document?
2. What processes beside call logging and problem management will this support group attempt to control in the support software?
3. What kinds of auto-fill fields are needed?
4. Can you tell if they are going to search old call records?

CASE PROJECTS

1. Design a User-Friendly Entry Screen

ClearVision Video sells and supports televisions. They have hired you as an independent consultant to streamline their call logging screen because their current software has too many required fields. This company sells directly to customers, but it also sells to distributors, who then sell the televisions in retail locations to the public. When the company sells directly to customers, they collect customer information. The distributors, however, do not collect any customer information.

Design an entry screen or additional screens for this company. Collect the customer's name and a description of the problem for every call. Be sure to allow the support staff to search for an existing customer record first. If the customer record doesn't exist, allow support staff to create a customer record. If you can answer the question or problem over the telephone, it is not necessary to collect a telephone number, just the customer's name. However, if you have to call the customer back and the customer record doesn't exist, be sure to always collect the telephone number. (*Hint*: Use a button or hyperlink to open a New Customer entry screen.) Don't forget to include a status and a priority field and place an icon on the entry screen to open a large, free text window if you cannot describe the problem in less than three lines of text.

Use Microsoft PowerPoint or a similar tool to draw a representation of the screen(s) with entry boxes and field labels.

2. **Create Categories for Organizing Calls**

   You are the support manager for the internal help desk. The company's training department plans to add some short, refresher courses to their Word curriculum. They want to know what kinds of questions your customers typically ask and what the customers' most common problems are, so they can create the appropriate classes. So far, your support group categorizes questions and problems only at a much higher level (for example, questions are categorized by products, such as Word and Excel, but no further). Define a set of six to eight subcategories that would be simple for the support staff to use during call logging and that would provide subjects for the training department. (Hint: Use the Word menus to remind yourself of common categories.)

3. **Build a Knowledge Base from Previous Call Records**

   You are a level two support staff member. Your support manager has assigned you the task of collecting information for a new knowledge base. The support group receives about fifty calls per day, and you decide to use closed call records to build some knowledge. Write a one- or two-page procedure that explains how you will begin this process. Decide how you will organize the raw data. Describe who will be involved in verifying that the information is correct. If you need to add to the existing call logging or problem management process, discuss the new steps that will make sure that knowledge is created regularly. Set a goal to create a reasonable number of knowledge documents every week.

4

SUPPORT PERFORMANCE AND REPORTING TOOLS

In this chapter you will learn:

♦ The benefits of measuring support performance

♦ Common support performance measurements

♦ Common features of report software

♦ New reporting tools

♦ Current report software applications

Support managers must demonstrate to higher levels of management that a support group meets its goals. Once managers select an appropriate set of support tools and deploy those tools in the support environment, they must demonstrate how the new tools help the support group accomplish its short-term and long-term goals. At the same time, they also must demonstrate the continuing value of the support group.

The best way to justify the value of a support group, and thus the expenses incurred to keep it functioning, is by using numbers. Numbers can demonstrate the need for more staff or for better control of existing resources. Numbers can provide early warnings that support services are not meeting customer expectations. Numbers show how a changing company environment, such as the introduction of new products or additional services, affects the business of support as well as all business users. To generate these numbers, managers use a **report writer**, which is software that allows users to select, manipulate, and present database information. Most support software includes a report feature that uses the same GUI as the rest of the applications. There are also other software applications, such as SAS and Crystal Reports, that perform advanced calculations and produce sophisticated graphical output.

REPORTS QUANTIFY PERFORMANCE

All business managers, including support managers, use statistical analysis to help them understand the business environment. The report writer is an important tool for this analysis because it helps translate general performance objectives into numbers that are easy to comprehend. For example, to understand a performance objective such as "provide skilled support staff that can respond to customer questions quickly," the support manager may track how many times support staff can answer questions while the customer is on the telephone. Initially, managers may find that the staff can answer 60% of all incoming calls the first time. If, over time, that percentage increases to 80% or 90%, it seems logical to assume that the staff really are "skilled," that the support group does respond to questions quickly, and that the group meets the performance objective.

A business handles an unlimited amount of data, resulting in hundreds of possible performance measurements every day. This jumble of numbers and statistics can be overwhelming, so managers also use software to translate reported data into graphs and charts. These "pictures" translate masses of data into relevant information about what is happening in the support group. The graph in Figure 4-1 clearly shows that there is a repeating pattern of call increases every other month for the months tracked.

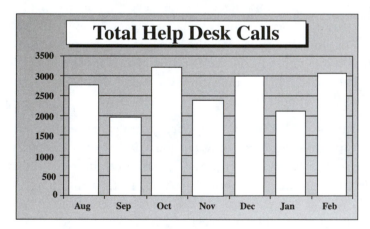

Figure 4-1 Total calls by month

The same information is presented in Figure 4-2, but it is more difficult to see the repeating pattern in the report.

Total Help Desk Calls							
	Aug	**Sep**	**Oct**	**Nov**	**Dec**	**Jan**	**Feb**
Total Calls	2769	1967	3237	2382	2990	2112	3074

Figure 4-2 Total calls by month report

4

 TIP Graphs and charts rely upon report tools to summarize data first.

Understanding which statistics to use in a graph and what those numbers mean takes thought and planning. Managers build reports from data that the support staff collect during the call logging and problem management processes. If the support staff don't understand which processes their managers measure and why, they may collect the wrong information. If support managers then interpret this wrong information, they can make incorrect decisions that affect staffing or the need for other support tools.

Managers monitor the support group according to the categories listed in Figure 4-3.

```
    ♦ Delivery cost
    ♦ Service performance
    ♦ Problem prevention
```

Figure 4-3 Categories for support analysis

Delivery Cost

One of the most common business areas that managers analyze is the cost of doing business. They expect all areas of the company, including the support group, to control costs as well as to meet business objectives, or the company won't be profitable. The **return on investment (ROI)** is a measurement that compares the dollar value of a support group's services and benefits to its operating costs. Support managers must demonstrate a positive ROI when they purchase new tools, as well as show that the support group continues to meet the company's business objectives.

One of the biggest costs is for staff salaries. Reports document the need for more staff. Managers compare the performances of trained and untrained staff members to justify the expense and time for training staff. Reports also quantify support staff skills and can indicate when support tools are effective, by tracking the performance of staff members who use tools to equalize skills and comparing the results with the performance of other staff members.

 Note Some support groups use support statistics as part of an employee's annual evaluation. When they do, it is important that support staff clearly understand the statistics being used to measure their performance. They need to understand which behaviors and actions to perform and how to perform them to achieve the required performance levels. Report writers make it simple for managers to compare statistics for the entire support group to an individual's performance. The average performance numbers can be used as the minimum score for a particular task. Support staff who are below the average may need more training or other coaching. Statistics from the call logging activities, however, won't show how effectively a staff member communicates or that staff member's attitude toward customers. Managers understand that they must evaluate each support staff member's technical skills, communication skills, and overall contribution to the support group to get the full picture about his or her performance. A staff member who resolves fewer calls than other team members may be rated very highly by team members and customers because of good communication skills or a pleasant, unflustered manner when solving problems.

Some support costs are not as easy to measure as the expense of hiring and training support staff. Indirect costs occur when support staff must handle preventable problems. For example, IT departments typically plan and implement software upgrades for large groups of computer users. Poorly implemented changes mean more support calls and more work later for the level two and three support staff (who are usually part of the IT departments). New products that are installed globally and without available user training are also examples of preventable problems. Managers frequently collect statistics from these types of problems and use them to ensure that more time and planning are devoted to later, related implementations.

Service Performance

Reports enable managers to monitor service performance and may indirectly measure customers' satisfaction. As discussed in Chapter 2, support groups prioritize, respond to, and resolve problems on the basis of the impact on customers in their day-to-day work. For example, the support group may attempt to resolve system outages (a priority 1 problem because data is no longer available) in four hours. If the support group meets that resolution time for every outage problem, managers can safely assume that customers are satisfied with the service they receive for outages. However, if ten outages occur during a month and the outages are restored within four hours for nine of those events, the managers cannot safely assume anything. In this latter case, the support group met the service levels 90% of the time.

Figure 2-6 showed a sample of call severities and target resolution times.

To determine the customers' levels of satisfaction, the support manager must review the details of the exception. If the resolution time of the exception is close to four hours, most likely the customers will still be satisfied, but a longer resolution could be disruptive enough for customers that they are unhappy with support. Customers won't be satisfied for long if the support group publishes a service level but doesn't deliver that service. **Accountability** means that someone has the authority to correct problems when he or she defaults on commitments. Support managers regularly review exceptions to performance to determine whether there are any types of problems that they can take steps to solve more quickly.

The availability of shared computer systems and networks and the response to outages have such a significant effect on business that most customers expect important business systems, such as e-mail and accounting software, to be available more than 90% of the time. Typically, support groups or IT departments must meet priority 1 service levels 97% of the time or more to guarantee customer satisfaction. Figure 4-4 is a sample report that compares the availability of several important systems for a four-month period.

System availability is calculated by dividing the total amount of time that a system was ready for customers to use by the total number of minutes it should have been available for use. An e-mail system that is supposed to run from 7:00 AM to 7:00 PM, Monday through Friday, but was not sending mail for four hours would have been available 93% of the time.

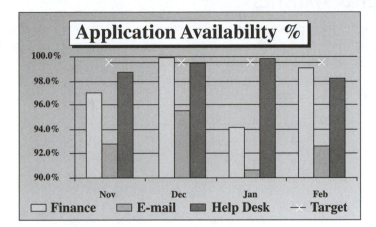

Figure 4-4   Application availability

Managers also use reports to determine the quality of the service provided by the support group's outsourcers. Most support groups manage their company's relationship with hardware vendors and telephone service providers. These outside vendors must meet their contractual obligation for responding to and resolving problems, or the support group isn't getting the service it paid for. Service levels apply to outsourcers as well. Reports show the support manager when a problem was reported initially, how long the support staff took to request service from the appropriate outsourcer, how long the outsourcer took to respond, and finally, the total amount of time it took to solve the customer's problem.

Reporting also points out the effect of product quality, because high-quality products don't usually generate as many call records. External customers expect to purchase products they can use. If they receive faulty products, they expect quick replacements or refunds. The number of product-related call records can be a good indicator of product quality. Because product quality, as well as service, affects customer satisfaction, an increased number of calls may predict increasing customer dissatisfaction, and eventually, the inability of a business to sell to new customers.

Problem Prevention

Support managers should take an active role in attempting to prevent problems. They can use reports to help them do this. As data comes into the support group, managers can use reports to isolate issues and identify problems in areas controlled by other departments. They can take these problems directly to other business departments, or to upper management when the problems affect large areas of the business. As they succeed in preventing problems, resources are freed to deliver new services as well. By removing preventable problems, through better planning and earlier corrective action, support groups decrease most of the risks involved in making system changes. As a result, level two and level three staff, who are most frequently affected by large system changes, have more time to plan and deliver new services (such as software upgrades or new installations).

COMMONLY COLLECTED STATISTICS

Both internal and external support groups collect statistics, but the support environment determines which statistics are used to compare a specific support group to others in the same industry. Also, because the support group's business goals are specific to each company, different support groups emphasize different measurements. Support statistics typically come from the data sources listed in Figure 4-5.

```
♦  Telephone calls
♦  Call records
```

Figure 4-5   Statistical data sources

Telephone Calls

Companies that have sophisticated telephone systems usually count the number of telephone calls to and from the support group. Customers call in to report new problems or ask questions. They also call back with more information about a problem they previously reported or to get an update on an outstanding problem. Support staff return calls left by voice mail, call other resources, and communicate with customers during problem management activities. The support staff collect a variety of data about every call.

Call duration is the length of a telephone call in minutes and seconds. Managers calculate the average call duration as a step in determining how many telephone calls a front-line person can handle in a day. Based on that number, managers estimate the number of resources they need. In other words, the number of telephone calls that come in to the support group during a normal day affects the total amount of staff needed.

Once they determine how many full-time support staff are needed, some support managers hire part-time or temporary staff. Managers convert the number of work hours that can be filled by full- and part-time employees into a **full-time equivalent (FTE)**. One full-time employee working 40 hours per week produces the same amount of work as two part-time employees who work 20 hours per week. The average number of calls handled per FTE determines the total front-line staff needed for the support group, which can be any combination of full- and part-time staff.

Whether full- or part-time, support staff are not always at their desks to take calls. All employees take daily work breaks and lunch breaks; they also may complete administrative activities, such as attending training classes and employee meetings. **Available time** is the amount of time in minutes and seconds when support staff can answer the telephone and deliver support services. This number is calculated manually by support managers or tracked electronically by the telephone system (Chapter 9 discusses telephone systems in more detail). **Hold time** is the amount of time that a caller remains on hold if no one is available to answer the telephone.

Hold time is usually calculated in seconds. Figure 4-6 shows how a sample support group has decreased the amount of time customers remain on hold from a high of 4 minutes to around 1 minute.

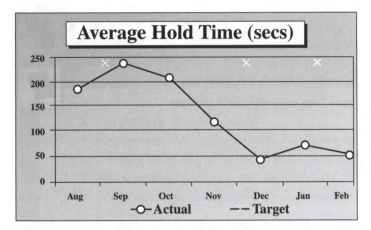

Figure 4-6   Average telephone hold time

If the caller hangs up before speaking with the support staff, the call is abandoned. The **abandon rate** is the percentage of abandoned calls compared to the total telephone calls received. The graph in Figure 4-7 shows that for one month, this support group had an almost 50% abandon rate. A high abandon rate tends to increase the number of calls coming to support; if the problem or question is important, the customer will call again. As a result, one problem is counted in the telephone statistics as if two problems were being reported. The number of actual problems for that month may have been roughly the same as in other months, but the telephone activity coming into support was much higher.

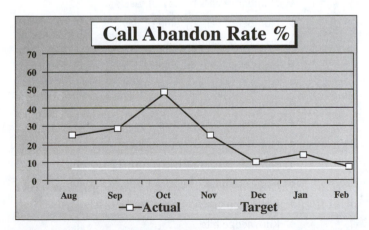

Figure 4-7   Call abandon rate

The more frequently customers call and wait on hold or abandon the call, the more likely it is that they will become unhappy. Customers get frustrated when they wait on hold for more than a minute or two. Most support groups consider an abandon rate of 8% acceptable, but individual customers may expect a response in seconds and will abandon earlier. A support group with a 20% abandon rate will definitely have unhappy customers.

Call Records

In addition to analyzing telephone call activity, support managers review statistics on the number of calls logged. It is important that support staff create call records for all problems and questions, so that the statistics accurately reflect what is happening in the support group. If the support software slows them down or if they have too many calls to take, support staff may be tempted not to log all the calls they handle. If the support software is too slow, affecting the ability to create timely call records, the support manager then has solid proof that the existing technology must be replaced. If the support staff take time to log all calls, but don't have any time left to resolve the problems, the manager also has evidence to justify hiring more support staff.

 It's easy to see when software is too slow. Support staff should be able to complete one or two screens of the required information to create a new call record in about 20 seconds. Query speed is the next area to examine for speed problems—can staff retrieve a record to update it in 10 seconds or less? Once software speed is addressed, increasing numbers of unresolved calls point to the need for more staff.

Statistical evaluations begin by comparing a cross-section of data to the total number of call records within a time period. As long as two or three time periods have roughly the same total number of calls, support managers can use this as a **baseline**, or starting point, for later comparisons. The total number of calls is the first number needed for all calculations. This number will be further refined and analyzed in a number of ways, as listed in Figure 4-8.

- Number of calls by day of week
- Number of calls by time of day
- Calls by severity
- Number of calls by origin
- Number of calls by customer
- Number of calls reopened
- Number of calls by type
- Number of calls by originator
- Number of calls by owner
- Response time
- Resolution time
- Knowledge hits

Figure 4-8 Call analysis breakdowns

A month is a good time period to use for statistical evaluation because many business processes are cyclic in nature. An entire month's numbers will even out any peaks of activity that might occur. For example, many companies pay their bills on approximately the tenth day of the month, so there may be questions about using the billing system several days up to and after that time.

4

Managers analyze telephone calls using some of the same categories as for call records.

Number of Calls by Day of Week

The **number of calls by day of week** shows the total number of call records that were created on a specific day of the week. This breakdown helps managers determine if they receive more calls on any particular workday. This information is important when managers hire both full- and part-time employees, and when they schedule employees for different shifts. If more calls are opened on Monday than later in the week, then managers can limit administrative activities on Monday or schedule more FTEs for that day. Business activities (such as weekly payroll processing or Monday staff meetings) determine when peaks occur, and they vary by company, by industry, and by season of the year. No matter when the peak is, support managers attempt to build their work schedules so they have sufficient staff coverage during peak call times. Figure 4-9 lists calls by day of week and calculates a weekly average. In this case, there are consistently more calls than average on Wednesdays.

Incidents by Day of Week
Report generated 4/6/2002

Week Ending	Mon	Tues	Wed	Thu	Fri	Total for Week	Average for Week
Mar 5	58	85	90	78	57	368	74
Mar 12	63	52	76	64	54	309	62
Mar 19	73	80	93	81	105	432	86
Mar 26	43	44	49	37	42	215	43
Apr 2	30	46	47	43	41	207	41

Figure 4-9   Incidents by day of week

Number of Calls by Time of Day

Number of calls by time of day is the number of call records created and counted for each hour of a workday. Managers use this number with the number of calls by day of week for support staff scheduling. Both numbers are particularly common when the support group provides 24 × 7 support. For example, the number of calls received on Saturday afternoon may be much lower than the number received on Saturday morning, requiring only a skeleton crew. Managers also schedule work breaks or lunch hours around peak call times during the day.

Calls by Severity

When a support group provides different service levels based upon problem severity, it is important for them to know how frequently high priority problems occur. Statistically, high priority problems should be fewer than 10% of the total calls received. If the percentage is higher, managers should determine whether this is because there are problems that could be controlled or because support staff don't prioritize the call records correctly. Most support groups calculate the priority 1 issues as a percentage of the total number of calls. It may not be possible for the support group to prevent all high priority problems, such as server outages, so support managers may define a **threshold**, or starting boundary, before they look for problem causes. For example, if the average number of priority 1 issues is about 5% of the total problems reported during a time period, managers may not become concerned until the percentage reaches 8% of the total calls. A larger number of high priority problems during a given time period will affect other support services, because managers shift resources to cover those problems.

 Statistical analysis is a branch of mathematics that uses data to make inferences and predictions in uncertain situations. A bell-shaped curve represents the probability of the occurrence of an event. Generally, it is considered that 80% of the time an event will occur normally, 10% of the time it will be below normal, and 10% of the time it will be above normal.

Call severity is also tracked by day of week and time of day to determine the problem's impact on the company. For example, employees won't notice a server outage at 3:00 AM because they don't arrive for work until later. However, the same server outage at 9:00 AM can prevent hundreds of workers from completing their tasks and has a greater business impact. Certainly support staff should consider that all outages are important, should be addressed quickly, and should be analyzed for future prevention, but the time of day affects severity.

Number of Calls by Origin

Support groups usually receive most problems or requests by telephone, but they may create call records from information provided by other electronic forms, such as voice mail, fax, and e-mail. **Origin of call** is the way a problem was reported. Origin is particularly important when support managers want to understand how their customers prefer to communicate, so they can provide support staff with appropriate skills. For example, a support group that receives almost half its call records from e-mail needs to be able to communicate well by writing. A high number of electronic origins may also indicate a need to bring in more automated tools (there are tools that can send automated responses to customers who use e-mail).

Some help desks set up a voice mail box where customers can leave a message instead of abandoning their telephone call. The percentage of voice mail messages to answered telephone calls is another type of abandon rate calculation. If the caller doesn't leave enough information, however, the support staff must then contact the caller to get the missing information. While on the telephone, the staff miss incoming telephone calls. As a result, a large number of incomplete voice mail messages can lead to longer hold times and higher abandon rates.

4

In situations when customers walk into the support center to report a problem or make a request, as occurs at some educational organizations or field service offices, they may get immediate attention. In other words, the support staff gives a higher priority to the needs of walk-in customers than to the needs of telephone callers. Support managers prioritize records created electronically from fax systems, Web pages, or e-mail at a lower priority than telephone calls, because telephone calls involve direct customer interaction. Call records automatically created through an interface from a tracking system for outages, however, are high priority because they affect many business users. Figure 4-10 is an example of how call records can be prioritized, depending upon the origin.

Processing Order by Origin	Origin
1	Person physically visits support office
2	Electronically generated outage records
3	Telephone calls
4	Overflow voice mailbox
5	E-mail messages or Web
6	Fax messages

Figure 4-10   Call origin processing order

Enabling customers to log their own problems or requests electronically can both help and hinder a support group. In some cases, it saves time because support staff don't have to transfer details from e-mail or fax to a call record before they work on the issue. In other cases, if customers don't provide enough information to complete a request or troubleshoot a problem, support staff have to make another telephone call or send another e-mail to get the missing information. Using e-mail to get missing information causes more interactions, because an answer may generate more questions. This results in an even longer time to resolve the issue. In most cases, a single telephone exchange is the most efficient way to collect the problem details and query for more information and gives support staff the opportunity to solve the problem sooner.

Number of Calls by Customer

The **number of calls by customer** is the number of call records created for a specific caller. This breakdown identifies users and abusers of support services. Managers can identify additional training needs or problem hardware by tracking the average number of problems by all customers and comparing that number to calls by individual customers. When calls are grouped by business department, managers can see where problems most affect the business.

Number of Calls Reopened

The **number of calls reopened** is the number of call records that moved from a closed or resolved status back to an open status. Managers always investigate this number because it can indicate some serious problems. Support staff reopen closed call records for several reasons:

- Support staff gave an incorrect resolution and didn't really fix the problem. This happens when staff need more training or don't use available resources. The more frequently this happens, the less credibility the support group has with customers.

- Support staff didn't confirm with the customer that the problem was fixed before they closed the call record. In this case, customers may specifically ask that the call record be reopened. This also happens when the support staff close call records just to reduce the number of outstanding issues. Again, customers lose confidence in the support group.

- The customer didn't follow the directions or understand the problem solution and needs help again. This identifies customers who need more training. It can also point out communication problems between staff members and customers.

Managers may also investigate more closely if there are no reopened calls. One reason for this may be because it is too difficult to find the closed record to reopen it. Instead of reopening calls, support staff create new call records. Not only does this inflate the call numbers, but it also hides the three problems mentioned above.

Number of Calls by Type

The **number of calls by type** is the number of call records by category. When support groups handle both problems and requests, they separate call records by these categories to show how support staff spend their time. For example, a support group that processes 100 problems a day is more reactive and stressed than a support group that handles 20 problems and 80 requests a day. Both have to meet service levels, but the amount of effort required to address requests is usually known in advance. The amount of effort needed to solve a problem isn't known until that problem is resolved.

Call categories help managers isolate problems they can prevent, because there are usually categories for outages. They also show the different skills needed by support staff. Many support groups assist customers using PCs and mainframe terminals. Troubleshooting steps are completely different for these types of computers. As mainframe terminals are replaced by PCs with mainframe terminal access, there must be enough staff to support these new types of problems. Figures 4-11 and 4-12 show samples of closed calls by type.

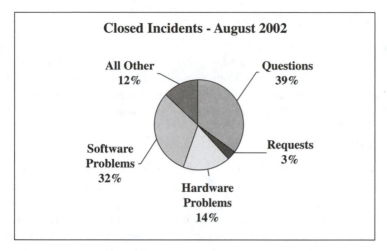

Figure 4-11 Closed calls by category

Closed Incidents — August 2002
By Cause and Region
Report generated 09/09/2002 06:00

Cause	Region						
	North	South	East	West	Europe	Asia	Total
Questions	182	83	271	89	10	245	880
Requests	20	2	31	10	0	16	79
Software Problems	202	46	234	75	15	223	795
Hardware Problems	66	26	144	60	5	136	437
Operating System Errors	20	1	2	2	0	24	49
Install Errors	3	0	28	3	2	31	67
Documentation	18	2	14	4	0	9	47
Other Vendors	11	18	47	11	0	21	108
Distribution	8	1	18	1	0	26	54
Total	**530**	**179**	**789**	**255**	**32**	**731**	**2516**

Figure 4-12 Closed calls by category report

When support determines the cause of a problem, records may also be grouped into hardware or software problems. This information is important for support groups that outsource hardware repairs, because it shows how much time they must spend managing work by others. It is also useful when the business has old or outdated hardware, because the number of problems related to that hardware will continue to rise. At some point, business managers will determine that the cost of replacing outdated hardware is less than the cost of lost productivity by business users and support staff.

Number of Calls by Originator

Number of calls by originator is the number of call records created by each support staff member. Because the originator of a record is usually the person who collected the information, this number is compared to telephone statistics and work schedules that show who was available to answer the telephone. This number can also be combined with call origin to verify that all staff share the task of monitoring a shared voice mail box or e-mail box.

Number of Calls by Owner

Number of calls by owner is the number of call records each support staff member owns. This number is reviewed daily and weekly to balance the support group's workload among staff members. The manager evaluates the number of call records, types of problems, and the skills of the FTE to determine whether a support staff member owns too many call records. For example, the effort needed to troubleshoot ten user login problems can be much less than the effort needed to troubleshoot a random PC lockup. To balance the support staff's workload, managers review all calls by priority, as well as an individual's calls, and estimate the effort required for each task. Support staff should also review their own assignments and request help resolving issues if they get behind. The objective of workload management is to make sure that all call records are processed within the service levels for the support group. Figure 4–13 is an open call report that a manager may use to review individual work assignments.

Open Incidents by Owner
Report generated 09/15/2002

Owner: Andy Henderson

Incident Id	Caller	Date Created	Incident Summary
1975	Jack Kouwenberg	15-Jul-2002	DB2 v5 connect error when edit product DDL doing an install

Owner: John Martin

Incident Id	Caller	Date Created	Incident Summary
3220	French Wilson	01-Sep-2002	ASM-SVDIS DOESN'T WORK

Owner: Lisa Roberts

Incident Id	Caller	Date Created	Incident Summary
4674	German Howard	01-Sep-2002	INP23 DISCONNECT GIVE SPEC ERROR 255 *NOT IN TRAN*
4676	German Howard	01-Sep-2002	INP311 WRITE TO INFORMIX CRASHES IPRUN
5007	Pia Bloom	07-Sep-2002	Cannot connect to Oracle 7.34. SQL server unknown error
5101	Leonard Scott	07-Sep-2002	How to create a blank database before running Setup

Figure 4-13   Open call records by owner

Figure 4-14 shows the workload for several different workgroups.

Workgroup	Month							Total
	Jan	**Feb**	**Mar**	**Apr**	**May**	**Nov**	**Dec**	**Total**
Desktop Support	37	88	261	122				516
Mainframe Tools	117	178	334	151				801
Network	67	107	171	71				418
DB Admin	167	193	253	79				717
Total	389	566	1019	423				2397

Closed Incidents by Workgroup and Month
Report generated 04/19/2002 07:00

Figure 4-14   Closed call records by workgroup

Response Time

Response time is the time it takes the support group to acknowledge a customer's problem or request and assign a resource. A support group commits to a maximum response time for most problems, based on priority. High priority problems are usually reported by customers directly to support staff, and if all support staff are unavailable, the customer should always have an option to page support staff or connect to a live person (a group administrative assistant or dispatcher). As a result, high priority problems are communicated to a person. However, if there are more calls than the support staff can handle by telephone, they may overflow into the voice mail or e-mail systems. Support staff then take turns transferring information from the voice mail or e-mail systems into call records. Support managers set a time limit for response to customers who leave voice or e-mail messages. This lets the customer know the maximum amount of time it will take for support staff to clear out the temporary backlog and return the telephone call, to either collect more information or begin troubleshooting.

Response time can also measure the length of time it takes to transfer call ownership from one team to another. For example, when level one support staff escalate issues to higher levels, they want to know that someone in the next support level has seen the new issue and will accept ownership within a reasonable time frame. If the other support levels don't respond within a reasonable amount of time, the customer may call level one support again to check on the problem status. Because records are frequently escalated using queues defined in the support software, the response time between two levels of support is called **queue time**.

 TIP   A new help desk should first set up support levels between different support groups. The support group must manage the response time between teams before it can manage the response time to customers.

Hardware vendors who dispatch field repair staff to the physical location also commit to response times as part of their service contracts with the company. If the vendor reports its progress with the problem to the support group, managers can more easily monitor the vendor's performance, and customers have a single point of contact (the help desk) to check the status of pending hardware repairs.

Resolution Time

Resolution time is the difference in days, hours, minutes, and seconds between the time a call record is created and the time it moves to a closed status. Resolution time can be calculated in two ways, depending upon the support group's hours. When support groups offer 24 $\times$ 7 support, a call record opened at 9:00 AM and closed the following day at 9:00 AM has a resolution time of twenty-four hours. When the support groups offer support from 9:00 AM to 5:00 PM (business hours), the same call has a resolution time of eight hours.

Resolution time is one of the most important statistics a support group can track and is always included in service level measurements. Support managers review each call record and compare the call's resolution time to the average resolution time of all records closed within a selected time period. Average resolution time is important, but the minimum and maximum resolution times are also useful to determine customer satisfaction.

 Time periods are usually days, weeks, or months. If there are extreme value differences between two time periods, managers will look at the next higher period to understand the total effect. For example, some support groups receive a large number of their calls on the first workday (Monday), and the smallest number of calls on Friday. Instead of looking at daily time, managers will calculate averages for the entire week.

First call resolution, an extension of resolution time, is the number of calls resolved while the support staff is still on the telephone with the customer. Support groups may not be able to provide first call resolution, because some problems require additional research to determine the cause. In that case, they may track **level one resolution**, which means that the level one staff either solved the problem with their own knowledge or used a knowledge base to solve the problem. The customer and support staff may have several interchanges, but the important indicator is that the problem was not escalated to a higher level of support. Both the first call resolution and level one resolution definitions are important indicators of customer satisfaction because these calls have lower resolution times than records that wait in a queue for higher-level support groups to accept ownership.

Although resolution is the most frequently used statistic, many variables influence it. Resolution times change during peak call times. Certain categories of problems take longer to close, and resolution time may vary depending on the support staff's skill levels.

Resolution time, by itself, won't guarantee that customers are satisfied with services. If staff members log call records after problems are solved instead of when they are reported, the numbers are skewed to show a short resolution (the call records are opened and closed within seconds). Because most managers expect staff to log calls as they are reported, this activity misrepresents true staff performance. In external customer support, software bugs also may seem to have a short resolution that is completely opposite from the customer's experience. This is because external support groups frequently close call records as soon as they discover that programmers are working on the bug. It makes sense to close the call records because there is nothing the support staff can do for the caller. However, customers won't be satisfied until the software bug is fixed. The resolution time for these calls appears to be seconds, but customers' overall impression is that it takes too long to fix their problems.

> **TIP** An important reason for logging all calls as they are reported is so that other support staff can find all outstanding issues, in case customers call in and can't reach the support person they reported the problem to originally.

Knowledge Hits

Knowledge hits means that support staff find the answer to problems in a knowledge base. Support groups that use knowledge bases build knowledge documents themselves or purchase solution data from vendors. The more times they find knowledge, the faster they can resolve calls (the lower the resolution time), and the greater number of calls they can answer.

SCOTT PICKARD
NETWORK SUPPORT SERVICES,
TECHNOLOGY ADMINISTRATOR
NORFOLK SOUTHERN CORPORATION
(INTERNAL HELP DESK)
ATLANTA, GEORGIA
MANAGERS USE REPORTS TO CONTROL
WORKLOAD

Norfolk Southern, a Virginia-based holding company with headquarters in Norfolk, Virginia, owns a major freight railroad, Norfolk Southern Railway Company, which operates approximately 21,600 miles of road in twenty-two states, the District of Columbia, and the Province of Ontario. The Network Support Services (NSS) group provides 24 × 7 support for employees. Support staff answer questions, handle problems for mainframe and wide area network computer users, diagnose software and hardware problems, and dispatch appropriate help.

In June 1999, the company began operating a substantial portion of the routes and assets of Conrail in the Northeast. The transaction added about 11,000 new employees to the support environment. More users suddenly were added to existing computer systems such as payroll, and there were significant increases in requests for login IDS and to troubleshoot security problems. Many of the new employees were using computer systems completely new to them. The number of daily telephone calls tripled with the transaction, and our new support management needed to be able to track and manage our performance during this rapidly changing time.

One of our most important management reports evolved from a summary report. Managers anticipated an increased call volume, but they needed more information. It was critical that support staff see how resources were allocated within the IT organization, and to pinpoint where they needed more staff. We expanded the daily, open summary report to include more details. Now the report lists open call records by criticality, and then summarizes it by workgroup. The detail follows and includes the ticket number, date opened, date last modified, owner, and short description. The report was run once a day, five days a week, but has been so useful that it is now generated twice a day and for all seven days. A subset of this report goes to higher levels of management, combining workgroups into the areas each assistant vice president manages, so upper management can see the distribution of the problems and any that aren't being addressed.

Another important report is our Mean Time to Repair (resolution time). This report helps support managers make sure that each customer's requests and problems are resolved within an acceptable time frame. We've used it to improve service and track problems that seem to reoccur.

When we were developing the reports, involving thirty to forty different workgroups, most were generated manually, a particularly labor intensive task. Now that the major reports are developed, they are scheduled to run automatically. Each workgroup manager receives his portion of the detail report through e-mail as an Excel spreadsheet. We are moving many of our reports to MS Access, rather than using an OLAP report writer, primarily because it is easy to automate Access reports and attach the reports to e-mail.

Our customers expect to speak directly with a skilled support person if they have a problem. One of our performance goals is to answer 93% of the telephone calls directly (no voice mail). We've started monitoring abandon rates, hold times, call lengths, and the number of times the calls roll over to voice mail. Our support manager used this number to calculate how many support staff we really needed. Our next step will be to integrate the telephone call statistics with the call management reports to determine how these numbers link to call management statistics, such as number of calls opened and average resolution time.

REPORT SOFTWARE FEATURES

Once a support group defines the performance measurements meaningful to their environment, managers use the support software's reporting features, or a report writing tool, to generate statistics. Originally, accessing the database tables and extracting meaningful data required a detailed knowledge of the database and its query tools. The task of generating reports was delegated to an administrator. This approach allowed managers to review only historical information; they couldn't use reports to manage workload or react to call peaks quickly.

Administrators are usually part of the IT staff, rather than the support group. Administrators support the support group and the tools they use.

As database software evolves, new technologies become available for managers and staff. **Online analytical processing (OLAP)** enables a user to extract and view data from different points of view. For example, a manager can display data in a spreadsheet that shows all the call records for a selected day. Then the manager can collect available times for staff members and telephone call numbers to compare call tracking activity and telephone activity. The primary advantage is that this database software provides an easy-to-use interface. It allows users to transform raw data into useful information and to examine the results without having to know programming.

Because of the popularity of OLAP, more support software includes report features with the same characteristics. Now, managers and support staff can use the same tools to examine data at any time. An **ad hoc** report is designed or improvised as needed. If an employee is sick, the manager creates an ad hoc report to list the call records assigned to that person, the problem categories, the record creation date, and the problem summary. Once the manager prints the report, he or she reviews each issue and reassigns it to another team member with appropriate skills.

Some report writer tools are easier to manipulate than others. With report writer tools, users can:

- Select fields on reports from a menu or drag and drop the field name onto the report page
- Create selection criteria from pull-down lists
- Use conditional operators, such as AND, OR, and NOT, to create complex queries
- Sort records by two or more fields
- Group records by categories, owners, workgroups, or other data fields
- Define simple calculations for data fields, such as count, average, minimum, maximum, sum, and percentage.

A **detail report** includes specific information about individual records. Support managers and staff use detail reports to manage workload. The report in Figure 4-13 that a manager uses to balance workload is also an example of a detail report.

A **summary**, or **flash**, **report** contains only calculations about many records. For example, a summary report could include the number of calls, average resolution, number of calls escalated, percentage calculations, and other statistics about a group of records.

Support staff use detail reports as worklists or to-do lists. Upper-level managers usually request only summary reports. The support manager uses both and evaluates details to explain why calculations on the summary report are high or low.

Detail and summary reports may begin as ad hoc queries, but over time managers may decide to review the information on a regular schedule. Rather than recreate the report each time, managers can save the report definitions to reuse them later. The same report can then quickly be run hourly, daily, weekly, monthly, or quarterly. Stored definitions save time and, when combined with scheduling software, enable support managers and staff to automate report generation.

A backlog report is an example of a regularly scheduled summary report. The backlog report shows how many call records were created during a selected time, how many were closed, and how many carry forward to the next time period. The report in Figure 4-15 summarizes the workload at the beginning of, during, and at the end of each week and compares the values over four weeks. Notice that the number of calls open at the end of each week carries to the next week as the starting number. Ideally, the backlog either stays the same or decreases.

Incident Backlog Report
Report generated 09/09/2002

	# Calls at Start of Week	# Calls Created During Week	# Calls Closed During Week	# Calls at End of Week	Average Resolution
Week 1 08/02 thru 08/08	200	315	400	115	3:10:35
Week 2 08/09 thru 08/15	115	431	420	126	3:13:50
Week 3 08/16 thru 08/22	126	632	480	278	4:06:33
Week 4 08/23 thru 08/29	278	517	460	335	4:10:18

Figure 4-15   Incident backlog report

Support staff may not be able to close everything that comes in each day, but over time, they should be able to manage the backlog. The support manager monitors the backlog to make sure it doesn't increase. If the backlog continues to grow, the manager investigates other areas (such as calls by category, to look for short-term peaks). An increasing backlog can indicate the need for more support staff.

At one time. reports could only be printed on paper, but today most report tools provide multiple output formats. The report can be saved as a file or forwarded electronically with e-mail or fax. Some report writers export the data directly to a spreadsheet so users can manipulate data further or graph the results. Many companies publish their recurring reports on Web pages, so interested parties can retrieve the information as needed. Support staff may be interested in the workgroup reports, whereas business managers are often interested in backlogs and call types.

Storing reports in a central location has several benefits:
- It ensures that everyone works from the same information and uses the same calculations.
- It saves resource and processing time because the report is generated only once.
- It saves the cost of printing multiple paper copies.

Other Report Software Trends

Some report software works with an **executive information system (EIS)** to present selected data graphically for quick interpretation. As data changes minute by minute, the graphs are updated. EIS charts and graphs are particularly useful for monitoring rapidly changing data that affects business. For example, the number of call records in a queue waiting for owners can be represented as a color graph. As the number of calls gets closer to a predefined limit (and the danger of exceeding the response time service level grows), the color of the graph changes. If the number of calls exceeds the predefined limit, the color changes again.

 TIP These graphical, real-time data interpretations are useful for many companies and all levels of managers and staff. Over time, the EIS term "executive" will most likely be replaced with a more generic description.

Another new technology in reporting is **real-time publish and subscribe**, or **push**. Just as Internet users subscribe to list servers and mailing lists, business users can subscribe to information "published" by the support center. Users decide which information they want to see, subscribe to the report as they would subscribe to an Internet mailing list, and receive an alert when a new version is available. Most of the information is viewed with a Web browser. The alert may inform the hardware repair manager that five new call records are in his queue. **Drill down** is the ability to take summarized information and progressively reveal more details. When you follow a Web link from a list of URLs on a page, you simulate the effect of drill down—the URL list is a summary report and each hyperlink takes you to a detail page. The first time managers drill down from a summary, they may see the call record numbers, the callers, and the problem summaries. They can drill down further on each record to find more details about the record, or return to any of the summarized versions.

REPORT APPLICATIONS

The simplest way to report on call records and activities is to use the built-in report writers that come with the support software. These tools usually interpret the database fields and present data so that it makes sense to the support software users. However, some support groups use other tools to generate reports.

Simple and Inexpensive Reporting Tools

One of the simplest and least expensive ways to refine and process business statistics is by using an electronic spreadsheet. Spreadsheets include built-in **functions**, program routines that complete a series of mathematical calculations. For example, the average function in Microsoft Excel automates three manual steps: (1) it counts the number of items in a range of cells, (2) it sums the values in the cells, and then (3) it divides the sum by the count. Functions perform arithmetic on dates (subtracting one day from another to determine the difference in hours, minutes, and seconds), complete financial calculations, convert text to numbers or numbers to text, and manipulate databases.

The electronic spreadsheet became a critical tool for all businesses that manage or manipulate numbers, replacing slide rules and preprinted statistical tables in the mid-1980s.

Spreadsheets also provide a way to view the values of database fields. The data pivot table feature was added to spreadsheets in the 1990s to perform common calculations on databases. A **pivot table** is an interactive table that quickly summarizes large amounts of data. You can rotate its rows and columns to see different summaries, filter the data based on selection criteria, or display different levels of detail. A user could take the data presented in Figure 4-14, which shows incidents by workgroup across months, and transpose the rows and columns to create the new report shown in Figure 4-16, which shows incidents by month across workgroups.

Closed Incidents by Month and Workgroup Report generated 04/19/2002 08:00					
Month	Workgroup				
	Desktop Support	Mainframe Tools	Network	DB Admin	Total
Jan	37	117	67	167	389
Feb	88	178	107	193	566
Mar	261	334	171	253	1019
Apr	122	151	71	79	423
Total	516	801	418	717	2397

Figure 4-16   Closed call records by month

Commercial Reporting Tools

Most reporting software can access different types of databases. It also allows users to create graphics and to include reports and charts in word processing documents. Many companies develop reporting tools. For example:

- Commercial applications developed by SAS Institute, Inc., and SPSS, Inc., enable users to perform advanced calculations on large databases. The software was introduced in the 1980s for researchers, physicians, and scientists, but is frequently part of the business environment also.

- Crystal Reports is one of the most common database report writers. It was one of the earliest report tools, and many PC database applications originally included Crystal Reports to manipulate records. Seagate Software owns the application.

- Information Builders, Inc., was originally a mainframe data-reporting tool, but it now has PC versions as well.

- As the need to manage and manipulate data increases, companies use more OLAP report writers. Cognos and Computer Associates were early entries in the OLAP market.

Commercial applications also import or manipulate many data formats. They can access spreadsheets, ASCII files, and several types of database software records (including Access, Oracle, and MS SQL Server). Once defined, report definitions in commercial applications can be saved. Most commercial applications include scheduling options and routing software as well.

 Several commercial reporting tool vendors are listed in Appendix A

Reports are a standard feature for all support software, and many support software vendors include commercial report tools as part of the application. Business managers, support managers, and support staff use reports to measure performance. Although most report tools are easy to use, it is important to understand how and when data is collected in order to analyze information correctly.

CHAPTER SUMMARY

- Business managers use reports to manipulate data as they attempt to understand changes in the business environment. The return on investment (ROI) is an important tool used to understand how quickly companies can benefit after introducing new tools. Upper managers expect support managers to show that they are accomplishing their business objectives. Numbers and graphs show this quickly.

- Performance measurements evolve over time because support groups add services and change processes. Managers use statistical analysis to document service quality, control delivery cost, and prevent problems. Workload management and basic call volumes determine the minimum number of staff necessary to do the job to the satisfaction of customers. Managers prevent problems by using call categories and priorities to identify trends. Eventually the time saved by not having to process preventable problems is devoted to delivering new services.

- Reports don't directly measure whether customers are satisfied, but they may provide early warning of situations when customer satisfaction or perceptions are at risk.

- Some telephone systems collect data about telephone calls between customers and support. Call duration indicates how long the average conversation lasts. If callers stay on hold too long, they abandon calls. They may call back later, which increases the number of calls coming into support.

- Support software provides a way to count the number of call records created and to analyze them by time of day, type, customer, and support analyst. The three most important numbers for support that are part of any service level agreement are the number of calls, the average response time, and the average resolution time.

❐ Online analytical processing (OLAP) makes it easier for everyone to view database information. Report writer software should have ease-of-use features that enable anyone to create ad hoc reports. A detail report lists individual records with selected fields. A summary report contains calculations about many records. Upper managers are most interested in summary reports. Support managers use detail reports to explain summary statistics. Support staff use detail reports to manage workload.

❐ Report tools are an important feature of support software. If the tools don't meet the support group's needs, users can use spreadsheets, which now include database manipulation tools such as pivot tables. Once data is summarized, users can display the summaries as charts or graphs. Commercial database report writers provide advanced calculations and support many data formats.

KEY TERMS

abandon rate — The percentage of abandoned calls compared to the total telephone calls received.

accountability — Someone has the authority to correct problems when he or she defaults on commitments.

ad hoc — Designed or improvised as needed.

available time — The amount of time in minutes and seconds when support staff can answer the telephone and deliver support services.

baseline — A starting point for later comparisons.

call duration — The length of a telephone call in minutes and seconds.

detail report — A report that includes specific information about individual records.

drill down — The ability to take summarized information and progressively reveal more details.

executive information system (EIS) — Presents selected data graphically for quick interpretation.

first call resolution — The number of calls resolved while the support staff is still on the telephone with the customer.

flash report — *See* summary report.

full-time equivalent (FTE) — The result of the conversion of the number of work hours possible by full- and part-time employees.

functions — Program routines that complete a series of mathematical calculations.

hold time — The amount of time that a caller remains on hold if there is no one available to answer the telephone.

knowledge hits — When support staff find the answers to problems in a knowledge base.

level one resolution — Level one staff either solved the problem with their own knowledge or they used a knowledge base to solve the problem.

number of calls by customer — The number of call records created for a specific caller.

number of calls by day of week — The total number of call records that were created on a specific day of the week.

4

number of calls by originator — The number of call records created by each support staff member.

number of calls by owner — The number of call records each support staff member owns.

number of calls by time of day — The number of call records created and counted for each hour of a workday.

number of calls by type — The number of call records by category.

number of calls reopened — The number of call records that moved from a closed or resolved status back to an open status.

online analytical processing (OLAP) — A method of accessing database information that enables a user to extract and view data from different points of view.

origin of call — The way a problem was reported.

pivot table — An interactive table that quickly summarizes large amounts of data.

push — *See* real-time publish and subscribe.

queue time — Response time between two levels of support. *See also* response time.

real-time publish and subscribe — A reporting technology that allows business users to subscribe to information "published" by the support center.

report writer — Software that allows users to select, manipulate, and present database information.

resolution time — The difference in days, hours, minutes, and seconds between the time a call record is created and the time it moves to a closed status.

response time — The time it takes the support group to acknowledge a customer's problem or request and assign a resource.

return on investment (ROI) — A measurement that compares the dollar value of a support group's services and benefits to its operating costs.

summary report — A report that contains only calculations about many records.

threshold — A starting boundary.

REVIEW QUESTIONS

1. _____ are the primary users of reports, but customers and support staff also benefit from report data.

2. What measurement compares the dollar value of services and benefits to the operating costs?

3. What three things do managers attempt to control with reports?

4. All of the following are used to manage service quality *except*:

    a. service levels.

    b. response by outsourcers.

    c. product quality.

    d. number of calls owned by staff members.

5. What effect can software upgrades have on support?

6. You can create a graph without running a summary report first. True or False?

7. _____ have a great effect on report numbers, especially when they don't understand what managers try to measure.

8. The amount of time when support staff can answer the telephone and deliver calls minus the time they take for breaks, lunch, and administrative activities is called _____.

9. What effect does a high abandon rate have on the number of calls to support?

10. It may be difficult to log all calls; however, support staff should log all calls for the following reasons *except*:

 a. This shows how much work support staff have to do.

 b. Managers want to see how well staff can write and describe problems.

 c. The time it takes to log calls can show how slow the support software is.

 d. Managers can see that they have enough people to answer the telephone, but still may not have enough to resolve all the problems reported.

11. What two statistics would be used by managers who schedule full- and part-time employees and who provide 24 X 7 support to customers?

12. How does tracking the problem origin help support staff?

13. Should all support groups allow customers to create their own call records? Discuss your answer.

14. A support group's problem management process clearly states that call records should be reopened if the customer has the same problem within twenty-four hours of closing. Customers frequently complain that they have to try several solutions before their problem is fixed. However, the number of reopened call records is very small. What is one thing the manager may determine from the low number of reopened call records?

15. What is the difference between number of calls by originator and number of calls by owner? When would these two numbers be the same?

16. Response time can be measured in two ways: as the response between _____ and customers or as the response between _____.

17. What two numbers are part of a support group's service level agreements?

18. Which of the following statements is *not* true:

 a. Queue time affects resolution time.

 b. Level one resolution is part of first call resolution.

 c. Level one resolution includes records resolved on the first call, as well as the resolution time of other call records, as long as higher levels of support don't work on the issue.

 d. Logging calls after they are solved results in incorrectly low resolution times.

19. The lower the knowledge hit rate, the lower the resolution time. True or False?

20. List three features a report writer should always have.

21. What is the difference between a detail report and a summary report? Which report do executives and upper managers use most frequently?

22. What are two advantages to distributing reports electronically instead of by printed paper copies?

23. Which business software has become a standard tool for manipulating numbers or other calculations?

    a. word processing software

    b. database software

    c. spreadsheet software

    d. e-mail software

HANDS-ON PROJECTS

Project 4-1

Calculating FTEs. Calculate the number of FTEs for the following support group. (*Hint:* Use 40 hours of work per week to represent one FTE.)

1. Twenty-four employees who work 40 hours per week.

2. Twenty-four employees who work 20 hours per week and twelve employees who work 40 hours per week.

3. Eight employees who work 30 hours per week.

4. Five employees who work 40 hours per week, four employees who work 20 hours per week, and four employees who work 30 hours per week.

Project 4-2

Filtering database records. The Excel spreadsheet **Project0402.xls** contains several thousand call records. Use the Excel AutoFilter feature to review selected rows of data. AutoFilter changes the column headings in row 1 to pull-down lists. The first three entries, enclosed in parentheses, are the same for all the pull-down lists and are used for predefined selection criteria. After the first three entries, the values of database records are listed in alphabetical order. If there are missing entries in a column, the last two entries of the pull-down list will be a way to filter records that are missing the data.

1. Open the Microsoft Excel file **Project0402.xls**.

2. Click **Data**, **Filter**, **AutoFilter**. AutoFilter turns on.

3. Select the **Category** column pull-down list. How many categories are used in this database?

4. Select the **Queue Assigned** column pull-down list. How many queues are used in this database?

5. Select the **Customer Dept** column pull-down list and select **(Blanks)**. How many records do not have a customer department?

6. Turn off AutoFilter by clicking **Data**, **Filter**, **AutoFilter**. Go to the last row of the database. How many records are in the database?

7. How many fields are in the database?

8. Close the database, and do not save any changes.

Project 4-3

Sorting records to find data. Use the Excel spreadsheet **Project0402.xls** for this project. The Excel Sort feature arranges data in the order you select.

1. Open the Microsoft Excel file **Project0402.xls**.

2. Move the cursor to cell **A1**. Click **Data**, **Sort**. Use the pull-down list to set the value of Sort by to **Ticket #**. Make sure the **Header row** option button is selected in the My list has area, and click **OK**. What are the lowest and highest ticket numbers?

3. Sort the database by **Date Created**. What are the earliest and latest date records that were created?

4. Sort the database by **Owner Login**. Scroll down the records and find calls owned by CMCBRIDE. How many call records are owned by CMCBRIDE?

5. Close the database, and do not save any changes.

Project 4-4

Finding call owners. Use the Excel spreadsheet file **Project0402.xls** for this project. Instead of sorting the database to find records for a selected owner, use AutoFilter.

1. Open the Microsoft Excel file **Project0402.xls**.

2. Click **Data**, **Filter**, **AutoFilter**.

3. Select the **Owner Login** column pull-down list, and click **SGEE**. How many records are owned by SGEE?

4. Select the **Owner Login** column pull-down list, and click **DLANE**. How many records are owned by DLANE?

5. Select the **Owner Login** column pull-down list, and click **(Custom...)** to open the Custom AutoFilter dialog box. Make sure that the value in the Owner Login box is set to **equals**. Select **SGEE** from the pull-down list on the same row. Click the **Or** option button. Select **equals** in the pull-down list below Or. Select **DLANE** from the pull-down list on the same row, and click **OK** to perform the query. Describe the results.

6. Close the database, and do not save any changes.

Project 4-5

Building complex queries. Use the Excel spreadsheet file **Project0402.xls** for this project. Instead of sorting the database to find records for a selected owner, use AutoFilter.

1. Open the Microsoft Excel file **Project0402.xls**.
2. Click **Data**, **Filter**, **AutoFilter**.
3. Select the **Owner Login** column pull-down list, and click **Aholland**.
4. Select the **Queue Assigned** column pull-down list. How many queues did Aholland work from and what are the queue names?
5. Select the **Category** column pull-down list and click **Paradox**. How many calls were logged for this category? What queues were they routed to?
6. Select the **Category** column pull-down list and click **MS Office**. How many calls were logged for this category? What queues were they routed to?
7. Close the database, and do not save any changes.

Project 4-6

Calculating resolution times and determining the oldest call records. Use the Excel spreadsheet file **Project0402.xls** for this project.

1. Open the Microsoft Excel file **Project0402.xls** and save it as **Proj4-6.xls** before you make any changes.
2. Move the cursor to column **D**. Insert a new column by clicking **Insert**, **Columns**. In cell **D1**, enter **Resolution Time**.
3. Move the cursor to cell **D2** and enter a formula to subtract column C from column E. Type **=**, press the right arrow key to highlight the cell in column E, type **-**, press the left arrow key to highlight the cell in column C, then press **Enter**. (*Hint:* Do not type the formula; you must use the arrow keys or mouse to select the cells, or you will get a #VALUE! error.)
4. Select column D and click **Format**, **Cells**. In the Format Cells dialog box, click **Custom** in the Category list box. In the Type box, enter **[h]:mm** (to represent hours and minutes), and click **OK**. (To verify your calculation and format, Ticket #1500 should have a resolution time of 2 hours and 46 minutes, or 2:46.)
5. Copy the formula to all cells in column D by highlighting the formula, clicking **Edit**, **Copy**, highlighting all the blank cells, and pressing **Enter**. This spreadsheet requires manual formula recalculations, so press **F9** to recalculate all formulas.
6. Save the file.
7. Find the call record with the longest resolution time. (*Hint:* Either sort the database or use AutoFilter and select the Top 10 records.) What is the Ticket #?
8. Find the call records with 00:00 resolution time. Review some of the problem descriptions. (Note that password resets are completed very quickly, so the call records will probably be created and closed at the same time.) Do any tickets appear to have been created after the problem was resolved (other than password problems)?

4

9. Is there an easy way to calculate average resolution time by category? If so, how would you do this?

10. Close the database, and do not save any changes.

Project 4-7

Using pivot tables to calculate and manipulate data. Use the Excel spreadsheet you saved as file **Proj4-6.xls** for this project. This project provides a count of call records by category.

1. Open the Microsoft Excel file **Proj4-6.xls**.

2. Move the cursor to cell **A1**, if necessary.

3. Click **Data, PivotTable and PivotChart Report**. In the Step 1 dialog box, select the **Microsoft Excel list or database** option button, then click **Next**.

4. The range of data, $A$1:$L$11816, should already appear in the Range box in Step 2 of the wizard, so click **Next**.

5. In Step 3 of the wizard, select the **New worksheet** option button, then click **Layout**.

6. Drag the **Category** button to the **Row** section. Drag the **Resolution Time** button to the **Data** section. Double-click the **Count of Resolution** button to open the PivotTable Fields dialog box. Type **Total Calls** in the Name text box. Click **OK** to return to the PivotTable and PivotChart Wizard — Layout dialog box. Click **OK**.

7. In Step 3 of the wizard, click **Finish**. The results appear in the new worksheet, labeled Sheet1. How many call records were logged for Hardware problems? How many were logged for E-Mail?

8. Save your workbook as **Proj4-7.xls**, and close the database.

Project 4-8

Manipulating a pivot table. Use the Excel spreadsheet you saved as file **Proj4-7.xls** for this project. Change the existing pivot tables to calculate records by category across queues. The resulting table will have the categories listed down the left column and the queue names across on the same row.

1. Open the Microsoft Excel file **Proj4-7.xls**.

2. In Sheet1, which contains the old pivot table results, click **Data, PivotTable and PivotChart Report**. You will see Step 3 of the PivotTable Wizard.

3. Click **Layout**. Drag the **Queue Assigned** button from the field names list to the **Column** section of the pivot table, then click **OK**. Click **Finish** in Step 3 of the wizard.

4. How many hardware calls were logged to the DC Support queue? How many Windows NT calls went to Wilson Center?

5. Save your workbook as **Proj4-8.xls**.

6. In Sheet1, drag the **Queue Assigned** title in the pivot table results to the row below the Category title, and release the mouse button. What kind of a report do you see now?

7. In Sheet1, drag the **Category** title to the empty cell to the right of **Total Calls**. What happened?

8. Close the database, and do not save any changes.

Project 4-9

Adding calculations to a pivot table. Use the Excel spreadsheet saved as file **Proj4-8.xls** for this project. Use what you learned in previous projects to create a table that shows by category the total number of calls, the average resolution time, and the maximum resolution time.

1. Open the Microsoft Excel file **Proj4-8.xls**.

2. In Sheet1, click **Data**, **PivotTable and PivotChart Report**. You will see Step 3 of the PivotTable Wizard.

3. Click **Layout**. Leave **Total Calls** in the Data section. Drag the **Queue Assigned** button out of the Column section.

4. Drag the **Resolution Time** button to the **Data** section. Double-click the **Count of Resolution Time** button. Type **Avg Res Time** in the Name text box, select **Average** in the Summarize by list, then click **OK**.

5. Drag another copy of the **Resolution Time** button to the **Data** section. Double-click the **Count of Resolution Time** button. Type **Max Res Time** in the Name text box, select **Max** in the Summarize by list, then click **OK**. Click **OK** to return to Step 3 of the wizard.

6. Click **Finish**. You will see a report grouped by Category with three rows of data.

7. Drag the **Data** title to the Total cell. This will pull up the three calculations so that they appear as one record per category.

8. The Average and Maximum Resolution times should be formatted to round the time to hours and minutes. Click **Data**, **PivotTable and PivotChart Report**. You will see the data from Step 3 of the wizard. Click **Layout**. Double-click the **Avg Res Time** button. Click **Number**, then select **Custom** in the Category list. Type **[h]:mm** in the Type text box, then click **OK** to return to the PivotTable Fields dialog box. Click **OK** to return to the layout dialog box. Repeat this step to correct the format for Maximum Resolution time.

9. Click **OK** to return to Step 3 of the wizard, then click **Finish** and review the final data.

10. Switch to the **Call Records** worksheet. Turn on AutoFilter and find the two MS PowerPoint problems. Is the average resolution correct?

11. Save the workbook as **Proj4-9.xls** and close the database.

Project 4-10

Adding columns to an existing pivot table. Use the Excel spreadsheet saved as file **Proj4–9.xls** for this project. You will add one more dimension to the pivot table for analysis.

1. Open the Microsoft Excel file **Proj4–9.xls**.

2. In Sheet1, click in the pivot table, and then click **Data, PivotTable and PivotChart Report**. You will see the data from Step 3 of the PivotTable Wizard. Click **Layout**.

3. Drag the **Owner Login** button to the **Page** box. Click **OK**, then click **Finish**. You will see a new label in cell A1 and a pull-down list of Owners.

4. In Sheet1, select **Aholland** from the Owner Login pull-down list, click **OK**, then print the results. Select three other owners, print the results, and compare the reports. Who has the best average resolution time?

5. In Sheet1, experiment by dragging the **Owner Login** label below the **Category** label.

6. Drag the **Category** label to cell **A1**. Compare the e-mail calls for all Owners, and print the report.

7. In Sheet1, select all rows of data and click **Data, Sort**. Highlight the cells in column **B**, and click the **Descending** option button, then click **OK** to see who owned the most calls.

8. Repeat Step 7 to change the sort order to see who has the longest Average Resolution Time.

9. Save the spreadsheet as **Proj4–10.xls**, and close the database.

Project 4-11

Finding OLAP software. Use the Web to search for OLAP report software. Visit the OLAP Council Web site at **http://www.olapcouncil.org** and review the list of companies that contribute to the standards. Also visit the Computer Information Center Web site at **http://www.compinfo.co.uk**, which has links to EIS, OLAP, and other report writers.

Find two companies that offer demos of their products. What are the product names? What database formats will they read or import?

Project 4-12

Finding EIS software information. Use the Web to find information about companies that provide EIS systems. Select a demo that gives a good overview of the use of an EIS. What areas in support would be appropriate to view with an EIS?

Project 4-13

Reviewing statistical applications. Visit the Statistics.com Web Site at **http://www.statistics.com** and select two statistical applications to review. Find white papers and compare the applications' features. (*Hint*: White papers are background or tutorial papers that explain a subject.) Describe the built-in functions or statistical calculations supported.

Project 4-14

Filtering and sorting records in Access. Use Microsoft Access and create an Access database from the Microsoft Excel file **Project0414.xls.** You will sort and filter records to obtain results similar to the Excel projects. Review the Help files on filters and queries.

1. Start Microsoft Access and create a new database with the filename **Proj4–14.mdb**.

2. Import the Microsoft Excel file Project0414.xls. Click **File**, **Get External Data**, **Import**. Select **Microsoft Excel** in the Files of type list, select the **Project0414.xls** file, and click **Import**.

3. In the Import Spreadsheet Wizard, select **Call Records** in the list box, then click **Next**.

4. Make sure the **First Row Contains Column Headings** check box is selected, then click **Finish**.

5. Click **OK** to confirm that the records finished importing. A new table named Call Records appears in the Proj4–14: Database object window. Double-click the **Call Records** table to open a datasheet window.

6. Select the **Date Created** column. Click **Records**, **Sort**, **Sort Ascending** to find the earliest and latest date records that were created. Repeat this step to sort the data by Owner Login.

7. Click **Records**, **Filter**, **Advanced Filter/Sort** to open a filter window.

8. In the filter window, type **SGEE** in the first cell in the Criteria row and press **Enter**. Switch to the Call Records: Table window. Click **Records**, **Apply Filter/Sort**. How many records does SGEE own?

9. Switch to the filter window and type **DLANE** in the first cell in the Or row. Click **Filter**, **Apply Filter/Sort**. Do you get the same results as you did in Project 4-4?

10. In the Call Records: Table window, click **Records**, **Remove Filter/Sort**.

11. Save the database and exit Access.

Project 4-15

Creating a crosstab report in Access. Use the Microsoft Access database you saved as file **Proj4-14.mdb.** You will create a crosstab query report using the Query Wizard to create the same information as in Project 4-7.

1. Open the Microsoft Access file **Proj4-14.mdb**.

2. In the Proj4-14: Table object window, select the **Call Records** table.

3. Click **Insert**, **Query**. In the New query dialog box, select **Crosstab Query Wizard**, then click **OK**.

4. In the first Crosstab Query Wizard dialog box, make sure **Call Records** is selected and then click **Next**.

5. In the second Crosstab Query Wizard dialog box, select the row heading **Category** in the Available Fields list, click the **>** button, then click **Next**.

4

6. In the third Crosstab Query Wizard dialog box, select the column heading **Resolution Time**, then click **Next**.

7. In the fourth Crosstab Query Wizard dialog box, select **Year** as the Date/Time, then click **Next**.

8. In the fifth Crosstab Query Wizard dialog box, select **Problem Resolution** in the Fields list, select **Count** in the Functions list, then click **Next**.

9. Leave the default query name, then click **Finish**. The results of the crosstab query appear in a new window.

10. Compare these results to the results from Project 4-7. What is the primary disadvantage to using the Access Query tool compared to the Excel pivot table?

11. Save the database, and exit Access.

CASE PROJECTS

1. Determining Call Volume

In a typical support group, front-line staff provide telephone support 8 hours per day. During the 8 hours, they take two 15-minute breaks and another 30 minutes to complete timesheets and read e-mail. They also spend about 1 hour researching information or working outstanding calls. If the average telephone call is 20 minutes, what is the average number of telephone calls a front-line person can process in a typical day?

2. Determining Individual Performance

As the manager of a support group, you want to review individual performance for the last 6 months for hardware and software problems. Design a report that lists the closed calls by month and group all calls into two major categories: hardware or software problems. (*Hint:* Network problems are considered hardware problems.) Use an Excel pivot table to create the report based on the raw data in the Excel spreadsheet file Project0403.xls. Use online Help to learn how to group categories and include subtotals by person in your report. Calculate each person's total hardware and software calls as a percentage of the total calls closed for each month.

3. Evaluating Reporting Tools

The Randolph company has hired you as a consultant to help them select a new reporting tool. They want to make sure they can access Oracle, MS SQL Server, and Access database files and can generate professional looking reports for their Board of Directors. They also want a tool that is easy to use for most people, but that has some advanced calculation capabilities. Create a requirements document using a spreadsheet or word processor that lists the requirements. Include sections for Data Access and Manipulation, User Interface, Charts and Graphs, Methods of Output, and any other categories that you think are useful. Use the Web to review features of current products and make sure you can evaluate two products for all the requirements you list.

5

CALL MANAGEMENT SOFTWARE

In this chapter you will learn:

♦ Which internal and external support functions overlap within call management software

♦ The well-known internal support software companies and products

♦ The well-known external support software companies and products

♦ How to evaluate call management software

♦ The setup or administrative activities for implementing call management software

Internal support groups experience tremendous growth as companies become more dependent on technology. Many companies enjoy the benefits of complex tools such as purchasing systems, resource management systems, scheduling applications, and sales and marketing applications. With technology, employees can complete more work and eliminate manual processes. As a result, companies expect employees to be more computer literate than they were a few years ago.

Company employees are also more likely to install their own software or customize their desktops with organizers or other desktop utilities. They frequently bring in software they use at home and download software from the Internet. These software applications may conflict with the company's business applications (because the business application requires specific graphics or memory settings). Software such as games and screen savers is sometimes not suitable in a business environment. Bringing in personal software also exposes the company to software viruses and potential lawsuits due to pirated software.

External support groups grow as they acquire new customers and retain current customers. The support group eventually adds services, depending upon the company's business. They may have to assist customers as they place orders over the Web, troubleshoot hardware or software that customers purchase, or handle questions from marketing campaigns. External support groups balance the cost of adding these services against keeping the expense of service delivery low.

Internal and external support staff use call management software to track support problems, questions, and requests, and many support groups use commercially developed software. All software companies compete in a rapidly changing and competitive environment. Support software companies must develop software that expands as support processes change and evolve. This software changes frequently as software companies compete by adding more features. As a result, support staff may use a variety of support software applications during their careers.

CALL MANAGEMENT SOFTWARE CHANGES RAPIDLY

It takes more and more time and effort to support computer systems. **Information technology (IT)** includes all forms of technology used to create, store, exchange, and use information in its various forms (business data, voice conversations, images, multimedia presentations, and other forms). Also the IT industry continues to grow and change overnight. Consequently, companies that provide support products and services for the IT industry change just as rapidly. Gartner Group, an IT market research firm, predicts that the market for customer service and support products will reach $1.4 billion by the end of 2001. **Market research** means to collect and analyze information about products, services, consumers, and trends.

 Market research firms research the companies that have not purchased this type of software or that plan to replace their existing systems, and estimate the value of these new systems and the amount of time it will take to purchase or implement them. Several market research companies are listed in Appendix A.

There is a lot of overlap in the activities internal help desks and external customer support groups perform, especially in the fact that both attempt to manage their relationships with their customers. Aberdeen Group, a Boston-based research group, categorizes software for both external and internal support as customer interaction software (CIS) rather than call management software. Companies recognize that both internal and external support groups deal with customers, and they empower their support staffs to address any kind of new question about any area of the company if they can. Help desks are as likely to answer questions about employee benefits and company procedures as they are about desktop software problems. As support staff demonstrate their expertise with technical or nontechnical customer questions, support managers can expand the support group's services.

There is an 85% functional overlap between internal help desks and external customer support operations—they identify customers, maintain customer information, enter questions and problems, solve problems, and manage unresolved questions or problems. The other functions they perform are usually specific to the processes for internal or external support. If the environmentally specific processes (such as asset management or contract management) are not very complex, internal and external support groups within a company may use the same call management software to support both kinds of customers. Software that serves both internal and external customers helps justify the cost of the software and reduces administration. As long as the software meets the needs of both groups, it really doesn't matter whether it was designed for internal or external support groups.

Software administrative tasks include setting up the software initially, installing new releases of software, backing up databases and files, adding and maintaining user login IDs for the system, and monitoring processing. Some of these tasks are discussed later in this chapter. Other administrative tools are discussed in Chapter 11.

5

CALL MANAGEMENT SOFTWARE FOR INTERNAL SUPPORT

The specific software companies that develop and sell help desk support software change annually. A current trend in support software is to integrate more and more applications to address all IT tasks in one software package. Software companies such as IBM, Computer Associates, and BMC Software provide integrated suites of products that the help desk can use to manage all the technological challenges that affect computer users. These larger software companies often acquire smaller software vendors that have good products to integrate with their suite.

The number of software companies tends to stay about the same. There are regular acquisitions, which reduce the number of major vendors. At the same time, the support software market is so profitable that new companies spring up to develop support software, and existing companies that have never been in this market add new software also. Call management software is still so new that no single software vendor has ever acquired more than 25% of annual call management software purchases.

Independent call management software vendors can compete with larger software suites as long as they meet the needs of the underfunded, midsized, workgroup-based IT help desk, which is still a majority of help desks working today. Most of these help desks still use internally developed applications to manage their support. They are usually still in a reactive mode of responding, rather than preventing problems, and won't use many of the sophisticated IT suites. These midsized help desks want to purchase the best software they can find from a mature, well-recognized software company. Midsized support groups usually have a staff of 5 to 200 people supporting at least 100 and no more than a few thousand employees.

Several call management companies became well known in the mid-1990s for their help desk support products. These companies are listed in Table 5-1.

Because the call management software market changes rapidly, the best way to find internal support software companies is to perform a Web search for "help desk software." More than 100 companies provide help desk and support software today.

Table 5-1 Internal support call management software

Company	Web Site	Background
Bendata, Inc. Colorado Springs, CO	http://www.bendata.com	Bendata was founded in 1982. The Heat help desk product offers a good level of out-of-the-box functionality for the price and can be implemented quickly.
Network Associates Santa Clara, CA	http://www.nai.com	Network Associates was founded in 1989 and acquired Magic Software in 1998. The product Support Magic can be implemented quickly and is a good match for midrange support groups.
Peregrine Systems, Inc. San Diego, CA	http://www.peregrine.com	Peregrine was a leading mainframe asset and change management company in the mid-1980s. The company went public in 1997, and soon after introduced ServiceCenter for internal support in the late 1990s. This company is best known for the range of environments the software runs in and the advanced integration with asset and change management modules.
Remedy Corporation Mountain View, CA	http://www.remedy.com	The product Action Request System (ARS) first shipped in December 1991. Remedy software became well known as an application with one of the highest levels of customization.

CALL MANAGEMENT SOFTWARE FOR EXTERNAL SUPPORT

External support processes change as rapidly as internal support processes. Many support groups offer their customers Web-based support as well as traditional telephone access. External support call management products focus on managing customer information, collecting market statistics, and following up on sales opportunities. External support software may also be integrated with database or sales software. Three of the most popular call management software packages for external support are listed in Table 5-2.

 External support software can be found with a Web search for "customer support," "customer management," or "CRM (customer relationship management)."

Table 5-2 External support call management software

Company	Web Site	Background
Clarify, Inc. San Jose, CA	http://www.clarify.com	Clarify, founded in 1990, provides internal and external support applications: ClearSupport and ClearHelpDesk. The initial release of call management software was designed to track product defects in the high technology market as software companies moved from free to fee-based service for product support. Both products are characterized by high levels of customization and control.
Siebel Systems, Inc. San Mateo, CA	http://www.siebel.com	Siebel was founded in 1993. The first products supported sales force automation (tracking customers, sales leads, and prospects) and marketing. In 1998, Siebel acquired Scopus, a leading vendor in the support center market. Since the acquisition, the Siebel Call Center product has become one of the largest in the market (roughly 25 percent). Their products offer extreme scalability and good out-of-the-box features, requiring little customization.
Vantive Corporation Santa Clara, CA	http://www.vantive.com	The Vantive Corporation was founded in 1990. This company provides both internal and external support applications: Vantive Support and Vantive HelpDesk. The initial product release focused on customer service and support (making it one of the oldest vendors for external support products). The software is also extremely customizable.

EVALUATING CALL MANAGEMENT SOFTWARE

The support manager works alone or as part of a team to select software for a new help desk. If the help desk is already in place, the selection team may replace an existing call management program that no longer fits the company's needs. Recall that processes are the building blocks of a support group's goals. Once support processes are defined, support software should automate and enforce the procedures and tasks. If possible, software should help balance staff skills and resources, while measuring the progress of each step for a performance report.

In most companies, the selected software must also work within the current IT environment. Businesses establish IT departments to maintain computer and telephone systems. As a group, IT managers will review the computing needs of their company and select technology that addresses those needs. This group will also review the proposed call management software to make sure they understand its hardware and software requirements, and that the software will work within the rest of the computing network.

 An internal help desk is usually part of the larger IT department. However, an external customer support group could be part of the sales or marketing departments, rather than IT management.

Selecting call and problem management software can be an overwhelming task, because several hundred companies develop and sell support software. Most support applications have the same core features presented with a different look and feel. Many emphasize related support processes differently. Selecting the wrong application wastes time and money, so managers are usually cautious when reviewing the available software. Support managers balance conflicting needs during the selection process, during which they evaluate:

- **The price of the software:** Depending upon the processes that the software automates, the price can range from $200 to $3000 per support staff member. There will also be a separate charge for customer support for the product.

- **The amount of customization the software allows:** Support groups **customize** software by adding or changing fields to match the values the company needs or wants.

- **The scalability of the application: Scalability** is the ability of a piece of computer hardware or software to expand to meet future needs. For example, scalable software can have more users or rescale to a greater number of records.

- **Support staff requirements:** In most cases, this means the GUI has clear labels, and support staff can record and retrieve call records quickly.

- **Management requirements:** Managers need flexible reporting tools and software that enforces procedures.

- **Software complexity:** The more processes the software addresses, the longer it will take to implement.

Once a support application is purchased, the support manager works with others to install the software and make it available for support staff. Just as other computer users need training to learn a new application, support staff should also work with the new software before the change is made, so they will be familiar with new screens and menus. Some support groups train a few support staff early so they can help train other employees.

Many employees don't like to change. The need to train on a new system and yet keep up with daily work can cause added stress. Because many help desks are already understaffed, the process of implementing new support software can lead to even more stress. It's important for all support staff to remember that the purpose of implementing new software is to improve the support environment.

5

DETERMINING FACTORS IN SOFTWARE SELECTION
HERB HAYNES
PROJECT MANAGER
CAMBRIDGE TECHNOLOGY PARTNERS (CONSULTING)

My support software experience has been during sales and product implementations for help desk and call centers. In some cases, I've helped support groups evaluate products; in others I've been part of the software company's sales team, supporting a product that was being evaluated.

Companies consider a lot of factors when they select one software package over another. Most companies are looking for a package that is simple to use, yet has a full set of predefined tables and fields to collect the data they need. One of the main factors is the ability to customize the package to meet their business requirements and workflow.

Companies need a package that has an open architecture that will adapt to their constantly changing system and network environment. This includes the ability to add tables and fields to the database. The system administrator should be able to easily change the fields displayed, the screen layout, and the tab order for all displayed fields on each screen. They also need to be able to customize the user interface to match their workflow any time their environment changes. The top vendor packages provide the ability to make these kinds of changes for both the desktop and web interfaces, without programmer evolvement. If necessary, software should also allow a support group to write and execute custom code for procedures that are unique to their organization.

One the biggest challenges for any support group is the ability to collect as much data as possible without slowing down the problem analysis and resolution steps. The fewer keystrokes an agent has to make, the more time they can devote to problem resolution or handling requests. As a company evaluates software, those packages that have default field selections where possible, and auto-fill data into fields, have a definite advantage over others during the selection process.

No matter how much data a support group collects, it doesn't mean a thing if you can't easily and quickly locate what you are looking for when you need it. Any package that wants to stand out among the competition must have flexible search functionality. This goes for both call records and knowledge base records, which should be separate records in the database. The point is to collect the answer to questions and problems only once, and easily locate the records when needed. A package that allows searching on any field with masking capabilities will increases the odds for selection.

Another area of importance is call escalation and notification. Most of the top support packages provide functionality that can be easily setup to notify a predefined list of agents and managers, based on the type of call and severity of the call. The better packages allow you to define custom rules around user-defined scenarios, with notifications to your choice of email, pager, fax or printer.

Certainly, no support software would be worth much without a reporting tools that allows the application administrator and upper management to easily define reports in a format useful to their organization. Most of the top software vendors provide an internal report writer with predefined reports, and the ability to use popular external report writers.

Support software packages vary widely in functionality, and it can be difficult to keep track of all the features to compare. Flashy demos and eye-catching user interfaces can hide some of the blemishes (and every software package has them). I always recommend that the support group make a list of requirements needed to meet their objectives and business requirements before they explore the software. This checklist should be used to match a product's features and functions to the business requirements.

CALL MANAGEMENT SOFTWARE TASKS

Support managers may assign one or two level two or three staff members to implement the software and train the rest of the support staff members. All staff members eventually work with the call management software. No matter what support environment or support application they use, support staff complete common tasks. These tasks are separated into two categories, which are listed in Figure 5-1.

- ◆ Setup tasks
- ◆ Daily support tasks

Figure 5-1   Common call management tasks

Setup Tasks

One person usually sets up the software for all the users, and setup tasks can vary, depending on the environment or application. This person is usually the application administrator. An **application administrator** is a person who defines important tables and fields used in a software application. The call management application administrator builds these tables to match the support group's processes, using a special GUI. Most of these fields and tables were discussed in detail in Chapter 3, but there are additional terms, fields, and tables specific to call management software. These include:

- **Customer information:** In many companies, other software applications collect and maintain customer information. Once the support group decides which information they will track (listed in Figure 3-4), they load the data electronically rather than enter the information one record at a time. Some support groups will load several thousand customer records before they use the software.

- **Support staff information:** Support staff should record not only staff members' names and login IDs, but also the skill sets or roles they may use as they update records. A **role** describes activities someone completes. For example, a level one role may allow support staff to update customer records, whereas a dispatcher role would not allow dispatchers to change customer information. The administrator adds all support staff information to the software and assigns them to roles.

- **Workgroups or queues:** If the support group routes call records to teams or workgroups using queues, administrators enter the values support staff see on a pull-down list. If there are a lot of workgroups, the information is kept in a table so support staff can search for information.

- **Categories:** A support group may support hundreds of products, and administrators either enter values for a pull-down list or add records to a table.

- **Statuses:** If calls are not solved on the telephone, the support staff may use different statuses to help manage the call records they still have to work on. Statuses are usually values on a pull-down list.

- **Priorities:** Recall that many support groups use similar priorities but with different names. Administrators add priority values to a pull-down list.

- **Other fields:** Support managers may decide that the support staff should collect additional information about customers or the calls. If the software doesn't have these fields, the managers can customize the software to track this information.

Administrators for small support groups complete most of the setup tasks once. It can take weeks to build these core tables. It can also take weeks to train all the support staff. As soon as they are trained, the support group will **go-live**, which means to begin using the new software. Support managers or application administrators will also add new support staff, workgroups, or categories, and will make other field or table changes if the support needs change.

Daily Support Tasks

Once the initial setup tasks are completed and the software is customized for the support environment, support staff will complete many of the same daily tasks. Both internal and external support groups use call management software to complete the following daily tasks:

- Add call records
- Search for call records by category, such as:
  - Call records waiting for owners
  - Call records by customer
  - Call records by owner
- Route call records to other members
- View their assigned work
- Update or change record information
- Update customer/employee information
- Generate reports

If given the opportunity, support staff can provide important information about whether the software is easy to use on a day-to-day basis. If the software is confusing or slow, employees will probably not use it as their managers want. Even during the evaluation phase, support staff should try to use the software to make sure it will assist them. Many support groups change procedures at the same time they change software, so it is important that staff can perform old and new procedures while still keeping up with daily calls.

 Support staff may not like the new support software, but for the wrong reason. The real problem may be with the underlying process, not with the software itself. Data entry should "flow" easily from the caller into the application. As support needs information to solve a problem, they can easily collect and save the data in the software.

Staff and managers should always evaluate new software as they perform the most common activities of support, to determine the software's relative ease of use. The best (and maybe the only) way to learn how to use a call management application is to use it regularly.

CHAPTER SUMMARY

- As companies continue to expand their use of technology, the IT industry and therefore the support business will continue to change in response. Support staff will most likely use a variety of software applications during the course of their careers.
- Internal and external support groups complete common support tasks that are about 85% the same. The largest market for internal support software is within the midsized, workgroup-based IT help desk. Many help desks still use internally developed applications and are underfunded.

❏ There are so many software vendors and support software is still so new, that no one vendor has a majority of the market.

❏ Managers try to select a support application that runs in the corporate environment, supports the business processes, meets reporting needs, and fits within the financial budget. If possible, support staff should validate the day-to-day usefulness of the application.

❏ Once support software is selected, many people work to set it up, adding customer information and setting up other tables of information to streamline use. Implementation may take weeks and depends upon the number of people to be trained and how many support processes are in place.

❏ Support managers should evaluate support applications by their ease of use in setup and daily tasks.

Key Terms

application administrator — A person who defines important tables and fields used in a software application.

customize — To add or change fields in software to match the values the company needs or wants.

go-live — To begin using new software.

information technology (IT) — All forms of technology used to create, store, exchange, and use information in its various forms (business data, voice conversations, images, multimedia presentations, and other forms).

market research — To collect and analyze information about products, services, consumers, and trends.

role — Describes activities someone completes.

scalability — The ability of a piece of computer hardware or software to expand to meet future needs.

Review Questions

1. The need for internal support groups will decrease as employees become more knowledgeable about technology. True or False?

2. _____ analyze products, services, and consumers and identify business trends.

3. The Aberdeen Group refers to support software as _____.

4. List three activities that may be common to both internal and external support groups.

5. A current trend in support software is to develop more and more individual applications that address one IT task. True or False?

6. The majority of internal help desks use commercially developed support software. True or False?

7. External support processes change as rapidly as internal support processes. True or False?

8. List four factors support managers consider when evaluating call management software.

9. A software application that can be used initially by twenty support staff members and then expanded for use by more than fifty support staff members is said to have a high level of _____.

10. How does new call management software add stress for support staff?

11. No matter what support environment or support application they use, support staff complete common tasks. True or False?

12. During setup, a(n) _____ defines tables and fields used in a software application.

13. What does it mean to go-live?

14. What is the most important contribution support staff can make when a support group reviews support software?

15. What is the best (and maybe the only) way to learn how to use a call management application?

HANDS-ON PROJECTS

 TIP Appendix A lists additional resources for all Hands-on Projects.

Project 5-1

Using demos to summarize software features. Complete a Web search to locate help desk or customer support software companies. Find three sites that offer demonstrations of their call management products. Download the demonstrations and try them, or complete the Web-based demos. Prepare a table or spreadsheet that compares the features and benefits of the three products based on what you learned from the demos.

Project 5-2

Locating vendors that provide other process applications. Expand the table or spreadsheet you created in Project 5-1 to include help desk or customer support software companies that provide other applications to handle appropriate internal or external support processes (such as sales, asset management, etc.). If none of the companies from your original list provides other software, then find three new companies that do. List the applications, and then discuss with your classmates how these programs complement support processes.

Project 5-3

Understanding implementation outsourcers. Several companies contract with businesses to implement IT and support software. Visit the Technology Solutions Company (TSC) Web site at **http://www.techsol.com**. Review the Web information, and then answer the following questions:

1. What are three different services this company provides?

2. Do they specialize in any specific support applications?

3. Do they work with internal or external support groups?

5

Project 5-4

Reviewing support software features. Install the HelpTrac software from Monarch Software, located on your Data Disk with the filename **HelpTrac6.exe**. This software is used for Projects 5-4 through 5-6. Run the demo slide show program and answer the following questions:

1. Can you customize this application?

2. What kind of database format does the application use?

3. Can you export data?

4. What does HelpTrac call the call records (for example, tickets, incidents, calls, problem reports)?

5. What fields can you use to find caller information?

6. How many reports are included with the product?

7. What are the methods of output available?

8. Can each support person personalize his or her view of data?

9. What commercial report writer works with the data?

10. What knowledge base works with the data?

11. What related processes (in addition to problem management) can you use this software for?

12. Is this software targeted for internal or external support groups?

Project 5-5

Completing internal support setup tasks. Use the HelpTrac Demo Supervisor application to complete setup tasks. Start the software, and then do the following:

1. Click **Options**, **General Options**, click the **General** tab, and turn off the equipment screens and solution documents. Click **OK** to close the dialog box.

2. Click **Lists**, **Status Codes**, **Ticket**. Delete or edit the existing statuses, leaving only the following statuses: Closed, Pending Hardware, Open, Pending Software. Click **OK** to close the dialog box.

3. Click **Lists**, **Priority Codes**. Rename the priorities from Critical, Rush, Normal, Low, and Inquiry to Critical, Serious, Important, When Possible, and Question. Click **OK** to close the dialog box.

4. You are not going to use Product fields, only Categories. Click **Lists**, **Category List**. Delete the categories for CPU, DOS, Monitor, and Peripheral Equip. Add Categories for **MS Word** and **MS Excel**. Click **OK** to close the dialog box.

5. Click **Lists**, **Technician Departments**. Add Level 1 and Network. Click **OK** to close the dialog box.

Start the HelpTrac Demo application and then complete the following tasks:

1. Add customers. Click **Profiles**, **User**, **Add**. Add five new callers and include their names, telephone numbers, and e-mail addresses. Assign them to different locations.

2. Add support staff or technicians. Click **Profiles, Technician**, **Add**. Add a record for yourself and select the **Level 1** department on the Identification Tab. Click the **Skills** tab and select **MS Word** and **MS Excel**. How many skills can you assign to a technician? Click **OK** to close the dialog box.

3. Add two more technicians and assign them to the Network Department.

4. Click **File**, **Exit** to close the application.

Project 5-6

Completing internal support daily tasks. Use the HelpTrac Demo application to log the call records saved in the Word file **Project0506.doc**. As specified below, some records you will complete while on the phone, and other records you will need to update.

1. Example #1 – Enter all text and the solution while still on the telephone, and set the status to Closed.

2. Example #2 – Enter the problem description, assign to Bill, and leave the Example record Open.

3. Example #3 – Enter the problem description, assign the problem to yourself, and leave the Example record Open.

4. Example #4 – Enter the problem description and assign to Bill. Add only the first Update to the solution, and set the status to Pending Software.

5. Example #5 – Enter the problem description, assign to Beth, and set the status to Open.

6. Example #6 – Enter all text and the solution while still on the telephone, and set the status to Closed.

7. Example #4 – Search for this call by category and status. Add the second update and set the status to Closed.

8. Enter the last two examples, leaving them open and without solutions.

Project 5-7

Accessing data with other tools. The HelpTrac database is stored in the HT6DEMO folder as **Cbtick.dbf**. Use Microsoft Excel to open the file. (*Hint:* You will have to change the Files of type list to dBase Files.) Create a PivotTable report of the calls by Category and Location.

Project 5-8

Reviewing additional support software. Install the SDS HelpDesk software from Scott Data Systems, located on your Data Disk with the filename **sdshlp40.exe**. This software is used for Projects 5-8 through 5-10. Open the Microsoft Word document with the filename **Tutorial.doc**. Complete the SDS Tutorial (skipping Tasks 8, 9, and 15) and use this product to answer the questions from Project 5-4.

Project 5-9

Completing external support setup tasks. Use the SDS HelpDesk application to complete the following setup tasks. Use the Setup Wizard to access the Tables you will set up. Start the SDS HelpDesk application (logging in as Admin) and then do the following:

1. Click **Issue Statuses**. Add new statuses and delete or edit the existing statuses, leaving only the following statuses: Closed, Pending Hardware, Open, Pending Software. Click **Exit** to close the dialog box.

2. Click **Issue Priorities**. Add new priorities and delete or update existing priorities, leaving only the following priorities: Critical, Serious, Important, When Possible, and Question. Click **Exit** to close the dialog box.

3. Click **Issue Categories**. Select **Product Support** and press the **Tab** key. Type **MS Word** in the Description text box and click the **Add** button. Select **Product Support** again and press the **Tab** key. Type **MS Excel** in the Description text box, and click the **Add** button. Delete the Complaint, Feature Suggestion, and How-to under Product Support. Select **Product Support** and press the **Tab** button. Change the description to **Products** and click the **Update** button. Click **Exit** to close the dialog box.

4. Click **Issue Conditions**. Delete the entries for Humidity, Pressure, Temperature, and Weather. Click **Exit** to close the dialog box.

5. Click **Issue Locations**. Press the Tab key to move to the Description text box, then add locations for Houston and Chicago. Click **Exit** to close the dialog box.

6. Click **Define Contact Types**. Add Level 1 and Network. Click **Exit** to close the dialog box.

7. Click **Define Skills**. Delete the Automotive, Carpentry, Electrical, and Plumbing skills. Add MS Word and MS Excel as skills. Click **Exit** to close the dialog box.

8. Add support staff or technicians. Click **Window**, **Work flow** to switch to the Work Flow window. Click **Address Book**, select the **Scott Data Systems Organization**, and type a new name in the contact text box. Select the **Level 1** department as the contact type. Click **Add**. In the Skills section, select the **MS Word** skill and click **Add**. Add **MS Excel** to your skills. Then click **Update** from the buttons above. How many skills can you assign to a technician? Click **Exit** to close the dialog box.

9. Add two more technicians and assign them to the Network Department.

10. Add customer records using the Address Book for all the people listed in the Word document **Project0506.doc**. Make sure their contact type is set to **Customer**.

Project 5-10

Completing external support daily tasks. Use the SDS HelpDesk application to log the call records included in file **Project0506.doc**. Complete the same daily tasks listed in Project 5-6 using the SDS software. Assign calls to the technicians you added in Project 5-9 instead of to Bill and Beth.

Project 5-11

Accessing data for reports. The SDS database is stored as the file **demo.mdb** in the same folder in which you installed the SDS HelpDesk application. You will save three of the database tables as Excel spreadsheet files.

1. Start Microsoft Access and open the **demo.mdb** database file. (*Hint:* Access 2000 users may see a message that this file is not Access 2000 compatible and no changes can be made unless the database is converted. Do *not* convert the database or you will not be able to use it again with SDS. Click Cancel to close the dialog box.)

2. Click **Tables** in the Object group, click the **Category** table, and then click **File**, **Export**. Leave the default filename (the table name), but select **Microsoft Excel 97–2000** in the Save as type list. Click **Save**.

3. Repeat Step 2 for the **Issue** and **Location** tables.

4. Close Access.

5. Start Microsoft Excel and open the **Issue**, **Location**, and the **Category** Excel files you saved.

6. You use the table lookup feature to look up the values of the CategoryID column in the Category workbook and replace them with the names of the categories. Switch to the **Issue** workbook and insert a column next to the CategoryID column. Label this column **Category**. In row 3 of the Category column (the first row with an issue), type **=Vlookup(**, click the first cell of the CategoryID column, type **,** (a comma), switch to the Category workbook and select columns **A** through **C**, type **,** (a comma),

and then type **3)**. Press the **Enter** key; the name of the category should be displayed correctly in the new Category column. Copy the formula to all the rows of the database. Review the Excel Help files for VLOOKUP if you have any problems.

7. Repeat Step 6 to add a lookup column for **Locations**.

8. Create a PivotTable report of calls by Category and Location.

9. Save the workbook as **Proj5–11.xls**, and exit Excel.

Project 5-12

5

Rating support software. Use the software evaluation worksheet, the Excel file **Project0512.xls**, located on your Data Disk. Rate the HelpTrac software application as Application #1 and the SDS software application as Application #2. You may need to customize the views to complete all the common tasks listed on the evaluation spreadsheet. Save the completed file as **Proj5–12.xls**. Which of the applications would you select if you were a support manager? Why?

Project 5-13

Reviewing additional support software. Complete a Web search of help desk or customer support software companies. Find a site that offers trial or evaluation copies of their software. Select an application that you wish to evaluate, install the software, and read the user documentation. Complete setup tasks and create problem records, with information similar to that used in Projects 5-5 and 5-6. Evaluate this application as Application #3 in your completed **Proj5–12.xls** software evaluation worksheet. Which of the three applications would you select if you were a support manager? Explain your decision.

CASE PROJECTS

1. **Evaluating Shareware and Freeware**

   You are the manager of a small help desk, which is beginning to receive enough support calls to justify a call management application. Unfortunately, you have a very limited budget, so you will have to show your manager just how useful call management software is. You decide to find either freeware or shareware to review the types of call management software features available. You discover several possible sources for software:

   - The Phil Verghis Web site at **http://www.philverghis.com**

   - The Ziff Davis Software Library Web site at **http://www.zdnet.com/swlib/** (search for "help desk software")

   - The HelpDesk.com Web site at **http://www.helpdesk.com**

   - The Help Desk Institute Web site at **http://www.helpdeskinst.com**

Prepare a list of available features. (*Hint:* It may be necessary to download two or three applications to prepare your list.) Write a short report that summarizes your comparison of features and licensing for each application, and explains which software you will use and why.

2. **Classifying Software Vendors**

Wilson Electronics has three internal support groups and two external support groups. The Vice President of Technology has decided that the company may be able to cut down on administration if all the support groups can use the same software. He has asked you to identify companies that provide call management software with features for both internal and external support. He wants to know if any of the support groups are already using call management software that would fit both groups. He also wants to know what databases these application run on, if Wilson Electronics can use Lotus Notes as the database, and which applications have a Web interface. Complete a Web search to locate help desk or customer support software. Build a table or spreadsheet that lists the name of the company, the name of the software, and whether the software is internal only, external only, or both. Include a column that lists the databases the software runs on and whether the software is Web-based.

3. **Call Management Vendor Changes**

The Gray Partners research firm tracks IT software and call management applications. You have joined the company as a new call management analyst, and you need to write a market review on companies that acquire support software vendors to add to their IT product suites. Complete a Web search and find at least two call management software company acquisitions in the last twelve to eighteen months. Review the software products the acquiring company had before the acquisition. Write a report that explains how the call management software acquisition adds to the acquiring company's product line and which products will work with that application.

CHAPTER

6

PROBLEM RESOLUTION SOFTWARE

> **In this chapter you will learn:**
> - The relationship of knowledge to problem resolution
> - The benefits of knowledge management
> - The obstacles to knowledge management and using problem resolution software
> - Methodologies for problem resolution
> - Commercial software used for problem resolution
> - Trends and available resources for problem resolution

In the early 1990s, support managers concentrated on establishing their support groups. At the time, the first priority was to track calls so managers could document the effects of implementing PCs and other technology in their companies. Reports helped them justify the need for support staff and showed the diversity of problems, questions, and requests they handled. Over time, support processes matured, and call tracking procedures evolved into call management systems. Outstanding calls may be separated into questions or problems that support staff know how to solve and problems that are new to the support group.

The next step in this support process evolution is the attempt to improve problem resolution. A problem resolution process includes identifying a problem's cause and preventing the same problem from happening in the future. Front-line staff may work with higher levels of support to research and troubleshoot problems. Once support staff discover the solution, they record this information so other staff members or customers can solve the same problem later. The information that staff use, and the new information they develop during troubleshooting, is valuable to a company because it can decrease support time the next time the problem happens.

Support software has evolved as support processes evolve. Many call management applications now include problem resolution features. Specialized problem resolution applications work alone or can be integrated with other call management applications. Support groups use problem resolution software to manage problem solving and solution storing.

PROBLEM RESOLUTION AND KNOWLEDGE MANAGEMENT PROCESSES

The problem resolution process attempts to identify a problem's cause and prevent the same problem from occurring in the future. This process has several steps:

1. Support staff collect as many details as possible about the problem and its scope. They determine whether the problem has a known solution or whether it is new to the support group.

2. The support staff look for quick solutions. They may investigate other, related areas, using their own personal experience, to determine the problem's cause. If necessary, the support staff work with other experienced staff members who might know the problem's cause.

3. If there is no quick solution, the support staff try possible solutions, discarding unsuccessful solutions until they find the right one.

This process happens once for each new problem. If the same problem happens again, the support staff members can draw upon previous troubleshooting experiences and can help other support staff who are new to the problem. If support staff record the troubleshooting steps in the call record, including the successful and the unsuccessful troubleshooting steps they took to resolve the problem, they can reuse closed call records when confronted again with the same problem. Solutions should be saved to provide problem resolution information for support staff as well as to document interactions with customers.

Many support groups use closed call records to help solve problems. The support staff can query calls by category to find related problems and read through the problem descriptions and resolutions. However, searching old call records is inefficient. First, it may be difficult to build a query that limits the number of records returned to a reasonable number. Queries for very common questions, such as login errors and printer problems, can return hundreds of records. Support staff will have to review the summaries and troubleshooting logs one by one to determine if previous calls have similar circumstances. Second, it is possible to miss records in a query because some support staff may use different search phrases than other staff members who have entered text in call records. In some support environments, a problem may seem different to two users, but have the same cause and resolution. Finally, call record solutions for software or hardware problems may be outdated. Solutions for one version of software don't always work for other versions.

Storing information is relatively easy, but stored information is useless if it cannot be found when needed. Problem resolution software attempts to address this issue by providing a tool designed for acquiring and sharing knowledge.

What Is Knowledge?

In its simplest definition, business-related **knowledge** is a collection of processed information that a company can use to accomplish tasks. Recall that data is raw numbers or facts collected in a database. Information is data organized into something meaningful and is derived from raw data. People process data or information to create knowledge.

People have knowledge when they either know the subject themselves or know where to find information about the subject. They acquire knowledge through experience, intuition, and research. They can also create new knowledge from existing knowledge, using logical **inference**. For example, if you know that Mike is Harry's son and that Will is Mike's son, and you know the rule that the son of one's son is one's grandson, then you can infer the new knowledge that Will is Harry's grandson.

 In philosophy, the theory of knowledge and how it changes is called **epistemology**.

Companies make multimillion dollar decisions based heavily on the knowledge possessed by key individuals. **Knowledge management** is a relatively new business process in which a company attempts to gather, organize, analyze, and reuse its knowledge. This process is still evolving, and there is a great deal of confusion over the terminology and the best way to manage knowledge with software.

A company uses several types of knowledge created through:

- information requests
- problem determination
- data mining

Information requests are relatively easy to collect because requestors (who may be customers or potential customers) know that they need information and know what to ask for. Examples of information requests are questions about procedures, how-to requests, and requests for data or known facts about computers, such as "What is the print resolution of this laser printer?" or "How much memory is installed in my PC?" Support staff may already have the information or can process these requests into knowledge when they discover the answer. Information requests are a large percentage of the calls the support group receives.

Support staff use problem determination knowledge when customers do not know what the problem is, or when customers don't know how to describe the problem. Support staff learn to **frame** a problem, organizing and refining the problem symptoms so they can search for a solution. Support staff collect the caller's answers to questions about the problem, so that a vague, general statement that starts out as "My PC is broken" eventually becomes explicitly framed as "When I turn on my PC, I don't see a Windows desktop, I see only some text." Problem determination knowledge is built after staff apply experience and inference to facts. In most support groups, level two and three support groups provide this knowledge.

Data mining is the analysis of facts, transactions, and reports about business activities to determine relationships between actions and results. It includes **structured data** (numbers and text that fit in separate fields in databases) and **unstructured data**, such as documents, presentations, or graphs that don't fit neatly into rows and columns of a database. Data mining is based upon recognizing patterns of information in data that may not be readily apparent without statistical analysis.

6

Data mining results in:

- Associations in which one event correlates to another (for example, beer purchasers buy peanuts a certain percentage of the time)

- Sequences of events that lead to later events (for example, a rug purchase is usually followed by a purchase of curtains)

- Classification and new organization of data (for example, profiles of customers who make purchases)

- Clustering, or finding facts not previously known (for example, women 16 to 25 years old buy not only clothing but also associated items such as shoes and jewelry)

- Forecasting, or discovering patterns that lead to predictions about the future (for example, if Web-based product sales continue to increase at this rate, it will be necessary to increase support staff by 20%).

Support groups who answer computer-related questions frequently find associations in support data. For example, a support manager may discover that a particular brand or model of hardware is more likely to break than another model. Using this new knowledge, the manager works with other company departments to educate customers. Internal support managers use this knowledge to standardize the brands or models of equipment the company purchases, so that problem hardware and software are limited in the company. External support groups also inform their customers if optional products they can purchase from other vendors work with the supporting company's products.

BENEFITS OF KNOWLEDGE MANAGEMENT

Support groups benefit when they collect and manage knowledge about the questions and problems they receive. Without a knowledge management process, information stored in individuals' memories is lost when they leave the support group. New support staff have to learn about the support environment as well as how to solve specific problems.

In many support environments, it can take staff members two months or longer to learn enough to be able to solve problems on their own (complex areas of support may require six to twelve months before support staff have enough experience). In the meantime, new staff members can solve problems they have never seen before, as long as they know how to search for a documented solution. Knowledge management also makes it easier for support staff to keep up with the increasing number of facts about products they support, so they can resolve information requests quickly. Most support staff quickly learn how to find information when they need it.

 It isn't always necessary to know a subject, as long as you know where to find information about the subject.

Teams of subject matter experts work together in the knowledge management process, and over time, a collection of knowledge becomes greater than any one person could have created. One person may begin with the solution to a problem, but as other people collect more examples, the support group accumulates a broader understanding of all the problem's characteristics (the different symptoms the problem exhibits, or events that may lead to this problem eventually). The problem solution is no longer the contribution of one person and his or her experiences, but of several people. It becomes a "living" resource and continues to change. Support staff are more likely to find a solution that isn't outdated if the knowledge management process ensures that the knowledge is maintained.

Higher levels of support staff may not need to use the knowledge themselves, but they also benefit from knowledge management. Level two and three staff members don't feel challenged when they have to address the same problems repeatedly, and they may decide to leave the support group to move into more interesting projects. When they develop knowledge that the front-line staff can understand, level one support staff don't escalate as many questions or problems to higher support levels. As the number of escalated calls decreases, level two and three support staff are free to handle more complex and challenging problems and projects. Their value increases, and they may remain with a company or the support group longer. This also helps the support group hold down costs: the percentage of calls resolved on the first call can increase, and higher-level support staff can be scheduled for other services.

Companies also benefit when they can share their knowledge with customers. Support staff can teach customers how to troubleshoot periodic problems, with knowledge support staff continually reuse and validate. As customers become more skilled with computers and software, they also learn to help themselves. Intranets, a rapidly growing source of shared information, are frequently the first step for customer self-service. An intranet page can contain many links to pools of company information. Customers can read FAQs and solve some problems themselves or review a list of support problems the support staff are already working on, before they call the support group. This can reduce the number of telephone calls to support and give support staff more time to work on outstanding problems.

External support groups use their knowledge to help make their company more competitive. Patterns of questions and requests for information help a company's upper management generate new business ideas and focus efforts in product development, marketing, and public relations. Call management records may be combined with invoice records to determine if there are any associations between support calls and purchases. Support managers may analyze customer attitudes and their comments about competing products to develop knowledge about the company's reputation in the marketplace.

KNOWLEDGE MANAGEMENT CHALLENGES

Although most business managers recognize the need for and benefits of knowledge management, few support groups actively enforce knowledge acquisition. Figure 6-1 shows the primary steps involved in a knowledge management process.

> 1. Collect data and identify sources of information.
>
> 2. Process and organize data and other information into knowledge.
>
> 3. Distribute the knowledge to support staff and/or customers.
>
> 4. Maintain and update the knowledge.

Figure 6-1 Knowledge management steps

Because problem resolution tools are also knowledge management tools, the same problems exist for both processes. Many of the processing and organizing tools are still immature and actually erode productivity. It takes time to classify and organize information, and under-staffed support groups may not be able to devote time to this activity. Although call management applications provide an easy collection method, support staff still have to review troubleshooting logs from call records to create knowledge. Support environments also change rapidly; new knowledge develops, existing knowledge changes, and other knowledge becomes outdated. In many support groups, all support levels create knowledge and must make time during other daily activities to concentrate on this activity. If the tools to create or maintain knowledge are slow or difficult to learn, staff will not use the knowledge tools as part of their daily work.

 TIP An immature software tool tends to automate manual tasks. Over time, the manual tasks will be streamlined into fewer separate steps by the software or will be replaced by new functions or features in the software.

Creating knowledge is also a "new" activity in many support groups. Successful support staff quickly learn what they need to log calls and manage their work. Support staff that create knowledge have to learn to structure the resulting knowledge in such a way that others can retrieve it. Initially, knowledge users are usually other support staff. Eventually, support groups allow their customers access to this same knowledge as a way to control their calls. Because this knowledge is no longer "internal" information, it needs to be presented with a standard format and written clearly so any customer can understand it.

People who have knowledge can also hinder knowledge collection. They are reluctant to share what they know because they want to be experts. If staff members who earn less can perform the same tasks as more skilled workers, the more skilled staff may believe that management will replace them with cheaper workers who can use their stored knowledge. These staff members and some managers fail to understand that knowledge is dynamic and usually based on more than just facts. People become experts because they know how to apply knowledge, experience, and intuition to create more knowledge. Successful support groups reward staff who share and maintain knowledge.

With many people contributing knowledge, it is more challenging to retrieve the required knowledge because of different writing styles or terminology. Problems and questions may not always be clearly defined: a how-to question can actually represent a problem, or a problem can really be just a how-to question. For example, a customer may say, "I can't print a Word document"; the solution may be to review the "how to print Word documents" knowledge, making sure that the customer completed each step correctly, before attempting more troubleshooting. Front-line staff have to learn new ways to look at problems, because knowledge is represented in different ways. If staff members discover outdated information or can't find answers easily, they lose confidence in the problem resolution tool and turn to older, slower ways to organize knowledge. It is harder for managers to enforce the use of knowledge tools when support staff cannot rely on them in all cases.

6

MANAGER ATTITUDES ON KNOWLEDGE CREATION BY SUPPORT STAFF
FRANCOISE TOURNIAIRE, FOUNDER
FT WORKS

Francoise Tourniaire has more than 15 years of experience as a Support and Services executive. Prior to founding FT Works in 1998, she was the Vice President of Worldwide Service at Scopus, which has since been acquired by Siebel, a leading Customer Relationship Management (CRM) software manufacturer.

Managers seem to have one of two predominant attitudes about creation of knowledge by support staff. Some support managers want everyone to contribute their knowledge. This works best if knowledge creation is integrated with issue resolution work. Many modern support tools have an integrated knowledge base for that purpose.

Unfortunately, many managers don't share this attitude. They give a variety of reasons why support staff shouldn't create knowledge:

- If it's everyone's responsibility, then no one is responsible. Everyone assumes that someone else will create the knowledge, so no one ends up doing it.

- Support staff don't have time. There aren't enough people to answer the phones now.

- Support staff don't have good writing skills.

This group of managers believes that the only way knowledge management will work is to dedicate people (moving staff from support) to do knowledge creation. This is good for a short time, but within a few months, these people lose touch with the real world. Knowledge is continually changing, and they need to continually refine information coming in from support processes in the knowledge system.

It's probably a good idea to have an editor review knowledge documents for format and grammar, but the real knowledge must come from people who do the work and integrate knowledge creation into their workflow.

PROBLEM RESOLUTION METHODS

Because there are so many forms of information and data, it has been difficult for software vendors to design software tools to handle both structured and unstructured data. Support groups primarily use problem determination knowledge to resolve problems. Problem resolution software is a subset of knowledge management tools that is specifically targeted for support staff. Companies frequently use several software applications to manage knowledge.

 TIP Knowledge management software is also known as groupware, because groups of people collaborate to create and share business knowledge.

Most problem resolution (and knowledge management) software evolved from **artificial intelligence (AI)**, the attempt to mimic human intelligence with computers. Many AI terms are used in problem resolution software to describe activities or similar concepts. For example, both AI and problem resolution software use the following terms:

- **Knowledge base:** An electronically stored collection of knowledge about a subject

- **Knowledge domain:** A specific area of knowledge covered by a knowledge-based system; for example, a collection of knowledge about MS Word would be the MS Word knowledge domain

- **Domain experts:** People who know a lot about a specific subject

- **Knowledge acquisition:** The collection and organization of knowledge from human beings

- **Knowledge engineer:** A person who obtains knowledge from human experts and organizes it into a knowledge base

- **Expert or knowledge system:** Software that imitates the problem-solving procedures human experts perform

- **Inference engine:** Software that imitates human inference in creating new facts from known facts, using inference rules

 John McCarthy, a computer programmer, coined the term "artificial intelligence" in 1956 at the Massachusetts Institute of Technology. AI is a branch of computer science that is concerned with making computers behave like human beings. It includes playing games, making decisions, understanding natural human languages, simulating brain activities, and robotics.

Support tools should allow multiple ways to retrieve the information and should assist knowledge creators by automatically structuring information to save time. Because there are different forms of structured and unstructured data, and people use different methods to retrieve knowledge, problem resolution software vendors use different methods to organize and retrieve knowledge. Figure 6-2 summarizes these methods.

> ◆ Text retrieval
> ◆ Decision trees
> ◆ Case-based reasoning
> ◆ Neural networks

Figure 6-2 Problem resolution methods

Text Retrieval

Most word processing users are familiar with finding text within documents, and text retrieval software is one of the easiest ways to organize problem resolution knowledge. A **text base** is a database of text files that are indexed for rapid retrieval. It handles structured and unstructured data and is ideal for how-to information or requests. Support groups use text retrieval to access written materials from word processing documents, journals, technical bulletins from hardware or software companies, Web pages, pieces of e-mail, help files, and other collections.

The text retrieval software uses a thesaurus to recognize synonyms and other related words. Because some words have different meanings when grouped together in a business context, the retrieval software also allows administrators to customize terminology to add phrases that have specific meaning for the support group. For example, electronic commerce companies may need to define terms for software that handles electronic transactions, such as "shopping carts" and "electronic wallets."

Adjectives, adverbs, articles, and pronouns, such as "big," "quickly," "the," and "it," respectively, occur so frequently that it doesn't make sense to search documents for these words. These common words, as well as numbers, are called **noise words** because they don't specifically help (they create "noise") during searches. An administrator maintains noise words for text retrieval software in a **stop file**. Words that are important to a search and are not included in the stop file are **keywords**. When a text base is created, the software breaks text in all the files into words, discards words that are stored in the stop file, and then creates an index of keywords for searching. The index tracks every word used and the documents each word appears in.

When support staff search the text base, they can combine keywords with comparison operators such as AND, OR, and NOT. As the retrieval software finds words, it assigns a mathematical **weight** to each document's importance, based on the number of times keywords or combinations of keywords appear. Figure 6-3 shows a sample search and the weighted results. Documents with a higher weight appear at the top of the search results list.

6

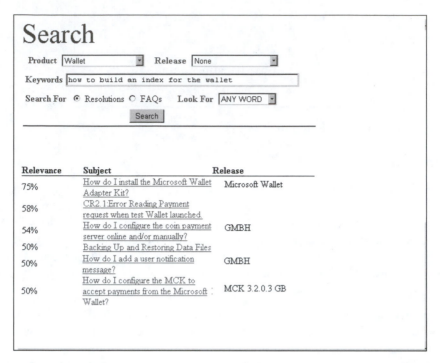

Figure 6-3 Weighted search results

Search engines are the core technology for all text retrieval software. A **search engine** is a software program that performs text searches. Problem resolution search engines frequently provide a way to automatically search for knowledge, using keywords from the summary of the call records. In many call management applications, support staff retrieve a call record, then select a menu option or button to start a search using words in the call summary. Users can then refine the searches or manually enter search words. Certain types of call records may be automatically stored within the call management software as a text base. In addition to the call summaries, support staff can search call record fields and the troubleshooting logs. Administrators determine whether searches are performed against the call management database or can include documents (such as word processing files) outside the software.

Web users rely on search engines to find information on the Internet. Search engines may look at the titles of documents, URLs, or the text of Web pages. A **knowbot** or **intelligent agent** is a software program that searches Internet sites and gathers information according to user-specified criteria. For example, a newsbot is a specialized knowbot that visits news-oriented Web sites each morning and creates a digest of stories based upon topics the user selects. Knowbots are a rapidly developing technology that enables personal data mining.

Software vendors customize their search engines to return as many relevant results as possible, so that nothing is overlooked. However, people become frustrated when their searches return thousands of references. Either they must learn how to refine broad searches by adding more selection criteria, or the software must do this for them by using additional information from other call record fields. The Search area of Figure 6-3 shows fields for keywords, and additional filters for Product and Release. These searches can also be constrained for any of the keywords. In this example, the search engine looks for the keywords "build" or "index" or "wallet," and returns documents with any one of these words. If the constraint is changed to Look For All Words, each document must include all three words before it appears in the results list.

Decision Trees

Decision trees, one of the earliest forms of expert systems, allow an interaction between the user and the knowledge through a series of yes/no or true/false questions. Figure 6-4 shows the decision tree for the "I can't print a Word document" problem. Each time support staff answer a question, they are provided with a new action to take and another question to answer, until they discover the cause and solution of the problem.

6

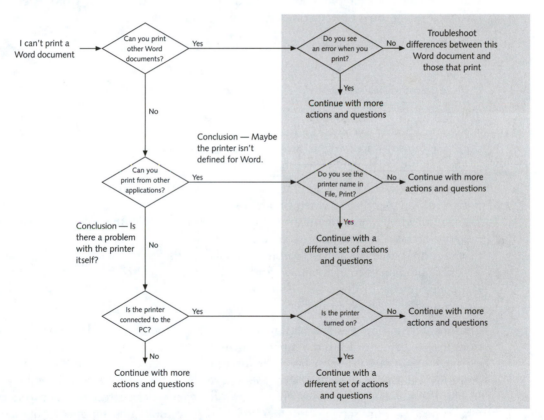

Figure 6-4 Sample decision tree

The most frequent causes of problems appear early in the series of questions and are at the top of the decision tree. The **root node** is the starting point (or first question or action) in a decision tree. Support staff begin by answering the question at the top node, and they progress through the questions until they reach a solution. More complex conditions are presented as multiple-choice options. Each question presents several possible choices, and the program presents different solutions for each option. A series of If-Then-Else statements or rules in the program logic eliminates possible problem causes until there is only one possible solution.

 TIP Decision trees and expert systems are also called **rule-based systems**.

In some situations, support staff may not be able to answer questions with a clear "yes" or "no" answer. **Fuzzy logic** is a way to represent values that are not completely true or false. Instead of a "yes" or "no" answer, there may be a "sometimes," "most of the time," or "I don't know" answer. For example, if you ask the question, "Do you exit your word processing software before you turn off the computer?" the answer could be:

- Yes, you *always* exit correctly.
- No, you *never* exit correctly.
- Sometimes you exit correctly and sometimes you don't.

The next questions presented will vary, depending upon whether you can give a complete answer or whether the answer is fuzzy. Depending on when fuzzy answers occur in the decision tree, the software weights these answers to determine which rules are true and which are false in an If-Then-Else statement.

Decision trees work well when there are logical connections between symptoms and solutions. They are very good when problem symptoms and causes are well defined and don't change, or when solutions must be consistent. For example, the rules to determine how many deductions to take for payroll taxes don't change more than once a year, and software that uses these rules must have consistent results. Users want to take as many deductions as possible, but taking too many deductions can lead to serious consequences with the Internal Revenue Service. In this case, a decision tree system could present questions to help them determine the acceptable number of deductions.

Creating decision trees usually requires experience and training in order to present the questions in the correct order. If the support environment changes, it may be necessary to add or rearrange questions. Whoever builds the decision tree needs to know the most likely problem causes so they can build related questions early in the decision tree. They may have to review the number of previous problems to determine the correct question order, which takes time away from solving customer problems. As a result, most support groups don't have time to build decision trees.

Support staff can approximate decision trees without expensive software by using hypertext documents. Answers to multiple-choice questions can hyperlink to other documents that go into more detail about similar information. Figure 6-5 is a hypertext document for some of the questions in Figure 6-4.

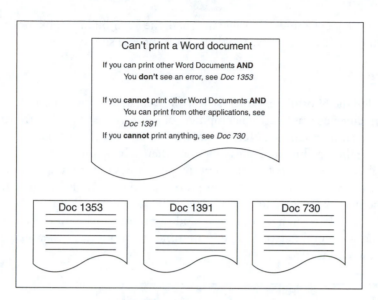

Figure 6-5 Hypertext decision tree

In this example, one master "document" summarizes the primary areas of knowledge for this problem. The three areas of knowledge are saved as separate documents and can be used to answer other related questions.

Case-based Reasoning

An expert frequently finds solutions to new problems by drawing upon past experiences in similar situations. **Case-based reasoning (CBR)** systems look for previous problem examples similar to the current problem. This software uses a sophisticated pattern recognition system to select case histories that fully or partially match a description of the current problem. Then, it presents a series of follow-up questions to narrow the search further. The order of questions, however, is not as important as it is with a decision tree, because patterns are used rather than If-Then-Else rules.

 CBR builds upon text retrieval and decision trees. Words are parsed and noise words eliminated, as in text retrieval, and patterns of data answer yes/no questions.

It usually isn't practical to use CBR software in support. Because CBR uses past experiences, the software may not recognize a rapidly developing problem situation until there are several solved cases. There are still many support areas (such as software application development) where the environment changes rapidly. When this happens, there are no existing cases to match the description patterns. Knowledge engineers, rather than support staff, develop CBR systems, because the software requires a lot of training and time to develop solutions. The best approach for implementing this kind of tool may be for level three support staff to use CBR to identify the most frequent causes of problems. Then, they can build troubleshooting documents or decision trees that solve these problems for front-line support staff to use.

Neural Networks

All of the knowledge methods discussed so far rely on human analysis. One of the original goals of artificial intelligence was to create computers or software that could learn new information without human intervention. **Neural networks**, or **neural nets**, learn new information by simulating the way human brains function when solving problems. Administrators build rules to weight connections between symptoms and causes (or inputs and outputs), and the neural networks "learn" to generalize about problems from examples. Neural networks are usually represented as layers: patterns of data enter the network through the input layer, processing is completed in a hidden layer, and the results make up the output layer. Figure 6-6 represents a neural network. The more times an input leads to a resulting output, the stronger the connection.

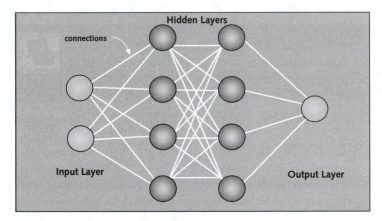

Figure 6-6   Neural network layers

Neural networks are used for data mining applications, to discover patterns and associations, and to predict results. Some of the network management applications discussed in Chapter 11 use neural net technology to reroute network transactions and predict connection failures. This powerful and expensive software requires knowledge engineers and domain experts.

COMMERCIAL SOFTWARE USED FOR PROBLEM RESOLUTION

Almost all call management software includes problem resolution features such as text retrieval or decision trees. Many of the commercial software companies discussed in Chapter 5 include problem resolution features in their call management applications. There are also standalone tools that provide these problem resolution methods. Appendix A includes problem resolution and knowledge management software commonly used by support groups.

Another type of knowledge management software promotes document publishing and sharing. These standalone collaboration tools (workgroup-oriented tools) enable groups of users to collect data and distribute knowledge among selected groups of workers. The software organizes word processing documents, spreadsheets, graphics, HTML pages, PDF files, and other file formats under a single interface. Special views show who created the information and who last updated it. Hardware and software development companies frequently use this kind of software to maintain user reference materials and training materials. Support staff can use text retrieval to review documentation when customers have questions.

Some vendors sell their knowledge and experience. Primus manages knowledge bases for different companies. Support staff create and use knowledge management software over the Web without worrying about the administrative tasks. Companies such as ServiceWare, Inc. and Knowledgebroker sell knowledge collections, which include thousands of documents on word processing, spreadsheet, and Windows-related how-to questions. For example, the Word domain may contain 600 common questions while the PC hardware troubleshooting domain includes more than 1000 documents. Because software and hardware manufacturers regularly upgrade their products, businesses can "subscribe" for periodic updates. Support groups can start their own knowledge base with these documents and can customize them to meet company-specific requirements.

Microsoft provides a knowledge collection called TechNet targeted for experienced support staff at level two or three support. Hardware vendors may also publish technical bulletins and troubleshooting documents specific to their products so support staff can easily narrow searches to complex setup and troubleshooting activities.

Trends

Market research firms agree that few companies are actually using knowledge management; those who do use it do not have enough historical information to show a return for the time and effort they've spent creating knowledge. Although most managers agree that creating knowledge for later use returns benefits in the future, many support managers find it hard to justify support staff time that isn't spent handling customer calls and that doesn't produce proven results. Some aspects of knowledge management, such as data mining, are definitely increasing, but the groups that tend to use this knowledge focus on product marketing and business analysis. Until more support groups can document their results, it will be difficult to prove the advantages of one type of problem resolution software over another, and it will be even longer before there are any clear standards for problem resolution software.

Several knowledge management resources are included in Appendix A.

Knowledge management is not successful unless upper managers support the effort. It takes time to build a knowledge base for staff to use. Subject matter experts need quiet, dedicated time to think through each problem-solving situation and to make sure they document everything. Right now, this activity takes time away from closing call records, but the same knowledge can be used over and over later for any number of new problems. Building knowledge is definitely a long-term goal with future benefits.

Fortunately, the growing volume of Web information shows managers that knowledge management and maintenance is necessary, because more customers expect Web sites to include relevant information. Companies are starting to treat their accumulated knowledge as an asset and to develop knowledge management plans and applications. Knowledge from data mining will continue to grow as well, as managers learn to develop knowledge about a company's business transactions.

Early adopters of problem resolution software found that dedicating resources to building or organizing knowledge produced better results. By restricting who can create knowledge, support groups control the process and introduce presentation standards. They define not only how knowledge is captured, but also how to determine when it needs to be changed or archived. Some support groups have technical writers assist them in writing solutions. Although technical staff understand the subject and should be included as subject matter experts, they may not always write clearly or explain in enough detail so that less experienced staff understand. Over time, more companies are creating knowledge engineering positions as part of the support career path.

Many support groups plan to allow customers to access their knowledge bases for self-service. Support groups need to ensure that they create solutions that are appropriate for a customer audience. In other words, they must not only correct the grammar and writing style in documents, but also ensure that confidential or proprietary information is not available.

CHAPTER SUMMARY

- ❑ Problem resolution centers on the way people solve problems. People process data and other information into knowledge. They can create new knowledge from existing knowledge. People possess subject knowledge or they know where to find information about a subject.

- ❑ Knowledge management is a relatively new business process that is still evolving. Business knowledge is developed because of information requests, through solving problems, or mining data and analyzing transactions and reports. Data can be structured, so as to fit the fields of a database, or unstructured, in presentations or graphs.

- ❑ Support staff benefit from problem resolution software in several ways. Experienced staff members can solve problems one time and then document the solution for later occurrences. When several people contribute to a solution, it eventually solves a wider range of related problems. Information is no longer lost when employees leave the support group. Over time, the knowledge collection helps staff teach customers to find knowledge and help themselves. Eventually companies can use patterns of questions to generate new products and services.

- ❑ Problem resolution tools must address the four challenges for knowledge acquisition: collecting data, processing the data, maintaining the data, and distributing the knowledge. Some experts are reluctant to share their knowledge or don't know how to explain how they solve a particular problem.

❑ Knowledge management software is a form of groupware developed from a branch of computer science called artificial intelligence (AI). Many of the terms created for AI apply to knowledge management.

❑ There are several approaches to structuring knowledge. Text retrieval software is one of the oldest and easiest methods to implement. Decision trees and expert systems, commonly called rule-based systems, are good ways to organize information when the results of problem solving must always be the same. Case-based reasoning systems use previous problem examples to "recognize" a similar situation. Neural networks are one of the most automated approaches. They simulate brain activities and "learn to" generalize about problems from examples.

❑ Almost all call management applications include a form of keyword or text retrieval of previous call records. Some problem resolution vendors collect solutions and sell these knowledge packages along with regular update subscriptions. Other vendors develop standalone problem resolution or knowledge management applications.

❑ Knowledge management systems are still evolving, and there are no clear examples in which one approach is better or easier to use than another. As information from the Web increases and companies attempt to remain competitive, there will be more emphasis on knowledge management and data mining to create new knowledge.

KEY TERMS

artificial intelligence (AI) — A software program that attempts to mimic human intelligence.

case-based reasoning (CBR) — A software program that looks for previous problem examples similar to the current problem.

data mining — Analysis of facts, transactions, and reports about business activities to determine relationships between actions and results.

decision tree — One of the earliest forms of expert systems, allows an interaction between the user and the knowledge through a series of yes/no or true/false questions.

domain experts — People who know a lot about a specific subject.

epistemology — In philosophy, the theory of knowledge and how it changes.

expert system — Software that imitates the problem-solving procedures that human experts perform.

frame — To organize and refine problem symptoms to search for a solution.

fuzzy logic — A way to represent values that are not completely true or false.

inference — The creation of new knowledge from existing knowledge.

inference engine — Software that imitates human inference in creating new facts from known facts, using inference rules.

intelligent agent — A software program that searches Internet sites and gathers information according to user-specified criteria.

keywords — Search words in a text retrieval system.

knowbot — *See* intelligent agent.

knowledge — A collection of processed information that a company can use to accomplish tasks.

knowledge acquisition — The collection and organization of knowledge from human beings.

knowledge base — An electronically stored collection of knowledge about a subject.

knowledge domain — A specific area of knowledge covered by a knowledge-based system.

knowledge engineer — A person who obtains knowledge from human experts and organizes it into a knowledge base.

knowledge management — A relatively new business process in which a company attempts to gather, organize, analyze, and reuse its knowledge.

knowledge system — *See* expert system.

neural net — *See* neural network.

neural network — A computer program that learns new information by simulating the way brains function when solving problems.

noise words — Common words and numbers that don't specifically help during searches.

root node — The starting point in a decision tree.

rule-based systems — *See* decision tree and expert system.

search engine — A software program that performs text searches.

stop file — A list of noise words in a text retrieval system.

structured data — Numbers and text that fit in separate fields in databases.

text base — A database of text files that are indexed for rapid retrieval.

unstructured data — Documents, presentations, or graphs that don't fit neatly into rows and columns of a database.

weight — During text retrieval, a document's importance based on the number of times keywords or combinations of keywords appear in a document.

REVIEW QUESTIONS

1. Problem resolution software is based on acquiring and sharing _____.

2. Which of the following statements is true?

   a. Information can be inferred from data.

   b. Data is processed information.

   c. Data is processed knowledge.

   d. Knowledge results in more knowledge.

3. Support groups have been performing knowledge management as long as they have logged calls. True or False?

4. What are the three types of support knowledge?

5. Which of the following items are considered unstructured?

   a. Word processing documents and video files

   b. Video files and database records

   c. Database records and spreadsheets

   d. Spreadsheets and word processing documents

6. Which of the following items is not part of data mining?

   a. Organizing and categorizing

   b. Publishing data

   c. Making associations between events

   d. Discovering facts not previously known

7. Many problem resolution applications are based on _____, which resulted from studies in artificial intelligence.

8. A(n) _____ is a computer program that discovers new facts using inference rules.

9. List the four primary tasks involved in the knowledge management process.

10. What may happen if knowledge in a problem resolution system becomes outdated?

11. Why would employees be reluctant to contribute knowledge to a knowledge base?

12. Which of the following problem resolution methods is the easiest to implement and covers most information request questions directed to support?

   a. CBR

   b. neural networks

   c. text retrieval

   d. document sharing

13. A database containing mostly word processing documents is called a(n) _____.

14. The core technology behind text retrieval systems is the _____.

15. The primary purpose of an intelligent Web agent is all of the following *except*:

   a. searching for knowledge.

   b. organizing results for presentation rather than searching.

   c. making it easier to find Internet information.

   d. searching large databases.

16. Explain the difference between a rule-based tool and a decision tree.

17. Which of the following are not examples of responses used in fuzzy logic?

   a. Cool, lukewarm, hot

   b. Sometimes, maybe, all the time

   c. 1, 2, and 3

   d. I don't know.

18. Which of the following problem resolution methods recognizes patterns of words?

   a. CBR

   b. neural networks

c. text retrieval

d. document sharing

19. Level _____ support staff, rather than front-line staff or customers, primarily use CBR tools.

20. Which problem resolution methods require knowledge engineers?

21. Which method of knowledge management is most frequently included as part of a call management application?

   a. CBR

   b. neural networks

   c. text retrieval

   d. document sharing

22. Some companies sell collections of knowledge. These knowledge domains usually include information for:

   a. frequently asked, how-to questions.

   b. common problem examples to help staff learn to frame the questions.

   c. statistical analysis of the company data.

   d. company policies and procedures.

23. An important trend in support groups, as companies implement knowledge management systems, is to:

   a. buy canned knowledge.

   b. dedicate resources to knowledge management.

   c. continue concentrating on the number of calls opened.

   d. increase Web use.

HANDS-ON PROJECTS

Project 6-1

Identifying knowledge management methods. Visit one of the Web sites listed in Appendix A and find white papers that explain knowledge management or problem resolution. Identify the method the selected vendor uses for knowledge management (text retrieval, decision trees, case-based reasoning, or other forms).

Project 6-2

Learning to frame questions. Visit the Ask Jeeves Web site at **http://www.ask.com**. Use any of the following problem summaries to complete a Web search. Complete three searches, using sentences to describe what you are looking for. Then, use one of the standard Web search engines (Netscape, Excite, Alta Vista, Lycos, etc.) and perform the same searches. Compare the results to the results you received using Ask Jeeves.

   ■ What is a neural network?

- What does problem resolution software do?

- Give some examples of fuzzy logic.

- Where can I learn more about data mining?

- Which call management software uses case-based reasoning?

Project 6-3

Understanding document management knowledge. Visit the Knowledge Management Magazine Web site at **http://www.kmmag.com** and the Pure PDF Magazine Web site at **http://www.purepdf.com**. Explain the different approaches to knowledge management these publications take.

Project 6-4

Using knowledge management demos. Visit two Web sites listed in Appendix A that provide online demos of their respective products. Try two online demos. Write a short summary of each product's features to present to your classmates, and identify the product you would prefer to use in support. Explain your decision.

Project 6-5

Identifying knowledge management methods. Visit the PC Docs Web site at **http://www.pcdocs.com** and complete one of the self-running demonstration. What approach to problem management does this software take? What are the limits to this approach to knowledge management?

Project 6-6

Using an expert system. Visit the MultiLogic Web site at **http://www.multilogic.com** and follow the Software Products and Support link to "Test Drive."

1. Complete the first sample expert system, changing your answers so the system identifies at least three different bears.

2. Complete the sample expert system for "QC of Computer Orders." Record the configuration options you chose and any potential problems the expert system identified.

3. Complete the fuzzy logic sample.

4. Complete the Disc Boot troubleshooting sample. Use the "Why are you asking this question?" button and display the rules that are evaluated at the first two steps.

List reasons why an expert system would not be used in a support group.

Project 6-7

Building an expert system. Visit the ZDNet Web site at **http://www.zdnet.com** and search for "expert system" software. Download an expert system application and develop a small expert system similar to the Bear sample in Project 6-6 (or create a sample of your own with three or four questions). Using the same problem scenario, prepare a word processing or HTML document with hypertext links that present the same decisions. Which application took longer to develop? Which application is easier for a user to understand?

Project 6-8

Using intelligent agents. Visit the Monster Web site at **http://www.monster.com** and sign up for a free account or visit Yahoo! or the Netscape home page and subscribe to the free e-mail News. How frequently does this intelligent agent send you e-mail with the results of searches?

Project 6-9

Understanding knowledge management terminology. Visit the Delphi Group Web site at **http://www.delphigroup.com**. Download a copy of the free knowledge glossary. Find three terms not discussed in this chapter that are used in knowledge management.

Project 6-10

Identifying call management software with problem resolution. Visit the Web sites for call management software vendors discussed in earlier chapters. Find two vendors that include problem resolution modules as part of their software. What knowledge approaches (text retrieval, CBR, etc.) do they use?

Project 6-11

Exploring data mining software. Visit the Knowledge Nuggets Web site at **http://www.kdnuggets.com**. Review the list of companies that provide data mining software and services. What IT subject(s) relate to data mining, according to this page?

Project 6-12

Using problem resolution in internal support call management software. Use the HelpTrac Demo software you installed in Chapter 5 and activate the problem resolution features of the software.

1. Use the HelpTrac Demo Supervisor. Click **Options**, **General Options**. In the Options dialog box, click the **Use solution tree** check box, then click **OK**.

2. Prepare ten solution documents, using common tasks you would perform using Microsoft Office products, beginning with a clear question and a clear solution or set of troubleshooting steps. Save these items as text or Microsoft Word files. Then, create tickets and enter the solutions in the software.

3. Prepare a separate list of just the questions that the solution documents will answer. Select a classmate to enter call records for each question, and see if he or she can find the solution documents you created.

4. Search for the call records you left open from Hands-on Project 5-6. Create solution documents from the solutions listed in the file **Project0506.doc** and close those call records.

Project 6-13

Using problem resolution in external support call management software. Use the SDS Demo software you installed in Chapter 5 and complete Steps 2 through 4 of Project 6-12. Which problem resolution software (HelpTrac or SDS) do you prefer? Explain your answer in a short report.

CASE PROJECTS

6

1. **Evaluating Knowledge Domains**

   You are a team leader in a new support group that will support several PC applications. Your support manager has decided your team will use some canned knowledge for common software questions. You will help evaluate the knowledge available. Visit the following content publishers (canned knowledge) and prepare a list of the knowledge domains they publish. Complete any online demos and describe any features that are unique to each application. Are there any other common software applications that should have a knowledge domain, that are not listed? Build a spreadsheet to compare the three publishers you reviewed.

   - Inference   **http://www.inference.com**
   - KnowledgeBroker, Inc.   **http://www.kbi.com**
   - Serviceware   **http://www.serviceware.com**

2. **Evaluating Text Retrieval Software**

   As the manager of the Bigfield Company's internal support group, you need to evaluate text retrieval software, but you don't have any experience with this type of software. Visit the Isys Web site at **http://www.isysdev.com** and download the evaluation copy of the software. Review the documentation on how to set up an initial database and how to add noise words (or common words) to the stop file. Select five word processing documents, five text files, and one spreadsheet and add these as a text collection. Practice searches against the text base, using phrases you have preselected from the word processing files.

3. **Comparing Text Retrieval Software to Problem Resolution Software**

   You are a level two support team leader for the Bigfield Company's internal support group. The manager of support thinks text retrieval software would be a good problem resolution method for the group, but you disagree. You fear that support staff won't use problem resolution unless it is integrated into the call management software. The support group uses HelpTrac software. You decide to build a few solutions for some sample problems, then search for the solutions with both applications, to understand the differences. Prepare a short report for the support manager that compares the number of steps necessary to use the Isys text retrieval software to the number of steps to use problem resolution in HelpTrac. (*Hint:* Create separate solution documents for Isys from the file **Project0506.doc**.)

CHAPTER

7

ASSET AND CHANGE MANAGEMENT TOOLS

In this chapter you will learn:

♦ The importance of asset management to companies

♦ The role of support groups in asset management

♦ Common features of asset management software and how support staff use them

♦ Well-known asset management software vendors

♦ The role of support groups in change management processes

Before 1980, the computing environment was limited to mainframe computers. These first computers were designed to handle large amounts of data. Their user interfaces were text based, and they processed data in large batches at a time. Most mainframes were placed in protected computer rooms with special cooling systems and raised flooring so that support staff could easily access the systems' cabling. Computer users worked with the system via terminals, which have no computing capabilities themselves. Unlike personal computer users, mainframe users cannot directly access the operating system to load data or software themselves—these tasks are completed by computer operators and system administrators. Each computer vendor manufactured the computer hardware, as well as terminals and printers, so only specific terminal and printer models could access the computers. Mainframe computers still make up a large part of a company's computing environment.

Today, computer users rely on desktop and laptop computers. Personal computers (PCs) are much simpler than most mainframe systems, so computer users have more control over how they use their computer systems. They can buy and load software, replace and add hardware, and access information on the Web. In the process, however, they may also expose their computers to **viruses**, software that produces undesirable and damaging events. When computer users lack the necessary skill, training, or experience to install software, replace hardware, access the Internet, or remove viruses from their computers, they turn to the help desk.

As the number of PCs increases, support staff are less likely to be able to visit each computer to collect troubleshooting information in person. Instead, they handle more problems by telephone. Support staff can better troubleshoot problems over the telephone when they have a clear understanding of the hardware and software installed. A support group may support thousands of computers, and customers may have diverse needs related to their business tasks; as a result, PCs may be very different throughout the company. Support staff can save troubleshooting time if they have a database of accurate information about each computer. Because the help desk frequently handles requests to install and move PCs, many support groups maintain an inventory of hardware components and software as part of their support activities.

Managing Business Assets

Companies use assets as they pursue their goals. **Assets** include any item of value owned by an individual or corporation that could be converted to cash. Physical assets include furniture, buildings, property, office equipment, and products to sell. **Asset management** is the process of collecting and maintaining a comprehensive list of items that a company owns. This list includes more than just the original purchase date, price, and description of a piece of equipment. For example, consider the purchase of a basic office desk. A manager buys the desk. Then, the manager pays someone to deliver it to the office. Later, the manager may add a lock to a drawer. The initial purchase plus the delivery charges and upgrades make up the cost of owning the desk. Because a desk should be useful for many years and the cost of maintaining a desk is much lower than its purchase price, the value of this type of company asset remains about the same as when it was initially purchased.

Technology-based assets don't maintain the same value over time; electronic equipment has shorter useful lives because technology changes quickly. **Total cost of ownership (TCO)** includes the initial cost of hardware and software, the cost of installation, user training and support, upgrades, and repairs. The initial cost of computer hardware may seem relatively small—only a couple of thousand of dollars. Buying software adds a couple of hundred dollars to the purchase price. Companies will also spend money training employees who use the technology, or supporting computer users who don't undergo training. Industry research groups estimate that the total cost of owning a PC is five to seven times its initial costs. Over the PC's short life, it may cost thousands of dollars for additional software or hardware to network the PC, maintain it, and/or troubleshoot it. Although computer prices are falling, a company that purchases hundreds of PCs still spends hundreds of thousands of dollars on technology with a shorter useful life than office furniture. Eventually, it can be more expensive to maintain old hardware than to replace it; the cost of replacements and labor to make repairs exceeds the expense of buying new equipment. Managers must understand when it is cost-effective to replace technology.

Financial managers used to conduct **physical inventories**, a survey to confirm existing assets by locating and identifying each asset. Traditional asset management processes assume that the assets are easy to recognize and remain in a specific area. Taking a physical inventory of assets such as chairs, filing cabinets, and desks is simpler than verifying technology assets. Desktop technologies are a moving and changing target—computer users frequently move to different offices, and the devices themselves consist of interchangeable components, such as memory, modems, and hard drives. Many of the components are also hidden from view (most computer users would not be able to recognize modems or memory), so a physical inventory can easily miss some of the components included in the full cost of the equipment. These memory boards, modems, and hard drives are also small, compared to older processors, and therefore are more portable than office furniture. A physical inventory won't prevent or account for theft.

Physical inventories for technology are also impractical when companies distribute their computing systems nationally or internationally in the form of desktop computers, laptops, cellular telephones, and other network and communications equipment. A single company may use thousands of PCs, acquired over several years. With rapid improvements in computing power, these PCs represent hundreds of levels of technology—a Pentium PC with extra memory, special software, and an unusually large disk drive may be worth three times as much as an older 486 PC, even though they both have the same outward appearance. As a result, it is impractical and almost impossible to complete physical inventories of technology in the same way that companies inventory office equipment or other property. IT organizations need sophisticated software to manage and track hardware and software installed globally.

THE ROLE OF SUPPORT IN TRACKING ASSETS

Support managers realized that the help desk, which is the central point of contact for computer users, is the best place to concentrate their asset management processes. Support staff receive requests to install new equipment, move PCs, and troubleshoot problems. Equipment also moves through the company as experienced computer users buy new equipment and recycle their old PCs to employees who need replacements or have no computers. Support staff are also in a position to identify when people and computers are mismatched. For example, experienced employees who work on a computer without enough memory to support their tasks may report this problem to the support group. If the support group also knows of PC memory that was removed from a compatible computer, the company can save money by recycling it instead of buying more memory.

The help desk is also involved when PC users upgrade their systems, which increases the value of each asset to the company. The modular components of PCs make it easy to replace parts, and thus save money. For example, computer users can easily order a larger local hard drive when they need more storage, rather than requesting a new computer. In addition, the original parts can be used to upgrade and repair other computers. For example, the still useful, but smaller hard drive can be used to replace a broken drive in another system. If support staff maintain a spare inventory database, the company can save money on replacement parts and save time by not waiting for hardware deliveries.

As mentioned earlier, most internal support groups are part of a company's IT organization. In addition to providing customer support, support staff will also share the IT department's business objectives, which are listed in Figure 7-1.

> ♦ **Acquisitions and disaster recovery**
> ♦ **Software license compliance**
> ♦ **Problem prevention**

Figure 7-1 IT objectives

Acquisitions and Disaster Recovery

IT managers monitor technology assets and take responsibility for acquiring technology. The managers can negotiate better pricing for bulk purchases and contracts when they have accurate inventories. Companies that outsource hardware repairs also base the cost of their services on the quantity, models, and ages of the equipment. Without accurate equipment inventories, the IT department does not know whether the outsourcer's service contracts are competitively priced.

Bulk purchasing is common in many retail areas. Some grocery stores allow customers to buy candy, nuts, and grains in bulk—customers weigh and bag the amount they want and save on packaging. Wholesale and discount stores buy in bulk and pass their savings on to their customers. Computer vendors also offer special discounts for bulk orders. IT managers may receive a 10% discount off the retail price for a single order of 50 PCs, but receive a 25% discount if they order 500 PCs at once. The 500 PCs can be stored in an IT storage location initially. As the company hires new employees, the PCs will be removed from storage and installed.

Upgrade planning is one of the most important TCO activities that IT managers complete. Software upgrades frequently require more memory and faster processors, so managers must identify PCs that don't have enough memory, purchase more memory, and install it, before the new software will work. For example, when Windows 95 became available and employees wanted to upgrade to this software release, many companies did not have accurate information about existing PCs. As staff members upgraded PCs from DOS or older versions of MS Windows to Windows 95, support staff discovered incompatible or inadequate hardware and software. Many companies had to buy new computers because hardware based on 80286 and 80386 processors wouldn't run the software. They also had to add memory to many 80486-based computers, which increased the TCO for those machines. Windows 95 was not expensive by itself, but some companies spent ten to fifteen times as much to upgrade hardware.

Obtaining accurate and current information about a company's technology assets will continue to be a big challenge for IT departments, particularly in companies that acquire hundreds of PCs each year. The need for accurate information is especially important as operating systems and core applications are deployed. With accurate asset inventory databases, IT managers can determine how many hardware upgrades are needed or identify potential software conflicts. They can also add more staff members to install the upgrades and train the help desk to handle questions related to the upgrades. Although the help desk will still receive calls related to the upgrades, the volume of calls may be smaller.

 The Year 2000 (Y2K) "bug" was the inability of some computer software to recognize dates past 1999. Many 386 and 486 computers could not "turn the century" because their Basic Input Output System (BIOS) was not designed to handle four-digit years (thus, the year 2000 was written as 00, which the older BIOS interpreted as 1900). The BIOS software in hardware made after 1997 handled this correctly, but a lot of older computers still needed to be upgraded before the end of the century. The hardware environment has always been competitive, and some manufacturers of older hardware were no longer in business to support their products. Software that calculated or stored dates was also susceptible to the Y2K bug. Spreadsheets and accounting programs required software upgrades or patches. Support staff and programmers were assigned to Y2K projects to make sure that commercial and homegrown software would continue to run in the twenty-first century.

Accurate records of software and hardware, as well as the configurations of individual computers, are also important for disaster recovery planning. **Disaster recovery** is a plan for restoring critical business functions after a disaster, to minimize loss of income. For example, if a fire destroys a company's office building, financial records, as well as assets, are lost. Not only will the company not be able to pay its bills, but also it won't know which customers owe money! If the company can't recover this information quickly, it may go out of business. To recover financial information, the company will have to buy replacement hardware, install the financial software, and recover the company's data from backup files. A disaster recovery plan identifies and prioritizes the information, computers, and software a company requires to stay in business, and IT managers attempt to replace critical technologies as quickly as possible. An inventory catalogs critical system configurations for disaster recovery as well as the value of hardware and software for insurance purposes.

Software License Compliance

Software is an asset, but it can also represent a liability for companies. Computer software is **intellectual property**—elements of human intellect that are unique and original, and have value. Software (along with books, art, and music) is protected by **copyright**, the exclusive legal rights granted to authors, artists, composers, or programmers to distribute or sell their creations. In the early days of the PC evolution, software companies used **copy protection**, software tools that prevented people from making unauthorized copies of software. One protection method required users to insert a key disk or enter a serial number each time they wanted to use the program. Other vendors designed software to work with a dongle. A **dongle** is a copy protection device that plugs into the computer or attaches to a printer port that enables software to run. This prevents the software from being used on other computers. A dongle is also called a **hardware key**.

Figure 7-2 shows several types of dongles.

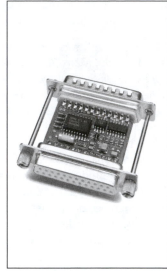

Figure 7-2   Sample dongles

 Software vendors still use copy protection when they distribute software in countries outside the United States because it is still difficult to enforce software copyrights internationally. Dongles are the most common copy protection used in Europe.

Early forms of copy-protected software were very unpopular with computer users and support staff. When employees left a company, new staff could not use software applications if they did not know the serial numbers to unlock the applications. Some copy protection methods interfered with other software. Other software installed hidden files at a specific location on the hard drive. If the file was moved during disk maintenance, or if the drive failed or was erased, the user could not run the software.

In the early 1990s, the FBI began to investigate **software piracy**, which is the act of illegally copying or using software. In 1992, the United States passed laws that protect software developers from piracy and stipulated heavy fines for making even a single unauthorized copy of software. Countries such as Canada, France, and the United Kingdom passed similar laws.

 There are several organizations geared to fighting software piracy, including the Software and Information Industry Association at http://www.siia.net and the Business Software Alliance at http://www.bsa.org. These organizations investigate software piracy reports and file lawsuits against companies, recovering millions in lost revenue. In most cases, they offer companies suspected of software piracy the opportunity to submit to a voluntary audit of software installed on their PCs. These new inventories are then compared to the companies' purchase receipts. If illegal copies of software are discovered, the companies have an opportunity to destroy the unauthorized copies and purchase legal copies, rather than face criminal charges. The audits are expensive and time-consuming for the companies, but less expensive than lawsuits.

To help prevent illegal copying, software vendors developed **license agreements**, which are legal statements that clearly define the terms under which a person can use software. There are three types of software licenses:

- **One license per PC:** Companies buy one copy of the software for every computer that will run the application. For example, if a company has twenty PCs, it buys twenty copies of software. Small businesses and individual computer users tend to license their software this way.

- **Concurrent licensing:** Companies install the software on a network and buy the right for a maximum number of users to share the software at one time. For example, a company with twenty PCs on a network may buy a license for ten users, because not all twenty users need the software simultaneously.

- **Site licensing:** Very large companies with hundreds or thousands of potential users pay a discounted amount for the expected number of users and agree to monitor themselves for compliance.

7

In most companies, the IT department purchases software licenses for applications all business users need. They track the number of licenses purchased as well as who uses the licenses, to make sure the company doesn't violate its software license agreement. Support staff maintain the inventory system as they process requests for moves or new installations of software, so they understand the software environment for each PC, in case there are support problems.

Illegally copied software understates the potential number of calls to support—the inventory may list 200 copies of an application (with at least 200 known customers using the software), but an equal number of unlicensed users also may call the help desk for support. Usually there are enough skilled support staff for applications that all company employees use, but only one or two staff members for specialized software. To ensure that there are enough trained staff, support must know the real number of software users for each application.

One of the most common forms of software piracy is employees bringing unlicensed software to work from home. For example, employees may bring to work copies of games they bought or received from friends (companies rarely purchase games). Some games overwrite important files used by business applications, causing errors. The employees then call the help desk to troubleshoot the problem or reinstall the business software.

Concurrent licensing can also generate more support calls. A company may purchase a concurrent license for 100 users. When the 101st user attempts to access the application, he or she gets a message saying that the application is not available. If the user doesn't see or understand this message, he or she may call to report a problem. The help desk usually tracks calls on concurrent license errors. When all licenses are used on a regular basis, managers may purchase additional concurrent licenses or switch to site licensing. Until the company can increase the number of software users through site licensing or additional concurrent licenses, the help desk will try to manage existing licenses for users. One way to do this is for the help desk to ask users who are logged into the application but not using it to log out. This frees a license for a waiting coworker.

Problem Prevention

One of the goals for a proactive support group is to prevent problems. It takes time to maintain hardware and software inventories, but the additional support benefits are worth the effort. If the help desk can identify which PCs are associated with customer problems, support managers can analyze this information for trends. Specifically they want to identify PCs with chronic hardware problems. The symptoms of these "lemons" may be indicative of hidden problems. For example, when a PC that needs new memory one month and a new hard drive the next, this could indicate a more serious problem with the motherboard or other low-level components. Managers can use statistics to document patterns of failures from selected vendors and to renegotiate prices and service levels. They can then purchase the most reliable equipment, which receives the fewest support calls. In addition, when a company limits the variety of equipment vendors, they limit the amount of troubleshooting knowledge that support staff need.

Maintaining an accurate software inventory can also prevent software problems. Large companies cannot upgrade all users at once to a new software release (either because there are so many PCs or because it will cost too much). Over time, a company can have several versions of spreadsheets or word processing applications on its PCs. Early software versions may have software bugs, which affect some of the software users. When support staff maintain an accurate software inventory, they can easily find the customers who need bug fixes when the fixes become available (even if the customer never reported a problem).

An accurate inventory also prevents support calls as customers add and upgrade software. Most Windows-based software uses common components from the operating system to print, file, and display information, but other applications can install their own versions that replace these standard components. These modified components may not always work well with other applications. Software inventory information makes sure the PC meets the minimum requirements for new software. Support staff can troubleshoot problems more quickly when they understand how different pieces of software interact.

COMMON ASSET MANAGEMENT SOFTWARE FEATURES

There is a wide range of software applications available for asset management. Support groups use asset software as part of a call management application or under a standalone application that interfaces easily with common support applications. Whether standalone or part of another application, asset management software has some common features, as listed in Figure 7-3.

The difference between an interface and integrated software was discussed in Chapter 3.

- ◆ Financial information
- ◆ Inventory
- ◆ Discovery
- ◆ Remote control
- ◆ Software distribution

Figure 7-3   Common asset management software features

Financial Information

Financial information is common to most asset management systems. Some companies employ financial analysts to maintain this information. An equal number of companies use their support groups to manage financial information. Important financial information to track in asset management systems includes:

- **Vendor:** Companies frequently change vendors to obtain better prices or service. Historical records enable managers to compare prices over time. Support staff also need vendor information in case hardware breaks during the warranty period, because vendors usually replace this hardware without charge.

- **Date of purchase:** Managers use the purchase date so they can compare prices over time and to calculate the useful life of an asset.

- **Initial cost:** Managers want to know exactly how much they originally paid for hardware. They use this information to negotiate better prices with hardware and software vendors and to budget for new hardware.

- **Additional costs:** Managers want to know how much was spent on enhancements and upgrades, to document the total cost of ownership.

- **Maintenance contract:** If the company purchases maintenance, managers need to know the length of the maintenance contract (another part of TCO) and to schedule maintenance renewals. The term and price of the maintenance contract is recorded in months or years.

- **Current value:** As equipment ages, its resale value decreases. Managers need to know the current value of hardware to make decisions about when to replace old hardware.

 Managers may sell old equipment to partially cover the cost of purchasing new hardware. Unfortunately, technology changes so quickly that old equipment may not have much resale value. Many businesses find the tax benefit of donating equipment to schools and nonprofit organizations greater than the money they receive from selling old equipment in auctions or to employees.

Nonsupport staff (such as an administrative assistant, purchasing agent, or financial analyst) record most of the financial information in the asset management system when the item is received.

Inventory

Help desk staff benefit primarily from the inventory information stored in the asset management system. The primary parts of an asset management inventory include:

- Warranty information
- Ownership
- Hardware elements
- Software elements
- Network information

Warranty

A **warranty** is written guarantee of the integrity of a product and of the maker's responsibility for the repair or replacement of defective parts. Several pieces of information make up the warranty information: the vendor that provides the warranty (either the manufacturer or the dealer), the warranty terms (whether the equipment is repaired or replaced), and the warranty period (how many months after purchase will the terms be honored).

If the item in inventory is hardware, the hardware manufacturer usually provides warranty repairs. Common PC manufacturers include Dell, Gateway, and Compaq, but there are hundreds of manufacturers for other types of hardware. Some companies buy equipment through resellers rather than directly from the manufacturer. In these cases, the manufacturers either handle hardware returns themselves or work through the resellers and authorized repair companies. Front-line staff review the appropriate service contract or warranty information before they dispatch hardware repairs.

Support groups that outsource hardware repairs don't have to worry about contacting the original vendor for repairs. The outsourcer will work through warranty requirements themselves. Unfortunately, some companies use more than one outsourcer for the same types of equipment. This happens when companies are merged during an acquisition or if an outsourcer doesn't provide service for some regions of the country. If there are several dispatch phone numbers, staff must know the correct regional repair center.

Support staff can save the company money because replacements or repairs during the warranty period cost less than buying new equipment. For example, many PC monitors and hard disk drives have one- or two-year warranties. As customers report hardware problems with these items, support staff can review the inventory to make sure that warranties have expired before new equipment is ordered.

Ownership

Hardware ownership identifies who will approve repairs and upgrade expenses. Support groups that complete their own hardware repairs order replacement parts and charge the expenses to the equipment users, rather than to the IT department. If the company uses an outsourcer, the support group charges expenses from the outsourcer to the business user.

Ownership also helps establish the physical location of hardware and the impact of problems. Some hardware, such as network devices, is shared by groups of computer users. When users share hardware, they may not know who else uses that equipment. Support staff need to know when shared pieces of equipment have problems, to determine the impact of a problem with that device. A printer that doesn't work shared by a group of fifty computer users may be a higher priority problem than a printer that doesn't work used only by one person. Shared equipment is tracked by using department names or codes. Hardware, such as printers, modems, fax boards, and CD-ROM drives, can be shared or dedicated to a single user. Support groups track single-user devices by recording the user's name and location.

 Software assets also have owners, but this information is usually only necessary to renew maintenance contracts or purchase upgrades; it's used for financial information rather than for support.

Hardware Elements

Hardware information is important because support staff use different troubleshooting methods, depending upon the hardware configuration. Specialized hardware can conflict with the BIOS or operating system, so one of the most common troubleshooting techniques is to determine whether the problem began before or after a particular hardware or software change. A quick review of the latest change or the results of regular maintenance activities can save time when identifying the problem's cause.

A current hardware inventory can also save repair time. Some error messages help support staff identify hardware problems with very little troubleshooting. Support staff can look up the asset directly to determine the model or manufacturer, and then order replacements without examining the PC. Support staff commonly track the following hardware information:

- **Asset number:** A unique number that a company uses to identify each asset. The company name and asset number are secured to the asset on a small tag. This tag is used to match records to equipment during a physical inventory.

- **Serial number:** A unique identification number that manufacturers include on all electronic items. Many manufacturers track sales by serial number, and they use serial numbers to locate stolen electronics for customers.

- **Make/model:** Identifies the hardware manufacturer's name and a specific equipment design. Examples include Compaq 4784, Toshiba Tecra 750, and HP (short for Hewlett-Packard) LaserJet 4. The make and model are critical for some upgrades, especially when adding memory, because the add-on components must fit uniquely designed sockets or slots.

- **Type:** A drop-down list of values that describes the hardware items, such as add-in board, disk drive, memory, modem, CD-ROM drive, mouse, CPU, monitor, plotter, printer, scanner, and workstation.

- **Description:** A short text field for additional details about the hardware.

- **RAM:** The amount of memory for the PC as a whole. Again, memory chips can be configured in different ways: two banks of 16-MB chips, four banks of 8-MB chips, one 32-MB chipset, parity or nonparity. This information has an impact on the cost of an upgrade, as well as on whether the memory can be expanded.

- **Disk size:** The total size of all drives in a PC or the size of an individual disk drive.

- **Operating system and version:** The default operating system that a PC uses. Although most desktop computers use Windows, there are exceptions. Older systems or software may use only DOS, and some newer computers run Linux or other forms of UNIX.

- **Device name:** Network administrators assign a unique name to hardware on a network to identify it. For example, network printers may be named PTR00315 or PRNACCT. If computers or printers don't communicate with each over a network, support staff need a device name to understand how each piece of hardware connects to the network.

Hardware configurations can be very complex, especially when several upgrades or additions are made to the same computer over time. Hardware inventories help support staff troubleshoot more quickly and prevent problems when customers upgrade equipment.

Software Elements

Software assets are more difficult to manage than physical assets—even when software is running, it may not be visible because some software doesn't interact with the computer user. As with hardware, support staff look at the mix of software when troubleshooting. Yet software interactions can be even more complex than hardware interactions. Troubleshooting software problems requires an understanding of the hardware, operating system, and interactions with other software running or installed on the desktop to determine a problem's cause. Software also requires sufficient memory to run and perform calculations.

To make matters worse, software vendors periodically publish patches to fix specific bugs, and the patches can cause new problems. A **patch** is a quick modification of a program, which is sometimes a temporary fix until the problem can be solved more thoroughly. Operating systems (such as Windows NT) and databases (such as Oracle 7.3.4) are frequently patched. Software is especially dependent upon the operating system for common actions, such as displaying, printing, and saving files, and problems in the operating system may affect many pieces of software.

Some of the software information tracked in an asset management system includes:

- **Product name:** The name of the vendor as well as the name of the product, such as Microsoft Word or Lotus 123.

- **Version:** A number that identifies the issue or release of the software. Version numbers include a major release number followed by a period and a minor release number, such as Word 97, Windows 3.1, Excel 2000, and Lotus Notes 4.5.

- **Patch level:** Most Windows-based applications include this information in the Help, About menu options, because patches are not displayed when the user starts the application. Other patches are identified by the date they were created.

- **Serial number:** An identification number that may be required to install the software or to receive technical support from the software vendor.

- **Installation type:** A specification of whether the software is installed directly on a computer's hard disk or on a network drive for users to share.

Over time, support staff may discover that some software versions cause problems with other applications. If support staff discover bugs in a certain software version and the software inventory shows that a lot of computer users have that version, they may delay additional requests to upgrade systems to that version until a patch is available.

Network Information

Some support problems aren't caused by hardware failures or software; they are problems with network hardware or traffic. When connected to a network, users may share large storage devices, hard drives, printers, mail servers, and mainframe computers. Different groups of users may share different hardware or software. Many company networks connect employees worldwide, so locating the source of a network problem is one of the most difficult types of support problems.

Network **connectivity** describes the connections between computers on a network. Figure 7-4 is a simplified example of how different computers can connect. (Keep in mind that large company networks include *thousands* of computers and network segments.) Connectivity helps support staff trace the source of a network problem and helps them understand the impact of a problem on a selected piece of hardware. In this diagram, a problem in the connection between the Web server and the local network would prevent all the PCs on the local network from connecting to the company intranet. A communication problem between the hub on the local PC network and the router it connects to means the PCs can't connect to the UNIX servers or the IBM S/370 mainframe.

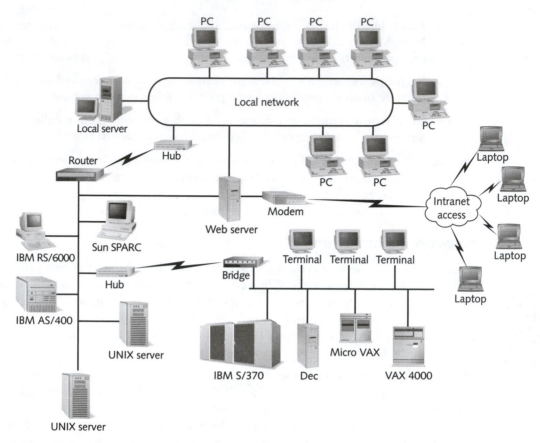

Figure 7-4   Network connectivity map

As more PCs are added to a heavily loaded segment of network, computer users may experience slow response time or outages later. Level two and three support staff use tools to monitor network traffic, identify connectivity issues, and prevent problems.

   Chapter 11 discusses network management software and how it is used.

Discovery

Inventory information helps support staff as long as it is accurate. Many asset management systems are complex and require more time to maintain the information than support staff have. Recently, new software tools have been designed to reduce the time it takes to maintain inventory information. **Discovery agents** are software tools that explore the devices on a network and collect hardware and software information in inventory files. Support staff can schedule the discovery agents to update inventory on a regular basis, or they can use the discovery agents to update the inventory on demand for a specific network device, provided that they know its name.

Discovery agents collect information about a network device as long as the network device is turned on and connected to the network. They collect information about hardware components, operating systems and versions, BIOS releases, disk capacities, and installed software in the background while computer users complete other tasks. Network administrators can build a list of "approved" software applications, and the discovery agents will flag unapproved and unknown software that may expose the company to a piracy investigation. Some discovery agents remove unauthorized software automatically. Discovery agents also complete background virus checking, which prevents the spread of viruses to other desktops on the network.

Support groups used discovery agents to check for Year 2000 compatibility. More advanced discovery agents map networks and display connectivity between devices. Other discovery agents monitor site-licensed software; they track the number of users, the applications they use, when they use them, and how long they use licensed software. Table 7-1 lists some of the software vendors that provide discovery agent software.

Table 7-1   Discovery agent software vendors

Vendor	Web Page
BindView	http://www.bindview.com
Computer Associates	http://www.cai.com
Hewlett Packard	http://www.hp.com
IBM Tivoli	http://www.tivoli.com
Microsoft (Systems Management Server—SMS)	http://www.microsoft.com
Network Associates	http://www.nai.com
Tally Systems	http://www.tallysys.com

Discovery agents cannot collect all the important information, only information stored in the software or hardware. Support staff must still maintain ownership information. However, ownership changes less frequently than hardware, software, and network elements, leaving the support staff more time to address issues.

Remote Control

Remote control software enables support staff to take temporary control of a remote computer. Remote control is a new technology that helps support staff reduce the amount of time they spend on the telephone with callers or in the field troubleshooting PCs. Support staff install client software on each PC. When a problem occurs that support staff want to observe, the computer user starts the remote control software from a menu. The support staff can then use their mouse and keyboard to open programs, files, or menus on the remote computer. The software can freeze the computer user's keyboard and mouse or allow dual control. Most remote software allows the computer user to watch what the support staff is doing. Software vendors that provide remote control software are listed in Table 7-2.

Table 7-2   Remote control software vendors

Vendor	Product	Web Page
Compaq	Carbon Copy	http://www.compaq.com
Computer Associates	Control I+	http://www.cai.com
Farallon Communications	Timbuktu Pro	http://www.farallon.com
Microsoft	Systems Management Server—SMS	http://www.microsoft.com
Symantec	pcAnywhere	http://www.symantec.com

Support staff use remote control software to save travel time and get more accurate problem information. They can install software, review a previous installation, collect log files, and read error messages as part of their troubleshooting activities. If they do not have discovery agent tools, a remote control application allows support staff to manually "discover" the hardware and software elements as problems are reported.

Support staff can also use remote control software to teach computer users complex tasks. The "trainer" takes control of the keyboard and completes the steps while the computer user watches the cursor move over the screen. The trainer can also open files on the user's computer or show customers software settings they need to change. Remote control also enables long-distance training to occur. For example, a support analyst in Dallas can train someone in Chicago over the network.

Software Distribution

Installing, updating, and removing software is time-consuming. These tasks can take weeks when thousands of computers are involved. Without remote control software, support staff have to travel to each PC, displace the user, and run the appropriate upgrade software. Remote control software can save travel time, but support staff can also cause problems if they do not configure the software correctly on every PC.

To save time and ensure consistency, support staff can use software distribution applications to automatically install, upgrade, or remove software. Software distribution applications save resource time when upgrading existing applications or installing new software because support staff do not have to visit each computer and wait for software to load from disks or CD-ROMs. They also don't have to track the PCs they visited or schedule access time with the computer users. Automated software distribution also eliminates follow-up support calls because the software is installed and configured correctly on every PC. Vendors that develop software distribution applications are listed in Table 7-3.

Table 7-3   Software distribution vendors

Vendor	Web Page
BindView	http://www.bindview.com
Computer Associates	http://www.cai.com
Globetrotter Software Inc.	http://www.globetrotter.com
Microsoft (Systems Management Server—SMS)	http://www.microsoft.com
Network Boss Ltd.	http://www.lanauditor.com

Level two and three support staff build a distribution "package," which includes the software to install and additional programs that install and configure the application. They copy the packages to different servers in the network. Then, they schedule the deployment during the users' off-hours. The installation program copies the existing configuration before it tries to complete the installation. Then, if the distribution application fails on a PC during the installation procedure, the software returns the PC to its pre-installation state and logs an error or alerts support staff by e-mail. Support staff follow up on any failures or errors; they can either reschedule the installation attempt for the next off-hour time period or manually install the application.

 One challenge software vendors have in creating distribution tools is that the distribution tools must work across all the operating systems in a network. Many companies have a mix of Windows NT, Windows 95, Windows 98, and UNIX machines on the network. Software distribution tools may need to travel over several forms of TCP/IP networks to get to all the desktop PCs. Some applications work only in single environments.

ASSET MANAGEMENT VENDORS

Asset management software tracks business assets such as equipment, vehicles, buildings, and furniture. Several vendors provide asset management software designed to collect information specifically about technology assets (network equipment, computer hardware and software, and telecommunications equipment). These applications usually include many inventory fields. As mentioned in earlier chapters, many call management applications also include asset management modules. Support staff use the same GUI to log calls, manage outstanding problems, and review or update assets such as PCs and printers. Table 7-4 lists technology-oriented asset management software vendors.

Table 7-4   Technology asset management vendors

Type of Software	Vendor	Web Page
Asset management (standalone)	Applied Innovation Management, Inc.	http://www.innovate.com
	Catsoft	http://www.catsoft.co.uk
	Eurotek Communications Ltd.	http://www.eurotek.co.uk
	Isogon Corp.	http://www.isogon.com
	MainControl	http://www.maincontrol.com
	Microsoft (Systems Management Server—SMS)	http://www.microsoft.com
	Miquest Ltd.	http://www.miquest.co.uk
	One Squared Productions	http://www.onesquared.com
	Softopia Development, Inc.	http://www.softopia.com
	System Support Associates	http://www.syssupport.net
	Tally Systems	http://www.tallysys.com
Help desk software with integrated asset management	Applix Inc.	http://www.applix.com
	Clarify Inc.	http://www.clarify.com
	Computer Associates	http://www.cai.com
	DK Systems Inc.	http://www.dksystems.com
	HelpDesk Expert	http://www.4helpdesk.com
	IBM Tivoli	http://www.tivoli.com
	Multima Corporation	http://www.netkeeper.com
	Network Associates	http://www.nai.com
	Peregrine Systems, Inc.	http://www.peregrine.com
	Remedy Corp.	http://www.remedy.com
	The Vantive Corp	http://www.vantive.com

CHANGE MANAGEMENT

Managers use change management processes to manage organizational changes such as new procedures or defining new business objectives. **Change management** procedures require employees who request changes to identify and evaluate risks to the company. They do this by projecting possible downtime and estimating resources required to complete the change. A change management committee reviews change proposals, collects approvals from the affected parties, schedules the changes, and coordinates the activities involved in a particular change.

Several types of technology changes affect support staff. A change request may begin with a request to add PCs to the network, add access to a shared printer, or assign a telephone extension for new employees. Eventually, employees also need login accounts and access to various software applications. These repetitive and relatively small changes to the environment are usually approved by one or two support managers and can be completed without affecting other business computer users. These change requests are tracked with the call management application.

If the company uses internally developed software, bugs and enhancement requests are forwarded from the call management system to a programming group. The developers will use software change management processes to review the problems or requests, schedule completion, and deliver the solutions. The help desk is usually involved in the initial stages of the software change management process. Their tasks involve:

- Collecting information from the computer user
- Verifying that the suspected bug is a software problem and not a feature of the product the caller just doesn't understand
- Requesting a program change on behalf of the caller

As the programming group makes software changes, they may deliver patches or new releases to the support group to distribute to the computer users. Once the patches or new releases are installed, the help desk assists users with any additional questions and closes the call record. If development changes cause new bugs, the help desk generates a new problem report and the cycle starts over.

IT operational changes can affect support staff and the computer users in a bigger way than single customer requests do. These changes are initiated by the IT department and benefit all computer users. Typical IT projects include upgrades to database software, reboots or maintenance of key pieces of network equipment, or deploying a Windows upgrade to hundreds or thousands of business users. These changes are riskier to a business because they have the potential to disrupt daily business. A mistake in planning or deployment will result in hundreds of new calls to the help desk.

These large IT change requests go through a formal review process. Level two and three support staff may participate in change review meetings to identify risks. They may also contribute directly to the planning or deployment to identify additional systems that are affected or ask groups to test changes on smaller systems, before the change is made for everyone. A change board reviews the change requests and schedules those that can be completed after business hours with other change requests. IT operational changes are tracked with special change management systems or project management tools.

7

Customers usually generate a Service Request (SR) to change software, but programmers can create an SR for the customer if they discover a problem that needs to be fixed. If a programmer creates the change request, the affected customers must approve it before the review board will even process the request. Programmers can't change software without documentation and the customer's approval. This is to make sure that every change identifies the business group or manager who is sponsoring the change (and funding the project), that the customer wants the change, and that Executive management approves the amount of effort and programmer resources that will be assigned to the task. Even a simple request to change information printed on a mailing label is documented to show the business objectives and the effect of not completing the requested change.

The change is forwarded to a development review committee. Members review requirements for the change to make sure it is consistent with the original program design and corporate software standards and to screen the requests for duplicates. Because software development can take weeks to schedule and complete, it is easy for our customers to forget that they already submitted the same requests earlier. Our customers don't have access to the service request application, so they can't review pending changes before they submit new ones, in case someone else already submitted a similar change.

The development group uses a Lotus Notes application to track pending changes and different statuses track whether a change was just requested, in progress, being tested, or completed and ready to install. This tracking system is separate from the rest of the company, which uses a homegrown application that runs on a mainframe. We manually coordinate upgrades with other groups, to make sure that important upgrades and conversions aren't affected by other network or software changes. Right now, the application and process meets most of the programmers' needs.

Front-line staff have to be trained if the change introduces new program features, before they can address questions. Support managers also schedule additional resources if they expect call volumes to be higher than staff can handle. Support staff should track any IT changes that cause new help desk calls, so planners can learn how to avoid the same problems in the future.

Asset management and change management processes are closely related. PC and IT change requests frequently involve adding or changing technology assets. A change request may also require changes in an asset management application to track the purchase, inventory the components, discover the network connectivity, and so forth. Support staff not only take requests for changes, but also take calls when problems arise because of changes.

CHAPTER SUMMARY

- Asset management software is important to companies because computers are more modular than in the past. The total cost of ownership (TCO) is a financial calculation used to determine the real cost of buying and using computers over the computers' lifetime to complete business objectives. A company invests a lot of money in hardware and software components, but those assets are more difficult to identify than other office equipment.

- Help desks maintain some asset management elements because they receive most of the requests to make changes.

- IT managers have the responsibility for upgrading software for business users. Without accurate inventories, the total expense and risk to the company is underestimated. As part of the inventory information, software must be monitored to prevent piracy. There are three ways to license software: one license per PC, concurrent licensing, and site licensing. Software piracy is a violation of copyright law and a federal offense.

- Asset management software includes financial information and inventory. Original prices and vendor information are recorded and maintained by financial analysts and staff. Help desk staff are more interested in warranty, ownership, and hardware and software inventory information.

- Discovery agents are new software tools that automatically update inventory information. They can also complete virus scans, identify unapproved software, or delete applications that violate license agreements.

- Remote control software allows support staff to take control of a PC monitor, keyboard, and mouse over a network. Staff can manipulate applications and read messages as well as if they were in front of the PC. This saves time in collecting troubleshooting information and in travel.

- Automated software delivery systems minimize support calls because all installations are completed the same way. They also decrease the amount of time required to upgrade software for thousands of PCs on a network.

- IT change management attempts to minimize disruption for computer users. Change requests are planned, reviewed, approved, and scheduled by a company's IT experts before they are completed. Software change management controls software changes so that new bugs aren't introduced as code is changed.

KEY TERMS

asset — Any item of value owned by an individual or corporation that could be converted to cash.

asset management — The process of collecting and maintaining a comprehensive list of items a company owns.

change management — Procedures that require employees who request changes to identify and evaluate risks to the company.

configuration management — *See* change management.

connectivity — Describes the connections between computers on a network.

copy protection — Software tools that prevented people from making unauthorized copies of software.

copyright — The exclusive legal rights granted to authors, artists, composers, or programmers to distribute or sell their creations.

disaster recovery — A plan for restoring critical business functions after a disaster, to minimize loss of income.

discovery agents — Software tools that explore the devices on a network and collect hardware and software information in inventory files.

dongle — A copy protection device that plugs into the back of the computer or attaches to a printer port that enables software to run.

hardware key — *See* dongle.

intellectual property — Elements of human intellect that are unique and original, and have value.

license agreements — Legal statements that clearly define the terms under which a person can use software.

patch — A quick modification of a program, which is sometimes a temporary fix until the problem can be solved more thoroughly.

physical inventories — A survey to confirm existing assets by locating and identifying each asset.

remote control software — Software that enables support staff to take temporary control of a remote computer.

software piracy — The act of illegally copying or using software.

total cost of ownership (TCO) — The initial cost of hardware and software, and the cost of installation, user training and support, upgrades, and repairs.

viruses — Software that produces undesirable and damaging events.

warranty — A written guarantee of the integrity of a product and of the maker's responsibility for the repair or replacement of defective parts.

REVIEW QUESTIONS

1. Assets include all of the following *except*:

   a. furniture.

   b. buildings.

   c. computers.

   d. people.

2. All business assets can be used over long periods of time. True or False?

3. Why is it harder to complete a physical inventory of IT assets than other types of assets?

4. Why is the help desk involved in tracking assets?

5. Managers evaluate the cost of replacements and labor to determine when it is _____ to replace technology.

6. What software upgrade of the 1990s demonstrated to IT managers the importance of maintaining hardware and software information?

7. All of the following organizations would be likely to investigate companies suspected of software piracy *except*:

   a. the FBI.

   b. the Software Information Industry Association.

   c. a software vendor.

   d. the Better Business Bureau.

8. _____ software from home is the most common example of software piracy in business.

9. Match the software licensing to its definition:

   a. Single licenses   1. A maximum number of simultaneous users

   b. Concurrent licenses   2. One copy for every user

   c. Site licenses   3. A large estimated number of users

10. What are two ways that software piracy or licensing causes more calls to the support group?

11. Who is most likely to maintain the financial part of an asset management application?

12. If a support group completes its own hardware repairs, why should they track computer hardware vendors?

13. The _____ of an asset determines who approves repairs.

14. _____ are software tools that explore the devices on a network and collect hardware and software information in inventory files.

15. _____ software can be used instead of a discovery agent to see installed software on a PC.

16. Which support group is most likely to use software distribution tools, level one or level two?

17. How do software distribution tools prevent calls to support?

18. What business group is the primary user of software change management applications?

19. All of the following are true *except*:

   a. requests are tracked in call management applications.

   b. IT changes are tracked in change management software.

   c. software enhancements are tracked in call management and software change management applications.

   d. knowledge documents are tracked in asset management applications.

20. Level(s) _____ support staff participate in IT change management meetings to identify risks.

HANDS-ON PROJECTS

Project 7-1

Evaluating asset management software features. Visit some of the asset management software vendors' Web sites listed in Table 7-4 or Appendix A. Collect product brochures from at least three different vendors and download any available evaluation copies. Open several screens of each evaluation software and review the sample data. What financial fields are tracked? What inventory type fields are tracked?

Project 7-2

Understanding copyrights. Visit the whatis.com Web site at **http://www.whatis.com** and look up the definition of copyright. Discuss the issues regarding Web page contents with your classmates. Research additional pages to determine the potential fines for convictions of software piracy.

Project 7-3

Locating trends in TCO. Search the Web for current white papers or review current PC magazines for articles on total cost of ownership. According to the Gartner Group or other IT research groups, what are three current trends in total cost of ownership? Are there any new costs, in addition to upgrades, user training, and support that they identify?

Project 7-4

Researching the effects of software piracy. Visit the Business Software Alliance Web site at **http://www.bsa.org**. What is the mission of this organization? What percentage of software does this organization believe is pirated?

Project 7-5

Understanding license requirements for different types of software. Visit the Software and Information Industry Association Web site at **http://www.siia.net**. What definitions do they use for commercial, shareware, freeware, and public domain software?

Project 7-6

Using remote control software. Open the file named **deskdivr.zip** located on your Data Disk, and review the **Readme.txt** file that describes the software features and requirements. You and a partner will practice using the remote control software either through an ISP or over a LAN. Install the software by running the **dd.exe** program. Use the software to open word processing files or to open other software on the remote computer. Describe what the screen looked like as you controlled (or were controlled) by the Manager part of the application.

Project 7-7

Evaluating IT suites with many asset management features. Visit the Microsoft Web site at **http://www.microsoft.com** and review the product information for Microsoft SMS. Search the Web for available training classes or Microsoft certification classes. How much training is required for this application? Does the application work with any existing help desk applications?

Project 7-8

Researching change management processes. Complete a Web search for articles on change management, or visit a library and find books or articles that discuss change or configuration management. What are the important elements in change management software? What additional business departments would use change management software? Prepare a short report with your responses to these questions.

Project 7-9

Using asset management software. Use the HelpTrac Demo Supervisor to turn on asset management features and search for hardware related call records.

1. Click **Options**, **General Options**. Click the **General** tab, and then turn on the **Equipment Screens**. Click **OK**.
2. Open the **HelpTrac Demo** and use the demo database.
3. Click **Profiles, Equipment, Edit**.
4. Retrieve all the equipment records for the selected user **Richard Henry**. Double-click to select any piece of equipment and use the tabs to review all inventory information.
5. Add a call record for a printer problem. Link the printer equipment record to this call record.
6. Add yourself as a user and enter records for the PC you use. Enter data on all the equipment tabs.
7. Run a report by clicking **Reports, Problem Category Reports**. Select **Change Filter**, and select **Printer Equip Type** from the Hardware Category. Make sure the call record you created in step 5 is in the report. Click **OK** twice.

CASE PROJECTS

1. Asset Management Benefits and Challenges

Your support manager has asked you to be the software administrator for the new asset management system. You want to make sure you understand what is required before you agree to accept the new responsibilities. Locate a company that is using asset management software and visit them. Prepare a list of questions to ask support staff and managers about their asset management procedures. Identify challenges as well as benefits that the support group has found since they started asset management. After your visit, prepare a report of what you learned.

2. **Designing an Asset Management Workflow**

You are the manager of a group of field service repair staff, and your company spends a lot of money replacing PC hardware. Most of the hard drives and monitors your company buys have a one-year, free replacement warranty. You need to design a workflow to make sure that support staff check the warranties for drives and computers before they order new equipment, and that they update the inventory after repairs. Customers report problems to a dispatcher. All PCs have an ID (the name of the employee who uses the equipment) and hardware warranty information. The dispatcher should retrieve the inventory information and check the warranty. If the equipment is still under warranty, field service must pick up the equipment and leave it in the shipping department; the shipping department will get an RMA (return merchandise authorization) and return the item. When the repair or replacement comes back, shipping updates the call, a dispatcher calls the customer to schedule installation, and the dispatcher dispatches a field repairperson. After field repair personnel make the change, they update the inventory system with the new hardware serial number and its warranty date, and close the call record.

3. **Evaluating Asset Management Software**

Wayne Industries has more than 5000 PCs on their network, and the company has decided to upgrade them to the latest version of Windows NT software. Most of the PCs are installed on Novell or NT networks, using TCP/IP, but there are several different versions of Windows software installed. To assist with the upgrade, your support group wants to use software distribution to upgrade as many machines every night as possible. Collect information on three software companies that provide discovery agents and software distribution. Prepare a spreadsheet that compares features and prices. Be sure to include the operating systems the software requires, whether the software can schedule software packages for future deliveries, and the types of databases the discovery agents use for the information they recover. Based on your research, which software would you recommend for Wayne Industries?

CHAPTER

8

ALERTS AND NOTIFICATION TOOLS FOR SUPPORT

In this chapter you will learn:

- ◆ The purpose of service levels
- ◆ How service level management uses alerts and notifications
- ◆ Different technologies for notifications and alerts
- ◆ Which notifications are customer-oriented
- ◆ Which vendors provide devices and software for alerts and other messages

Managing outstanding problems is an important support process. **Notifications** are updates about the support environment forwarded to customers, support staff, and managers. Support staff can notify other team members manually with handwritten notes or telephone calls, or by e-mail. Call management software may allow software administrators to define "rules" to automatically generate electronic notifications as events happen within the software.

Alerts are a special type of notification used to inform selected staff or managers when there is an error condition. Because they refer to errors, alerts are time-sensitive. They must be delivered quickly so that the receiver can correct or prevent the error. Higher-priority support problems must be handled promptly and by appropriate staff. Lower-priority items must still be resolved within time frames defined for their performance levels. Managers rely on alerts to identify outstanding issues that need more attention and to meet service levels.

 TIP   Alerts can also be called "alarms," "bulletins," "escalation notices," or "warnings."

A support group uses many types of notifications or alerts to inform support staff and other interested parties (customers, other support staff, support managers, or higher-level business managers) of new issues. They are useful communication tools between different support analysts, between different levels of support, and between the help desk and its customers.

SERVICE LEVEL MANAGEMENT

Service level agreements, which define the services that a support group delivers and when and how they will be delivered, are one way to measure help desk performance. These agreements also explain the way that customers can escalate issues to managers if performance is not acceptable. Many customers expect support staff to be able to immediately answer their question, solve their problem, or complete their request. These customers frequently get angry if support takes longer than *they* want or need. They forget that the support group must respond to all customer needs for the good of the entire company. To help meet customer expectations, support groups attempt to prioritize incoming work into levels of service. The more likely that a customer cannot complete business tasks, the higher that customer's problem or request is placed on the support group's priority list. For example, a problem accessing a shared drive on which many customers' work is stored is a higher priority than a problem formatting text. Similarly, fixing a printer that several people use is more urgent than fixing a printer that one person uses. On the other hand, if the person who prints payroll checks has printer problems, the support group assigns it a higher priority, because that person's primary assignment cannot be completed and many employees are affected. Support groups define and publish service levels to help customers understand the urgency of their problem in relation to all customers' problems.

 TIP The impact on customers isn't the only thing that determines a high priority item. For example, database errors may not seem important to customers, but they can indicate serious problems that may affect information in the database and, ultimately, the customer.

There are four steps involved in managing service levels, as illustrated in Figure 8-1. The support group begins by defining the service. Support staff may be notified as new items come in, to deliver the service. As services are delivered, managers rely upon alerts to make sure services are delivered as promised to customers (if not, they may assign other staff members to the outstanding problems or re-prioritize other issues). Over time, support managers analyze support performance and will attempt to improve delivery for all services if possible.

As customers call the support group, staff members make sure that they can deliver what the customers request and identify additional information they need. It is important for level one support to identify the real problem, to avoid reopening a problem several times. Staff and managers monitor service deliveries to make sure that they prioritize calls correctly and that they assign calls to someone who can complete the request.

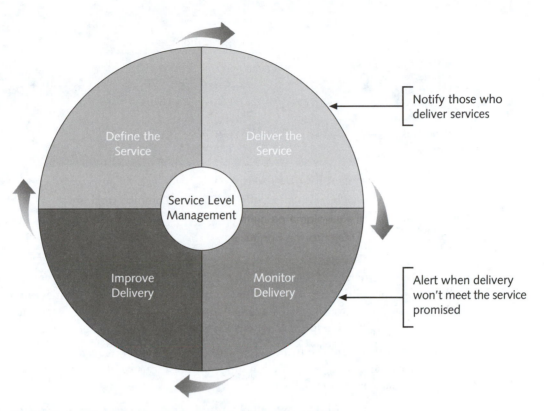

Figure 8-1   The four steps of service level management

If services promised don't match customer expectations, the SLA describes ways to escalate issues. Support managers attempt to minimize the difference between promised performance and actual performance by monitoring outstanding issues. Reporting tools may not be effective for monitoring because a report showing average call resolution is too late in the call management process. Managers and staff rely on alerts and notifications while the request is still open to warn them if delivery may not meet customer expectations.

The customer-support relationship isn't the only area that needs a service level agreement. The arrows between groups in Figure 8-2 illustrate other areas in which it is always best to clearly define service and set expectations. Service level agreements exist not only between support and customers, but also between different levels of support and with external vendors and service providers.

Companies purchase services and deliverables from outside vendors with legal contracts or purchase agreements. A purchase agreement often includes the type of services, how and when they are delivered, and how they are measured, just as a service level agreement will. Customers notify higher levels of management when vendor performance is consistently below the published agreements, and SLAs may establish penalties for

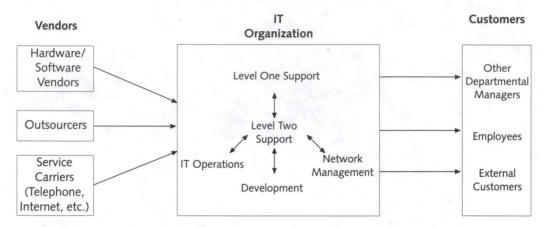

Figure 8-2   Possible service level agreements

unacceptable performance. Services levels between IT departments (level one support, level two support, development, operations, and the network management group) usually rely upon written escalation procedures. If any group doesn't respond or resolve escalated items quickly, issues are escalated to that group's management.

Alerts or notifications are the main tools used for service level management. As support staff manage outstanding problems, they rely upon notifications or alerts to improve communications. For example:

- A notification to the new call record owner can prevent him or her from overlooking the item in pending work. Support staff hand off items to team members who are working on related items or when they can't continue working on the problem themselves. When managers reassign items from overloaded support staff to other resources, a notification informs support staff that they are now responsible for the problem.

- Notifications keep the original support analyst in the communication loop. As higher support levels update text, front-line support can track the progress of the problem. In some support groups, higher-level support staff delegate activities back to level one support. Depending upon the workflow, an alert may inform the level one call record owner to collect more information from the customer or to follow up with the customer. If level two or three support staff close call records themselves, notifications help the original call owner learn how to solve the problem the next time, so he or she won't need to escalate that problem.

- Notifications are a way to collect information. Other staff or management may be interested in problems or questions about a selected topic, such as anything related to a specific product, release, or subject. For example, an analyst who works in a support group that has both Windows 98 and Windows NT desktops may want to review all Windows NT problems to learn more about that subject. As NT problems are created or closed, the staff member receives a notification.

- Alerts can prevent errors. Managers or team leaders want to be warned before an outstanding item exceeds its service level. For example, if support promises to install a new PC within fifteen days of the customer's request, an alert thirteen days after the request will remind the staff that this item is due shortly. If the item remains open sixteen days after the request, managers may reassign the item to someone who can complete the item immediately or reprioritize other outstanding items.

- Follow-up alerts remind staff to communicate regularly with other departments when they escalate items. A follow-up alert can remind staff to call an outside vendor just to make sure that the vendor is able to meet its agreed time frame. If not, support then can communicate this information to the customer before the request or problem is past due.

TECHNOLOGIES FOR SUPPORT NOTIFICATIONS AND ALERTS

8

Notifications for service level management take many forms. Some notifications are completed manually, such as calling the new call record owner on the telephone as you reassign a call record that you created to them. Many business users prefer receiving electronic notifications, such as voice mail or e-mail, because they can control interruptions. The sender can be a support staff member or a special feature of the call management software, and can dispatch an electronic notification at any time—but the receiver decides when to retrieve it.

Alerts can be designed to escalate through different management levels. Support managers or team leaders may receive alerts for a problem that exceeds its service. The longer the problem remains outstanding, the more frequently alerts are generated. As the item ages, higher-level managers are alerted.

Support groups can use several tools for notifications and alerts, including those listed in Figure 8-3.

```
    ♦ Support software flags and messages
    ♦ Message boards
    ♦ E-mail
    ♦ Voice mail
    ♦ Pagers
    ♦ Wireless telephones
    ♦ Handheld devices
    ♦ Badge locators
```

Figure 8-3 Types of support notifications

Support Software Flags and Messages

Support software usually provides a visual marker or flag as an alert or notification. The flag can appear as a special icon by the call summary information, or the record may appear in a different color from other records, based on its priority, type, or age. Consequently, flagged items are easy to see, whether support staff sort outstanding call records by date created, date last modified, or by customer. Some software includes service level definitions so that call records change color as they get closer to exceeding the service level for that priority.

Many call management applications let support staff create messages (similar to e-mail messages) that stay within the support software GUI. Support staff see incoming messages or alerts across the top of the PC screen, as a scrolling message on the bottom of the screen, or in a special window. As staff log in to the support software application, they see a list of messages issued while they were logged off. The advantage to keeping these messages within the call management software is that they won't get overlooked as easily as they might if the messages were routed to an e-mail application.

Color-coded flags or icons may also appear on daily reports generated by the support software. Items exceeding their service level may print in boldface or italic text, or in a different color. Even software without special colors or fonts can allow managers to schedule reports of high-priority items and distribute them automatically by e-mail to support staff and team leaders. Managers commonly send all team members a list of priority 1 outstanding calls and the names of the individuals working those calls every two to four hours until the problems are resolved. This information helps all staff members, because they know who is free to handle other calls and they can manage their own time better.

Message Boards

Support groups use a variety of messages boards for notifications and alerts. One of the simplest, most cost-effective ways to notify groups of people is to post messages on an erasable whiteboard. Used like a blackboard, these nonmagnetic boards are cleaner, cheaper, and lighter than traditional chalkboards. Managers can use different colored dry erase markers to post "hot" issues and daily reminders, such as current system outages, server trouble, planned maintenance of important systems, or staff members out of the office. To be effective, staff should be able to see the whiteboard from their desks or as they move around the office. Good places to hang a whiteboard are near the break room, restrooms, or the entrance to the help desk. Although information on the whiteboard must be updated manually, this form of notification has the advantages of low cost and ease of use.

Electronic display boards, or **reader boards**, are more advanced versions of whiteboards, that display information on a digitized board or television monitor. Some display boards can even create graphs of the data they receive. Most display boards show the data as color-coded information, and some display boards include audible alarms that ring when certain events happen, to grab the support staff's attention. With display boards, staff and managers can move freely between desks or other work areas and still see important alerts as they appear. Display boards can work with the telephone system to show the number of calls waiting, the length of the longest waiting call, and the number of support staff who are on the telephone. Figure 8-4 shows some of the telephone information that can be displayed on a reader board. This real-time information helps level one staff manage their telephone time and managers determine when to assign more staff to handle incoming calls.

Figure 8-4 Electronic reader board

 Some telephones display call information in a way similar to display boards, for example the number of calls waiting for a selected support team and the longest hold time. Managers' telephones may also show the number of employees on the telephone and the hold time for each workgroup. Chapter 9 discusses these telephone displays as part of automatic call distribution (ACD) systems.

If support staff have individual offices or if the support center has high cubicle partitions around agents, not everyone may be able to see a wall-mounted display board. Some vendors offer software that creates a display board on each computer in the support area. A smaller version of the display board, with color-coding and alarms, scrolls data across the top or bottom of each monitor. A few PC-based display board systems allow managers or staff to broadcast special messages, such as the name of a server that is down or a section of the network where users report slow response.

E-mail

One of the most commonly used notification methods is e-mail. **Electronic mail**, or **e-mail**, is the exchange of computer-stored messages by telecommunication. Some e-mail applications will send only text messages; others forward graphic images, sound files, or other items as attachments. Public and private networks (companies have private networks among computers, but the Internet is a public network) can exchange e-mail because standard sets of rules, called **protocols**, regulate the way data is transmitted between computers. E-mail is one of the protocols (called SMTP) included with the Transport Control Protocol/Internet Protocol (TCP/IP) suite of protocols. A popular protocol for receiving e-mail is POP3.

On the Internet, there are a variety of TCP/IP protocols, which include:

- **TCP (Transmission Control Protocol)**: The set of rules used to send data in the form of message units between computers over the Internet. TCP keeps track of the individual units of data (called **packets**) that a message is divided into for efficient routing through the Internet.

- **IP (Internet Protocol)**: The set of rules used to send and receive messages at the Internet address level. IP handles the actual delivery of data.

- **HTTP (Hypertext Transfer Protocol)**: The set of rules for exchanging text, graphic images, sound, video, and other multimedia files on the World Wide Web.

- **SMTP (Simple Mail Transfer Protocol)**: A protocol for sending e-mail. It is used with one of two other protocols—POP3 or IMAP—that let the user save messages in a mailbox.

- **POP3 (Post Office Protocol 3)**: The most recent version of a standard protocol for receiving e-mail. POP3 is a client-server protocol in which e-mail is received and stored by an Internet server. Periodically, you (or your client e-mail receiver) check your mailbox on the server and download any mail. POP3 can be thought of as a "store-and-forward" service.

- **IMAP (Interactive Mail Access Protocol)**: An alternate e-mail receiving protocol. With IMAP, you view your e-mail at the server as though it were on your local computer. Any e-mail messages deleted locally remain on the server. IMAP can be thought of as a remote file server mail system.

E-mail is an effective tool for sending notifications—it can be created manually, and most call management software includes tools to send software-generated notifications out to the company's e-mail tool. However, e-mail is ineffective for sending alerts because the recipient must open the mail window or must retrieve messages from a server. Also many companies generate thousands of pieces of e-mail among employees every hour, so important messages may be temporarily "lost" in the flood of incoming messages—the recipient may not see the important message, because he or she is receiving so many messages, or messages may not get to the recipient in a timely way because there is so much e-mail traffic. Some companies save money by storing their e-mail messages destined for the Internet and sending them periodically instead of as they are created (not all companies connect to the Internet continuously). As a result, e-mail is not always up to date for many users.

E-mail can be distributed to lists of people as well as to individuals. It is one of the earliest applications used through the Internet and is popular because it takes little effort for the sender to create or send a piece of e-mail.

E-mail can, at times, be used effectively to request more information about a problem. But e-mail can extend the amount of time it takes to solve a problem because it is a one-way communication method (there is no interaction with another person). Consider the following exchange of e-mail messages. A business user sends an e-mail describing a problem to the support group. Support logs the call, and then uses e-mail to ask a follow-up question. The business user answers the question, which leads to another question from support, and so on. The greater the number of information exchanges, the more delays there will be in solving the problem. It is always fastest for support to communicate directly with a customer to ask questions, record the answers, and generate the next set of questions.

Voice Mail

Telephone messages are another form of notification. **Voice mail** is the business term for sending, storing, and retrieving audio messages, similar to a telephone answering machine. A voice mailbox is typically associated with a telephone number or extension. When someone calls a number and the line is busy or not answered, the caller hears a recorded message. The message may tell the caller how to page the individual or how to speak to another person or operator. The owner of a voice mailbox can change the outgoing message or listen to incoming messages after entering a security code. Members of a voice mail system can generally forward messages to other members' mail boxes or create distribution lists (similar to an e-mail distribution list), to send the same message to a group of people.

 TIP The telephone system is sometimes called the **voice net** by business telecommunications staff.

Voice mail is one of the simplest and fastest methods for sending notifications, but it has the same limits as e-mail. Most business users check for voice mail messages several times a day, and a company may generate thousands of individual and group messages daily. Unless the sender has a way to flag a message as a higher priority, it can be "hidden" among other voice mail messages that might be less urgent.

Voice mail is also a form of one-way communication, because the sender leaves a message and waits for the recipient to listen and call back. Voice mail can be used to notify a call owner or to escalate a problem, provided that the notification is not time-sensitive. As long as the receiver checks voice mail regularly, voice mail is useful for support.

 TIP The experience of two people trying to reach other by telephone but always reaching each other's voice mail is called "(tele)phone tag." One way to avoid telephone tag is to leave a message with your available schedule or to ask the person you are calling specifically when you should try to call back. If you are trying to resolve a reported problem and need more information, leave a message that explains what information you still need so the caller can be prepared or can leave the information on your voice mail when he or she return the call.

EFFECTIVE SUPPORT MESSAGES AND COMMUNICATIONS

Support staff will attempt to contact customers with questions or problem updates by telephone, but they may not always be able to achieve direct, person-to-person communications. When this happens, they can avoid "telephone tag" by structuring voice mail messages, similar to the way they would structure an e-mail message. When you leave messages for customers, be sure to do the following:

- **Identify yourself:** Include your name, explain where you work, and leave your telephone number or extension (or the number for the support group). Speak telephone numbers slowly or pause before you continue to allow listeners time to write down the numbers.

- **Summarize the purpose of the call:** Describe the problem in one sentence first. Some voice mail systems allow users to scan the first ten seconds of a voice message. A clear voice mail "subject" will help customers decide whether to listen to the details or skip to the next message. If you are leaving an update on a problem, include both the call record number and a problem description.

- **Deliver the message:** Organize your message so you can deliver it quickly and so customers can listen to it quickly. Customers have their own sources of stress and they will skip rambling, unorganized messages that waste time when they have many voice messages to review.

- **Repeat your telephone number:** If you need a response within a specific time frame, explain why. Inform them if they need to speak to you directly, or whether they can work with another support staff member.

If you need several questions answered, explain this when you deliver the message. You may be able to leave a short list of two or three questions that they can respond to with voice mail. If there are more than three questions and you have not been able to reach customers directly, ask to schedule an appointment to collect the information. Be sure to explain how long it will take (five minutes, fifteen minutes, thirty minutes, and so on) to answer your questions, so they can plan their time. It may also be helpful to forward an e-mail message with a written list of the same questions so they can prepare in advance for the appointment. (Some managers may be able to delegate a list of questions to an assistant who can handle the call in their absence.)

Voice messages leaving problem updates are much simpler. In many cases, it will not be necessary for customer's to contact the support group, but be sure you clearly explain this ("This is just an update on call number 3515 and it isn't necessary for you to call us back"). If the problem is still unresolved, explain when the support group can provide another update ("We should have another update in about four hours" or "We don't expect to receive your replacement hardware until the end of the week").

When staff members do finally make direct contact with customer's, they should be protective of the customers' time. Support staff should always ask customer's if they have time to hold before they place customer's on hold to get other information or to discuss with other support staff offline. If support staff use a speakerphone, they should always identify who is listening to the conversation for customer's and inform them if others enter or leave the room.

Pagers

A pager is a wireless telecommunications receiver with a small screen to view messages. Originally, messages could only be triggered by the sender via a telephone call, and the devices allowed only number messages because message entry was limited to sounds generated from a telephone touch pad. Today's pagers are more complex and can accept text messages of 250 characters that can be saved and reviewed later. Companies that provide paging service may provide PC software to send pages directly from a PC by modem; others use special e-mail addresses to route text messages from e-mail or over the Internet to receivers.

8

 Pagers are also called beepers because they beep to alert the person carrying the pager that there is an incoming message. Most pagers can be switched from an audible beep to vibration. The person carrying the pager must place it in a pocket or on a holder attached to a belt so that he or she can feel the vibration if the pager is triggered. This enables people to receive pager messages in locations such as churches or movie theatres without disturbing others.

Generally, pagers are used by people who are continually changing their location or who are not able to answer a phone call immediately. Support groups use pagers in several ways:

- Support staff who handle customer problems reported after office hours may carry pagers. Support groups that provide twenty-four-hour support may use an answering service to contact support staff after normal business hours. Customers call the regular support telephone number, but the call is routed to an answering service that collects the information. The answering service then pages the support person on call for the week, who then calls the customer and begins troubleshooting. Using pagers for after-hours support saves the expense and inconvenience of staffing an office twenty-four hours a day and over holidays. Support staff take turns covering the off-hours, yet can still enjoy many hours as if they were off-duty.

- Programmers and other IT staff or managers also carry pagers so they can be alerted to outages and problems that happen during weekends. Mainframe computer operators may need to alert their managers if important programs or reports don't complete on time. Programmers support both computer operators and customers as level two or three support.

- Some higher-level support staff may work away from their desks, installing computers or software in different locations. These support staff won't see an alert within the call management application. Dispatchers or level one staff can use pagers to alert them to new items routed to their queue. These items aren't always high-priority; the pager can provide notifications like an e-mail system as well as alert them to high-priority problems. Field repair staff rely almost entirely on pagers for notice of new assignments.

- Support staff managers receive alerts for all high-priority items via pagers. Even when managers are in meetings, they can remain informed of critical activities that support staff are working on.

> **TIP** A pager system requires an electronic pager and a telecommunications service provider (which is similar to a telephone service provider). Most companies also provide paging software that works with their specific equipment. The software enables users to store a searchable list of names and pager numbers for frequently paged employees and keeps a history of sent pages. The software also allows the sender to type in a text message, or paste text from another window (such as the call management software) to save time.

Pager systems are usually very reliable, and service providers can page people regionally, nationally, and internationally, depending on the customer needs. There are also more ways now to send a page message: a paging dispatcher may answer telephone calls and type the text message for the sender, senders can route pages through e-mail, from Internet Web pages, by PC-based paging software, or by calling a personalized pager number. Newer pagers also support interactive paging, which means that the page recipient can reply to the person who sent the page by choosing from a predefined list of responses and broadcasting the response directly from the pager device without a telephone.

Pagers are effective for notifications and are the oldest and most reliable method for delivering alerts. Unfortunately, some office buildings are in locations that make it difficult to receive wireless transmissions. Staff may also miss some pages if they don't ensure that they have charged batteries in the pager. Pager functions continue to expand, but pagers could eventually disappear as separate devices as more people use cellular telephones and other handheld devices.

Wireless Telephones

Cellular telephone service is a type of short-wave analog or digital transmission in which a subscriber has a wireless connection from a mobile telephone to a nearby transmitter. The transmitter's span of coverage is called a **cell**. A cellular telephone has a wider cell range than a cordless telephone (which has a very short wireless connection to a local telephone outlet). As the cellular telephone user moves from one cell to another, the telephone signal is passed from one to another local cell transmitter. Generally, cellular telephone service is available in urban areas and along major highways. Field repair staff and outsourcers were the original support users of cellular telephones because they traveled between locations or cities.

Personal communications services (PCS) is a newer telephone service for mobile users that is similar to cellular and is sometimes referred to as digital cellular (although cellular can also be digital). Like cellular, PCS requires a number of transmitters to blanket an area of coverage. It generally requires more cell transmitters for coverage, but has the advantage of fewer gaps or blind spots between covered areas. The PCS telephone itself is slightly smaller than a cellular telephone. PCS started in urban areas with large numbers of users.

Technology for wireless telephones continues to improve rapidly. As prices for hardware and telephone services drop and coverage areas expand, more companies are replacing pagers with wireless telephones. Wireless telephones provide the same effective communication as a normal telephone call and can store messages in voice mail systems when the person called is unavailable. Some support managers and staff forward their desk telephone calls to their wireless telephone when they leave their office so they can receive telephone calls wherever they happen to be. As a result, cellular and PCS telephones are effective for alerts as well as for notifications.

Handheld Devices

Personal digital assistants (PDAs) are small, mobile, handheld devices that provide computing and information storage and retrieval capabilities for personal or business use. They are most commonly used for keeping appointment calendars and address book information handy. Some PDAs have a small keyboard for data entry. Others have an electronically sensitive pad that the user writes on with a special pen or stylus. PDAs may run with a variation of the Microsoft Windows operating system, called Windows CE, or another operating system.

As they have become more common, some PDA vendors combine other electronic features such as wireless communications with the calendar and address book programs. Several PDAs receive pages. When a new message is received, a pager card turns on the PDA and sets off an audible alarm. Instead of carrying a pager and a handheld computer, the user need carry only one device.

New PDA software also lets users receive e-mail or send and receive faxes. Although it may not be practical to read long e-mail messages from the smaller PDA screens, short messages and notifications are appropriate. A few wireless telephones also include PDA software, again consolidating multiple devices into one piece of equipment. PDAs with paging options can function well for alerts.

Some call management software vendors have discovered a way to allow field staff to update records remotely through a PDA. In the past, field service support staff relied upon dispatchers or other support staff to relay problem details. To keep track of the details for each visit, they also printed call records to carry with them. When they finished repairs, they either called a dispatcher who manually updated the records or returned to their desk to close the

8

tickets. At best, field staff updated all tickets at the end of the day, which meant that the resolution times were not accurate. Now, a few call management software vendors provide software that enables field staff to download call tickets to a PDA. As field staff complete work or need to update records, they make the notes in the PDA. At the end of the day, they can update the call records with their PDA notes from their desk or remotely via a wireless modem. The advantage is that the synchronized records include updated information and true resolution times. Field staff can receive alerts about urgent calls via the paging board in the PDA, download the record details remotely, and then use the PDA to organize and sort outstanding work. If they discover new problems while working on a known problem, they can create new call records on the PDA as needed.

Badge Locators

Infrared locators on employee badges provide a way to find and alert field support staff. Incorporated as part of an identification badge, employee-tracking systems eliminate telephone tag and overhead audio messages. A dispatcher uses a software application to select a field staff member, finds his or her location (which is updated every five seconds with infrared signals from an employee badge), and then calls the field staff member's wireless telephone or pager. The dispatcher uses the location information to determine whether the support staff member can be interrupted (because they aren't in a meeting room) and to coordinate or prioritize visits by location. The support analyst can take care of other calls in the same area, avoiding repeat trips to the same location and saving travel time. Figure 8-5 shows the computer system used to track employees.

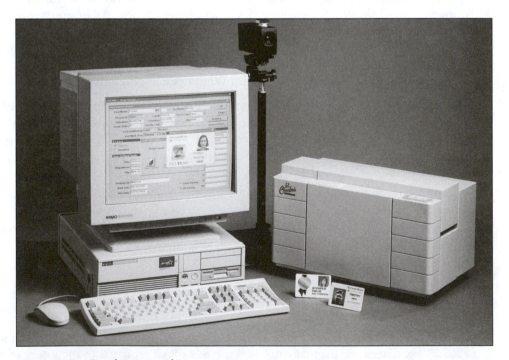

Figure 8-5   Employee tracking system

Some offices allow employees to page anyone in the office through speakers in the ceiling rather than through wireless pagers. Employees use the telephone, which is connected to the overhead speaker system, as a microphone for the message. These overhead audio messages interrupt everyone at work, but they are a useful way to deliver a timely message to a group of people in the building (for example, lunch is now being served, the training class is ready to begin, or the building needs to be evacuated because it is on fire).

Employee-tracking systems don't track employees to restrooms, but they can indicate when employees enter or leave a building and who they are with. Support groups must be careful to emphasize that these tracking systems are not an attempt to invade employee privacy, but are a way to help support respond to customers more quickly. This technology is closely related to paging and may be included with other paging devices in the future.

8

TECHNOLOGIES FOR CUSTOMER NOTIFICATIONS

Most of the technologies used to notify support staff are also appropriate ways to update customers about the progress of a problem. Support staff can post the same types of messages on Web pages for customers to access as would be displayed on a message board. Customers can access the Web page before they call the support group. Support must update information regularly (every two to four hours); otherwise customers will not check the Web pages before they call to report a problem.

Some call management systems allow customers to directly access their outstanding problem reports. Depending upon how the software is implemented, customers may also be able to add information themselves. Although they won't see the alerts or notifications generated by the call management software to support staff, customers can see status changes and text updates.

A support group that allows customers to view and update their own problem records can benefit or suffer, depending upon how they manage the information. When support staff regularly record their behind-the-scenes activities, customers can see that their problems are getting attention and they may not initiate follow-up calls. When customers can see that a call record is unassigned or has not been updated in several days, they may escalate their problems to support managers. They may also call the support group to ask why no one is working on their problem.

E-mail systems are a very good way to forward progress reports to customers. Some call management systems automatically generate progress reports to customers or support managers when the call record status or history changes. E-mail may be one of the most reliable ways to reach someone who is always on the telephone, because they may be able to see new messages on the computer screen. E-mail also provides a written record of the communication.

Voice mail systems are a standard tool in most companies. They are also good for giving progress reports to the customer. If support needs additional information and must leave a message, they should indicate the exact information they need and when they will try to call back to collect that information. This way the customer can be better prepared when they do actually talk with support. Some customers may want to be paged when the support staff are ready to work on their problem. It may also be appropriate to page customers *once* if the support staff have been unable to contact them directly. When appropriate, support staff should always ask how customers want to be contacted and if there are other ways (besides voice mail) to reach them.

 Some call management systems store multiple telephone numbers for each customer, including a primary telephone number or extension, a cellular telephone number, and a coworker's or manager's number.

Another way to notify customers is to use an announcement system with a voice mailbox. Customers call support, but instead of being placed on hold, their calls are routed to a voice mailbox. A recorded message informs callers about already reported system-wide problems or known outages. If the customer has the same problem, he or she does not have to leave a message. Announcement systems are frequently part of an integrated voice response (IVR) system, which allows customers to choose from a set of options before it routes their call to an appropriate support staff member. (Chapter 9 discusses IVR systems in more detail.) When the IVR answers the telephone, it plays a recorded message about known problems, and then asks callers to enter a number from the telephone touch pad to categorize the type of service they need.

Web-based message boards and recorded announcements can improve support service and save customers and support staff time because they can answer repetitious questions. Support staff don't need to personally communicate with all users affected by a network outage, because the telephone system disperses appropriate and updated information, as customers need it.

ALERT AND NOTIFICATION TECHNOLOGY VENDORS

One of the most important features of a call management application is to provide internal alerts and to communicate with other technologies such as e-mail, fax, and pager systems. The call management software vendors discussed in previous chapters provide these basic methods for notifications. Some software also includes features to automatically generate alerts, based on rules. Software administrators build the rules, determine the method for delivery (within the call management software, to external e-mail, or to a pager), and maintain a list of alert recipients.

Other vendors provide hardware, software, or telecommunications services that work with call management software. These technologies often have their own set of features as well for tasks that are specific to each type of message or alert.

Vendors for the following technologies are listed in Appendix A.

Message Boards

Whiteboards and blackboards are available from any office or school supplies vendor. Electronic displays, or reader boards, are sold by standalone vendors and by some automatic call distribution (ACD) system vendors (discussed in more detail in Chapter 9).

E-mail

There are hundreds of e-mail applications, but most companies standardize on a few PC-based applications, such as:

- Lotus Notes Mail
- Microsoft Internet Explorer Mail
- Microsoft Outlook or Outlook Express
- Netscape Messenger Mail
- Novel Groupwise
- Qualcomm Eudora

All e-mail software between systems uses the TCP/IP protocols mentioned earlier.

Pagers, Pager Services, and Pager Software

Pager, pager services, and pager software vendors may also describe their services as "wireless messaging services," "wireless paging," or "messaging services." Most of the service companies provide national or regional service, but many smaller companies provide local (within a state or major city) paging services. Pager service providers provide their own hardware devices.

Cellular and PCS Telephones and Service

Local and regional companies provide wireless telephone services such as cellular and PCS. The best source of information is the local telephone directory. You will need a wireless telephone and a service provider as well. Some of the latest cellular telephones are also covered regularly in technology newsletters.

Handheld Devices

As mentioned earlier, some call management vendors have developed interfaces to PDAs, so that support staff can download call records. PDAs already include some text notifications; users can either connect the PDA to a modem or use wireless communication to receive e-mail or fax. Telephone vendors are also adding pager features, such as text messaging and PDA software, to their telephones. Over time, these integrated devices may eventually replace voice mail systems or e-mail for notifications.

Apple Computer introduced the first handheld computer, called the Newton. The original Newton was withdrawn from the market because of design problems. There are two dominant operating systems for the majority of PDAs or "palmtop" devices—Palm OS and Windows CE. Although Windows is a dominant desktop operating system, the Palm OS PDAs represent the largest number of devices sold—roughly fives times as many as its next competitor. This new technology continues to change rapidly, so some vendors offer PDAs that will run either the Windows CE or Palm OS operating system.

CHAPTER SUMMARY

- Service level agreements (SLAs) prioritize incoming work and set customer expectations for performance. Managers and staff use alerts and other notifications to make sure that services are delivered as promised. Notifications are generated to inform staff of assignments. Alerts must attempt to reach the receiver immediately to be effective.

- Written service level agreements define the services, priorities, and available hours for support. They also document ways for customers to escalate issues. Service level management attempts to minimize the difference between promised performance and actual performance.

- A service level agreement exists between customers and level one support. An IT department should also have agreements between groups that escalate items to each other, and between the support group and outside vendors.

- Call management applications include several ways to flag records as they age. This can include built-in message boards and color-coded displays. They can also generate reports and flag exceptions in a different type or color.

- Manual message boards or whiteboards are inexpensive and communicate hot issues, provided that they are in a location where staff can see them regularly. Electronic messages boards may be integrated with telephone systems or call management software and are constantly updated to keep staff informed about pending calls and other issues. If there is not a clearly visible location for the display board, PC message boards will pop up the same information on each computer in the support workgroup.

- E-mail is an effective way to notify people, but it is not as effective for alerts because messages do not always reach the recipient immediately. Voice mail is a standard business tool, useful for notifications, but subject to the same problems as e-mail. Both provide one-way communication and can delay problem resolution.

- Pager systems are currently the most reliable way to send alerts. As the price of wireless telephones comes down, more vendors are combining pager, telephone, and e-mail features, so that users only need to carry a single device. PDAs can be combined with pager boards or cellular telephones. In addition some call management vendors download call records to PDAs for field support staff to collect and maintain data.

- The same notification methods can be used to keep customers informed on the progress of problems. Web-based message boards communicate some of the same information to customers that reader boards provide to support staff. In addition, recorded announcements and IVR systems inform customers of serious problems already being worked on by support staff.

◻ There are many vendors providing alert or notification systems. The difficulties in maintaining a current list are that the technology is still changing and many terms are used for the same devices.

KEY TERMS

alert — A special type of notification to inform selected staff or managers when there is an error condition.

cell — The span of coverage for a mobile telephone transmitter.

cellular telephone service — A type of short-wave analog or digital transmission in which a subscriber has a wireless connection from a mobile telephone to a nearby transmitter.

electronic display board — An advanced version of a whiteboard that displays information on a digitized board or television monitor.

electronic mail — The exchange of computer-stored messages by telecommunication.

e-mail — *See* electronic mail.

Hypertext Transfer Protocol (HTTP) — A set of rules for exchanging text, graphic images, sound, video, and other multimedia files on the World Wide Web.

Interactive Mail Access Protocol (IMAP) — A set of rules for receiving e-mail and storing it on a file server.

Internet Protocol (IP) — A set of rules to send and receive messages at the Internet address level.

notifications — Updates about the support environment forwarded to customers, support staff, and managers.

packets — Individual units of data.

Personal Communications Services (PCS) — A newer wireless telephone service that is similar to cellular and is sometimes referred to as digital cellular.

personal digital assistant (PDA) — A small, mobile handheld device that provides computing and information storage and retrieval capabilities for personal or business use.

Post Office Protocol 3 (POP3) — A set of rules for receiving e-mail and saving in a mailbox.

protocol — A standard sets of rules to regulate the way data is transmitted between computers.

reader board — *See* electronic display board

Simple Mail Transfer Protocol (SMTP) — A set of rules for sending e-mail.

Transmission Control Protocol (TCP) — A set of rules that controls data in the form of message units sent between computers over the Internet.

voice mail — The business term for sending, storing, and retrieving audio messages, similar to a telephone answering machine.

voice net — Another term for a telephone system.

8

REVIEW QUESTIONS

1. _____ are a way to measure help desk performance.

2. List the four steps in service level management.

3. Why are reporting tools ineffective in managing service levels and performance?

4. Support groups should have service level agreements between all of the following *except:*

   a. operations and the payroll department.

   b. level one and two support.

   c. level two support and development.

   d. support and service providers

5. Notifications are a subcategory of alerts. True or False?

6. Which technologies are appropriate for notifying staff that a high-priority item has been assigned to them?

7. Which technologies are considered customer notifications?

8. What are the possible formats available for message's within the call management software?

9. Message boards should be located so that they are visible. Physical locations that are likely to attract the attention of support staff include all of the following *except:*

   a. next to the restrooms.

   b. by the reception area.

   c. next to the break room.

   d. in someone's office.

10. Is it necessary for support staff to understand how e-mail protocols work? Explain your answer.

11. List five reasons why e-mail is such a popular method for communication in business.

12. Equipment for voice mail systems are advanced versions of _____ (which many people use at home).

13. What are three types of wireless messaging systems?

14. List three reasons why pagers are a popular way to notify support staff.

15. Pagers may be used by all of the following businesspeople except:

    a. field staff.

    b. managers of support or IT organizations.

    c. level one support.

    d. administrative assistants.

16. Which notification technologies are most likely to merge in the future?

17. An announcement system is used only to advertise products and other customer information and cannot be used to inform customers of important support topics. True or False?

HANDS–ON PROJECTS

Project 8-1

Understanding service level agreements. Search the Web for two sample service level agreements. Each SLA should be from a different service organization (such as internal support, external support, a university or college, government services, or an outsourcer). Make sure that the three primary elements (services provided, levels of service or priority, and available hours) are included. Identify additional elements within the service level and discuss the reasons that these items were added. Possible sites to locate SLAs include:

- **http://maps4.cr.bcit.bc.ca/bis/sla.htm**
- **http://web.missouri.edu/~ue/sla/**
- **http://etc.nih.gov/pages/etcservicelevelagreement.html**
- **http://www.supportresearch.com/Fry/tpl-SLA.htm**
- **http://www.everestsw.com/accountability/example.html**

Project 8-2

Learning more about e-mail applications. Visit the Whatis.com Web site at **http://whatis.com** and click the **Email for Beginners** link. Do the following:

1. Identify the primary areas of an e-mail message.
2. Look up in the Word List the definitions for the following words: alias, ascii art, attachment, BTW, draft's, emoticon's, flame, header, HTML email, LOL, quote, ROTFL, rules, snail mail, and thread.
3. Describe how these concepts might affect support staff.

Project 8-3

Understanding acceptable uses for e-mail. Search the Web or review magazine articles or textbooks to find definitions or discussions on "e-mail etiquette" or "netiquette." Identify some of the common rules and limits for e-mail. List examples where violations of these rules would affect support staff as they work with customers. Possible Web sites include:

- **http://www.sitecrafters.com**
- **http://www.becrc.org/etiquette.htm**
- **http://www.emailaddresses.com/guide_etiquette.htm**

- http://www-no.ucsd.edu:9323/mail/etiquette.html
- http://www.webfoot.com/advice/email.top.html

Project 8-4

Understanding acceptable uses for voice mail. Search the Web or review business magazines or textbooks for definitions or discussions on "voice mail etiquette" or "voice mail." Identify some of the common recommendations for effective communication between support staff and customers. Possible sites include:

- http://www.justsell.com/content/printnroute/sales/prgs0002.htm
- http://www.qut.edu.au/computing_services/hit/advice/voicemail/
- http://www.seattletimes.com/news/lifestyles/(follow the links to Archives)

Project 8-5

Researching pager basics. Visit the Web site at **http://www.notepage.com/basics.htm** and answer the following questions:

1. How many different ways can pages be sent?
2. Follow the links to the glossary and find the definitions for ASCII, cap code, analog, digital, PCS, and silent alert. How are these terms used by support staff as they complete their work or as they support customers?

Project 8-6

Learning about pagers in the real world. Interview someone who has to carry a pager. Use the following questions to collect information and prepare a report that explains the advantages and disadvantages this person describes for carrying a pager.

1. Does your pager save or store messages?
2. Can you control when or how you receive pages?
3. Have you ever received a page by mistake (someone sent it to the wrong number or person)?
4. How many pages do you get in the course of a day or week?
5. Are the pages you receive alerts or notifications?
6. Have you ever lost messages or your pager? If so, what were the consequences?

Project 8-7

Converting voice messages to text. There is software that works with paging or e-mail to convert voice messages to text (allowing users to forward important e-mail messages to text pagers or e-mail systems. Search the Web for companies that sell voice-to-text conversion software (*Hint:* Search for speech-to-text or text-to-speech conversion software. One Web site available is **http://www.wildfire.com**). Find a demo or tour and write a report that explains some of the benefits this software provides and how it could be used by support staff or customers.

Project 8-8

Researching PDA capabilities. Visit the 3Com Web site at **http://www.palm.com**, the IBM Web site at **http://www.direct.ibm.com**, and the Symbol Technologies Web site at **http://www.symbol.com** and review the information about the Palm Pilot brand of PDAs. (*Hint:* Workpad is the name of the IBM model.) If you are unfamiliar with these devices, take any tours or demos. Then, answer the following questions:

1. What term or application is used to share information between the PDA and a PC?
2. How is data entry completed?
3. How much text can you receive via the e-mail feature?
4. How big is the device?

Project 8-9

Using PDAs for field support. Visit the AvantGo Web site at **http://www.avantgo.com**. Search for **Demonstrations**, and then find and review the PGD demo. What additional useful support information can field staff receive with this system?

Project 8-10

Researching badge location systems. Visit the Arial Systems Web site at **http://www.arialsystems.com** and complete the online tour. Then, answer the following questions:

1. What is the primary advantage the vendor cites for using a personnel locator system?
2. What two ways can you search for staff, according to this page?
3. What other application does this vendor provide, relative to support groups?

Project 8-11

Defining flags within call management software and paging staff. Use the HelpTrac application to flag call records and to practice sending pages to support staff.

1. Flag a ticket so you can easily find it again. Double-click any ticket to open it. Click the **Show Flag** button near the bottom of the screen. Click OK and notice the change in your display.
2. Set up your preferences so a beep sounds if there are new high-priority tickets assigned directly to you. Click **File**, **Preferences**, **Run Control.** Click the **Operation** tab. Make sure the **My high priority tickets** option is selected, and then click OK.
3. Change your profile to indicate you have a pager and enter a pager number and PIN. Click **Profiles**, **Technician**, **Edit** and select your profile from the list of technicians. Click the **Comm** tab and select **Alpha pager**. Enter a fictitious pager number and Pager ID (this would be the pager PIN). Click **OK**.

4. To page someone, you would click the Pager button on that screen. Select any open ticket assigned to Bill@Hardware or Bill Miles. Select the pull-down list for the Assign to field, as if you are going to reassign the ticket. When you see the picklist of technicians and their workloads, click the **View Tech** button for the technician profile. Make sure there are a pager number and Pager ID for this technician and click the **Pager** button. In the Pager Message Selection window, select the Message option button, type **Call me ASAP**, and click **OK**. A dialog box informs you that in the actual program the modem dialer would be invoked (which sends the page).

Project 8-12

Defining escalation and alerts within call management software. Use the HelpTrac Supervisor application to set up escalation periods and create alerts when call records remain open too long. Notify technicians Beth, Bill, and your login name when high-priority items are two-hours old.

1. Click **Lists**, **Priority Codes**. Click the **Generate Exception for Aged Ticket** option button.

2. Click the **Change** button in the Escalation Control list. Drag the names of **Beth**, **Bill** and your login record to the **Controllers** list.

3. Change the priorities at the bottom of the window to the values listed in Table 8-1 and test the new settings:

Table 8-1

Priority	Days/Hours Until Exception	Method of Notification
1	0 days / 1 hour	Display
2	0 days / 8 hours	Display
3	3 days / 0 hours	Display
4	5 days / 0 hours	Display
5	21 days / 0 hours	Email and Display

CASE PROJECTS

1. **Finding Call Management Software with Service Level Management**

Your support group has been using a homegrown call management application. The support manager has finally decided to replace this system with a commercial application. Not only must the new software meet the needs of support staff, but it also needs to include features that help monitor service delivery per your customer service level agreements. As part of the evaluation team, your task is to review the service level features for several applications. Identify at least three call management software vendors (*Hint:* Several vendors were discussed in Chapters 5 and 6). Prepare a report for the rest of the software evaluation team that compares the products. List the features that will help manage service levels. Determine whether the software lets staff members create messages or alerts within the software and if the messages can also be forwarded externally to pagers or e-mail. You also want to determine how frequently the software checks escalation rules (every hour, half hour, or fifteen minutes) to determine if it is time to send an alert.

2. Subscribing to Pager Services

The Johnson Brothers software company, in Denton, Texas, has been growing rapidly, and managers have decided to increase IT staff availability by giving pagers to staff members. They have hired you as a consultant to help them understand the available technology and to make recommendations for software to use from their PCs for sending pages. One of the first tasks you need to complete will be to collect tutorials or glossaries to teach the decision makers about the available technology. You also need to collect at least two samples of paging software that they can evaluate. Your final task will be to prepare a list of service providers for north Texas (*Hint:* Several resources are listed in Appendix A).

3. Electronic Display Boards for PC Screens

You have worked as a team leader in the internal support group at Wayne Industries for several years. Your support group has been growing very rapidly, and the support group is going to have to relocate to a temporary office building. For the short term, facilities management has found office space in another building, but at least half the support staff will have to work in offices and will not be able to see the electronic display boards that are mounted in the main support center. Because this technology has been very helpful, you decide to see if you can find software to simulate a reader board on each PC screen. Search the Web or review office supply catalogs for electronic displays or message boards that are displayed on PC desktops. Collect demos or other marketing materials and compare the types of information they present. You need to find at least two applications that can display telephone information as well as allow managers and staff to send messages. You also need to be able to color code messages, based on priority. Prepare a short report to present to the support manager that includes prices and features for each package.

8

TELEPHONE-BASED TECHNOLOGY

In this chapter you will learn:

♦ The core features of modern telephone technologies

♦ Products that distribute calls automatically to support staff

♦ What technologies combine telephone information and database records

♦ Features of voice response systems and speech recognition software

♦ Vendors that provide telephone-based technology for support groups

Although computer users more and more frequently forward their problems and requests to the help desk electronically by e-mail, fax, or the Internet, the telephone continues to be the most common source of new call records. This is because nearly everyone knows how to communicate by telephone. Improvements in telephone equipment and service, and reasonable rates, ensure that most people have a telephone at home for personal communication with friends and family. Likewise, telephones are essential for business communication. Telephones and related technology link a company to customers, employees, and vendors. As companies expand worldwide, they need special telephone features that can save time when connecting employees between offices and decrease the average time of each telephone call.

Support groups have the same needs as the rest of the company. Their customers call a single telephone number that all support staff share, and the volume of calls that the group receives grows daily. Efficient telephone systems and related technologies enable support staff to streamline their work. Telephony-based devices can collect information from customers before a support person answers the telephone. This saves time so staff members can handle a greater number of calls. The integration of telephone and computer systems is a major development in the evolution of the automated office.

BASIC TELEPHONE TECHNOLOGIES

The telephone is the preferred device for one-to-one communication; it is easy to use and enables a company to complete its business worldwide. Many companies open offices in several major cities or in other countries to increase support and distribution of their products and services. Frequently, employees who work in one part of the country never meet employees who work in a city in another part. Also, when companies merge to consolidate products or eliminate competitors, managers need to disseminate information to all employees, no matter where they are located. Even companies that remain in one location may have so many employees that their offices reside in multiple buildings in different locations within a city. Telephone systems are the most economical way to support all of a company's communication needs.

The internal components of the telephone haven't changed much since Alexander Graham Bell invented the telephone about 100 years ago. A base unit contains the mechanical components: a receiver that translates electrical waves to sound and a speaker that converts sound to electrical waves. The only change that most home telephone users have seen is in dialing methods (pressing individual number buttons instead of turning a round, rotary-based dialer that generates pulse signals).

Business telephone equipment is more complex than personal telephones because a company engages in thousands of one-to-one telephone interactions every day. Office telephone equipment may have a significantly different appearance from home telephones. Many office telephones have connections to multiple telephone lines. Special buttons place callers on hold (so the connection isn't lost) or direct sound from the handset to a speaker (so a group of people can hear the same message). Telephone systems continue to evolve into sophisticated tools for retrieving information.

 Alexander Graham Bell originally worked with the deaf and hoped to find a way to limit their isolation and improve their communication with others. He was studying voice and sound patterns when he realized those patterns could travel over electric lines. This then became the basis for the telephone. Many areas of business, technology, and science have sprouted from this core technology, including computer networks.

Business-oriented telephones include the elements listed in Figure 9-1.

♦ Private telephone networks
♦ Specialized desktop equipment

Figure 9-1   Business telephone components

Business users rely upon internal support groups to manage corporate telecommunications technologies, just as they manage computer systems. Many support groups process requests for telephone additions, moves, and changes. Support analysts troubleshoot telephone problems and answer questions about advanced features in voice mail systems or on telephone sets. Level two and three support staff maintain the telephone network in much the same way as they maintain computer networks. Telephone system administrators define privileges for internal extensions (for example, they allow or deny some extensions the ability to make long-distance telephone calls). They also add users, change connections, delete users, monitor traffic, and maintain the connections from within the company to the outside world.

Private Telephone Networks

Telephone service companies operate public exchanges or connections between cities or regions. An exchange eliminates the need for separate connections between individual telephone users. The telephone company uses a different number code to identify each exchange. In a telephone number, such as 555-3451, the first three digits of the telephone number (555) go through one exchange or connection. A small town may have only one exchange, in which case all seven-digit telephone numbers in the town would begin with the same three numbers.

A business telephone system begins with a device to connect callers outside the company to people within the company. Unlike a telephone at home, which has a direct phone line from the telephone to the public telephone network, companies save money on phone lines by sharing connections. A **private branch exchange (PBX)** is a system that brings telephone signals into a company from the public telephone network and routes them to local telephone lines inside the company. The PBX also generates signals to send calls back to the public telephone network (signals include telephone and network tones such as busy signals, no answer, connection, ringing, no ringing, and modem tones). The business owns or leases the PBX. Many of the early PBXs were manual, which required switchboard operators to route incoming calls to the appropriate desks by using assigned extension numbers. Almost all PBXs are automatic now.

There are several, separate pieces of hardware that are part of a PBX system, including:

- Telephone trunk lines that terminate at the PBX (physical telephone lines are called **trunk lines**). These lines can remain within a single building or extend nationwide to many locations. Trunk lines enable users to transfer calls easily from one location to another by dialing an extension number rather than the entire ten- or seven-digit telephone number.

- The network of lines within the PBX

- A computer with memory that manages the switching of the calls within the PBX and in or out of it. This computer is similar to a PC—it has a cabinet with slots for cards, and different cards provide different types of connections. It also has call control software and routing information because some calls go directly to desks, fax machines, or other devices. Some PBXs run from a PC or interface to a PC so that other applications, such as fax services, can be included.

■ A console or switchboard for a human operator

Appendix A includes a list of some common PBX vendors.

Local telephone companies frequently provide blocks of telephone numbers to call into a company's PBX. This service, called **direct inward dialing (DID)**, allows customers to call a separate telephone number for each person or workstation within the company without requiring the company to install a physical line into the PBX for each possible connection. For example, a company might rent thirty telephone numbers from the telephone company that could be called over eight physical telephone lines. This would permit up to eight ongoing calls at a time; additional inbound calls would receive a busy signal until one of the calls was completed. The PBX automatically switches a call for a given telephone number to the appropriate telephone workstation in the company, which can support voice or fax transmissions. DID service eliminates the need for a switchboard operator. Calls connect faster, and callers feel they are calling a person rather than a company.

Call control software can help process telephone calls by analyzing telephone signals. Each key of a touch-tone telephone generates a unique signal called **dual tone multiple frequency (DTMF)**. The signal is composed of two tones of specific frequencies, which cannot be imitated by voice. Fax machines and modems use DTMF signals to establish communication between computers and equipment. **Automatic number identification (ANI)** is a telephone service that sends the DTMF tones along with the call to identify the telephone number from which the call originates. When the call is routed to a telephone display, staff members can see who is calling before they answer the telephone, and they can decide whether to answer the call immediately or to let the call connect to their voice mail system.

ANI, commonly referred to as **caller ID**, is often used by emergency center dispatchers to save time collecting information and, when necessary, to help locate callers. A telephone company's 911 service usually includes the ANI feature, but calls from another internal extension also show. Home telephone users also may use caller ID to screen calls.

Other call control software may use the source of the telephone call to determine how to process the incoming call. Companies may use different local support telephone numbers, so customers don't pay long-distance charges, but calls to all the telephone numbers route to the same destination. **Dialed number identification service (DNIS)** is a telephone service that identifies the source of calls that are routed to the same destination. DNIS is also used if a company has multiple 800, 888, 877, or 900 numbers that connect to the same destination (possibly as the result of a merger). Calls can be routed to support or marketing groups in the company based on the toll-free number the customer dialed.

Specialized Desktop Equipment

Once the telephone call enters the company's internal telephone network, additional equipment and software routes or stores the telephone calls. Callers who dial in to a single telephone number can use centralized telephone number directories to connect to a specific person. Most automated systems link to voice mail systems (which were discussed in Chapter 8), which enable callers to receive information or leave a message. Callers can also listen to music while they are on hold or waiting to be transferred to other connections.

With appropriate telephone hardware, display lights indicate when new voice mail messages arrive. Some telephone sets, such as the one shown in Figure 9-2, include small displays that show the caller ID information, such as the caller's name or company name, or the caller's internal extension and employee name, for all incoming calls. Larger telephone displays are similar to reader boards: they list the number of callers for a workgroup who are on hold and the average hold time for all callers.

Figure 9-2   Sample telephone with display

TIP Many directories allow callers to locate a person in the list by his or her name, in case they don't know the person's direct telephone number.

AUTOMATIC CALL DISTRIBUTION

Some support groups receive as many calls as a small business—for example, as many as 2000 calls per day may be routed to nearly 400 support staff members. Some telecommunications switches such as PBXs aren't sophisticated enough to process that many calls quickly. Many support groups rely on an **automatic call distributor (ACD),** a technology that manages incoming calls and routes them according to the number called and an associated database of handling instructions. Frequently the most important piece of technology in support, ACDs are designed to route large numbers of incoming calls to people on the basis of rules. If all support staff are busy, the ACD plays a message to inform the caller that all lines are busy and that they are in a queue waiting for staff to become available.

An ACD can work with a PBX or stand alone. Companies that offer sales and service support use ACDs to identify callers, make outgoing responses or calls, forward calls to another party, and gather usage statistics. ACDs can also balance the use of phone lines by switching outgoing calls to different trunk lines. High-end ACD systems include data management and reporting tools. ACDs also provide some form of caller identification similar to that provided by automatic number identification (ANI) or dialed number identification (DNI).

ACDs can be network-based for multiple locations or service a single department. Support groups that have ten or more level one support staff often use an ACD to distribute calls because it is faster and less expensive than a live receptionist. When support staff are available to take telephone calls, they "log in" to the ACD. When they leave for lunch, breaks, or meetings, they log out, and calls are routed to other team members. A complex set of business rules determines how the ACD routes calls. Some ACDs send a new call to the next free agent on a list; others route calls to staff members who have been idle the longest time. Most ACDs route calls to a workgroup or queue of people.

Table 9-1 lists some common automatic call distributor vendors.

Table 9-1   Automatic call distributor vendors

Company	Web Page
Ameritech	http://www.ameritech.com
Aspect	http://www.aspect.com
AVT	http://www.avtc.com
BCS Technologies	http://www.bcstechnologies.com
Call Center Systems	http://www.aaccorp.com
CenterForce Technologies	http://www.cforcetech.com
Cintech	http://www.cintech-cti.com

Table 9-1   Automatic call distributor vendors (continued)

Company	Web Page
Davox (AnswerSoft)	http://www.davox.com
Executone	http://www.executone.com
NexPath	http://www.nexpath.com
NICE, Dees Call Center Division	http://www.dees.com
Nova CTI	http://www.novacti.com
PakNetX	http://www.paknetx.com
Perimeter Technology	http://www.perimetertechnology.com
Rockwell Telecommunications	http://www.ec.rockwell.com
SoftBase Systems	http://www.softbase.com
Teloquent	http://www.teloquent.com
Telrad	http://www.telradusa.com
Teltronics	http://www.teltronics.com

9

Skills-based routing is an ACD feature that matches the requirements of an incoming call to the skill sets of available analysts or analyst groups. The ACD then sends the call to the next available, most qualified analyst. The callers' need may be determined from their caller information using DNIS or ANI and is matched against a list of support skills. In addition to qualifications, skills-based routing can distribute calls according to other rules. International support groups may need to route calls on the basis of language skills. Other support groups route high-priority calls differently from other calls. If all level one support staff are on the telephone or not available, calls may be routed to level two support staff who are designated to pick up overflow level one calls. Many ACD vendors integrate information about waiting calls with reader boards or other electronic displays to alert staff when they are on the telephone with other calls.

ACD administrators can also give callers additional choices if they cannot reach a support analyst immediately. Delay announcements tell callers what the average wait time has been for the last hour and how many callers precede them in the queue. Callers then have the choice of staying on the line or leaving a voice mail message. When a support staff member becomes available, the ACD automatically routes the voice mail to the available analysts rather than waiting for the support staff to retrieve the message.

ACDs have an advantage over PBXs in routing calls because they collect and store call statistics. A support manager or team leader can check the ACD at any time to see how many staff members are logged in, who is logged off, and how long they have been logged off. Large support centers use these statistics to schedule staff and predict call volumes. Basic call statistics include the:

- Number of telephone calls per shift

- Number of times a call was transferred from one analyst or workgroup to another

- Average time in seconds to answer a call

- Average time callers spend on hold (an acceptable hold time is thirty seconds or less; most callers won't wait on hold longer than about three minutes)

- Average length of each call

- Number of times calls are abandoned (callers who don't reach an analyst may hang up rather than remain on hold or leave a message)

As discussed in Chapter 4, support managers use these statistics to understand how often their customers request services and whether there are enough support staff to answer telephone calls. The more frequently customers call and wait on hold or abandon the call, the more likely it is that they will become unhappy.

Some ACDs allow managers to monitor calls for quality assurance. Random telephone calls are recorded and replayed to ensure that support staff are courteous and have clear pronunciation and proper inflection. These tapes can also be used to teach staff members how to handle difficult customer situations. External support staff can learn how and when to discuss new products or services for add-on sales when customers call for other information. Sophisticated ACD systems allow managers to interrupt a telephone conversation if necessary to calm down a customer or provide supervisor-level assistance. Other ACDs allow managers to view the computer screens support staff navigate, while the managers monitor the telephone conversation.

Appendix A includes a list of vendors that provide real-time telephone system monitoring.

COMPUTER TELEPHONY INTEGRATION

Computer telephony integration (CTI) software links telephone-originated information—such as caller name, the telephone number the person called from, and the number the person dialed—to other computer information systems. Much overlapping functionality exists between PBXs and ACDs because vendors continually add more features to both. CTI enables telecommunications devices, PBXs, ACDs, and corporate databases to work together. Software, such as CTI, that links common hardware technologies is called **middleware**. Telephony middleware was developed as telephone vendors and computer manufacturers standardized ways to link computers to telephone systems. IBM provided one of the first workable CTI applications, now sold as "CallPath."

Automated attendants are CTI applications that play a recorded message according to defined criteria. For example, customers who call after business hours may hear a message with the company's usual business hours. Some messages explain the caller's options if the number called is busy or if the recipient has logged out of the system temporarily.

CTI applications can integrate caller messages with databases and word processors. Using automatic number identification (ANI) or dialed number information services (DNI) from the ACD, a CTI application can provide information about the caller pulled from databases or other applications before a support analyst answers the telephone. Displaying records based on ANI or DNIS from a call management or marketing application is a feature commonly called a **screen pop**. As the ACD routes a telephone call to an available support analyst, the CTI software compares the ANI to the customer records. It can retrieve either the customer profile or a list of all open call records for that caller. Screen pops can shave thirty to sixty seconds off a call. However, ANI cannot be relied on all the time because customers may place calls from other users' telephones.

> Some CTI support software enables analysts to dial customers directly from the call record screen by selecting a button within the application.

As support staff transfer telephone calls to other support persons, the caller and the database information about the caller transfer to the new analyst at his or her workstation. Intelligent call transferring saves time because customers don't have to repeat themselves to another support person. Transferred calls also carry with them the history of the telephone call—such as the support persons involved, when the call started, and how long the customer has been on the phone or was waiting on hold.

> CTI applications enable companies to save money by decreasing the length of telephone calls made to the support groups' toll-free numbers. As the length of calls decreases, support staff can also handle more calls.

The latest CTI applications integrate voice mail, incoming fax, and e-mail systems with other telephone-based activities in a single application program. Support staff can use a single inbox for any kind of message and process items in the order they were received. They can receive fax messages from several incoming numbers and route those to departmental printers or electronic inboxes. They can also use a graphical user interface (rather than a telephone keypad) to initiate or receive calls, forward telephone calls to higher support levels, and have conference calls with other support staff. Support staff can drag the customer's name to a telephone icon on their PC to dial the customer, retrieve the latest call record, and open a log file in one step. While looking at a customer record, they can drag a file to a fax icon, and the CTI software automatically retrieves the customer's fax number. CTI applications can also be used to automatically forward call-related information, such as the date and time of support calls, to billing or invoice systems.

CTI was originally used in large telephone networks because only very large call centers could justify the costs of the required equipment installation. This has changed. Most local telephone service companies now offer ANI or DNIS more frequently and inexpensively. Also, many ACD systems are now PC-based. Microsoft Windows CTI applications use **Telephony Application Programming Interface (TAPI)**, which is a standard program interface between PCs and telephone-based communication devices. TAPI provides a way for a program to detect dual tone multiple frequency digits and covers a wide array of services, ranging from initializing a modem and placing a call to directing the voice through a

9

microphone to the telephone system. Using TAPI, programmers can take advantage of different telephone systems and PBXs without having to understand all their details.

 TAPI was developed jointly by Intel and Microsoft and is included with the Windows 95/98/2000 and NT operating systems. **Telephone Services Application Programming Interface (TSAPI)** is the telephony interface used on Novell networks.

Table 9-2 lists some common CTI vendors.

Table 9-2 CTI software vendors

Company	Web Page
Converse Network Systems	http://www.comversens.com
CTiTEK	http://www.ctitek.com
Dialogic Corporation	http://www.dialogic.com
EasyRun Communication Software Systems	http://www.easyrun.com
Genesys	http://www.genesyslab.com
IBM	http://www.ibm.com
N-Soft	http://www.n-soft.com
Periphonics	http://www.peri.com

Voice Response Units

An **Interactive Voice Response (IVR)** system is a combination of hardware and software that allows people to ask questions and provide answers through a telephone. IVR systems automate data entry and eliminate the need for twenty-four-hour staffing for noncritical questions. These customer-oriented applications can actually increase the number of calls a support group receives without increasing its voice mail messages. The IVR can pass data entered through the telephone keypad, so customers can query databases without support staff assistance.

Nearly everyone who has ever called a utility company or bank has experience using an IVR system. Many businesses, as well as support groups, use IVR technology to provide customer information. Customers can retrieve information about:

- **Available services:** Customers can quickly access common information such as a list of services in their selected area or a company's business hours. In most cases, callers enter their area code or ZIP code to personalize the IVR response.

- **Account balances:** Customers use bank IVRs to check account or credit balances over the telephone. To maintain security, customers must enter either a Social Security number or a personal identification number (PIN) to validate their right to access the selected account.

- **Government agencies:** Federal and state agencies establish toll-free numbers that use IVRs so callers can find answers to questions and reach the correct office for service.

- **Special product offers:** Some vendors set up temporary numbers for customers to order a single selected item or reserve products until they can pick them up. The number passes callers to an IVR where the customers enter credit card information and the number of items they wish to purchase.

- **Insurance claims:** Callers can check the status of insurance claims and the payments they make to insurance companies and medical offices.

- **Stock trades:** Customers use IVRs to place trade orders and check account balances with their brokers.

- **Educational programs:** Colleges and universities use IVRs to direct calls about student services and educational programs.

If any of the customer queries listed above can't be handled automatically, IVRs route the calls to support staff, or use recorded messages to inform customers when support staff are available.

Companies can place IVR systems in different locations in a telecommunications network. Some IVR systems prompt customers to indicate a preferred language, and then route calls to bilingual support staff or present additional questions in the chosen language. An IVR can accept telephone calls as they come in to the company, preprocess common questions with prerecorded answers, and then route the remaining calls to an ACD (which has its own rules for routing calls directly to staff members). An IVR can also receive calls from the ACD and allow customers to select voice mail or fax systems from a list of options.

There may be several points in IVR processing at which customers can listen to prerecorded announcements. When a caller is following up on an existing service call, some CTI applications use an IVR to accept a call record number from the customer before completing a screen pop. Ultimately, a well-designed IVR workflow handles as many repeat calls as possible and routes telephone calls that need human skill and intellect to an agent.

Table 9-3 lists some common IVR vendors.

Table 9-3 IVR vendors

Company	Web Page
Aculab	http://www.aculab.com
Aspect Telecommunications	http://www.aspect.com
Bicom	http://www.bicom-inc.com
Brite Voice Systems	http://www.brite.com
Corepoint	http://www.corepoint.com
Crystal	http://www.crystalpc.com
Edify	http://www.edify.com
Envox	http://www.envox.com

Table 9-3   IVR vendors (continued)

Company	Web Page
GM Voices	http://www.gmvoices.com
Interactive Digital	http://www.interactivedigital.com
InterVoice-Brite	http://www.intervoice.com
Lucent Technologies	http://www.lucent.com
MediaSoft Telecom	http://www.mediasoft.com
Nortel Networks	http://www.nortel.com
Periphonics	http://www.peri.com
Syntellect	http://www.syntellect.com
TALX	http://www.talx.com

The functionality of IVR systems can be enhanced with additional features. Figure 9-3 lists the add-on options that can expand IVR support services.

◆ Voice recognition

◆ Speech synthesis

◆ Fax services

Figure 9-3   IVR add-on options

Voice Recognition

One of the distinctions between an ACD and an IVR is that many IVRs can process voice signals in addition to dial tones. **Automatic speech recognition (ASR)** is computer software that recognizes certain human speech and translates it to instructions other computer programs can process. The speech most easily "understood" by these programs is usually discrete numbers and short commands, such as credit card numbers, telephone numbers, or a limited group of words spoken together. Callers speak their answers to questions, instead of using the telephone keypad, which may be easier to use for some people who may not always have their hands free to interact with the IVR, for example, travelers. A customer who wants to find the correct airport gate may be prompted for a multiple-choice response ("Do you want arrivals or departures?"), can confirm that the IVR understood the request ("Did you say departures?"), and can provide specific information ("What is the flight number?") by speaking answers.

Voice recognition is certainly more user-friendly than other automated systems. It provides access for callers without touch-tone telephones, and enables callers who can't see or push buttons well to communicate. It is definitely easier to speak the name of a person you are trying to reach than to spell the last name using the telephone touch pad. Not only are voice systems easier to use, they are also closer to the way we usually interact and require less time to learn.

Some companies are experimenting with voice recognition and voice imprints to prevent fraud and telephone theft. Each person has a unique voiceprint as well as a fingerprint. In the future, this unique voiceprint will be recorded and saved to control access to personal information.

Text to Speech

IVR systems that access personal account information frequently use text-to-speech applications to return the requested information. **Speech synthesis** systems translate written text (retrieved from a database, e-mail, or other file) to audio sounds. Text to speech is appropriate when it is not practical to prerecord all the available options or information. For example, a checking account balance could be any amount, ranging from a few cents to thousands of dollars. It would take much longer to find the correct answer in a recorded list of possible answers than it would to synthesize an answer based on the numbers that represent the amount found in a database. A speech synthesis application is also cheaper than having an attendant read information from a database.

Telephone directory assistance was one of the first applications to benefit from text-to-speech conversion. However, as the Internet and e-mail become more popular, more people are using text-to-speech systems to access their e-mail boxes or fax mail boxes when they are away from their computers.

Appendix A lists some voice recognition and speech synthesis vendors.

Fax Services

IVR systems can integrate both incoming and outbound faxes. Customers can request written product or support information through a fax back or **fax-on-demand** application. An IVR prompts callers through a list of questions as they decide which documents to receive. Additional prompts collect the caller's fax number and schedule the fax on the fax server.

A **fax server** is a computer with fax software. The fax software accepts requests from other computers on the network and attempts to send the fax through a modem (rather than a dedicated fax machine). The software also records errors that result when the receiving fax is busy or the telephone number doesn't connect to a fax device. The fax server can also receive incoming faxes.

Fax-on-demand applications answer questions quickly because customers don't have to wait for someone to return a phone call or mail them information. Fax services can reduce common support questions about how to install or set up computer hardware or software. Faxes may also be easier for customers to use than a recorded announcement if they request a lot of detailed information and are more informative than spoken answers because they can include pictures or diagrams. The IVR can collect the callers' fax numbers or telephone numbers so support staff can follow up later. CTI applications also collect detailed records of the specific documents requested.

Support staff can also use fax systems to broadcast service bulletins, product announcements, or customer-oriented newsletters. Broadcast faxes can be scheduled for after business hours (to take advantage of lower telephone rates) and sent to large groups of customers.

Fax services are more frequently used in external support groups for technical support and in call centers to forward product information. Internal support groups most frequently use intranet Web pages to distribute the same information. Internal support groups will supplement the Web pages with fax services for remote offices that cannot access the intranet or do not use computers.

> **TIP** Additional software is now available to convert fax information to other forms. Incoming faxes can be converted from graphical formats to text and may automatically update an existing call record. There is also software that converts fax documents to speech, similar to systems that convert e-mail to speech.

MARK THISTLEWAITE, ARCHITECT
CALL CENTER AND SUPPORT CONSULTING FOR A LARGE CONSULTING COMPANY
LAKE FOREST, CALIFORNIA

GUIDELINES FOR GOOD IVR DESIGN

An IVR can be considered an extension of the support group—when it is designed well, it functions as another member of the support team. In many cases, the voice that customers hear when they call the support group is the voice recorded on the IVR, it is important to make sure that the interactions between customers and IVR options are efficient and designed with the customers' (not the support group's) needs in mind.

There are several guidelines I recommend when setting up an IVR for support:

- **Professional voice:** Because the first point of contact is a recorded voice, it's important that the voice sounds professional and courteous. The yellow pages of any phone book will list companies that provide professional "voices." If someone within the company can provide this, it's important that they speak quickly, but clearly.

- **Menu options:** Most people can keep a limited number of items in their short-term memory (usually four to six items), so don't put more options on a menu than they can remember. Three options is the ideal because they can be delivered in a few seconds.

- **Menu levels:** Once you select the first option, it should not take more than a couple of additional sets of menus before the customer is routed to a real person.

- **Expert mode:** The IVR should support dial through, which means that menu options can be selected before the entire menu finishes. Any menu options that are more commonly selected by all customers should be listed early in the menu (as options #1 or #2) and the less frequently used options should be listed later in the list.

- **Warn users of changes:** Managers and administrators need to review call statistics regularly and make changes to IVR menus or prompts if necessary. If many customers use the IVR repeatedly, it's important to warn them for a short time (one or two weeks) that the order of menus may have changed, in case they are used to using expert mode.

- **Option to exit:** In some cases, it may not be readily apparent which option the customer should select. If he or she is confused, a way to exit from the IVR menu system in order to reach a "live" person should be provided. Many systems use the "0" menu option to route these callers to someone who can either answer their questions, or who can find someone in the support group who can.

Behind the scenes, it is also important that support managers and system administrators make sure that the IVR connects and disconnects properly with the telephone system. Customers may abandon calls (just as they will when on hold) at any point in the IVR menu system. Failure to have a reliable disconnect method can result in significant costs in line charges and lost customer goodwill (especially if another customer can get a previous customer's session). This should be reviewed carefully when setting up the IVR.

As the business needs change, the interactions between the IVR or support group and the customer may need to change as well. The IVR can handle repeat questions about system availability for different groups of users. There may also be different messages for different times of the day. The IVR should also generate some statistics that the support manager can evaluate to see which options are used and how long it takes to traverse through the longest set of menus before the customer reaches a live person.

A poorly designed IVR is *worse* than a bad support staff member. Menus that are confusing or that take too long will result in lost calls. For external support groups and call centers, this can mean lost revenue. For internal support, it means customer frustration and more problems that are escalated to support management.

9

INTERNET PROTOCOL TELEPHONY

Internet protocol telephony (IP telephony) uses the same telecommunications connections that support the Internet to exchange voice, fax, and other data that usually are carried over the public telephone network. Using the Internet, calls travel as packets of data on shared lines. Voice data delivered this way is called **voice over IP (VoIP)**, and many PC modems now support data, fax, and voice transmissions.

> **TIP** An advantage of voice over IP is that it avoids the tolls charged by ordinary telephone service. Customers with local phone numbers to their Internet provider are also making local calls over the Internet.

Customers can use a single telephone line at home for simultaneous Internet and telephone access. They begin a VoIP by browsing a vendor's Web site, using their Internet connection and Web browser software. If customers need help or want more information about something they see on a Web page, they select a button to contact support. A CTI application connects customers to the support group, passes the Web information to the support center, and opens a telephone line to the customer, similar to intelligent call transferring through an ACD.

The customer speaks to a support staff member through the modem using a PC microphone. At the same time, support staff receive an image of the Web page the customer is browsing, similar to the way they can see a PC screen when using remote control software (although support staff can only watch as customers visit Web pages; they have no keyboard control). They can direct customers to other Web pages or answer questions using other standard support tools.

CHAPTER SUMMARY

❏ Managing telephone calls is a by-product of support. All business users rely on telephone technologies to conduct day-to-day business. Telephone systems have changed little in the 100 years since Alexander Graham Bell invented them, but new technologies are required to handle the increasing numbers of telephone calls coming into a business (or support group).

❏ PBX systems allow businesses to share connections with the rest of the telephone network community. A PBX system includes telephone trunk lines, a network of lines within the PBX, a computer with memory, call control software, and a console or switchboard for a human operator. Additional technologies, such as voice mail and fax systems, pick up activities that PBX systems cannot complete. Standard telephone services provide caller information that can be passed to other systems and processed with CTI software.

❏ ACD systems distribute a large number of incoming calls to a large number of business users more quickly than a human operator. Most systems provide basic statistics on the telephone calls as well, so managers can analyze call volumes.

❏ CTI software is middleware that connects computer information with telephone information, and then presents or processes it. Some call management applications accept this data in the form of screen pops—as the analyst answers the telephone the data appears on the PC desktop. Microsoft Windows-based computers use the TAPI protocol to initialize modems, send DTMF signals, and generate ringing sounds, so users know what is happening during the connection.

◻ IVRs present lists of questions and accept data, usually from a telephone keypad. They can increase the number of processed telephone calls by helping customers find their own answers to common questions and directing calls. An IVR can forward calls from a PBX to an ACD or accept calls from an ACD for more processing. IVR systems are already used by many businesses and can be enhanced further with speech recognition or fax back options.

◻ New technologies, such as IP telephony, convert voice transmissions to data packets and use Internet lines to forward any kind of data. IP Telephony allows a customer to communicate over a single telephone line and can forward both voice and data, similarly to an ACD system with screen pops.

KEY TERMS

automated attendants — CTI applications that play a recorded message based on defined criteria.

automatic number identification (ANI) — A telephone service that sends the DTMF tones along with the call to identify the telephone number that the call originates from.

automatic call distributor (ACD) — A system that manages incoming calls and handles them according to the number called and an associated database of handling instructions.

automatic speech recognition (ASR) — Computer software that recognizes certain human speech and translates it to instructions that other computer programs can process.

caller ID — *See* automatic number identification.

computer telephony integration (CTI) — Software that links telephone-originated information—such as caller name, the telephone number the person called from, and the number the person dialed—to other computer information systems.

dialed number identification service (DNIS) — A telephone service that identifies the source of calls that are routed to the same destination.

direct inward dialing (DID) — A telephone service that allows customers to use individual telephone numbers for each person or workstation within the company without requiring a physical line into the PBX for each possible connection.

dual tone multiple frequency (DTMF) — A unique signal generated as you press the telephone's touch keys.

fax-on-demand — An application that allows customers to request written product or support information from a network fax system.

fax server — A computer with fax software.

interactive voice response (IVR) — A combination of hardware and software that allows people to ask questions and provide answers through a telephone.

Internet Protocol telephony (IP telephony) — Uses the same telecommunications connections that support the Internet to exchange voice, fax, and other data that are usually carried over the public telephone network.

middleware — Software that links common hardware technologies together.

9

private branch exchange (PBX) — A system that brings telephone signals into a company from the public telephone network and routes them to local telephone lines inside the company.

screen pop — Displaying records based on ANI or DNIS from a call management or marketing application.

skills-based routing — An ACD feature that matches the requirements of an incoming call to the skill sets of available analysts or analyst groups.

speech synthesis — Translates written text to audio sounds.

Telephony Application Programming Interface (TAPI) — A Microsoft Windows program interface between PCs and telephone-based communication.

Telephone Services Application Programming Interface (TSAPI) — The telephony interface used on Novell networks.

trunk lines — Physical telephone lines.

voice over IP (VoIP) — Voice data delivered over the Internet.

REVIEW QUESTIONS

1. List three reasons why a business telephone may look different from one used in someone's home.

2. IT staff manage telephone systems in ways that are similar to _____.

3. It is important to understand what a PBX provides in a business setting because:

   a. all business users must understand PBXs to use the telephone.

   b. additional technologies pick up calls from a PBX for further processing.

   c. customers must interact directly with a PBX when they call for support.

   d. support staff manage the PBX.

4. List three signals that a PBX sends to a public telephone network.

5. If everyone in a company has a direct telephone number rather than just an extension, the telephone company is providing what type of service?

6. A PBX is a computer system that works with the telephone network. True or False?

7. What part of the telephony system works with voice mail to show a light on a telephone, indicating that there is a new voice mail message?

   a. the ACD

   b. the IVR

   c. the PBX

   d. call control software

8. Which telephone service indicates the toll-free telephone number that a caller dialed?

9. Which telephone service is commonly known as caller ID?

10. Which of the following technologies is the most important for a support center of fifty support analysts?

    a. an ACD

    b. a problem management application

    c. a call management application

    d. a fax server

11. List three support skills that might be used in skills-based routing.

12. Because technologies overlap, there are some common features between ACD and PBX systems. Identify one feature that is provided only with an ACD system.

13. Which of the following statements is true?

    a. CTI is software that connects telephone systems.

    b. CTI is a category of software that connects telephony hardware and other applications.

    c. CTI merges telephone and database information into a single database.

    d. All support groups use CTI applications.

14. When would saving thirty seconds per call become significant in a support group?

15. What is one small but real problem about using ANI to generate screen pops?

16. What is the greatest savings from a CTI application?

17. The most common telephony system used in business is a(n) _____. Many businesses use these for repeat questions.

18. An IVR system is a special form of CTI that can query a database for information. True or False?

19. An IVR cannot:

    a. route calls from a PBX to an ACD.

    b. completely replace support staff for common questions.

    c. interface with voice mail.

    d. route calls according to language requirements.

20. List two examples of common speech patterns that are frequently understood by automatic speech recognition applications.

21. What is one of the oldest applications of text to speech? When is text to speech used?

22. What are two advantages of using fax-on-demand systems to provide customer information?

9

HANDS-ON PROJECTS

Project 9-1

Understanding telephone basics. Brantford Ontario is known as the place where Alexander Graham Bell invented the telephone. Visit the town's Sesquicentennial Festival Web site at **http://207.61.52.13/comdir/festivals/sesqui** and follow the links to **History**. Review an article about Alexander Graham Bell and what led him to invent the telephone. There are additional links at the How Stuff Works Web site at **http://www.howstuffworks.com** and the Telestra Web site at **http://www.telstra.com.au/learnit/sec_3_1.html** that explain how the telephone exchange was originally designed and developed. Write a short report that summarizes at least three significant developments in telephone technology.

Project 9-2

Comparing telecommunications and computer terminology. Visit the Claremont Internet Press Web page at **http://clp.net/clp-dict.html** for telecommunications terminology or the Tribute to the Telephone Web site at **http://telecom-digest.org/tribute**. How many telecommunications terms are also used in the computer industry? Prepare a list of ten common terms. What can you surmise from this?

Project 9-3

Understanding CTI components. Visit the Genesys Web page at **http://www.genesyslab.com**. Review the diagram of the complex CTI hardware framework. What telephony and nontelephony technologies can be integrated under this framework? What statistics are collected? (*Hint:* Search for DART and Call-Center Pulse papers.)

Project 9-4

Using integrated voice and fax software. Use the **Visual Call Management** application from Key Voice (http://www.dialogic.com/free/4894web.htm) located on the Data Disk. Run the executable file and unzip all the files. Load the Help file and follow the links to view **Visual Call Management (VCM) and Fax from the Desktop.** Select **VCM Call Control Features (click here to see this now)** and answer the following questions:

1. What options are available when you get a telephone call?

2. What other tools are accessible from this application?

3. Search the help and play the Email reader. What are your impressions of this feature?

4. Play back the sample mailbox greeting. What options are given for immediate assistance?

5. What feature(s) are available for employees who may be away from the office?

Project 9-5

Understanding CTI basics. Visit the Dialogic Web site at **http://www.dialogic.com**. Find the white paper titled "Basic Capabilities of Automated Computer Telephony Systems." Review three features that are not covered in this chapter and give practical examples of how they could be applied in a support group.

Project 9-6

Finding current telephone articles. Review current magazines for articles on telephone-based technology, or visit the Hello Direct Web site at **http://www.hellodirect.com**. Select an article, tutorial, or product review about a subject related to this chapter and then summarize the additional information you learn.

Project 9-7

Using integrated CTI software. Visit the Dialogic Web site at **http://www.dialogic.com** and follow the links to the free software, Interactive demos. Download the **Call Management: CallXpress Desktop Call Manager (Interactive Demo)**. Run the executable file and then answer the following questions:

1. What information is included in the call list?
2. What are the options for incoming calls?
3. How do you determine the caller's ID?
4. What PC Personal Information Manager applications are supported for tracking customer database information?
5. What performance statistics are collected by the application?
6. What is another term that this vendor uses for IVR?

9

Project 9-8

Reviewing automated agent software features. Visit the AVT Web site at **http://www.avtc.com** and follow the links for CTI software. Search for **Automated Agent (Demo)**. Download and install this software. This multimedia presentation walks you through the features and benefits of the AVT product.

Answer the following questions:

1. What technologies can be integrated with this application?
2. What are the benefits summarized from the overview?
3. What examples of text-to-voice information are provided?
4. How does the caller interact with this application?
5. How are customizations completed?

Project 9-9

Using speech synthesis software. Visit the Dialogic Web site at **http://www.dialogic.com** and follow the links to free software. Download a copy of **TextTalk**, the text-to-speech conversion software. Extract the files from the .exe file and answer the following questions:

1. Load the **sample.txt** file. Experiment with the different voices. Which sound more mechanical?

2. Open the Dictionary and add your name (or the name of someone incorrectly pronounced in the dictionary). Experiment with different examples until it sounds like your name.

3. Enter a short sentence. What happens if you change the sentence to a question? How do commas change the pronunciation of a sentence?

4. Load one of the e-mail text files. What is the difference when you select **Intelligent Preprocessing**?

Project 9-10

Experimenting with voice recognition. Visit the Altech Web site at **http://www.altech.com** and search for demos. Try the **Stock Quotes** demo. Change your voice several times. Were you able to confuse the speech recognition system? How do you know when the application understands you?

Project 9-11

Using IVRs with voice recognition. Call one of the two telephone systems listed below, follow the prompts, and write a short report describing your experiences.

▫ Bell South's Val system—(904) 248-1496

▫ Sears Store Directory—call a local Sears store

Project 9-12

Understanding fax-on-demand software features. Visit the Surecom Web site at **http://www.surecom.com** and follow the links to the **Fax on Demand** software. Review the product documentation and then answer the follow questions:

1. What hardware is required for this service?

2. What customer information can be collected? Why would this be important for a support group?

3. What support-oriented statistics can be collected?

CASE PROJECTS

1. Justifying an ACD purchase

As a team leader for your support group, you have identified several repeat calls that could be answered with an automated system. You want to prepare a report for your manager that will document the benefits that an ACD brings to support groups. You decide to look for companies that already use ACDs to get firsthand information. Visit the library for support and telephone magazines and prepare a report of four companies that use ACDs. Be sure to include the number of calls these companies receive per day, the types of products or services they support, and the performance statistics they collect. (*Hint:* You can find many of these articles in the archives of CallCenter, Support Management, Teleconnect, and Computer Telephony magazines.)

2. Designing a Good IVR

You are the manager of a support group that uses ACD and IVR technology. One of the most common customer complaints is that your IVR takes too long to use. Your ACD statistics also show that although many calls come into the support group, at least half of the calls are abandoned. You suspect that the IVR prompts and menus are too complex. Using IVR magazines, market research reports, and Web sites, locate articles that discuss how to design a good IVR system. Look for discussions that explain what encourages customers to use an IVR. Identify two key elements for an effective IVR that you can use to evaluate your current system. (*Hint:* The Call Center Web page at **http://www.call-center.net** includes a tutorial link to "IVR/VRU User Interface Design Best Practices.")

3. Teaching Support Staff about IVRs

You are an employee-training specialist at the Jefferson National Bank. The company's new Web page has caused an increase in the number of questions customers have about bank services. The support group is small, but now it must add technology to help handle the additional telephone calls. The support manager would like install an IVR, but most of the support staff fear that the technology will be too hard for customers to use or will lead to even more telephone calls. The manager asks you to find some tutorials on IVR technology that demonstrate how easy it is to use an IVR for banking information. Collect at least two magazine articles about financial organizations that successfully use IVR systems. Also, locate a Web-based tutorial or demo that demonstrates how an IVR works. (*Hint:* Bigcat Systems at **http://www.bigcat.net** has an IVR demo that creates a bank account.)

9

CHAPTER

10

OFFICE SPACE IN THE SUPPORT ENVIRONMENT

In this chapter you will learn:

♦ How common work areas affect employee efficiency and health

♦ Ways to improve comfort within an employee's individual work area

♦ Techniques to improve the support environment

Support groups buzz with activity. Telephones ring. Visual alarms appear. Automated notifications sound. Staff arriving or leaving cause heavy traffic, especially in large support groups that stagger work shifts. Staff members meet in hallways or open areas close to other employees to discuss problems. With all this activity, support staff can be distracted easily. Other aspects of the job can lead to additional stress. Impatient, frustrated, and even hostile customers can become abusive and raise their voices over the telephone. Support staff must remain proficient in the applications they support and keep up with the workload. At the same time, they have to remember different procedures for each kind of problem.

Sophisticated technology enables support staff to handle more problems, but the physical environment can affect employees' productivity as well as their health. Environments that minimize physical and mental stresses make it easier for front-line support staff to remain friendly and patient with callers. In high-stress occupations, such as support, employees must develop ways to manage stress. Because much of their work requires computer interaction, support staff must also develop good work habits to remain healthy and prevent injuries.

The physical design and location of the help desk or customer support center can add to or detract from the support staff's efficiency. Although staff members have little control over the physical location and type of equipment their company selects, they can control their immediate workspace to reduce the effects of stress and improve productivity.

SHARED WORKPLACE ELEMENTS THAT AFFECT EMPLOYEES

The **Occupational Safety and Health Administration (OSHA)**, an agency of the U.S. Department of Labor, is dedicated to reducing hazards in the workplace and enforcing job-safety standards for all employers. OSHA educates companies on their responsibilities to their employees. Federal laws require all employers to provide adequate lighting, ventilation, and sound control. Not only do employers face government fines if they fail to meet these standards, but they also risk legal costs from workers' compensation claims and other work-related liabilities.

Support groups are at greater risk for these basic violations. When understaffed, support staff may work additional hours to pick up the unanswered calls or to resolve outstanding problems. As a result, staff members may sit in the same place for hours at a time without physical rest breaks to prevent eye and back strain. If staff members type for long periods or work where they cannot properly align their bodies to the keyboard and mouse, they may overwork their hands and arms.

Not every manager has the luxury of redesigning the physical layout of the support center. Many support groups begin as small organizations and grow as they add services or merge with other help desks after a corporate acquisition. At that time, the support group may have the opportunity to move into a larger office area. Companies that specialize in designing support centers or help desks assist in addressing those special challenges for the support environment. These companies work with the support manager to maximize the available space and create an attractive workplace that easily meets workplace standards.

 Many support center design companies, after redesigning the support center, have helped support managers show productivity increases and better employee retention. Employees frequently stay in a job or location longer when they enjoy their surroundings.

Employees may share some elements of the workplace, which are listed in Figure 10-1.

> ♦ Offices or cubicles
> ♦ Lighting
> ♦ Noise level

Figure 10-1   Shared workplace elements

Offices or Cubicles

The number of support staff, the way they work together, and the available space determine whether support staff work in offices or cubicles. Individual offices are usually too expensive. Most help desks have a few offices around the outside of the building and open areas for cubicles in the center. Common spaces, such as meeting rooms, break rooms, and restrooms, may be in the center of the building, away from staff member desks. Copy machines, fax machines, and shared printers are usually placed within easy access of the groups of people who use them.

Cubicles are attractive and functional work areas. Figure 10-2 shows a standard cubicle arrangement that can be used for any workgroup, as well as for support staff.

10

Figure 10-2   Office cubicles

Cubicles provide a definite advantage when support staff need to work together as teams. The walls between individual workspaces are low, usually only three to four feet tall so staff can easily interact and view electronic reader boards. Partition walls between cubicles may be taller to reduce noise, but taller walls inhibit easy collaboration. A five-foot partition wall is an acceptable compromise; it is short enough for most employees to look over to ask a quick question, yet tall enough to reduce noise. Figure 10-3 shows cubicles with low partitions. Some cubicles include sections of glass in the partitions rather than fabric. The glass reduces noise, but allows others to see if employees are on the telephone or already working with others.

There are several ways to arrange cubicle offices. A traditional layout has the cubicles arranged in straight rows with even aisles. This creates the most employee space and easy access to each employee. Support staff who support common products are physically close to each other. A modification to the traditional arrangement places cubicles diagonally. This diagonal layout uses space better, because aisles can be narrower, and helps reduce noise, because there are few long, clear aisles for sound to move through. Large companies may cluster cubicles. The clustered cubicles are square, but grouped together with shorter aisles between them to fit more people into less space. Clusters also allow very good communication between groups but result in more confusing access to employees because aisles are not regularly spaced.

Figure 10-3   Cubicles with low partitions

A new cubicle layout is the star arrangement (also called a pinwheel or pod configuration). Cubicles are attached in the center and are wider at the outer edges of the arrangement. Star arrangements include three to six workspaces, depending upon the number of team members. Managers or team leaders can easily walk around the outer edges to review terminals and offer assistance. The partition walls between workspaces are low, so staff members can look at other team members with little effort and they can easily stand up to attract a manager's attention when necessary. Figure 10-4 shows a star cubicle arrangement.

Figure 10-4   Star cubicle arrangement

> Most office design standards recommend at least 35 square feet of personal work area per employee, which translates to a 5 by 7-foot cubicle. If an employee needs more computer equipment or space for frequently used reference materials and manuals, the space should be larger.

Level two or three support staff may work in cubicles grouped next to the front-line staff area or in offices. Depending upon the type of problems or requests they handle, several people may share an office or each employee may have an individual office. Offices provide a quieter problem-solving environment. Support staff can control interruptions and reduce distracting noise by closing the door when they work on difficult problems. However, offices diminish the synergy of team problem solving unless support staff leave their offices to join the group.

Lighting

Bad lighting isn't an obvious workplace problem because it doesn't directly cause physical injury. However, it can lead to employee discomfort. Too little light will make analysts squint and strain to see paperwork or the computer monitor. Too much light causes eyestrain, headaches, and fatigue. Office workers may not immediately realize that they are suffering from improper light, they just know they have headaches and are tired and stressed. The OSHA standard recommends indirect lighting in soothing colors (soft white rather than bright white); employees may need to supplement overhead lighting with a small, adjustable desk lamp.

Computer terminals and PC monitors that face windows usually have a lot of glare, which is a symptom of too much light. If possible, monitors should be placed with their sides to the window. To soften glare, the support group should either provide an antiglare screen for the monitor or spray the glass with an antiglare coating.

The contrast between images displayed on a terminal also causes eyestrain. Text and pictures (which are called foreground objects) appear against a solid color (called the background). If support staff can control their monitor's color display, they can change the background and foreground colors to create a greater contrast and reduce eyestrain. Yellow, cyan, or white letters on a black or navy blue background provide a change from black letters on a white or gray background.

> Some employees regularly change their Windows desktop themes to display different colors, patterns, or images. Not only do some color combinations provide better contrast, but also nature-oriented pictures of trees or waterfalls may help employees relax. Laughter is another stress reducer, and some employees prefer cartoon characters or animated objects for a mental break.

Lack of natural light affects some people's moods. Well-designed offices provide break rooms accessible to windows, or outside break areas so employees can enjoy some natural light during the day. It is especially important for people to be exposed to some natural light during the winter months, when exposure to natural light before and after work hours may be limited.

10

Spending five to ten minutes outside or just looking outside several times a day can help reduce stress and mood swings.

> **Seasonal affective disorder (SAD)** is a type of depression some people experience when they do not receive enough natural light. Almost everyone experiences "cabin fever" when they have been indoors too long in the winter or if the weather has been cloudy for an extended time. SAD is an extreme version of cabin fever.

Noise Level

Noise is particularly difficult to prevent in support groups. Support managers want to control unwanted sound because noise disrupts interactions between customers and support staff. Support managers also want staff members to work together as teams, which requires communication between staff members. Talking is the fastest, most convenient way for staff members to interact. Because support still receive the majority of problems and requests by telephone, staff members also speak to customers. A support group of fifteen front-line support staff may generate fifteen separate conversations at the same time.

The office setup helps control the amount of noise in the help desk. Cubicle walls deaden noise. Most cubicle partitions are covered with fabric to absorb sound. Also, acoustic wall and ceiling panels soften reflected sound. Most offices are carpeted, which is quieter than bare floors and provides added warmth. Unfortunately cubicle partitions, acoustic tiles, and carpeting are expensive. The support manager may not be able to afford assistance from a professional design company to evaluate the proposed layout and make sure that the new cubicle arrangement blocks noise.

Employees can help reduce noise in several ways. One way to turn down some of the noise is to use silent alerts for incoming telephone calls. As long as the telephone display is visible to the support analyst, it isn't necessary to leave the telephone on audible ring. Although speakerphones enable multiple people to participate in a telephone conversation, most Automatic Call Distributions allow three-way conferencing to other lines. Plants also absorb sound. Some companies provide large potted plants, but employees can supplement these with smaller plants on their desks to absorb sound as well as to refresh the air.

> Three-way conferencing enables multiple people to communicate over a telephone line. A normal telephone conversation is two-way—it involves the caller and receiver. If those two people need to speak to a third person, one person's connection is placed on hold while a new connection is made to the third person. When the new connection is complete, a button on the telephone allows the people on the new connection to reconnect with the person on hold.

In extreme cases, employers may use white noise generators to reduce noise levels. **White noise** is sound that contains every frequency within the range of human hearing. It is generated on a sound synthesizer and masks other noises. Most people hear this sound as a slight background buzz but eventually they "tune it out" completely.

> **TIP** Sound "designers," such as artists and musicians, use white noise generators to create sound effects such as wind, ocean surf, space whooshes, and rumbles. **Pink noise** is white noise that has been filtered to reduce the volume at each octave.

INDIVIDUAL WORKPLACE ELEMENTS THAT AFFECT EMPLOYEES

A **workspace** includes the furniture, equipment, and tools necessary for an employee to complete assigned tasks, as well as the physical arrangement of these items and the space they occupy. Support staff may have very specialized workspaces, depending upon the level of support they provide or the types of services they deliver. Typical support workspaces include:

- A **workstation**, which is the computer, keyboard, mouse, processor, monitor, and all required software to complete assigned tasks

- Chair

- Telephone equipment

- Desk space with areas for writing or opening reference materials

- Storage for reference materials, writing supplies, and personal items

Staff members arrange these components within an office or cubicle to meet their needs and personal preferences. The interaction between people and computer systems, programs, and other devices is part of the study of **ergonomics**. An ergonomically designed workspace is designed for maximum work efficiency and maximum worker comfort, health, and safety. Employees using poorly designed workspaces may suffer from headaches, wrist pain, backaches, shoulder pain, or swollen ankles.

> **Note** The study of ergonomics also includes physical characteristics such as the height, weight, and strength of people and how they function in their working or personal environment. Offices are usually designed for "average" physical characteristics of employees, so a workspace ergonomically suited to one person can be completely wrong for someone else. The Ergo World Web site at http://www.interface-analysis.com/ergoworld/ includes multiple links to ergonomic subjects.

In 1999, OSHA published a formal standard for office layout and furnishings to reduce eye, back, and wrist injuries. According to OSHA, eye, back, and wrist injuries lead to more days absent from the workplace than any other workplace injury. **Repetitive stress injuries (RSIs)** include symptoms of tenderness, swelling, tingling, numbness, and loss of movement in joints and are caused by repeating small strenuous actions with arms, wrists, and hands for long periods of time. Spending many hours performing movements in a fixed or awkward position increases the risk of RSIs. **Carpal tunnel syndrome (CTS)** is a common form of RSI that affects hands and wrists. It is linked to typing, but other occupations (assembly workers, tennis players, and artisans) are susceptible as well. Other forms of RSI include bursitis and tendinitis. RSIs can damage muscles, tendons, and nerves. PC users in particular

10

often suffer from aches and pains in the fingers, hands, wrists, arms, elbows, shoulders, neck, and back.

Even children are susceptible to CTS. They repeat small, strenuous hand movements when they use joysticks to play video games.

There are several simple, effective ways to reduce RSIs. The simplest method to avoid RSIs is to take short, regular breaks from typing or mouse activity. Stretching exercises that include the hands, shoulders, and the neck can flex strained muscles and reduce pressure. Knee bends and walking reduce ankle swelling and leg cramps.

It's easy to recognize employee safety hazards in occupations such as manufacturing or construction where large equipment is involved, but when employees work in office environments, safety hazards like RSIs are harder to identify. State and federal laws attempt to ensure that employees are protected from physical dangers in the workplace, but employees should take steps to protect themselves from all injuries when possible. In most cases, they can make simple, no-cost adjustments to their workspace that will help them prevent these injuries. They can also identify small, low-cost improvements that will help their employer increase productivity. Areas that employees should look at include their workstation, chair, telephone, and desktop surfaces, and storage.

Workstation

The primary technology in a workspace is the workstation. From here, support staff use call management software to record calls, search for solutions, remotely control other PCs, and use common office applications to read or send e-mail and track tasks. Workstation components such as monitors, keyboards, and mice must be properly aligned to ensure the employees' health and productivity.

The body should be aligned with the monitor, so that the computer user can read text and review images without straining. The monitor should be at or slightly below eye level. To accomplish this, adjust the height of the monitor or the chair (discussed below). If there is enough overhead space, raise the monitor off the working surface, which is usually too low to prevent neck strain. Most office supply stores sell small, plastic monitor stands, but a few outdated software manuals or a box will do in a hurry (as long as they can support the weight of the monitor). Some experts recommend placing the monitor 18 to 24 inches from the eyes. This can vary when using a larger monitor with a high-resolution display, as long as you can read the screen without straining or squinting. As mentioned earlier, staff members may need to use antiglare screens or additional desk lights to reduce glare. According to one call center design firm, flat panel monitors not only save space, but they also provide fewer flickers (which also cause eyestrain) and are cooler than traditional computer monitors.

TIP   A general guideline is to place the top edge of the computer monitor even with your forehead while you are sitting.

Note   Most PCs with Windows allow monitor resolutions of 800 × 600, 1024 × 768, 1152 × 864, or 1280 × 1024 pixels. The higher resolutions provide the best contrast, but make objects on the desktop appear smaller. Many computer users set the monitor resolution lower to enlarge the Windows objects, but this increases eyestrain. Although many employees still use 14-inch or 15-inch monitors, support staff frequently must use many pieces of software and need larger screens to work with multiple applications at the same time. Almost all support applications require a minimum resolution of 800 × 600, but users with 17-inch, 21-inch, or larger monitors should be able to easily see 1024 × 768 resolution or higher.

Depending on their size, support staff may need to raise or lower the height of their desktop to position the keyboard and mouse correctly. Most workstations have adjustable desktops. The typing and working surface should be positioned so that the forearms are horizontal to the desktop and wrists are straight. The goal is to avoid resting the wrists on the hard surface of a desktop. If the support group uses desks rather than cubicles, it may be necessary to raise the keyboard.

10

TIP   You can raise the keyboard with thin blocks of wood or a few narrow notepads.

The mouse may also need to be repositioned. Carpal tunnel syndrome is not restricted to typists; people who point and click with the mouse are also at risk. The mouse should be comfortably close to the keyboard. In addition, there should be a clear area of about 6 inches by 6 inches in which to move the mouse. Grip the mouse loosely. Some vendors make a larger-sized mouse for people with large hands, so the fingers curve slightly over the top of the mouse. Sometimes, a mouse may not be suited to an individual's hand movements. Touch pads require different hand movements and are no more expensive than a mouse. A wrist rest will help hold the wrist straight when using the mouse.

TIP   Some people learn to use a mouse with their nonwriting hand to ease strain on their writing hand and so that they can take notes. The Windows environment enables users to change the functions of the left and right mouse buttons. If you need to use the mouse with your left hand, switch the button actions so the click and double-click actions are done with the index finger.

Chair

Support staff usually sit for most of the day to answer telephone calls. Although the chair isn't a high-tech component, it can affect productivity more than the workstation. An uncomfortable chair not only causes back injuries, but it also adds to mental stress, which makes it much harder to remain helpful and cheerful when talking on the telephone with customers.

Office chairs should have adjustable seat heights, backs, and armrests. The seat should be low enough that the feet rest on the floor, the chair back should support the lower back, and armrests should be even with the elbows. With most chairs, the tilt of the seat itself can be adjusted and the back can be unlocked to allow rocking back while seated. It should be easy for anyone to adjust the chair without special equipment. The base of the chair should be no larger than the seat, so it will not interfere with foot placement while sitting. Five legs (rather than four) with rollers prevent the chair from easily tipping over. Most chairs swivel and roll with minimal effort. These features enable support staff to move easily within their work-space to retrieve books or files.

Staff members can enhance a chair's back support by placing a lumbar pillow or a rolled-up towel behind their back. When sitting, legs should be relaxed and comfortably in front of you. A footrest can relieve some back pressure from the sitting position, but it should be large enough to permit a relaxed leg and foot position.

Back strain and injuries are included in OSHA guidelines. An employer should be able to provide a good chair with good support. Broken chairs are an employee hazard and should be removed from the workspace.

A chair should be personalized to fit an individual's physical requirements. If you need to work away from your workspace for an extended period, take your chair with you and be comfortable. Likewise, if you borrow someone else's chair, return the chair to its original position.

Telephone

The telephone is a significant source of incoming work for support staff. The telephone deskset (discussed in Chapter 9) may be quite sophisticated and include message panels and multiple telephone lines. The telephone should also be within easy reach, about 10 inches from the most common position of your hand. It should not require stretching to reach the telephone number pad (or to connect or disconnect a call when using a headset).

If you use your right hand for your computer mouse, you may want to learn to answer the telephone or dial with your left hand to reduce the number of actions you make with the same hand.

An important accessory for the telephone is a headset. Headsets free the hands for typing or writing and eliminate the need to balance the telephone receiver between your tilted head and shoulder. Headsets also enable support staff to answer the telephone in a shorter time because it is faster to click the "connect" button than to move the receiver from the base to the ear.

There are a variety of headset models with different features. Some companies let employees try all the available models to decide which is most comfortable for them. **Monaural headsets** cover only one ear, which allows support staff to hear what is going on around them. Even when off the phone, analysts can leave monaural headsets in place and still speak to other support staff. Monaural headsets have a variety of designs:

- A headband style fits loosely over the top of the head, holding the earpiece and microphone securely in place. The earpiece is covered with a foam cushion for extra comfort and to help block out noise. Figure 10-5 shows a headband-style headset, which connects to the telephone deskset with a cord.

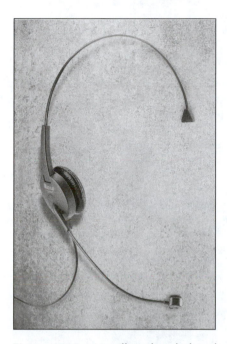

Figure 10-5   Headband-style headset

- An over-the-ear-style headset is smaller and lighter than a headband-style one (and doesn't disturb the wearer's hair). Some analysts don't like these because it is harder to keep the attached microphone in the proper position. Figure 10-6 shows an over-the-ear-style headset.

10

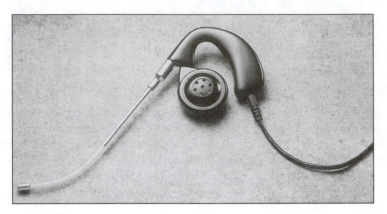

Figure 10-6   Over-the-ear-style headset

- An in-the-ear headset is a variation of the over-the-ear style. The microphone is attached to the earpiece and an earplug fits in to the ear. This style filters noise. An in-the-ear headset is shown in Figure 10-7.

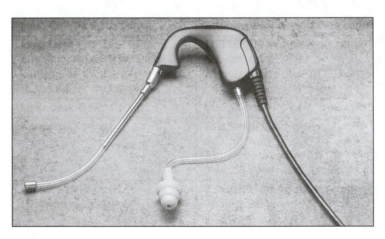

Figure 10-7   In-the-ear-style headset

- An earplug with a microphone clip is the smallest headset. A small plug fits loosely in the ear to reduce noise. Further down the cord is a small microphone with an adjustable clip that is clipped to the collar. Figure 10-8 shows this style.

One company markets a combination microphone and earphone set with both components included in the earpiece, which uses "bone" transmission. As you speak, sound is transmitted through the jawbone to the earphone/microphone earpiece.

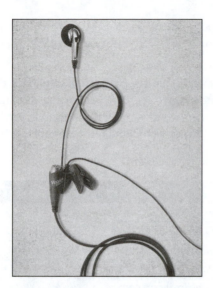

Figure 10-8   Earplug-style headset

Binaural headsets cover both ears and offer the greatest noise reduction. Binaural headsets use either a headband or two earplugs. Figure 10-9 shows a binaural headband style headset.

10

Figure 10-9   Binaural-style headset

Most headsets include noise-canceling technology in the earpieces and microphones. They also include extra foam cushions and connector cords. Wireless models enable support staff to stand up and move around.

Headsets should be adjusted so they fit comfortably and support staff can hear the caller clearly. The cushions and microphones should be cleaned regularly to remove dirt and germs. Microphones should be sensitive enough that callers do not know that the analyst is speaking on a headset. Table 10-1 lists companies that sell headsets for different telephone systems.

Table 10-1   Common headset vendors

Company	Web page
ADCOM/BHS	http://www.adcombhs.com
ClearVox	http://www.clearvox.com
CommuniTech, Inc.	http://www.communitech.com
Headsets Direct	http://www.headsetsdirect.com
Hello Direct	http://www.hello-direct.com
KAAAS	http://www.kaaas.com
Plantronics	http://www.plantronics.com
Progressive Ideas	http://www.progressiveideas.com
Spectrum	http://www.spectrumtec.com
Telex	http://www.computeraudio.telex.com
Tri-Tel Technical Services	http://www.tritelchicago.com

Level two and three support staff usually do not spend as much time on the telephone as front-line support staff. Consequently, they may find headsets uncomfortable because they are not used to wearing them. During long telephone conversations, however, it is still important for them to avoid neck and shoulder cramps. Speakerphones are another way to free analysts' hands as they talk and to enable other support staff to join the telephone conversation. Speakerphones are effective when used in individual offices, where it is easier to control background noise and where other employees won't be disturbed. Callers should be able to hear support staff who speak in a normal tone of voice and a short distance away. They may need to adjust the sound volume on the speakerphone so that the caller can still hear them clearly.

Desktop Surfaces and Storage

Work areas and storage don't necessarily prevent RSI injuries, but the use of the desk space contributes to employees' overall comfort at work. Support staff should always have a clear desk area in which to write comfortably or to place an open reference manual. If space is limited, look for ways to create it temporarily. The following are some ways to create extra space:

- **Place PC processors on the floor:** The only areas support staff need to be able to reach easily are the disk drive, CD-ROM drive, or power switch; otherwise, the box with the computer processor should fit under the desk and out of the way of their feet.

- **Move the keyboard out of the way for short periods:** This will usually free up at least a 6-inch deep section of desk for reading or writing. If the top of the monitor is flat, place the keyboard on top temporarily. Keyboards may also be stored on edge against the monitor. Some workstations have swing-out keyboard shelves, but these may not be in the correct position for typing.

- **Move the mouse when not needed:** Small, clip-on holders can be attached to the side of a monitor for storing mice when they're not in use. A small, stick-on hook attached to the side of the monitor also provides a place to hang the mouse up temporarily.

- **Raise the printer:** Most companies set up printers in common work areas. However, support staff who have a printer in their work area can use a desktop printer stand to raise the printer off the desktop. Papers or other work items can be stored under the stand.

- **Add a shelf:** A small shelf—7- to 9-inches high, 9-inches deep, and 2- to 3-feet long—can raise items usually stored on the desktop and create free space beneath. Most office supply stores carry these for about $40.

- **Hang the telephone headset from a hook:** There are stands that store a telephone headset when it is not in use. A small clip or hook hung next to the monitor or telephone also provides a handy place to store a headset.

10

When support groups use multiple shifts for support, staff members may share cubicles with other employees. Some cubicle styles come with small free-standing sets of lockable drawers; office supply companies also sell smaller versions. The drawers are low, to fit under a desk, and are on rollers. Personal items and desk equipment such as pencils, staplers, and tape dispensers can be stored in an organizer or caddy and moved aside temporarily.

Some cubicle designs include an over-the-wall hanger for coats, umbrellas, or bags. Household supply stores also sell over-the-door hooks or coat hangers (next to the ironing boards and clothes hangers) for a couple of dollars. These should fit over the top of a cubicle partition or over the top of an office door without requiring nails, pins, or tacks that damage walls or partition fabric. These hooks will free space that is often used to store items not used indoors.

OTHER TOOLS THAT IMPROVE THE WORK ENVIRONMENT

Employees may not be able to directly address some workspace problems or sources of stress because of understaffing. However, support staff can take action to limit the frustration the environment produces. These areas are divided between the items listed in Figure 10-10.

◆ Traditional office tools
◆ Personal touches

Figure 10-10 Workplace tools

Traditional Office Tools

Although support staff may not have much say about the computer tools or telephones assigned to them, they can take steps to ensure that these items don't add stress or frustration. Support staff don't have to know how to use all the features of traditional office tools, but the sooner they are comfortable with the most common tasks, the less stress they feel.

Although answering a telephone is simple, other telephone-oriented tasks can take a bit of practice to master. It should take only a few minutes to learn how to transfer a telephone call. Practice with a coworker a couple of times to ensure that the caller won't be disconnected. Another handy task to learn is how to add a third caller to a conference call. Again, practice this task before using it with a customer to prevent stress.

Learn to use PC software effectively. Most businesses rely on e-mail to communicate with employees. Employees can create different folders to store messages. Decide up front how to best organize information and then use those categories to move messages out of the inbox. Only keep messages in the inbox as long as there is something in the message that requires action (such as read, reply, forward, and so forth). Set up a daily routine for reviewing, replying to, and storing messages in the e-mail inbox.

Many e-mail applications have calendar programs that support to-do lists and appointments. Some companies use shared calendars to plan meetings for groups of people. Learn to set up personal appointments or reminders. For example, if you have a doctor's appointment on Tuesday, create a pop-up reminder for Monday to help you mentally prepare for being away the next day and reassign work before it is due. If you have to prepare for a meeting, be sure to schedule time at least the day before the meeting to create slides or handouts, so you are not rushed.

Word processing applications, spreadsheets, and other desktop applications have many features to automate tasks. Regularly schedule a few minutes to learn a new feature that will help you be more efficient. Twenty to thirty minutes once a week should be sufficient. During breaks with coworkers, ask them about shortcuts they have learned that can save time.

There are also PC applications that remind you to take exercise breaks to prevent stress. Some include sample exercises to stretch arms, hands, and shoulders to release tension. The exercises are simple enough that you can practice them while on the telephone. Even if you don't take a regular coffee break in the morning and afternoon, you should still take ten to fifteen minutes of physical activity as a refreshment break. Studies have shown that employees who take regular breaks produce more work than employees who don't.

DONNA HALL, PRESIDENT
THE RIGHT ANSWER
WASHINGTON, D.C.
HTTP://WWW.THERIGHTANSWER.COM
PREVENTING SUPPORT BURNOUT

Good CSR (customer support representative) skills come from within and without. Individuals who want to stay in a support profession need to constantly monitor themselves and evaluate their attitudes while performing their jobs.

It is especially important to try to stay in control of your telephone personality. It's relatively easy to determine when you are starting to be less patient or helpful (like when you personalize or internalize comments from customers or your coworkers). This is especially important if you have to handle a lot of customer complaints; it's difficult to take in negativity without feeling overwhelmed by other people's problems. Internal support groups probably receive more negativity than those who support external customers (how many times have you heard the help desk referred to as the "helpless desk"?). It's one thing for external customers to treat staff badly (because we can't control our customers), but when fellow employees do the same, CSRs may question their value as a person.

As a customer service person you are frequently told that you have to understand everyone else (or at least the people you are dealing with) so you set yourself up with the expectation of being the perfect person. You can't always do this. It's good to strive for high goals, but when you are not on your best game—admit it and take steps to redirect frustrations and refresh yourself.

You have to believe that what you are doing is important and work to address these negative feelings. When others don't display good manners, try to rise above them and display professionalism. If you feel you have reached your limit, you may need to rotate off the telephones to another activity. One activity could be to follow up with good news messages for customers—to put yourself on the giving end of making people happy.

One of the first steps you should take is to take a break. Use this as an opportunity to get some fresh air and relax. Physical activity counters frustration, so try taking a walk at lunch or take the long way down to the cafeteria (I worked with someone who would stand up and exercise next to her cubicle, just to release tension). Other people may calm down with a cup of tea or by listening to calming music for a few minutes (remember a song is only two to three minutes long).

Support staff need to take extra steps to ensure they stay in the best mental and physical health. Schedule vacations or a long weekend regularly. I always suggest investing in a massage (a full hour, at least) every six months to really relax all those tense muscles. Even a short, ten minute, professional massage of the neck and shoulders can work wonders. (If you're a team leader or support manager, this makes a great recognition reward.)

10

It may also help to develop your own support group to have group discussions and share thoughts or ideas on how to work through these issues with others on the team. Be careful when you "vent" your frustrations, because others can buy into your negative feelings. If morale is down, it may not be good to go to a coworker, so find a sympathetic friend who can listen while you talk out the issues. You need someone who can put you back in place—not join you.

The most important thing is to remember what is important—this is a job, not your entire life. Sometimes there aren't happy endings, but that doesn't mean you are bad.

Personal Touches

There are other simple ways for support staff to control stress and increase productivity. These low-tech and low-cost solutions contribute to a feeling of well-being.

- **Mouse pad:** A mouse may move more smoothly over a mouse pad than directly on a desk surface. Mouse pads are available in a variety of shapes and colors and can be personalized with photos of your favorite places or family. Some also come with built-in wrist pads.

- **Writing implements:** A small pencil cup with about three or four good pens and pencils saves time because you don't have to hunt for something with which to take notes.

- **Images:** A favorite nature photo or computer screen saver can quickly provide a mental break from problems at work.

- **Glassware:** You will feel more comfortable if you have a favorite coffee cup, mug, or drinking glass handy. Take breaks to refill the glass with fresh water, juice, or lemonade for a quick pick-me-up.

- **Eating utensils:** If you bring lunch or other snacks to work, bring a real plate and silverware to improve the appearance of food (and help you relax). Keep a fork, spoon, and knife at your workspace to use with take-out food.

- **Comfortable shoes:** Some staff find it refreshing to change into soft-soled shoes or fancy slippers when they sit at the desk, to prevent ankle swelling.

- **Pets:** Small, desktop-sized aquariums and water fountains don't take a lot of space. Many people are soothed by the sound of running water and relieve tension by watching the antics of a pet fish.

- **Power strip:** If you have several electronic devices, set a power strip on top of the desktop, so you don't have to crawl under the desktop when you need to change outlets or plug in a new device. Make sure the cord from the outlet at the floor is long enough to place the on and off switch within easy reach. Use a grounded electrical power strip, with six to eight plugs, for computer equipment.

- **Fans and heaters:** Temperature is sometimes a problem in offices. Building owners usually control thermostats, and attempt to find a temperature that is comfortable for the majority of people. Outer offices may be colder during the winter and inner offices may be overheated because of temperature variations within a building. If a sweater doesn't provide enough warmth, purchase a small, personal thermal heater. If there is a lot of computer equipment generating heat in an area, or if the work area is too warm, personal fans can be clipped to a wall or shelf and take very little space.

- **Physical breaks:** Take breaks away from the desk as frequently as possible. Periodically, get up and visit other coworkers at their desks rather than calling them on the telephone. Take a short walk out the front door or around the building for some fresh air. If your office building has multiple floors, schedule a quick walk up the stairs to increase blood flow and relieve some stress.

 TIP Electronic aquariums—screen savers with moving fish or videos of aquariums you can play from the computer—are available if you don't want to worry about caring for live fish.

Smart support managers allow support staff flexibility in their immediate surroundings to combat stress and increase productivity. The law regulates physical safety and employee health, but support staff can improve their work environments when they take time to evaluate and remove small frustrations and annoyances. Not only are they healthier, but they are more productive.

10

CHAPTER SUMMARY

- ❐ Laws require employers to provide adequate lighting, ventilation, and sound control to prevent employee work-related injuries. Support groups have an additional need to control noise because of the nature of service they deliver.

- ❐ The physical layout of an office can be designed to increase productivity, while still meeting employment requirements. Cubicles allow office designers to attractively arrange large groups of employees so they can collaborate on problems more easily. Offices are more expensive, but may be used by level two and three support staff so they can control noise as they work on complex problems.

- ❐ Too much or too little light does not cause physical damage, but leads to tension and stress. Glare should be reduced from computer screens. Changing the foreground and background colors of the PC software can also add contrast. In some cases, lack of natural light can cause mood swings.

- ❐ Noise can be controlled with fabric-covered cubicle partitions, acoustic panels, carpeting, and plants. In extreme cases, white noise will mask out background sounds.

- ❐ Employees should take responsibility for controlling their workspaces. Repetitive stress injuries affect all computer users. Workstation components, such as monitors, keyboards, and mice, should be aligned properly so support staff can work without straining. The heights of the desktop and the chair can contribute to back, hand, and arm injuries. Telephone headsets are primarily used to prevent neck and shoulder strain.

❑ Support staff should learn all common features of their telephones and PC software. This will help reduce their stress and improve their productivity.

❑ Other areas of the workspace don't directly induce injuries, but affect the overall well-being and mental health of support staff. When necessary, individuals can use different techniques to control temperature, clear the desktop to create writing space, and remove clutter.

❑ With some creative thinking, support staff can find low-cost, low-technology "tools" to remove stress and improve productivity.

KEY TERMS

binaural — Telephone headsets that cover both ears.

carpal tunnel syndrome (CTS) — A common form of RSI that affects hands and wrists.

ergonomics — The study of the interaction between people and computer systems, programs, and other devices.

monaural — Telephone headsets that cover only one ear, which allows support staff to hear what is going on around them.

Occupational Safety and Health Administration (OSHA) — An agency of the U.S. Department of Labor dedicated to reducing hazards in the workplace and enforcing job-safety standards for all employers.

pink noise — White noise that has been filtered to reduce the volume at each octave.

repetitive stress injuries (RSIs) — Symptoms of tenderness, swelling, tingling, numbness, and loss of movement in joints caused by repeating small strenuous actions with arms, wrists, and hands for long periods of time.

seasonal affective disorder (SAD) — A type of depression some people experience when they do not receive enough natural light.

white noise — Sound that contains every frequency within the range of human hearing.

workspace — The furniture, equipment, and tools necessary for an employee to complete assigned tasks as well as the physical arrangement of these items and the space they occupy.

workstation — The computer, keyboard, mouse, processor, monitor, and all required software necessary to complete assigned tasks

REVIEW QUESTIONS

1. What is OSHA?

2. List three things employers are required to provide for all employees.

3. _____ promote the most team collaboration and are less expensive than individual _____.

4. What is the minimum amount of personal workspace required for each employee?

5. Glare is a symptom of too little light. True or False?

6. Employees can change their monitor's foreground and background colors to provide better _____.

7. All companies are required to provide some form of natural light in their employees' workspaces. True or False?

8. List two ways employees can help control noise.

9. What is white noise and how is it used?

10. A workstation includes all of the following *except*:

   a. computer processor.

   b. keyboard.

   c. writing surface.

   d. monitor.

11. Name three forms of repetitive stress injuries.

12. List four symptoms of repetitive stress injuries.

13. Describe the correct position of the computer monitor.

14. Describe one way to reduce the combined stress of writing and using the mouse with the same hand.

15. You can relieve some back pressure while sitting by using a(n) _____.

16. What occupational hazard is minimized by using a telephone headset or speakerphone?

17. Describe a situation when it would be more appropriate to use a speakerphone than a headset or handset telephone.

18. _____-style headsets are best suited for very loud work environments.

19. List three ways to increase the amount of open space on a desktop.

20. List three reasons to spend time learning PC software tools provided to you.

21. List five personal tips or items that support staff can use to contribute to a feeling of well-being.

HANDS-ON PROJECTS

Project 10-1

Understanding OSHA ergonomics standards. Visit the OSHA Web site at **http://www.osha.gov** and follow the links to **Ergonomics**. Answer the following questions:

   1. What are work–related musculoskeletal disorders (WMSDs) as defined by OSHA?

   2. What solutions are best to reduce pain and prevent disability?

   3. What group of workers are the first targets for the Ergonomics Program Standard?

Project 10-2

Identifying ergonomics issues at work. Visit the Combo Web site at **http://www.combo.com** and follow the **Ergonomics At Work** link. Then do the following:

1. Read the article entitled "Ergonomics and Economics." What is the minimum productivity increase documented for any of the studies listed?

2. Review the article entitled "Improving Productivity and Efficiency." Why is productivity increased when good furniture is used?

3. Locate an ergonomic topic that was not covered in this chapter and summarize three key points in a short report.

Project 10-3

Learning the truth about common stress injuries. Visit the Office Ergonomics Web site at **http://www.ur-net.com/office-ergo**. Review the articles provided and then list three myths of ergonomic wisdom that you might have believed that have been disproved. Use the document entitled "A Checklist" to match the symptoms to the possible solutions listed in Table 10-2.

Table 10-2

Symptom	Possible Solution
1. Light sources that can be seen	A. Adjust backrest.
2. Neck flexed downward	B. Bring viewed item closer to centerline of view.
3. Raised or tensed shoulders	C. Create a regular break schedule.
4. Twisting the head to the side	D. Lower chair or add footrest.
5. Prolonged sitting in one position	E. Lower work surface or keyboard.
6. Lumbar back area not supported	F. Move monitor so light enters from a side angle.
7. Feet dangling	G. Raise document or monitor to comfortable height.
8. Twisted torso	H. Rearrange work area or lower viewed objects to lower field of view.
9. Reflected glare on the screen	I. Rearrange work or swivel chair.
10. Monitor image dim, fuzzy, flickery, small, or otherwise difficult to read.	J. Use software to enlarge image.

Project 10-4

Learning additional names for RSI injuries. Search the Web for other terms for RSI. (*Hint:* Different countries use different terms, but all the terms basically describe the same types of injuries.)

Project 10-5

Discovering other resources for ergonomics. Visit the Center for Office Technology Web site at **http://www.cot.org** and follow the **Mission** and **Ergonomics Basics** links. Answer the following questions:

1. What is the purpose of this organization?
2. What is this group's definition of ergonomics?
3. What sciences are related to ergonomics?
4. What human factors must be considered when designing an ergonomic solution?

Project 10-6

Learning correct workstation placement. Visit the IBM Healthy Computing Web site at **http://www.pc.ibm.com/us/healthycomputing**. Read the overview. Follow the link to **Setup**, **Workstation Ergonomics** and download the animated version (http://www.pc.ibm.com/us/healthycomputing/we-download.html). Install the application and review the animation. Answer the following questions based on the animation:

1. What is the appropriate viewing angle for the monitor?
2. How high should the desktop be from the floor?
3. When is a wrist rest actually used?
4. How far away should the monitor be?
5. In addition to cleaning the monitor, what personal items should also be cleaned regularly?

Project 10-7

Finding technology for injured workers. Visit the Typing Injury FAQ Web site at **http://www.tifaq.org** and review the links or Site Map. What technology is useful for workers suffering from RSI or who cannot use their hands? Review the article entitled "When Your Voice Means Business"(http://www.tifaq.org/articles/voice-novdec98-barbie_scott.html). Although this article discusses voice as it is used for speech recognition, there are several helpful hints for support staff who must use their voices for long periods of time. List five recommendations from this article.

Project 10-8

Using RSI prevention software. Visit one of the Web sites listed below and download shareware or evaluation software that monitors keyboard use or offers exercise breaks.

- Typing Injury FAQ at **http://www.tifaq.org** (follow the links for Software, Shareware/Low-Cost Programs)
- Niche Software, Ltd., at **http://www.workpace.com/niche**
- Omniquad at **http://www.omniquad.com** (follow the links to ErgoSense)

10

Over the next week, use the software every time you use the computer. Keep a journal and record how you feel during and after each computer session. Was the software successful in helping you avoid fatigue during this time?

CASE PROJECTS

1. **Designing a New Help Desk**

You are a level one support staff member working in an internal company help desk. Your group has doubled in two years, and many of the employees are in cramped offices. Upper management has identified a new area for the group and wants a team of support staff and managers to help design the new offices. Work with a team (three or four classmates) to identify ways to reduce stress. Visit at least one support group and ask the managers and staff to describe specific benefits that their office designs provide. If they use cubicles, review how those are arranged and the types of partitions between workers. Evaluate the overhead and natural lighting and ways they control glare. What technologies help control noise? Visit several employee workspaces and take notes on the arrangement of the workstations, chairs, and telephones. Are employees allowed to personalize their areas? Design the help desk for your company. Use drawings to illustrate how to arrange cubicles and list design features important to a help desk.

2. **Troubleshooting Monitor Ergonomics**

The Northwest Consumer Organization recently established a new support group, and you are its team leader. Support staff members work in a new office and have telephone headsets and new computers with 17-inch computer monitors that rest on the desktop with the keyboard and mouse. Many of the employees are new to support and previously used computers for only a small part of their job. Within a few short weeks of the move, at least half of the support staff complain that they have shoulder and neck pains. You suspect several things are causing this, including the position of the monitors. Visit the OSHA Web site at **http://www.osha.gov** and locate any documents that discuss Video Display Terminals. Review the documents and list at least ten ergonomic items that you need to check to eliminate the monitors as a source of the neck and shoulder pains.

3. **Identifying Hidden Causes of Stress**

Some level two support staff in your support group work from home or telecommute. Most of their fellow employees are envious and have hinted that these employees don't experience as much stress because they work from home. As the support group manager, you want to educate all the employees so they understand that the benefits of telecommuting are balanced by their own sources of stress. Create a presentation that discusses in detail two or three challenges that telecommuters face, so you can explain this to all employees. (*Hint:* One list is available at the IBM Healthy Computing Web site at **http://www.pc.ibm.com/us/healthycomputing**. Follow the links for Comfort, Exercises, and Stress for Telecommuters.)

11

ADDITIONAL LEVEL TWO AND LEVEL THREE SUPPORT TOOLS

In this chapter you will learn:

♦ The objectives for IT systems management

♦ Common system management software features

♦ The components of a managed system

♦ The primary software vendors for level two support tools

L evel one support staff are the principal users of the software tools and processes discussed in Chapters 1 through 10. Ideally, the support staff who answer the telephone directly address 80 to 90 percent of all customer problems. The remaining problems, however, take more time to troubleshoot or require the technical expertise of well-trained analysts. IT staff members who work as level two or three of the support group solve specific technical problems as well as maintain most of the company's computer systems.

In addition to using the same tracking and management tools as level one support, higher support levels use other utilities and tools. These applications are specialized for specific hardware and operating systems. In most cases, IT organizations use these applications not only to resolve problems, but also to prevent interruptions in service for computer users.

WHAT IS SYSTEMS MANAGEMENT?

As a company's needs grow through expansion or acquisitions, they expand their computer networks. Companies continue to add new technologies—Web pages, intranets, and Internet links—as they expand their business worldwide. These "global enterprises" compete internationally. Over time, it becomes almost impossible for IT staff or managers to remember all the interconnections, and increasingly difficult for them to maintain a computer network that contains tens of thousands of devices. As a result, IT managers and system administrators rely on systems management tools to automate common tasks, provide troubleshooting information, and prevent problems.

In its broadest terms, **systems management** is the process of protecting the integrity of business applications, the company's data, and the technology assets that connect those applications and data. A company's network can be composed of hundreds or thousands of individual devices that are connected. A system can be one application on a single server or LAN that connects dozens of PCs for a workgroup, or it can include several applications on one or more computers that must work together. Connections between devices and the successful transfer of data between systems are high priorities for the support group. If problems with connections aren't corrected quickly, computer users will encounter errors as they try to complete their work, and will call the support group to fix the problem.

Systems management is also called **enterprise management**, which emphasizes that a company's technology, in all locations worldwide, is managed through a single support group. This support group may not reside in one place, but the management of systems is done consistently in all locations and with the same management tools.

IT staff are specialists in managing certain types of systems, and often have "administrator" as part of their titles. The telecommunications administrator manages office telephones and network lines between computers. The e-mail administrator keeps the e-mail system in working order by adding new users, changing passwords, deleting terminated employees, and making sure that enough storage space is available. Level one support may escalate difficult problems to the appropriate administrator who has detailed knowledge of that system.

Some support groups are structured so that level two support staff complete systems management tasks. Other support groups refer these tasks to level three support staff.

As with help desks, there are two approaches to systems management—reactive and proactive. The reactive approach focuses on maintenance, diagnostics, and problem resolution, similar to a level one support group's reactive approach to handling customer problems. Reactive administrators are concerned with whether the network is working correctly. When there are problems, level one support staff must escalate these calls because they usually don't have either the correct training or the security to resolve the problems. This approach works, provided that there are enough level two support staff to handle the escalated calls.

The proactive approach to systems management looks at the current network and tries to anticipate growth and enhancements in the network. Proactive administrators attempt to prevent problems before they happen. They also analyze network activity to determine how effectively the network is working. In some cases, proactive management tools enable support staff to correct a problem or contact customers before the customers even know a problem exists. In a proactive environment, the support group does not wait for customers to report problems because their management tools alert them seconds after a problem occurs.

The main performance measure for higher levels of support is system availability. **System availability** compares the time it took to repair a failure to the time the system was accessible before the failure. Failures are usually critical problems, such as an inability to access a database that all employees use daily or an e-mail system that won't deliver messages. The formula for system availability is:

system availability = MTBF / (MTBF + MTTR)

where

MTBF = mean time between failures, measured in hours
MTTR = mean time to repair a failure, measured in hours

For example, if the e-mail system has had only one outage in two years (one year equals 8760 hours) and that outage took four hours to correct, then the e-mail system availability was 99.98 percent.

e-mail availability = 17,520 / (17,520 + 4)

As a rule, access to networked systems is critical for many companies, and users expect most computer systems to be available 95 percent of the time or more. Figure 11-1 is an example of a system availability graph for several systems.

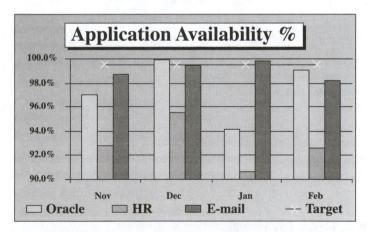

Figure 11-1   Sample system availability statistics

System availability is also included in SLAs between the support group and customers. As mentioned earlier, service level agreements define services and the performance measurements for those services. The support group will define service levels for systems that large groups of customers share, so that customers understand which problems qualify as a system failure and the amount of time a problem will be open before managers are notified.

SYSTEMS MANAGEMENT SOFTWARE FEATURES

Systems management software is a set of tools or utilities used by administrators that monitors hardware and software applications. These applications may be separate programs dedicated to specific tasks or part of an integrated suite of software. To be effective, the software must communicate with and track every network device, server, workstation, operating system, database, and application in a company, including mainframe computers that are centralized in a data center, distributed systems (such as LANs or WANs) that connect desktop devices, and laptops for mobile employees. It must also track devices that are not traditionally part of the IT environment, such as telephone switches, modem banks, long-range radio receivers, satellite communications equipment, encryption devices, ATM machines, and point-of-sale systems.

A modem bank is a group of modems that are shared. When a computer needs a modem, a software switch connects the requesting system to an available modem.

A network may start out with a single type of device and operating system (such as IBM-compatible PCs with PC printers). Over time, additional types of equipment and operating systems may be added to meet the company's business needs, creating a **heterogeneous computing environment**, which is a mix of different computing devices and operating systems. A heterogeneous computing environment may use a combination of mainframe computers running OS/390, UNIX computers, IBM AS400s, PCs running Microsoft Windows NT or several versions of Windows, network gateways, and routers. Each individual device, or **node**, has a unique identification, or **address**, on the computer network. Addresses are unique within a network, whether they are assigned permanently to one device or randomly assigned to devices, such as PCs, connected to the network.

One of the most important features of systems management software is the ability to discover new devices on the network, assign unique addresses, and detect configuration changes. This systems management software feature works much like the asset management tools discussed in Chapter 7. It can be difficult for support staff to understand the patterns and connections between all the devices, especially when there are thousands of addresses on the network. The systems management software builds a **topology**, a graphical representation of the network nodes and the links between them. A topology can be rendered in 2-D view or 3-D view to help administrators better understand and troubleshoot the network. Also, devices are color-coded—a green device is operating normally, a yellow device has noncritical errors, and a red device has failed. Figure 11-2 shows a sample network topology.

There are several ways to represent the topology graphically:

- **Logical connections:** Administrators may need to see the logical connection of devices. This representation shows how to get from one device to another through gateways. A **gateway** is a network point that acts as an entrance to another network.

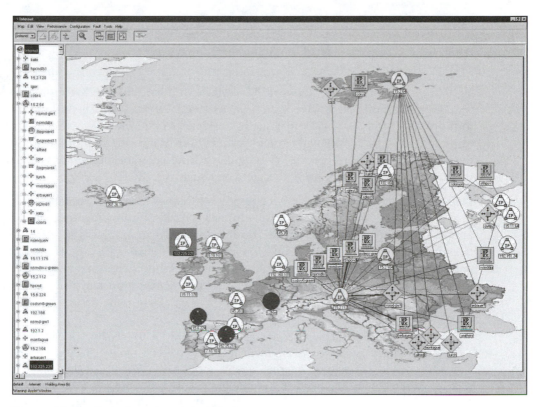

Figure 11-2   Sample network topology

- **Geographical connections:** The chief information officer (CIO) or other upper managers may want to see a picture of the main connections worldwide. Level two support staff may monitor devices that have peak levels of service according to the time zone in which they're located. They may view these devices on a geographical map.

- **Physical locations:** Hardware repair staff and telecommunications analysts may need to see a floor-by-floor representation, so that they know where on the network to find the device with a problem.

- **Customers:** The vice president of communications may need to see the e-mail servers arranged by organization chart. Because the organization chart lists the number of employees in different departments within a company, a graphical representation will show which departments are the heaviest users of e-mail services.

The systems management software continuously checks and updates the network topology. The software will **poll** the entire network to check the operational status of each piece of equipment and the connecting telephone lines. The type of device or line determines whether the topology registers an error if the device or line does not respond to the poll. For example, laptop computers connect to the network temporarily, during which time they can exchange data with other computers. However, the poll results won't show an error when the laptops disconnect from the network. A database server, however, must be accessible to the network as long as employees need to use the data. If the poll for a selected database server results in an error, support staff should be alerted to correct the error.

Software polls for devices depend on the type of network connections (mainframe network or TCP/IP) in place. **Simple Network Management Protocol (SNMP)** is a set of standards for communication with devices connected to a TCP/IP network. The systems management software may send an SNMP message to a printer to determine whether it is online and ready to print. The printer will respond with an SNMP message. Mainframe networks communicate using different, proprietary protocols. Most mainframe computer vendors use gateways to transfer information to other networks such as TCP/IP.

Polling generates thousands of device response messages every few minutes, which is more than support staff can examine manually. Instead, special software programs, called **intelligent agents** (or simply **agents**), collect and process this information. Agents are created for specific tasks. An intelligent agent can make decisions about the information it finds and communicate with other agents. Agents execute commands for NT, UNIX, and other programs; log data for historical analysis; set flags; record data in a database; page an operator; and/or create color-coded alerts on a topology.

An agent program can use parameters you provide to search all or part of the Internet, gather requested information, and present it to you daily or periodically. Examples of Internet agents include the PointCast Network and Netscape's daily news services. Other agents watch specific Web sites and inform you when the site or related information has been updated. For example, you can describe the types of jobs you are interested in at the Monster Web site at http://www.monster.com, and the agent sends daily postings to you by e-mail. The practice of receiving information from an agent is called **push technology**.

An agent is also called a **bot**, which is short for robot. The definitive Web site about bots is BotSpot at http://botspot.com.

Support staff use special workstations or monitors to review and monitor polling results and error messages. The **console** is a workstation that can access computers on multiple networks. Support staff use the systems management software from the console to perform a variety of tasks. For example, they can remotely control applications, analyze data collected by agents, and troubleshoot problems. They can also launch specific management applications to control different systems on the network.

TIP

In the days of mainframe computing (before client/server computing), specially trained computer operators worked in the computer room so they could change tapes on tape drives and directly manipulate computer equipment. The console was secured behind locked doors in the computer room. This privileged location conveyed godlike powers (such as stopping programs while they ran or moving files on the mainframe) to anyone with fingers on the console keys. Now, under UNIX and other modern operating systems, such as Windows NT, the console is the main screen and keyboard, and passwords guard access to the operating system.

MANAGED SYSTEMS COMPONENTS

A shared system can contain different components that higher-level support groups manage. As they monitor network performance and other problems, they concentrate on specific events. An **event** is an action or activity that has significance to a task or programs. Error messages are a significant event, but software messages that signal the end of important processing steps are also significant. Many management applications record events as entries in a log file. The log is a sequential list of events that includes the date and time of each event, the type of each event, the program that caused each event, and the resulting message. For example, programs that run when a user starts a computer with Windows NT prepare the computer to run other software. As these programs execute (or if they cannot execute), they record errors and messages in a system log. Other events, such as printing, add entries to the system log when they are completed successfully.

Figure 11-3 shows a Windows NT system log file. The system log, behind the Event Detail dialog box, shows several events with a source of "NETLOGON," "EventLog," and "Serial" as well as informational messages about print jobs. The selected event—a print job—occurred on November 22, 2002, at 6:46:27 PM. The Event Detail dialog box specifies that a Microsoft Word document named form.doc and owned by dmcbri was printed on a printer labeled Home Printer on the printer port LPT1. The entry also includes the file size and the number of pages printed. Other entries in this log may be warning messages—events that won't stop all processing, but that should be reviewed to prevent further problems. There are also error events.

11

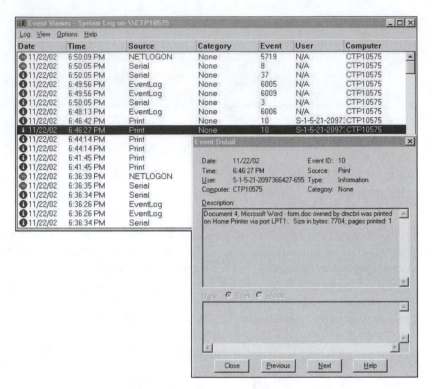

Figure 11-3   Sample Windows NT system log file

Software agents can process warning and error events automatically. Some agents page support staff to alert them to serious problems. Other agents create call records in the support group's call management application. Level two support staff then may pick up the calls from a pending queue and record the steps they take to resolve the problem. Eventually, support staff can use call records for these events to create new agents.

Performance is another important item that support staff monitor. Performance management processes evaluate the effectiveness of a computer or network device. Staff members gather statistics and historical information and evaluate system performance under a variety of conditions. Modern computer systems are closely interrelated, and, as data moves between slower computers, transactions may temporarily back up between network connections. A **bottleneck** occurs when a resource reaches its maximum capacity and cannot keep up with the demands placed on it. A bottleneck in one area can quickly overload another area. For example, a computer with too little memory or processing power may not be able to keep up with requests as additional computer users try to access it. Delays between requests and responses grow longer, resulting in timeout errors over the network. As the number of errors over the network increases, it takes longer and longer for all computer users to complete any work on the network. Bottlenecks can occur quickly, making it time-consuming for support staff to isolate the real cause of a problem.

Timeout errors occur when one computer attempts to communicate with another, and the receiving computer is so busy that it can't respond to the communication attempt within a predefined amount of time. For example, if customers attempt to log in to a UNIX server and it is too busy, they may see an error message such as "Your request to login to server DGA031 has timed out."

Support staff track events and monitor performance for many types of networked equipment and software. The most common components that support staff manage are listed in Figure 11-4. Each of these systems experiences different problems.

- ◆ Network management
- ◆ Server management
- ◆ Application and database management
- ◆ Desktop management
- ◆ Security management

Figure 11-4   Systems management areas

Network Management

Slow response is one of the most common calls a support group receives about the network. **Network traffic** describes the transactions that pass between devices on a network. A node on a network may have hundreds of users. If only one communications line exists between a computer and a device (such as a printer) that it communicates with regularly, that section of the network may become overloaded. Network management support staff use protocol analyzers and data collision detectors to analyze network traffic during normal and peak activity periods. Normal traffic takes into account weekly and monthly computing activities. For example, if month-end billing occurs around the tenth day of every month, a network traffic increase of 10 percent at this time would be considered a normal activity, and systems management software should not generate alarms. However, a 10 percent increase in traffic on the twentieth day of the month unrelated to a specific activity should generate alarms and be investigated.

If a section of a network is regularly overloaded with traffic, the IT staff will find ways to reroute traffic through additional devices to try to balance the increased traffic. In most cases, these network changes will be transparent to computer users.

Server Management

Many common support calls are caused by servers, and level two support staff with special privileges on these systems must resolve most of these problems. The problems differ, depending upon the type of server they manage.

11

One type of server is a computer that provides a service for other computers or workstations connected to it via a network. The most common example is a file server, which has a local disk and receives requests from remote clients to read and write files on that disk. Also common in many companies is an e-mail server, which needs enough disk space to store all sent and saved e-mails, as well as space for the e-mail software to complete its internal routines.

A common problem for computer-based servers is to run out of disk space. If the e-mail server runs out of space, all e-mail activity stops. E-mail administrators may create an agent to alert them when the available disk space falls below 15 percent of the total disk capacity. With advance notice, the administrators can compress files or ask users to delete old messages before the e-mail system fails completely.

One way to avoid using all the available disk space on an e-mail or file server is to set up storage quotas for users. Management decides the maximum amount of file space to be reserved for each user, and the system software prevents the user from exceeding that amount of space. Quotas are very common with free e-mail services on the Web.

Other file servers enable computer users to store personal work files or share files with a workgroup. These servers must have enough space to add new files. File server administrators may schedule jobs to back up these files or compress the files on disk so they can be retrieved faster. They may also set up agents to look for duplicate files across machines. File management utilities help system administrators locate files that have not been accessed recently so that rarely used files may be moved to lower-cost storage media, such as tapes.

Print servers also need storage space. There must be enough storage space to temporarily write a file to disk in a format that the printer will understand. When the file prints successfully, the temporary file is deleted from the disk. If the printer malfunctions and cannot print all the files spooled to disk, support staff may need to remove spooled print jobs or free up disk space.

Files are spooled or written to disk because printers can't print as quickly as a computer can send data.

Fax servers are similar to print servers. They use temporary space to generate a file on the file server.

A second type of server is a program that provides services to other computers. A **daemon** is a program server that runs continuously, waiting for requests for service. Daemons occupy server memory and are dormant while they wait for some condition(s) to occur. (An Oracle database has several daemons to handle different types of database requests.) The message transmitted between the requesting machine and the server passes over the network. If a fatal error occurs at either end of the communication, the daemon stops running and users won't be able to access data until the daemon is restarted. A system administrator usually restarts the daemon, but agents can also automatically restart it.

Daemon and **demon** can be used interchangeably. The mythological meaning of daemon is that of an attendant spirit, which may have resulted in the acronym "Disk And Execution MONitor."

As long as the server has enough memory, most users won't experience performance issues. However, if other programs require memory at the same time, the computer will use virtual memory by swapping programs to disk. When this happens, processing speed gets slower. Support staff manage server memory and track the number of times a selected computer runs out of memory. To balance the workload, they will either move programs to other computers or increase the computer's memory. A poor server configuration can also lead to network faults.

Virtual memory allows a computer to use more random access memory (RAM) than it actually has. When a computer fills RAM completely, it moves or "swaps" instructions and data between the active storage in memory and the hard disk temporarily. As programs end and RAM becomes available, the instructions and data are read back into memory from the hard disk.

Application and Database Management

Databases and applications frequently use program servers, which are also managed by systems management software. Errors are recorded in event logs and agents warn staff before more serious problems develop. If the database or other software is licensed for a limited number of users, staff members will track the number of times someone cannot use the program because all licenses are taken, to justify purchasing more licenses. Software administrations also manage disk space, defragment files, and optimize a database so access and retrieval performance is very rapid.

Software administrators also schedule maintenance programs. For example, payroll processing usually requires a series of steps. First, payroll staff enter the number of hours each employee worked. Next, the payroll software calculates payroll taxes and employee deductions. After payroll staff or administrators review these preliminary calculations, another software routine updates the year-to-date earnings and deductions. Finally, a job prints the payroll checks.

Although most series of jobs can be run manually, special systems management software enables administrators to run them automatically. The administrators define rules in a scheduling application that determines which jobs can run at the same time and which should run sequentially. If an early job doesn't run successfully, the scheduling software will generate an event or alert so support staff can fix the problem and the following jobs can be restarted or the entire sequence rerun.

11

Desktop Management

Software such as Microsoft Systems Management Server (SMS) and Intel LANDesk include proactive utilities to detect problems. Agents may monitor individual PCs for available disk space, review errors in log files, and back up critical files. Virus scanning programs can look for viruses on any device on the network before they spread to other computers. The most useful application is remote control—support staff can update a Windows registry file, reconfigure a PC to an original installation copy, or reboot the PC from the systems management console. Some support groups restrict remote control of desktop computers to level two support staff because staff need either special training or security privileges to correct many PC problems. This is common for NT networks, where administrator privileges are required to correct security and file sharing problems.

 Remote control software was discussed in Chapter 7.

Security Management

Security management is more than setting up user accounts and resetting passwords. Network security is more important now that companies are using the Internet to share information with their customers. Most support groups restrict security maintenance to level two or three support staff, because adding and changing accounts incorrectly can prevent all users from accessing the network.

 Internet-specific security software will be discussed in more detail in Chapter 12.

Systems management software manages security by reviewing events and logs and scanning for errors that indicate unusual password activity. Log files may have records showing login failures because passwords don't match or repeated attempts to log in at a single location unsuccessfully. Agents can also be added to monitor changes to certain system files or other restricted areas that don't change under normal conditions. Some security applications can also be configured so that users can reset their own passwords without gaining access to other areas where they might cause problems.

 Some systems management applications list the Internet as another type of system. Internet management is actually the combination of all the systems types listed above. Security on a Web server is greater because corporate data must be protected. Web pages are managed as an application, and data may be stored in a database for further analysis. The Web server and other daemons need to run without problems, and disk space must be monitored on file servers or the Web application will fail. Finally, network traffic must be monitored and any bottlenecks to the company's Web page removed immediately.

PHILIP VERGHIS, CUSTOMER SUPPORT MANAGER
AKAMAI TECHNOLOGIES, INC.
CAMBRIDGE, MA
HTTP://WWW.AKAMAI.COM
PROACTIVE SUPPORT REQUIRES SELF-HEALING TECHNOLOGY AND SPECIALIZED SUPPORT STAFF

My company provides network services to some of the most well-known Internet and eCommerce sites in the world. As a company, our goal has been to create the world's most efficient Web delivery network--by removing Web congestion and guaranteeing continuous accessibility for our customers and their customers.

Our service guarantee sets a very high standard for customer support. If we don't deliver faster service (1.5 to 10 times faster) than other providers, with 100 percent reliability, regardless of the number of users on the network, they don't pay for service. Every employee in every department of the company, from the Chief Executive Officer and Chief Founder to the newest employee, is committed to this mission (there are many times I have called company executives at 3:00 in the morning just to let them know about developing issues with a customer). We want to make Akamai as well known for customer support as for our technical brilliance.

To achieve our company goals, our product depends upon a large network of over 1500 servers and 100 networks in 30 countries. Because no hardware can ensure that all pieces of the network are continuously available, our scientists have developed a self-correcting system that automatically routes Web content when individual networks are overloaded or out of service. Our Network Operations Center (NOC) monitors all servers in the network 24 hours a day, 7 days a week and 365 days a year.

When one of our customer's Web sites starts experiencing a lot of traffic, the site owner runs a utility that redirects calls from their Web server to the Akamai network. As our network picks up the request, our software determines the most efficient connection between the individual user and the Akamai server. Our customers have very little problems using the tools we provide. Our network was designed from the beginning to include self-correcting features and every server is an intelligent probe that can collect data.

We rely upon many intelligent agents to alert us before our customers realize they are having network problems. Our call volumes are actually low, but behind the scenes, support staff will examine gigabytes of data collected from the network to determine or prevent problems. We can't just "reboot" a server to correct network problems because our network interacts closely with our customers' networks to route traffic.

11

Our support staff (the Customer Care department) would be considered a third level support group in most companies. The "entry" level staff member usually comes to us with an engineering degree (we have a lot of MIT graduates because of our location and company history) and at least a year or two of network experience. More senior staff members usually have a master's level degree in engineering or programming with five to ten years of management experience. Customer Care staff members could easily work in Research and Development (R&D) because of their technical skills. We attract skilled candidates because the network challenges we have to solve are unique.

We retain our support staff because of the company's attitude toward support – our founders are passionate about going the extra step to make sure our customers are successful. We have built our own support system, the Akamaized Relationship Management System (ARMS), which is a Web portal that connects every company employee with customer information, based upon their role with the customer. It ties together homegrown software and commercial tools, providing data exchange between our sales force automation tools, customer management software, issue tracking, and knowledge base. Customer Care may receive e-mail from the customer and can get the history of interactions from the pre-sales engineer, as well as the history of interactions with the account manager. We provide constant feedback to R&D, so they understand just how customers use the features they work hard to develop.

Eventually, ARMS will also allow us to link more closely with our customers. We are working closely with the Distributed Management Task Force (http://www.dtmf.org) and the Customer Support Consortium (http://www.customersupport.org) as they develop and publish standards for exchanging call records and solution documents electronically. As more vendors adopt the Service Incident Exchange Standard (SIES) and the Solution Exchange Standard (SIS), companies will be able to exchange call tracking records between different software applications to reduce the time it takes to escalate issues between support groups. We will be able to work even more closely with our business partners, our customers, and their customers. As we help them become more successful, we'll be successful as well.

SYSTEMS MANAGEMENT SOFTWARE VENDORS

There are several common systems management software vendors. Table 11-1 lists software vendors that provide systems management applications.

As mentioned in Chapter 5, many of these vendors acquire smaller companies to enhance the features and tools they can provide their customers. Integrated system management suites of tools offer the advantages of a common user interface and consistent menus to higher levels of support. Many of these products also include call-tracking features.

Table 11-1 Common systems management software vendors

Company	Product Name	Web Site
BMC Software	Patrol	http://www.bmc.com
Cabletron Systems	Spectrum	http://www.cabletron.com
Cisco Systems	CiscoWorks	http://www.cisco.com
Computer Associates	TNG	http://www.cai.com
Hewlett-Packard	OpenView	http://www.hp.com
IBM	NetView	http://www.ibm.com
Intel	LANDesk	http://www.intel.com
Microsoft	Systems Management Server (SMS)	http://www.microsoft.com
Network Associates	Sniffer	http://www.nai.com
Seagate Technology	NerveCenter	http://www.seagate.com
Sun Microsystems	Solstice	http://www.sun.com
IBM Tivoli	TME	http://www.tivoli.com

CHAPTER SUMMARY

11

❐ Systems management attempts to protect all business applications and data. Levels two and three support staff administrate many IT systems and take calls escalated from level one support.

❐ There are two approaches to systems management. Reactive management addresses problems as they come in, which is similar to the way in which level one support works. Proactive management attempts to prevent problems before they happen. The primary performance measurement for networked systems is availability.

❐ Most networks are heterogeneous—a mix of different computer platforms and operating systems. Each individual device is a node of the network. A graphical topography represents the physical or logical connection of nodes.

❐ Many network messages use the SNMP protocol. Software agents collect and process thousands of messages, because the number would be too great to manage manually. An event is an action or activity that has significance to a task or program.

❐ Network management tries to prevent bottlenecks between devices. Network performance problems may be difficult to diagnose because so many systems are closely interrelated.

◻ There are two types of servers. One is a computer that provides services, such as storage, for other computers on a network. The second is a program that provides services. Some servers (called daemons) run continuously, waiting for requests.

◻ Databases and applications also use servers. The easiest problems to manage on a network are specific application or database problems.

◻ Security is more than adding logins and setting passwords. System management applications can monitor password failures and changes in files that don't occur under normal conditions. Companies that connect to the Internet need increased security to protect their corporate data, while still forwarding selected data and e-mail to the outside world.

KEY TERMS

address — A unique identification on a computer network.

agent — A software program that collects and processes information.

bot — An abbreviation for robot. *See also* agent.

bottleneck — Occurs when a resource reaches its maximum capacity and cannot keep up with the demands placed on it.

console — A workstation that can access multiple computers on multiple networks.

daemon — A program server that runs continuously, waiting for requests for service.

demon — *See* daemon.

enterprise management — *See* systems management.

event — An action or activity that has significance to a task or programs.

gateway — A network point that acts as an entrance to another network.

heterogeneous computing environment — A mix of different computing devices and operating systems.

intelligent agent — *See* agent.

network traffic — The transactions that pass between devices on a network.

node — An individual device on the computer network.

poll — To check the operational status of a piece of equipment and the connecting telephone lines.

push technology — The practice of receiving information from an agent.

Simple Network Management Protocol (SNMP) — A set of standards for communication with devices connected to a TCP/IP network.

system availability — The comparison of the time it took to repair a failure to the time the system was accessible before the failure.

systems management — The process of protecting the integrity of business applications, the company's data, and the technology assets that connect those applications and data.

topology — A graphical representation of the network nodes and the links between them.

REVIEW QUESTIONS

1. What is the difference between an enterprise and any other business organization?

2. E-mail administrators and database administrators will most likely be part of level one of the support group. True or False?

3. The _____ approach to systems management focuses on maintenance, diagnostics, and problem resolution.

4. Is level one support reactive or proactive? Explain.

5. There are 720 hours in a 30-day month. If an e-mail system took eight hours to fix a problem one month, what is the monthly availability of the e-mail system?

6. A(n) _____ network has many different operating systems and platforms.

7. Why may a topology map be represented in different ways? List the different ways.

8. All computers use SNMP to communicate on a network. True or False?

9. Hotbot.com is an example of a program _____.

10. Which of the following would not be considered an event?

    a. A message that a document printed successfully.

    b. A message that a document did not print successfully.

    c. A warning that a laptop could not connect to the network.

    d. An error that a file system is full.

11. When activity on a device or between devices occurs at a rate that exceeds the capacity, support staff attempt to find the _____.

12. Match which administrator would resolve each of the following errors. (*Hint:* Some administrators solve multiple problems, and some problems require multiple administrators.)

    1. E-mail administrator   a. It takes a long time to retrieve payroll records.

    2. Network administrator   b. I haven't received any e-mail all day.

    3. Database administrator   c. My print jobs won't print on the printer.

    4. Application administrator   d. My fax isn't going out to my customer.

    5. System administrator   e. I can't access a file in the department's shared file folder.

    6. Security administrator   f. I need a printer added to the network so our department can use it.

    g. I get an error that there is no more space when I try to file an e-mail message.

    h. I get an ORA-1400 error when I try to retrieve a database record.

    i. I get an error that says the application has timed out.

    j. I get an error that says I can't connect to the database

    k. I can't log in and I have typed my password carefully.

    l. I discovered a virus on some files I received in e-mail.

11

HANDS-ON PROJECTS

Project 11-1

Reviewing a topology. Visit The Atlas of Cyberspaces Web site at **http://www.geog.ucl.ac.uk** and follow the link **The Atlas of Cyberspaces** (to view computer network topologies). View the examples and identify the geographical locations involved. Print three topologies and identify them.

Project 11-2

Understanding performance management issues. Visit the SolarWinds Web site at **http://216.60.197.203** and follow links to papers on performance management. Or, find articles on network performance management in back issues of computing magazines. Identify at least three common performance measurements and write a short report that describes how support staff would use these measurements.

Project 11-3

Describing SNMP protocol features. Visit The Simple Times Web page at **http://www.simple-times.org** and follow the links to the archives of past issues. Answer the following questions:

1. When was the protocol created?
2. What are some of the security issues?
3. What organization maintains the protocol standards?

Project 11-4

Evaluating performance analysis tools. Glance is a UNIX performance analysis tool that is common on Hewlett-Packard, Sun, and IBM systems. Visit the Hewlett-Packard Web site at **http://www.openview.hp.com** and follow the links to the library of papers. Review the white papers for "Using Glance Effectively." List five of the specific performance problems the software may discover. What operating systems does it run under?

Project 11-5

Identifying administration tasks. Interview a level two or level three support person who administers a system (such as e-mail, database, network, or some application). Prepare a list of daily and weekly activities that the administrator performs.

Project 11-6

Understanding performance reports. Visit the MCI Web site at **http://www.vbns.net**. Follow the Network Traffic and Performance Monitoring link. Review some of the Daily Performance reports and statistics for network performance and compare the statistics for round trip speed (averages in milliseconds) for two systems for five days. Calculate the average, maximum, and minimum values for those days.

CASE PROJECTS

1. **Creating a Network Topology**

   Computers in the computer lab of your university have been suffering from slow system response. You have been asked to map the topology of the lab, before the problem is escalated to the university's support group. Use a map of the university campus to create a small part of the network topology. Create a topology that shows all the PCs in the lab and link those computers to the appropriate Web or file servers. Contact the university's support group for basic information and the locations of the main computing facility and the servers that support your computer lab.

2. **Calulating Mean Time Between Failures**

   As a team leader in a newly established level two support group, your manager wants to establish a service level agreement for system availability for the e-mail and database systems your customers use. You decide to interview several internal support managers and review their targeted percentages for system availability. Interview at least two different support groups that track system availability. Be sure to ask when they were able to commit to a published percentage for their customers and what influenced them in selecting the specific measurement (for example, why would they commit to 95 percent or 98 percent availability)? Use this information to suggest appropriate e-mail and database system availability to your manager.

11

3. **Adding Proactive Support Services**

   You manage a level three support group that supports internal customers at the Anderson Training company. Your support group has improved rapidly and you want to begin being more proactive in preventing problems, rather than just responding to network problems. Contact the software vendors or visit the Web sites for at least two integrated systems management suites of tools. Prepare a spreadsheet comparing the features for modules that monitor disk space and network or server events. Be sure to include a column that lists the operating systems and network protocols supported. Create a short report for your manager that explains how you will move into proactive support. Include the system management software you need to purchase and the amount of training needed by your support staff to use the new tools.

CHAPTER

12

SELF-HELP TOOLS

In this chapter you will learn:

♦ The advantages of self-service support for customers and support groups
♦ The primary self-service tools
♦ The challenges that self-service technologies present to support groups

---

Support groups continue to grow as technology becomes more ingrained in daily work and personal life. Internal support groups increase their services so computer users can be more productive and companies more competitive. External support groups expand their service hours to address worldwide needs and customers' expectation of answers at any time, whether day or night. Both internal and external support must solve the problems of understaffing and handling a greater variety of incoming questions and problems.

Although customer self-service won't completely replace a staffed support group, it is a growing component of the support environment. Customer **self-service** is the initial troubleshooting that a customer attempts, using knowledge or support tools that a support group maintains. Customers use self-service technologies for a variety of reasons: they are more convenient, they are available around the clock, and customers can use them to pursue solutions at their own pace without having to wait in line.

Support staff interact with these self-service tools as well. They may provide some of the initial knowledge in a knowledge base or use the same tools when customers cannot (or will not attempt) to help themselves. They also support these technologies just as they would any other business application by monitoring their use, evaluating customer successes, and making changes to features. If a customer has already tried self-service, support staff can begin their troubleshooting attempts at a later stage of the problem resolution process.

ADVANTAGES OF CUSTOMER SELF-SERVICE

Support groups face many of the same problems as the IT profession. Technology changes require managers to train their staff constantly. The demand for skilled technicians is growing, and most support groups are short staffed. The work pace and environment are stressful.

Each call to an internal help desk costs approximately $1 per minute in staff time and resources. One way internal support groups can control costs is to provide self-service tools for their customers. In some internal support environments, as much as 10 to 30 percent of repetitive calls can be resolved by customers using self-service tools. These tools don't eliminate the need for support staff, but they enable the support group to keep up with increased demand for services.

There are no formal studies on the average costs of support for external support groups because external support is not a business expense (as an internal support group is). This was discussed in Chapter 2.

Self-service tools work because a small percentage of callers would rather solve their own problems. Callers who attempt to help themselves do so for several reasons:

- They want to avoid the telephone hold times and begin troubleshooting immediately. Self-service tools mean that they don't have to navigate through an impersonal IVR, but can take action immediately.

- They like to solve problems themselves and learn by doing. They view problems as a challenge and use them to expand their understanding of an application. They can also explore at their own pace, making sure they understand everything. Busy level one support staff members may not have time to thoroughly explain why a particular problem happens, because their objective is to answer each question as quickly as possible. If the help desk has solved the problem previously, they already know an answer exists and just want to get to it as quickly as possible.

- They may have a better understanding of the problem than the support group. They don't have to describe what they were doing or the sequence of tasks they took to a support analyst.

- They may feel embarrassed to call the support group. They may have taken shortcuts or experimented with software settings and are embarrassed about their current situation. Or, they may want to determine which support group they really need before calling, so they don't waste the support staff's time.

Customers of external support groups have different reasons for using self-service rather than internal customers (remember, a large number of external customers buy products and services that are not technology-oriented). The growth of the Internet has provided a new way for customers to review company information and products. By using the Internet, the support group can expand its service hours and receive customer requests in forms that customers prefer. Customers can review product information, send e-mail requests, print or fax documents from Web sites, schedule training, and request that a salesperson contact them. Because questions frequently arise about products, companies use self-service to promote additional products and to expand business by listing related products or services, or by promoting products their business partners sell. As more companies offer self-service options, their competition finds that they must offer the same services just to compete.

 Internal support groups may also allow internal customers to use e-mail, fax, or Web pages to submit requests or report problems.

SELF-SERVICE TOOLS

There are several types of self-service tools that a support group can use, depending on its budget and needs. These tools are listed in Figure 12-1.

```
♦ Telephony
♦ Mailing lists
♦ Desktop and server software
♦ Internet support
```

Figure 12-1   Self-service tools

Telephony

12

As discussed in Chapter 9, many telephone-based technologies enable customers to directly retrieve the information they want. Fax-back services are one of the oldest ways to get detailed, specific answers to computer setup or troubleshooting questions. From a touch-tone phone, users select an option to retrieve a document that either explains how to find other documents or lists all available documents. Intel and Microsoft were among the earliest computer vendors to offer fax-back, self-service information. Computer magazines, user groups, and Web pages publish toll-free telephone numbers for fax-back services.

 In the rapidly changing technology environment, "old" really isn't a very long time. Fax-back services have been in place since the early 1990s, when companies began acquiring fax machines as standard office equipment.

Telephone-based support services (such as IVRs and message systems) are also commonly used by everyone for business and personal needs. Noncomputer businesses, such as banks and brokerages, have increased public acceptance of IVRs and intelligent message systems. To remain competitive, many of these companies had to add telephone-based support services because their competitors added them. Airlines and travel services also use IVRs to organize static information, including flight schedules, weather conditions, or changes due to construction. Companies add after-hours messages to their telephone systems to provide an informational message with the office location and the business hours.

Companies receiving calls nationally also include the time zone as part of their after-hours message.

Mailing Lists

Automated e-mail processing applications, such as mailing lists and newsgroups, are well–established forms of self-service tools. A **mailing list** is a list of e-mail addresses used to distribute e-mail to a large number of recipients. **Listserv** is an automated e-mail discussion list that processes e-mail requests for addition to or deletion from mailing lists. Some listserv programs provide other facilities, such as those for retrieving files from archives and performing database searches. Users receive details of available services by sending a message with the word HELP in the subject or body of the e-mail message to the listserv address. **Majordomo** is a freeware mailing list processor; **listproc** is another mailing list processor that runs primarily on UNIX machines. They both work similarly to listserv.

Listserv was initially written to run on IBM mainframes. It now runs on UNIX servers and other platforms.

Computer users with e-mail accounts can "subscribe" to virtual mailing lists. **Usenet** is a collection of notes on various subjects that are posted to servers on a worldwide network. A **newsgroup** is a Usenet collection of topic groups, similar to a mailing list that is maintained on a news server. Members of the newsgroup submit or post questions or opinions about items the group members discuss. Subscribers browse through the postings as they browse e-mail or they can choose to receive a separate message for every posting through their e-mail. Depending on the type of newsgroup, subscribers receive tips and tricks, regularly published newsletters, or problem reports. Internet newsgroups are one way to subscribe to a newsgroup, but companies can also create internal newsgroups specifically for their customers.

Usenet was originally implemented in 1979–1980 at Duke University as a distributed bulletin board system for UNIX machines. It encompasses government agencies, universities, high schools, businesses of all sizes, and home computers. Usenet groups are distributed to news servers periodically as digests, which have groups of postings collected into a single large posting with an index. Examples of Usenet groups include alt.computers, comp.Unix.wizards, and rec.arts.sf-lovers (for science-fiction fans). There are thousands of newsgroups ("groups" for short), and Usenet contributors add at least 40 megabytes (the equivalent of several thousand paper pages) of new technical articles, news, discussion, and chatter every day.

To participate in Usenet, you need a newsreader. Several Web browsers include newsreaders, and URLs that begin with "news:" refer to Usenet newsgroups. Not all Internet hosts subscribe to Usenet, and not all Usenet hosts are on the Internet, but there is a large overlap.

Usenet's original protocol was UNIX-to-UNIX Copy (UUCP), but today the Network News Transfer Protocol (NNTP) is used to transfer news articles between a news server and a newsreader.

Desktop and Server Software Solutions

There are two types of self-service tools available for PC users—optimization software and self-healing diagnostic software. Optimization software reviews system files and hardware on a PC. The software looks for compatibility problems or internal errors that aren't visible as people use their computers, and uses rules to determine settings that may improve PC performance. Some examples of optimization software are listed in Table 12-1.

Table 12-1 Optimization software

Company	Product	Web Page
Network Associates	First Aid, PC Medic, and Nuts & Bolts	http://www.nai.com
Symantec	Norton Utilities	http://www.symantec.com

After the optimization software analyzes the system, it presents a set of recommendations to the computer user, who then decides which changes to make. (These applications require direct interaction for changes.) Although optimization software is sometimes effective for first-time users, most of the recommended solutions are generic, so that they apply to all computer systems. The software cannot tell if a problem exists with a specific piece of hardware, or make a recommendation specific enough for users to fix the problem themselves.

Self-healing diagnostic software can diagnose problems, determine appropriate corrections, and complete the corrections without user interaction, by collecting information as the computer user works. Many hardware manufacturers are including these applications as part of the software bundled with each PC.

12

 Windows 98 scans the computer's hard disk and fixes file problems that occur when Windows isn't shut down correctly. Windows 95 runs the same programs, but the user must select which corrective action to take to fix file problems.

Self-healing diagnostic software is still evolving rapidly. There are three basic categories of self-healing software:

- Preemptive diagnosis
- Data collection
- Administrative automation

Preemptive diagnostics software find problems before they happen, by reviewing installed software and making sure the appropriate software patches and releases are installed. These applications fix problems without user intervention. Examples of this software are listed in Table 12-2.

Table 12-2   Preemptive diagnosis software

Company	Product	Web Page
Aveo	Attune	http://www.aveo.com
Network Associates	Oil Change and Repair Engine	http://www.nai.com
Support.com	Healing System	http://www.tioga.com
SystemSoft	SystemWizard	http://www.systemsoft.com

The preemptive diagnostics can be launched automatically by a critical system event, such as a general protection fault (GPF), or started manually by the computer users clicking an icon. The software compares the symptoms and setup information from the PC against information in a knowledge base. Some software resolves problems through software version control—these programs identify installed software by name and version and review current patches and releases available on the Internet. Users are then alerted that a more recent software version is available, and the download begins.

Data collection applications automate and improve the exchange between users and support technicians by collecting relevant information. These products collect information about the state of a system and deliver the appropriate self-service resolution. If the software can't solve the problem using information in the knowledge base, it uploads problem details to a remote server. Support staff are alerted that a user is connected, and they begin troubleshooting, using the problem details saved on the server. Data-collection-oriented software can automatically log the number of times that a user invokes it, the nature of problems fixed, and whether the problem was solved, uploading the details every time the user calls the remote server.

 When PCs are initially configured, the support staff make sure that software works with the available hardware. Over time, customers may add additional software or hardware. Many hardware companies report that in more than half of their service calls, the hardware is functioning but the installed software is incompatible.

Talkback is an example of this type of data collection self-healing diagnostic application. Talkback is built into the Netscape Communicator Web browser. It captures information when users have problems and feeds that information via the Web back to Netscape, which records it in a database. Netscape support staff analyze the collected data to determine what problems occur most frequently. Product engineers then use this information to create program routines that can work during these problem situations without errors when they design future versions of the software. Talkback pinpoints the exact code that was running when a crash occurred so that programmers know exactly which routines have problems. Table 12-3 lists examples of automated data collection software.

Table 12-3   Data collection software

Company	Product	Web Page
Courion Corporation	Password Courier	http://www.courion.com
Motive Communications	Motive Solo and Motive Duet	http://www.motive.com
NetManage	SupportNow	http://www.netmanage.com
Full Circle Software	Talkback	http://www.fullsoft.com/test_drive

The last type of self-healing diagnostic software enables users to perform support activities traditionally completed by support staff, such as resetting passwords. Many systems "lock out" users if they make repeated errors when they try to log in (this is a security feature that attempts to stop unauthorized users from logging in with someone else's ID and password). In large support environments, as much as 5 to 10 percent of all requests the support group receives are to reset passwords for customers. In most cases, it takes only a few seconds to reset a password, provided the support staff have the correct security access. Automating password resets (by allowing customers to reset their own login IDs) gives support staff time to handle more difficult problems. Customers can access these automated administration applications through specially structured e-mail or from an intranet Web page. Courion Corporation and Computer Associates have security products that also enable system administrators to delegate password resets or new user account setups to level one support or employee managers. Gasper Corporation has a voice-activated application—computer users call an IVR system, follow prompts to get to the appropriate password area, speak a unique identifying string, and then reset their own password.

12

SOME CUSTOMERS PREFER SPECIAL ATTENTION

Although more companies are expanding their customer self-service options, there is also a good argument for improving and expanding personal services a support group offers. Expanding services makes sense because it helps companies stand out from their competition.

When was the last time you walked into a department store and were offered helpful information as you shopped? Consumers demand lower prices and longer business hours (many retailers and supermarkets are already open twenty-four hours a day) and in return they accept the fact that they are less likely to find service representatives who can answer questions about products or point them to related products. As a result, retailers who offer the same types of products are hard to distinguish--when no one offers special services, it really doesn't matter where customers buy products, and they usually select the most convenient supplier. Because this is the norm, in the few cases when service representatives make suggestions or offer information based on the customer's unique situation, customers are more likely to remember these services and return for later business.

As more companies implement Web-based support services, additional technology helps companies interact with their customers if the customer wants the interaction. Some examples include:

- LivePerson (http://www.liveperson.com) is a simple service that lets customers click a button and open a new browser window for a text "chat" with an actual customer service representative.

- NewChannel (http://www.newchannel.com) allows support staff to initiate chats with customers as they move through Web sites. If a customer has been moving back and forth between product pages and the support page, support staff may push a text message specific to that customer, such as "We have more information about this product, if you would like to ask me any questions. Just press the Chat button, and I'll be glad to help you."

- BroadVision (http://www.broadvision.com) and NetPerceptions (http://www.netperceptions.com) attempt to personalize a customer's Web experience. Both products link real-time Web activity to historical customer information so support agents have relevant information in the event the customer calls the support group. Support staff can also push related information to the customers or call them to make special offers.

Market research continues to indicate that, as far as customers are concerned, support services from Web retailers are usually very poor. As more companies establish their Web presence, customers will most likely remember the companies who make purchasing convenient and offer support when the customer really needs it.

Internet Support

The Internet is an ideal way to present self-service information and tools. The Yankee Group, a Boston market research firm, reported in late 1999 that 57 percent of its customers already used the Web for customer support. Support groups receive 10 to 15 percent fewer repeat questions as long as they publish and maintain a good knowledge base for customer access. The Internet is especially popular for presenting product information or technical support reference material.

Employees frequently have access to restricted Web pages. An **intranet** is a network modeled on the World Wide Web, used by members of an organization and usually inaccessible to outsiders. Intranets are not necessarily connected to the Internet. Much of the information collected in these Web pages is confidential and not shared with the general public. Since 1995, intranets have become more common in companies because of the availability of cheap or free browser and server software. From intranets, employees can review Human Resources information, order office supplies, take online tutorials, and review marketing materials.

In some cases, it is necessary to share confidential information with customers. An **extranet** is an extension of a company intranet that allows selected customers, business partners, suppliers, and mobile employees to access the company's private data and applications. A **firewall** is a security system intended to protect a company's network from external threats. Firewalls prevent hackers from communicating directly with computers in the company's network through the Internet. All communication is routed through a proxy server outside of the organization's network, and the proxy server decides whether it is safe to let a particular message or file pass through to the organization's network. The firewall computer forms a gateway between the company intranet and the Internet, as shown in Figure 12-2. Users with the correct software and security connect to the internal network through controlled points in the firewall. Once inside the firewall, customers can only access a few, predefined files, programs, or databases.

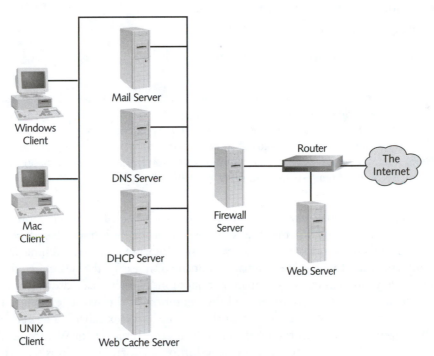

Figure 12-2   Extranet with a firewall

Companies that sell products by catalog orders, telephone orders, or from Web pages may eliminate calls by allowing customers access to their extranet. For example, Federal Express customers can check on the status of packages they have shipped by using a shipping ID, which was issued to them when they shipped the item to protect the information. Software vendors also allow customers access to technical support information and other services that are available to special accounts.

Support groups typically begin building Internet (or extranet) support by publishing lists of frequently asked questions (FAQs). They later add additional types of information. Well-developed Web sites incorporate several features, including:

- FAQs
- Hints and tips for using the Internet more effectively
- How-to articles or tutorials on common tasks
- Links to other sites
- Online reference manuals
- Security policies
- Important telephone numbers
- A search tool
- A feedback tool (to report problems)

TIP Educational institutions have used Internet Web sites to publish a wide variety of unchanging information, such as computer lab hours, tutorials, institution-specific information, historical information, and community-oriented programs. A university or college that supports thousands of students and faculty members can handle hundreds of requests for user accounts and questions with fewer than a dozen support staff; they receive a lot of requests that are repeated with each new group of students.

There might be additional ways to collect feedback or search for information, depending upon the targeted users and whether the Web site is Internet- or intranet-based. For example, the Ask Jeeves Web site at http://www.ask.com assists Internet users in searching Web sites for specific information. To help users retrieve information easily, the search engine accepts queries that are written in the way humans ask questions, which is called **natural language**. For example, if a user wants to understand the definition of the word "extranet," he or she might ask the question, "Where can I find the definition of extranet?" The search engine parses the important words in the question, searches the Internet for Web pages that contain the words, and presents the data organized into categories to help isolate the results. Figure 12-3 shows the results of this search. Typically Web pages with definitions (for example, dictionaries or thesaurus pages that are most likely to "define" things) are grouped together at the top of the results, and Web pages for search programs (for example, AltaVista and WebCrawler that contain general references such as white papers or newsletters) are grouped later in the results.

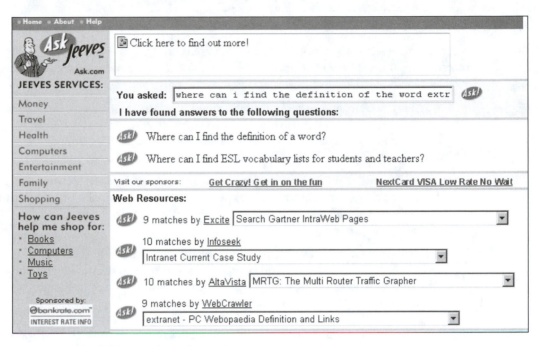

Figure 12-3   Ask Jeeves search results

 Toshiba America purchased rights to a special version of Ask Jeeves to handle customer support questions. They wanted customers to use the natural language engine to query the company's knowledge base with simple questions. Natural language queries are more likely to find the correct results because customers don't have to worry about special query construction rules.

There are other activities that support groups can allow customers to complete using Internet support, besides sharing support knowledge bases. Some companies allow customers to create their own call records and to follow the calls' progress as support staff research them. For example, an energy company in San Antonio, Texas, allows internal users to log problems, verify the status of their requests, and search for answers from the call management application. Telephone calls from internal users have dropped significantly, since they can track their ongoing status from the Web. Call logging by customers is a big timesaver for support staff because support staff are often interrupted by new telephone calls as they try to complete problem details. Eventually, they must return to finish the problem descriptions so they can move the call record through the support process to other support levels.

 In a broader interpretation of self-service tools, some companies also consider computer-based training (CBT) as a self-help tool. When CBT is easily accessible from a Web page or shared file system, employees can launch CBT for a specific topic to answer procedural questions before they call the support group.

SELF-SERVICE CHALLENGES

As promising as self-service tools are, these tools aren't always successful in every company. First, customers must accept the tools and use them. Customers may not accept self-service tools for several reasons:

- Many people are not technically inclined. They use technology because it is part of their job and because it is necessary to complete their work. When they have problems with technology, they prefer to talk to another person.

- Customer support includes handling complaints as well as solving problems and completing requests. Software applications don't understand a customer's frustration or disappointment like a real person can. Interpersonal communication helps support staff understand when it is appropriate to elevate a problem to a higher level of urgency.

- Customers have to be able to find what they need quickly. Web-based self-service is unsuccessful without good content. Support groups must collect, publish, and maintain knowledge resources regularly. Web visitors quickly abandon a site after they search a few times unsuccessfully.

 Most support experts agree that support groups can expect only about 25 percent of their customers to use self-service tools.

 Web sites that receive a lot of e-mail from customers asking for information already on the Web site should ask themselves why customers are sending e-mail. Is it because customers can't find the answers on the Web site? Some Web knowledge base applications provide a rating button so that customers can indicate whether the specific information they looked at solved their problem or pointed them to more useful material.

Self-service tools are also unsuccessful if they increase telephone calls to support. Self-healing diagnostic applications must be able to handle all types of hardware or software configurations and be able to resolve different combinations of problems. Self-service tools are another product the support group maintains (similar to telephone systems and other technology), and won't be effective if customers require support staff to answer questions about the tools themselves.

CHAPTER SUMMARY

- Self-service tools are used by a minority of callers who either prefer the challenge of solving their own problems or who want service at their own pace. If a caller knows what information he or she needs, he or she probably understands more about the question than the support staff.

❐ Fax-back services and IVRs are self-service tools that noncomputer users may be familiar with.

❐ Newsgroups and mailing lists have been used longer than other self-service tools. Several mail-processing programs automate common administrative tasks, such as adding e-mail addresses, retrieving files, and performing database searches.

❐ Special PC software, called self-healing diagnostic applications, prevent problems or diagnose problems and take appropriate corrective actions. Other applications enable computer users to perform tasks usually completed by support staff, such as resetting passwords after repeated login failures.

❐ The Internet is a rapidly growing way to enable customers to support themselves. Similar network applications, such as intranets, provide data within a company or to a selected list of customers and business partners. Well-developed support sites provide as much information as possible about alternate resources and search options.

❐ Most support groups share knowledge base information with their customers. A few allow customers to log and track their own problem reports. Customer call logging saves support staff time. Customer Web access to call tracking systems decreases follow-up calls to check problem status.

❐ Self-service tools are an important way for support groups to keep up with increasing demands for service. Some people will never use self-service tools because they prefer communicating directly to a person. Self-service tools must be deployed carefully and maintained well or they can also generate more work for the support staff.

12

KEY TERMS

extranet — An extension of a company intranet that allows selected customers, business partners, suppliers, and mobile employees to access the company's private data and applications.

firewall — A computer with additional security that serves as a gateway between the company intranet and the Internet.

intranet — A network modeled on the World Wide Web, used by members of an organization and usually inaccessible to outsiders.

listproc — A freeware mailing list processor that runs primarily on UNIX machines—similar to listserv.

listserv — An automated e-mail discussion list that processes e-mail requests for addition to or deletion from mailing lists.

mailing list — A list of e-mail addresses used to distribute e-mail to a large number of recipients.

majordomo — A freeware mailing list processor, similar to listserv.

natural language — Queries that are written in the way humans ask questions.

newsgroup — A Usenet collection of topic groups.

self-healing diagnostic software — Software that can diagnose problems, determine appropriate corrections, and complete the corrections without user interaction.

self-service — The initial troubleshooting that a customer attempts using knowledge or support tools that a support group maintains.

Usenet — A collection of notes on various subjects that are posted to servers on a world-wide network.

REVIEW QUESTIONS

1. List three reasons why some computer users choose to use self-service tools.

2. Which types of self-service tools would noncomputer users most likely use?

3. A(n) _____ is a Usenet collection of topics where subscribers post messages and remarks.

4. Name two automated e-mail processors.

5. Self-healing diagnostic software prompts computer users before it makes changes. True or False?

6. Name a common software application that includes a form of self-healing diagnostic software.

7. Which of the following network statements is true?

   a. All companies allow employees access to the Internet.

   b. A remote employee would use an extranet to access Human Resources information.

   c. Once they are behind a firewall, a company's computers are accessible to all network users.

   d. A company's business partners could use an extranet to review product information that many customers may not have access to.

8. The most common item shared with customers on the Internet or an extranet is the support group's _____.

9. What percentage of customers is likely to use self-service tools?

10. List three reasons why self-service tools aren't more widely adopted.

HANDS-ON PROJECTS

Project 12-1

Using self-healing software. Visit the Motive Communications Web site at **http://www.motive.com**. Follow the **products & technology** links to take a Product TestFlight of the Motive products. Complete either Testflight simulation. If the software determines a problem is caused by outdated software, what actions occur?

Project 12-2

Applying self-healing diagnosis to support problems. Visit the Support.com (formerly known as Tioga Systems) Web site at **http://www.tioga.com**. Follow the links to the **eSupport link** and take the Enterprise Healing System tours (complete the first three chapters). What are three common help desk problems covered in these support tools?

Project 12-3

Reviewing administration automation software. Visit the Courion Corporation Web site at **http://www.courion.com**. What operating systems and network applications can be supported with the password reset modules? What common call management applications are integrated with Password Courier? Take the demo for Password Courier. Is this product intranet-based or Internet-based?

Project 12-4

Understanding   preemptive   software. Visit   the   Aveo,   Inc.   Web   site   at **http:// www.aveo.com**. Review the Web pages about Attune. What category of self-healing software is this product? Who are some of their business partners?

Project 12-5

Using   data   collection   diagnostic   software. Visit   the   Web   site   at **http://www.fullsoft.com/test_drive**. Follow the links to locate the Talkback test drive for Call Avoidance. In the example, what would have happened if Janet, the computer user, had spoken to a support technician? What does this demonstrate about the need for hardware and software inventories?

Project 12-6

Using e-mail based self-service tools. Visit the Island Data Web site at **http://www.islanddata.com**. Follow the **Products** links to ExpressResponse and take the online demo. Do customers have to structure their e-mail before sending messages to ExpressResponse? When a query finds possible answers, how do customers indicate which answer they need more detail on?

Project 12-7

Researching Internet-based self-service products. Visit the Quintus Web site at **http://www.quintus.com** and download white papers on "Web-Based Customer Service" and "Ten Reasons Your Ecommerce Website Needs Live Help." Answer the following questions:

1. What is the primary advantage of a Web-based ACD?

2. How does "follow the sun" support improve when provided by the Web?

3. What is the primary reason that adults shop online?

12

CASE PROJECTS

1. **Subscribe to Support Newsgroups or Mailing Lists**

   You have recently been promoted to support manager for the internal support group of Eden Valley Enterprises. You want to make sure that your support group is following common procedures and that the issues you face regarding hiring, staffing, and support burnout are similar to those that other support groups experience. Select two mailing lists or newsgroups from Table 12-4 and subscribe for two weeks. Group the posting summaries by subject and summarize the major topics discussed during this period. Which topics are discussed most frequently?

Table 12-4   Newsgroups and mailing lists

Topic	Newsgroup or Mailing List and Message
Computer Training subjects	**listproc@bilbo.isu.edu** Subject: none Message: subscribe Computer-Training your_first_name your_last_name
Heat Call Tracking Software	**http://www.heatsoftware.com/heatforum/index.html**
Help Desk List (Digest) (one e-mail message daily, which contains all the messages sent to the list for that day)	**LISTSERV@wvnvm.wvnet.edu** Subject: none Message: subscribe HDESK-L your_first_name your_last_name
Help Desk News Group	**bit.listserv.hdesk-l** or **uwo.comp.helpdesk**
Knowledge bases	**listserv@list.nih.gov** Subject: none Message: subscribe knowbase your_first_name your_last_name
McAfee Help Desk (Network Associates)	**subscribe-mhd@alldata.com** Subject: none Message: none
McAfee's ZAC (Zero Administration Client) and desktop management products	**subcribe-zac@alldata.com** Subject: none Message: none
Newsgroups on technical support	**alt.management.tech-support** or **alt.managing.techsupport**
Remedy ARS	**listserv@listserv.acsu.buffalo.edu** Subject: none Message: subscribe arslist your_first_name your_last_name
SupportMagic Software	**listserv@cfrvm.cfr.usf.edu** Subject: none Message: subscribe smagic your_first_name your_last_name

Table 12-4   Newsgroups and mailing lists (continued)

Topic	Newsgroup or Mailing List
University-specific Help Desk list	**listserv@vma.cc.nd.edu** Subject: none Message: subscribe hdi-edu your_first_name your_last_name
University-specific list for support professionals who support computers and students in residence halls and computer clusters	**listserv@vma.cc.nd.edu** Subject: none Message: subscribe resnet-l your_first_name your_last_name

2. Using a Virtual Help Desk

Your company is considering purchasing a product called AutoCad, which is produced by AutoDesk. Part of your product evaluation includes a review of the company's support options. AutoDesk uses a "virtual" help desk concept on their Web page to provide customer self-service options. Visit the AutoDesk Web site at **http://www.autodesk.com**. Follow the Tech Assist link to the AutoCad product. List some of the different information topics. How would you submit an enhancement request? How would you report a problem that you think is a software bug? If you still can't find what you are looking for, what other options would make this site more customer friendly?

3. Understanding Successful Self-Service Web Sites

Your external support group is considering offering your customers a self-service Web site. The Vice President of Technology wants your Web site to represent the company well and mentioned that many technology companies consider Cisco Systems to have one of the best self-service Web sites. In particular, Cisco Systems answers 77 percent of all questions via their online support center, including those about hardware repair shipments, and allows their customers to set up a profile so they are notified whenever a new bug might affect them. Visit the Cisco Web site at **http://www.cisco.com** and follow the links to Service & Support, Online Support Benefits. Read the overview to learn what the company's support objectives are. What does this company call its knowledge base? In the event that you still want to speak to a human support analyst, is it easy to find an appropriate telephone number? What other types of questions or requests can be handled by this Web site, besides questions about the products?

12

13

SERVICE TECHNOLOGY TRENDS AND CAREER RESOURCES

In this chapter you will learn:

♦ The developing changes in IT and support environments

♦ The emphasis on certifying support professionals

♦ IT and support staff career development resources

Information technology is a set of "young" business processes, as opposed to processes in other business departments. Technology improvements have occurred so quickly during the last twenty years that it has been difficult for companies to develop and refine their information processes. However, Information Management is becoming an important company department, just like Accounting, Payroll, Finance, and Sales.

Most support groups provide services for the technology used by companies and their customers. In the coming years, IT support groups will begin to work more behind the scenes, like the other business areas. Technical problems will be more time-sensitive because customers will rely on technology and support even more than they do now.

CHANGES IN IT AND SUPPORT ENVIRONMENTS

In the last fifteen years, IT environments have evolved from mainframe-based applications to network systems with many different types of technology (LANs, WANs, telecommunications equipment, and UNIX or PC file servers). The industry is evolving toward round-the-clock availability, which requires that key systems remain operational continuously. Previously 24 × 7 processing was a consideration for only multinational companies and other very large organizations. Today, all moderately sized businesses are beginning to adopt 24 × 7 system availability so that information is continuously available; a company's collected information is becoming more important than the products it sells. In other words, employees need access to systems at all times—it's no longer enough to just sell products without analyzing the results of the sales and customer interactions. Some of the trends represented by these IT changes are listed in Figure 13-1.

```
♦ eCommerce
♦ Remote access
♦ Self-Service
```

Figure 13-1   IT trends

eCommerce

Electronic commerce (eCommerce) is business communication and transactions that occur over networks and through computers. Activities include buying and selling goods or services over the World Wide Web and the Internet, transferring electronic funds, and exchanging data. The software used for eCommerce tends to be UNIX- or NT-server-based. Internet traffic is expected to grow tremendously in the next five years, as more small and medium businesses join the Internet community. When applications can be used by any number of customers over the Internet, it is hard to predict how many users will attempt to use the application at any time.

 In the late 1990s, corporate managers began to push their companies to use their Web pages to increase business. Marketing and IT departments worked together to change their companies into a "dot.com" (or .com) type of company, which meant they were well known on the Internet.

As companies exchanged more data among different types of computer systems, it became apparent that they needed to standardize data. **Electronic data interchange (EDI)** is the direct computer-to-computer transfer of business information. While EDI was originally designed for purchasing systems, companies now rely on standardized document forms, such as e-mail, fax, and video conferencing, for data they receive from their business partners.

In 1993, President Clinton signed an executive order to all departments and agencies of the U.S. federal government on streamlining government procurement through electronic commerce. This order required civilian and noncivilian agencies to convert to electronic commerce by January 1997, to move the U.S. government from a paper-based to an electronically-based system. All companies that do business with the government must have EDI capabilities. EDI standards now exist for financial and health care data.

As more companies connect to the Internet and network traffic increases, computer systems and network management will become more complex. Companies will allow selected business partners access to more systems *behind* their firewalls. Extranets may become more common as businesses link internal information with data from their suppliers and business partners. Connections with customers and trading partners already focus on simple commerce activities, such as sales and order-status tracking. Support staff will troubleshoot not only their own company's networked systems but also their company's customers and business partners' connections to the company's network. Support staff will need a good understanding of connectivity technologies just to isolate problems.

Already help desks and support centers have been relabeled "contact centers" to emphasize the fact that they are more directly involved in company business. The duties for staff members are expanding, according to market research groups. Customer service representatives will not only answer questions and solve problems, but also perform sales roles and promote new products and services. Forrester Research projects that by the year 2001, 50 percent of all new hires will be selected for their process and change management capabilities and that 25 percent of all IT staff will be relocated to business units. Troubleshooting and communication skills, which are key support staff skills now, will be part of the minimum skills that all employees need to help companies achieve their goals.

Remote Access

Remote network access will also change many of the traditional work environments ("Technology Marches On," *InfoWorld*, 7/21/99). Information systems and applications will be accessible at any time of the day or night (commercial databases such as Oracle and SQL Server now allow IT staff to back up database records without requiring all computer users to exit). More business computer users will work remotely because of better connectivity; modems are faster and local telephone and cable companies provide faster connection services such as DSL or ISDN at more affordable prices. Improvements in networking and telecommunications will also allow support staff to work remotely and globally. Help desks won't be concentrated in a single, physical location, and many customers won't realize that support staff are actually working from home offices. Instead, virtual support centers will provide follow-the-sun support.

13

Telecommuting is the practice of connecting a computer to a business's network through a modem. Originally, the term described people who worked from home occasionally (for example, parents who had sick children who couldn't go to school or day care would telecommute, or system administrators who needed to access the company computer systems after business hours would do so), but the meaning has expanded recently to include all remote workers. Not only do many employees prefer telecommuting as a lifestyle, but also local and state governments encourage companies to promote telecommuting as a way to reduce parking and pollution problems. The U.S. Office of Personnel Management (the federal government's human resources agency) at http://www.opm.gov/wrkfam helps other federal agencies develop family-friendly programs such as telecommuting. An interesting story on the history of telecommuting is located at the Hireability Web site at http://www.hireability.com (follow the links to Resources).

With the increase in continuous accessibility, support groups must be proactive. The number of transactions that software processes will increase, and processing will have to continue behind the scenes, rather than after-hours, as companies expand globally. Business impact will be too great to wait for problems to happen, so IT professionals and automated systems will have to identify potential problems early. New types of automated agents will query databases and follow online transactions until they are successfully completed, preventing errors that can lead to downtime. Companies that minimize their recovery time between problems will be the most competitive.

TELECOMMUTING COMPLICATES SECURITY AND REMOTE ACCESS

A study in late 1999 by InfoBeads, the market research arm of Ziff-Davis Corporation, found that the number of telecommuters was almost 7 million people (an increase of 30 percent from the previous year). Although most employees telecommuted part-time, the survey also revealed that the number of full-time telecommuters had increased 78 percent to almost 1 million workers. Telecommuting has become an important benefit for many IT workers and, as telecommunications services and equipment improves, the number of full- and part-time telecommuters will continue to rise.

Although companies that offer telecommuting and remote access may attract or retain more employees, new IT issues have arisen. Laptop computer thefts not only deprive employees of remote access, but also expose the company to higher risks with loss of important and confidential data. Support staff also have to be able to support employees remotely, which requires software tools for remote control and diagnosis for problems and to push software upgrades. In some cases, someone (the remote employee or support staff) will have to travel to complete hardware upgrades or repairs. People outside the confines of a company also want access to the same internal resources that onsite employees have, and they need fast remote access. Previously, employees could dial-in to a company network behind the firewall, but dial-up access to a central location was slow and employees who traveled between locations incurred significant long distance charges.

As service providers offer public cable and satellite access to the Internet, many IT groups have looked to national service providers who can produce fast and secure links to company networks. One IT solution that provides secure, local access is a virtual private network (VPN). A VPN gives users access to corporate networks over the Internet or other public or private networks and includes security features for encryption, authentication, and tunneling. Companies use VPNs instead of traditional dial-up connections that use the public switched telephone network or dedicated leased lines, for remote users and telecommuters, to connect LANs in different sites and to provide extranet services to customers and business partners. VPNs have higher security than extranets, and require data encryption between the user's PC and corporate servers.

Companies can save money several ways by using a VPN:

- They reduce the number of access lines into a corporate site. Many companies pay monthly charges for two types of access lines: (1) high-speed links for their Internet access and (2) frame relay, ISDN, or T1 lines to carry data. A VPN can consolidate data traffic over the company's Internet access and reduce the number of leased lines needed.

- They outsource the management of remote access equipment to a service provider. This eliminates some operational costs when the company can get rid of modem pools and remote access servers, and support staff can maintain other equipment.

- They reduce long-distance phone charges by remote employees. The user dials a local call to an ISP rather than place a long-distance call.

Although security is enhanced, the amount of administration is not necessarily increased. Many ISPs support a range of authentication techniques using products such as Kerberos, tokens, and software- and hardware-based dynamic passwords. A few vendors can link VPN access rights to security already defined in Windows NT Workgroup lists, Novell Directory Services, or Binderies.

In general, service is reliable and competition between providers is fierce. Most of the service providers with nationwide access guarantee that the network will be available at least 99.6 percent of the time, which translates into a maximum outage time of about 6.5 minutes a day before refunds or credits kick in. Some offer higher availability with refunds or credits kicking in for outages of 3 minutes a day or longer. As more IT organizations outsource specialized tasks as activities to specialized providers, new services develop. Some national service providers have added other services to provide remote workers with hardware and software upgrades as well as equipment repair.

13

Self-Service

Knowledge bases are already becoming increasingly important because employees no longer stay with one company or job for more than a few years. As employees move from company to company, there will be a growing need for company-specific and historical knowledge. New staff members can use this stored data to look up old problems and their solutions and to understand the business reasons for some customer interactions. International Data Corporation industry analysts project that the market for problem resolution software will reach $657 million by 2002. As a result, support staff will spend less time directly answering questions and more time creating and organizing knowledge for self-service applications for customers. Customers have become more successful searching knowledge bases because there have been advances in natural-language processing and search engines.

 Forrester Research projects that by 2001, online self-service tools will handle 50 percent of all external requests for help.

Self-service tools, such as knowledge bases and computer-based training, will continue to increase in use. Some experts estimate that 85 percent of all calls coming into support are actually usability issues—the customer is trying to figure out how to use the product. Most of the usability issues relate to documentation or training. Customers could have found the solution themselves if they had just read the manual, completed the tutorial, or gone to a training class. Most people won't use software documentation. In response, software manufacturers have been eliminating user manuals and improving online help systems. For example, many Windows applications include "wizards" that lead the user through common or complex tasks. Computer users who are willing to read printed reference manuals can purchase books by third-party publishers about most commercial PC products.

Some companies are reducing interactive telephone support in favor of automated systems. Over time, many companies will change the free and fee-based services they offer. Free support will be available through self-service tools for anyone who buys products. Customers who prefer human telephone support will be able to purchase a "premium" support option.

PROFESSIONAL CERTIFICATION

Professional certification already exists for many professions. Public accountants, electricians, engineers, and mechanics are certified to ensure that they understand and can complete all the requirements for their profession. These people are considered experts, and they understand the best processes and practices for their profession. As a rule, certification builds credibility with customers. Certified individuals often get better jobs, receive higher salaries, and advance more quickly than people who are not certified. Most certifications are based on a combination of test scores, academic credit (in the case of students), and/or job experience.

Managers recognize the importance of certifying IT and support professionals because customers need assurance that support staff can address increasingly complex technical problems. As mentioned earlier, many support staff move from IT back into business departments.

Not only must staff be able to troubleshoot technical problems, but they must also be able to effectively determine the business impact of problems and the effect on a company's customers. Certification is becoming a part of the ongoing training and education of all support staff. The different levels of professional certification are listed in Figure 13-2.

```
♦ IT certification
♦ Support certification
♦ Product certification
```

Figure 13-2   Certification levels

IT Certification

Two organizations are involved in certifying individuals in specific IT areas—the Association of Information Technology Professionals and the Institute for Certification of Computer Professionals. The **Association of Information Technology Professionals (AITP)**, at http://www.aitp.org, is a professional association that emphasizes training for employers, employees, managers, programmers, and computer operators. AITP was founded in the 1950s as the National Machine Accountants Association (NMAA) and evolved into the Data Processing Management Association (DPMA) in the 1970s, before the organization took its current name in 1996. The association attempts to provide a way for all members to be teachers as well as students, through its mentoring programs. It also provides a resource where members can make contacts with other IT professionals. A special interest group works with universities and colleges to ensure that IT-specific courses continue to address current technology.

The group helped establish the ICCP, which focuses on certification. The **Institute for Certification of Computer Professionals (ICCP)**, at http://www.iccp.org, develops and maintains examinations to certify individuals as either Associate Computing Professionals (ACP) or Certified Computing Professionals (CCP).

 Certifications change as the IT environment changes. In the 1980s, there were Certified Data Processor (CDP), Certified Computer Programmer (CCP), and Certified Systems Professional (CSP) certifications.

Other IT organizations and support groups provide a way to network with individuals with common interests by coordinating regional and national meetings. Table 13-1 lists professional associations and their related Web sites. Most have local or regional chapters that meet regularly.

13

Table 13-1 IT organizations and support associations

Organization/Association	Web Page
American Teleservices Association, Inc.	http://www.ataconnect.org
Association of Information Technology Professionals	http://www.aitp.org
Association for Women in Computing	http://www.awcncc.org
Association of Support Professionals	http://www.asponline.com
Association of Windows NT Professionals	http://www.ntpro.org
BackOffice Professionals	http://www.bopa.org
Call Centre Managers Forum	http://callcentres.com.au
Call Center Network Group	http://www.ccng.com
CSM Group	http://www.hug.co.uk
Customer Care Institute	http://www.customercare.com
Customer Service Management	http://www.csm-us.com
Customer Support Consortium	http://www.customersupport.org
The Direct Marketing Association	http://www.the-dma.org
Direct Selling Association	http://www.dsa.org
Distributed Management Task Force	http://www.dmtf.org
Help Desk 2000	http://www.helpdesk2000.org
Help Desk Institute	http://www.helpdeskinst.com
Incoming Calls Management Institute	http://www.incoming.com
Institute for Certification of Computer Professionals	http://www.iccp.org
Interex (The International Association of Hewlett-Packard Computing Professionals)	http://www.interex.org
International Customer Service Association	http://www.icsa.com
SHARE	http://www.share.org
Society of Telecommunications Consultants	http://www.stcconsultants.org
Software Support Professionals Association	http://www.supportgate.com

Support Staff Certification

All support staff should have some level of communication training so that they can work with customers effectively. It is easy to find one- or two-day training seminars to improve basic communication and listening skills, to learn how to work with difficult support issues on the telephone, and to learn ways to improve customer service. There are also organizations that promote and provide support-specific training, including:

- **Help Desk 2000:** Certification programs include Certified Help Desk Professional, Certified Help Desk Manager, and Certified Help Desk Director

- **Call Center University:** Certification programs include managers, supervisors, and Technical Manager/Specialist

- **Support Services Career Certification (S2C2):** Certification programs include Certified Support Services Representative (CSSR), Certified Support Services Associate (CSSA), Certified Support Services Specialist (CSSS), as well as other technical and managerial certifications.

- **Computing Technology Industry Association (CompTIA):** Certification programs include the A+ certification that certifies competency of entry-level service technicians, and the Network+ certification for networking technicians.

Depending on the level of support they provide, some support staff may have degrees from colleges or universities. Many universities, colleges, and technical trade schools offer associate degrees for support professionals. Level two and three support staff may have a Bachelor of Science degree in computer science, or a Bachelor of Arts degree in management information systems (MIS).

Product Certification

Product certification has been increasingly important for levels two and three support staff. Many products are very complex, and software vendors want to make sure that the people who install their products understand them completely. Certification in these areas includes the ability to install, implement, and administer the application as well as the ability to provide support services. The vendor defines program requirements. Each vendor has training and testing centers, and they certify third-party instructors and training centers. Some of the most common product certifications come from companies such as:

- Novell
- Microsoft
- Cisco
- Oracle
- Lotus

Some software vendors, such as Novell and Microsoft, require sales staff to be certified before they can sell the company's products.

Novell

Novell, Inc., at Web site http://www.novell.com, provides PC network software. Novell software was one of the first PC technologies to recommend certification. They have several individual tests for each level of certification. Some of the Novell certification titles include:

- Certified NetWare Administrator (CNA)
- Certified Novell Engineer (CNE)
- Master Certified Novell Engineer (MCNE)
- Certified NetWare Instructor (CNI)

13

Microsoft

Microsoft Corporation, at Web site http://www.microsoft.com, provides PC software, e-mail software, networking software, Internet servers and browser software, and database software. Microsoft certification programs are not restricted to support or IT professionals. Microsoft certification titles include:

- **Microsoft Office User Specialist (MOUS):** Validates expertise with desktop applications

- **Microsoft Certified Professional (MCP):** Validates expertise with more complex applications such Exchange and system management tools

- **Microsoft Certified Professional + Internet (MCP+Internet):** Validates expertise in administering security, server setup, and resource management as it is affected by Internet access

- **Microsoft Sales Specialist (MSS):** Identifies business partners trained in selling Microsoft products

- **Microsoft Certified Systems Engineer (MCSE):** Identifies staff qualified to effectively plan, implement, maintain, and support information systems in a wide range of computing environments using NT Server

- **Microsoft Certified Systems Engineer + Internet (MCSE+Internet):** Identifies IT professionals who can enhance, deploy, and manage sophisticated intranet and Internet solutions that include browser, proxy server, host server, database, and messaging and commerce components

- **Microsoft Certified Database Administrator (MCDBA):** Identifies professionals who implement and administer Microsoft SQL Server databases

- **Microsoft Certified Trainer (MCT):** Identifies trainers qualified to deliver Microsoft courses to computer professionals

Cisco

Cisco Systems, Inc., at Web site http://www.cisco.com, provides networking hardware and software. The Cisco Certified Internetwork Expert (CIE) requires individuals to recertify every two years.

Oracle

Oracle Corporation, at Web site http://www.oracle.com, provides database software. There are several levels of training and certification oriented toward database administrators and developers. Certifications are available for:

- Oracle Database Administrator (for each specific software release)

- Oracle Application Developer

- Oracle Database Operator

- Oracle Financial Applications Consultant

Lotus

Lotus Development Corporation, at Web site http://www.lotus.com, provides Web server, e-mail, and database software. Lotus certifications include levels for developers, administrators, consultants, and user specialists. Certification programs include:

- Certified Lotus Specialist (CLS)
- Certified Lotus Professional (CLP)
- Certified Lotus Instructor (CLI)
- Certified Lotus End-user Instructor (CLEI)

Other Certification Programs

Most call management applications include user, administration, and implementation training programs. Companies such as Siebel Systems, Inc., who partner with consulting companies to sell and deliver products and train other customers, require consultants to be certified as Siebel Certified Consultants or Siebel Certified Instructors. The Remedy Skilled Professional Program ensures that administrators and consultants are experts in all areas of ARS software. Technical-level product certification is designed to help administrators and service technicians provide quality support for specific products.

Support centers, especially those that provide support services as an outsource vendor, can be certified just like individual employees. The Support Center Practices (SCP) Certification program establishes the service quality for all IT support centers and help desks. The program covers eleven major areas, which are broken down into detailed elements with specific measurable results. Points for each element determine the overall effectiveness of the support center.

13

ADDITIONAL CAREER DEVELOPMENT RESOURCES

The most important trend in support is change. Support for IT products changes as fast as technology itself, and only informed individuals will be aware of how others in support use technology. As in all professions, support staff can use additional resources to increase and maintain their understanding of support trends.

Market Research Companies

Market research companies analyze trends and predict business changes for different industries. Many require membership fees to access special reports or use knowledge bases, but some provide white papers and general trend discussions on their Web sites free of charge. Table 13-2 lists some common market research companies.

Table 13-2   IT market research companies

Company	Web Site
Datamation	http://www.datamation.com
Forrester Research	http://www.forrester.com
Frost & Sullivan	http://www.frost.com
GartnerGroup	http://www.gartner.com
International Data Corporation	http://www.idc.com
Ovum	http://www.ovum.com
RealMarket Research	http://www.realmarket.com
META Group	http://www.metagroup.com
The Robert Franceis Group	http://www.the-rfg.com
The Yankee Group	http://www.yankeegroup.com

Publications

Publications, including magazines, newsletters, and Web pages, discuss general IT trends as well as support-specific issues. Web pages and newsletters are usually free, whereas printed magazines are available through paid subscriptions (although, some magazines give free copies to IT managers or staff if their positions require them to recommend or approve purchases for products that are advertised in the magazine).

Appendix A includes some available publications.

A few companies and individuals have consolidated information specifically for customer and technical support professionals on their Web pages. These special resources are good sources of information about standard processes, software, and support issues for all levels of support and management. These Web sites are listed in Table 13-3.

Table 13-3   Support and help desk resources

Resource	Web Page
Bruton Consultancy	http://www.pcug.co.uk/~bruton
Help Desk FAQ	http://www.philverghis.com/helpdeskfaq.html
Help Desk Funnies	http://www.mcpi.com/ff
Helpdesk.Com	http://www.helpdesk.com
Internet Resources for Help Desks	http://www.rgu.ac.uk/~sim/research/helpdesk/hdlinks.htm
The Resource Center for Customer Support Professionals	http://www.the-resource-center.com

User Groups and Web Support Sites

Most call management and problem resolution vendors have user groups. Customers gather at least once a year to meet other customers and to share their experiences and learn from each other. At the same time, vendors may also provide additional training sessions and communicate information about upcoming hardware or software enhancements. Most vendors include user group and conference information on their Web pages.

There are also local computer user groups, in which volunteers organize group meetings and schedule presentations. Because these groups are independent of vendors, they control the topics they want to discuss (including their experiences with vendors and their support groups). In the spirit of sharing, some free technical support Web sites have also sprung up. These volunteers frequently answer questions about problems that may be hardware-related (which most software vendors won't address).

 Sample user groups and other free support services are listed in Appendix A.

Because technology continues to change rapidly, support professionals need to use additional resources from trade publications, user groups, and Web sites to stay informed of changes as they occur. Books and reference manuals are quickly outdated. An ongoing challenge for support professionals and their managers is to stay current on education and events in the support business.

CHAPTER SUMMARY

13

- More companies will move to 24 × 7 system availability in the next few years. This will increase the complexity of network problems and may make these issues more time-sensitive. Support staff will have to understand connectivity technologies as well as product-specific information.

- Help desks and support centers are being relabeled as contact centers. They handle telephone calls as well as e-mail, fax, and Internet-based contacts with customers. The role of many support staff is also expanding to include add-on sales and marketing activities.

- Remote network access will continue to improve. Support staff will work in virtual support centers and many will be home-based.

- Over time, support staff will spend more time creating and maintaining knowledge bases of information for customer self-service. Knowledge bases will include answers to product and procedure questions in addition to historical company information.

- ❏ Customers will use more self-service tools and online help systems for applications to answer many how-to questions. Over time, customers who purchase products may receive free self-service support, but will have to pay for more expensive, human telephone support.

- ❏ Certification ensures that IT and support professionals are qualified and competent. Novell and Microsoft already have certification programs in place for their network software. Several support groups also train and test support staff to ensure that they understand the business impact of customer problems. Formal education options for support professionals include university degree programs, general IT certifications, support certifications, and product certifications.

- ❏ IT technology and processes continue to change rapidly. Support staff need to maintain their technical expertise and stay informed of current trends so that they can plan and develop their careers.

KEY TERMS

Association of Information Technology Professionals (AITP) — At http://www.aitp.org; a professional association that emphasizes training for employers, employees, managers, programmers, and computer operators.

eCommerce — *See* electronic commerce.

electronic commerce — Business communication and transactions that occur over networks and through computers.

electronic data interchange (EDI) — The direct computer-to-computer transfer of business information.

Institute for Certification of Computer Professionals (ICCP) — At http://www.iccp.org; develops and maintains examinations to certify individuals as either Associate Computing Professionals (ACP) or Certified Computing Professionals (CCP).

telecommuting — The practice of connecting a computer to a business's network through a modem.

REVIEW QUESTIONS

1. Processing for 24 × 7 operations was traditionally only pursued by _____ companies or _____.

2. Describe three activities typical of eCommerce.

3. Electronic data interchange was originally developed for _____.

4. In addition to product and technology knowledge, support staff will need a good understanding of _____.

5. Call centers and help desks will most likely evolve into _____ to handle many types of requests and add-on services.

6. Explain two consequences of improved remote connectivity for support staff.

7. Telecommuting is encouraged by state and local governments as a way to reduce _____ and _____ problems.

8. What is the estimate for the amount of requests that will be handled by self-service tools by the year 2001?

9. Are software or hardware vendors likely to include user manuals with their products? Explain your answer.

10. List three levels of certification.

11. Describe a benefit that IT professional organizations provide, besides training classes and certification tests.

12. List four types of training available for support staff.

13. The oldest certification program is provided by:

   a. Microsoft NT server

   b. Oracle

   c. Novell

   d. Lotus Notes

14. Why are market research groups important to IT managers and support staff?

15. What program certifies that an entire support center follows standard business practices within measurable guidelines?

13

HANDS-ON PROJECTS

Project 13-1

Understanding market research forecasts. Visit one of the market research groups listed in this chapter or review IT and support publications and look for articles on current IT trends. Describe at least two current trends that will affect support professionals.

Project 13-2

Promoting certification. Visit the Help Desk 2000 Web Site at **http://www.helpdesk2000.org** or read other support-oriented publications and review articles on certification for support professionals. List three reasons that these articles give about why support staff should pursue certification.

Project 13-3

Analyzing certification programs. Visit the Microsoft Web site at **http://www.microsoft.com**, follow the links to their certification programs, and review the descriptions for the different Microsoft certifications. There are two special,

Internet certification levels. Explain some of the challenges that Internet access presents to IT professionals. Which certification(s) would be appropriate for programmers? Which would be appropriate for computer users?

Project 13-4

Utilizing different types of support resources. There are specific Web sites devoted to support or help desk issues. One of the entries in Table 13-3 may seem out of place, but is actually an important site. Identify the table entry that seems out of place and explain why it is important to help desk professionals.

CASE PROJECTS

1. ALTP Student Membership

You are a student attending college for an associate degree as a support professional. You decide to join a professional organization to get a better understanding of the real challenges and issues that IT professionals face. Visit the AITP Web site at **http://www.aitp.org** and search the Web site for a local, student branch of this organization. If there is a local branch, attend the next scheduled meeting. After the meeting, prepare a short report for your class-mates, describing the meeting discussions and the types of people who attended the meeting.

2. Current Articles on eCommerce

The president of your company has decided to allow customers to support themselves and order products from your company Web page. He has asked you to prepare a presentation on the five top challenges that companies and their support staff face when they implement eCommerce. Visit several IT publication Web sites or review articles from current maga-zines on eCommerce. Prepare a short presentation using a presentation graphics program, such as Microsoft PowerPoint, to create five to ten slides that list the challenges that eCommerce presents and possible ways of addressing those challenges.

3. Free Support Resources

Your family has decided to set up a small, home-based business. Although you have used a computer at work, you want to make sure you can find answers to problems you may encounter in Microsoft Word or Excel, which are the applications you plan to use to record sales and customer information. You decide to test some of the free PC support Web sites. Submit three questions or problems to two different sites. Track the length of time it takes to receive a response or answer from each site. Could this be a reliable resource for your support group? Explain your decision.

APPENDIX

A

WEB SITE RESOURCES

The Internet provides a wealth of information about help desk tools, technology, and techniques as well as other topics relevant to support group professionals. This appendix includes all the Web sites listed in this book. It also includes additional Web sites related to the topics discussed in the chapters.

Be aware that Web sites frequently are restructured, URLs change, and companies merge. Although the following URLs were current when the book was written, some of them may have changed. For the most recent version of these Web page listings, visit the Course Technology Web page at **http://www.course.com**.

CHAPTER 1

Support Terms and Background

Ask Jeeves	http://www.ask.com
Call Center Glossary	http://www.incoming.com/resources/glossary2.html
Help Desk FAQ	http://www.philverghis.com/helpdeskfaq.html
Whatis.com	http://whatis.com

Vendors

Support Technologies	http://www.supporttechnologies.com

CHAPTER 2

Hotline

The National Food Safety Database	http://www.foodsafety.org

Vendors

3Com	http://www.3com.com
Hewlett-Packard	http://www.hp.com
Netscape	http://home.netscape.com/support

CHAPTER 3

Free PC Help

Ask-A-Tech	http://www.ask-a-tech.org
Experts Exchange	http://www.experts-exchange.com
HelpMe.com	http://www.helpme.com
Myhelpdesk.com	http://www.myhelpdesk.com
NoWonder	http://www.nowonder.com
The PC Guide	http://www.pcguide.com
Tom's Hardware Guide	http://www.tomshardware.com

CHAPTER 4

Commercial Reporting Tools

Actuate	http://www.actuate.com
Cognos	http://www.cognos.com
Comshare	http://www.comshare.com
Hyperion	http://www.hyperion.com
Information Builders	http://www.ibi.com
Oracle	http://www.oracle.com
Pilot Software	http://www.pilotsw.com
SAS Institute	http://www.sas.com
Seagate Crystal Reports	http://www.seagatesoftware.com
SPSS	http://www.spss.com
Strategic Software Systems	http://www.sss1.com

OLAP Information

Computer Information Center	http://www.compinfo.co.uk
OLAP Council	http://www.olapcouncil.org
Statistics.com	http://www.statistics.com

CHAPTER 5

Market Research Companies

Datamation	http://www.datamation.com
Forrester Research	http://www.forrester.com
Frost & Sullivan	http://www.frost.com
GartnerGroup	http://www.gartner.com
International Data Corporation	http://www.idc.com
Ovum	http://www.ovum.com
RealMarket Research	http://www.realmarket.com
META Group	http://www.metagroup.com
The Robert Francs Group	http://www.the-rfg.com
The Yankee Group	http://www.yankeegroup.com

Additional Support Resources

Call Center Solutions Magazine	http://www.tmcnet.com/ccs
The Computer Information Center	http://www.compinfo-center.com
Help Desk Institute	http://www.helpdeskinst.com

Call Management Software

Bendata	http://www.bendata.com
Clarify	http://www.clarify.com
Monarch Bay Software (HelpTrac)	http://www.helptrac.com
Network Associates	http://www.nai.com
Peregrine Systems	http://www.peregrine.com
Remedy	http://www.remedy.com
Scott Data Systems	http://www.scottdatasystems.com
Siebel Systems	http://www.siebel.com
Vantive	http://www.vantive.com

Software Integrators (Implementation Consultants)

Anderson Consulting	http://www.andersonconsulting.com
Cambridge Technology Partners	http://www.ctp.com
Deloitte & Touche	http://www.dttus.com
KPMG	http://www.kpmg.com
Support Technologies	http://www.sti-help.com
Technology Service Corporation (TSC)	http://www.tsc.com

Shareware and Freeware Software

HelpDesk.com	http://www.helpdesk.com
Help Desk FAQ	http://www.philverghis.com/helpdeskfaq.html
Help Desk Institute	http://www.helpdeskinst.com
Ziff-Davis Software Library	http://www.zdnet.com/downloads

A

CHAPTER 6

Knowledge Management Resources

Association for Information and Image Management (AIIM) International	http://www.aiim.org
Customer Support Consortium (CSC) International.	http://www.customersupport.org
The Delphi Group	http://www.delphigroup.com
International Institute for Knowledge Management (IIKM)	http://www.iikm.com
International Society for KnowledgeOrganization (ISKO)	http://www.isko.org
Knowledge Management Consortium International (KMCI)	http://www.kmci.org
Knowledge Management Magazine	http://www.kmmag.com
Pure PDF Magazine	http://www.purepdf.com

Knowledge Management Software

Text Retrieval

Excalibur Technologies	http://www.excalib.com
PC Docs	http://www.hummingbird.com
Relevance Technology	http://www.relevance.net
Verity	http://www.verity.com
Virage	http://www.virage.com

Collaboration Tools

Dataware	http://www.dataware.com
Documentum	http://www.documentum.com
Enigma	http://www.enigmainc.com
The Haley Enterprise	http://www.haley.com
inFact Technologies	http://www.infact.com
Intellisystems	http://www.intellisystems.com
IntraNet Solutions	http://www.intranetsol.com
Plumtree Software	http://www.plumtree.com
SageMaker	http://www.sagemaker.com

Semio	http://www.semio.com
Verano	http://www.verano.com

Case-based Reasoning

Inference	http://www.inference.com
MultiLogic	http://www.multilogic.com

Content Publishers

Inference	http://www.inference.com
KnowledgeBroker	http://www.kbi.com
ServiceWare	http://www.serviceware.com

Knowledge Management Demos

CustomerSoft	http://www.customersoft.com
Emerald Intelligence	http://www.emeraldi.com
The Haley Enterprise	http://www.haley.com
Inference	http://www.inference.com
KnowledgeBroker	http://www.kbi.com
Primus	http://www.primus.com
Servicesoft Technologies	http://www.servicesoft.com

CHAPTER 7

Software Piracy Watchdogs

Business Software Alliance	http://www.bsa.org
Software and Information Industry Association	http://www.siia.net

Discovery Agent Software

BindView	http://www.bindview.com
Computer Associates	http://www.cai.com
Hewlett-Packard	http://www.hp.com
IBM Tivoli	http://www.tivoli.com
Microsoft Systems Management Server (SMS)	http://www.microsoft.com
Network Associates	http://www.nai.com
Tally Systems	http://www.tallysys.com

Remote Control Software

Compaq Carbon Copy	http://www.compaq.com
Computer Associates ControlIt	http://www.cai.com
Farallon Communications Timbuktu Pro	http://www.farallon.com
Microsoft Systems Management Server (SMS)	http://www.microsoft.com
Symantec pcAnywhere	http://www.symantec.com

Standalone Asset Management Software

Applied Innovation Management	http://www.innovate.com
Catsoft	http://www.catsoft.co.uk
Eurotek Communications	http://www.eurotek.co.uk
Isogon	http://www.isogon.com
MainControl	http://www.maincontrol.com
Microsoft Systems Management Server (SMS)	http://www.microsoft.com
Miquest	http://www.miquest.co.uk
Softopia Development	http://www.softopia.com
Systems Support Associates	http://www.syssupport.net
Tally Systems	http://www.tallysys.com
Technology Equipment Asset Management	http://www.techassetmgmt.com

Software Distribution Vendors

BindView	http://www.bindview.com
Computer Associates	http://www.cai.com
Globetrotter Software	http://www.globetrotter.com
Microsoft (System Management Server)	http://www.microsoft.com
Network Boss	http://www.lanauditor.com

Help Desk Software with Asset Management

Applix	http://www.applix.com
Blue Ocean Software	http://www.blueocean.com
Clarify	http://www.clarify.com
Computer Associates	http://www.cai.com
DKSystems	http://www.dksystems.com
HelpDesk Expert	http://www.4helpdesk.com
IBM Tivoli	http://www.tivoli.com
Multima	http://www.netkeeper.com

Network Associates	http://www.nai.com
Peregrine Systems	http://www.peregrine.com
Remedy	http://www.remedy.com
Vantive	http://www.vantive.com

CHAPTER 8

Electronic Displays and Reader Boards

Callware Technologies	http://www.callware.com
Centergistic Solutions	http://www.aaccorp.com
Daktronics	http://www.daktronics.com
Data Masters	http://www.data-masters.com
Design Computer Systems	http://www.designcomputer.com
INOVA	http://www.inovacorp.com
LED Signs OnLine	http://www.led-signs.com
PaceCom Technologies	http://www.pacecom.com
Salescaster Displays	http://www.salescaster.com
Showtronics	http://www.showtron.com
Spectrum	http://www.specorp.com
SYMON Communications	http://www.symon.com
Telegenix	http://www.telegenix.com
Texas Digital Systems	http://www.txdigital.com
Visual Electronics	http://www.digital-fax.com

E-mail Software

Lotus Notes Mail	http://www.lotus.com
Microsoft Internet Explorer Mail	http://www.microsoft.com
Microsoft Outlook or Outlook Express	http://www.microsoft.com
Netscape Messenger Mail	http://www.netscape.com
Novell Groupwise	http://www.novell.com
Qualcomm Eudora	http://www.qualcomm.com

Pager Software and Pager Services

Amcom Software	http://www.amcomsoft.com
AT&T	http://www.att.com
GTE	http://www.gte.com

MCI	http://www.mci.com
Motorola	http://www.motorola.com
PageNet	http://www.pagenet.com
SkyTel	http://www.skytel.com
Sprint	http://www.sprint.com
Telamon	http://www.telamon.com
WebLink Wireless	http://www.pagemart.com

Telephones

Mitsubishi Electric	http://www.mitsubishi.com
Motorola	http://www.motorola.com
Nextel	http://www.nextel.com
Nokia	http://www.nokia.com
Qualcomm	http:// www.qualcomm.com
Samsung	http://www.samsung.com
Sony	http://www.sony.com
Sprint	http://www.sprint.com

PDA Hardware

3Com	http://www.palm.com
Casio	http://www.casio.com
Hewlett-Packard	http://www.hp.com
IBM	http://www.direct.ibm.com
Symbol Technologies	http://www.symbol.com

Call Management Software for PDAs

| Bendata | http://www.heat.com |
| Remedy | http://www.remedy.com |

Telephones with PDA Software

NeoPoint	http://www.neopoint.com
Nokia	http://www.nokia.com
Qualcomm	http://www.qualcomm.com

Examples of SLAs

http://etc.nih.gov/pages/etcservicelevelagreement.html

http://maps4.cr.bcit.bc.ca/bis/sla.htm

http://web.missouri.edu/~ue/sla

http://www.everestsw.com/accountability/example.html

http://www.supportresearch.com/Fry/tpl-SLA.htm

E-mail Etiquette

http://www.becrc.org/etiquette.htm

http://www.emailaddresses.com/guide_etiquette.htm

http://www.sitecrafters.com/support/netiquette.asp

http://www.webfoot.com/advice/email.top.html

Voice Mail Etiquette

http://www.justsell.com/content/printnroute/sales/prgs0002.htm

http://www.qut.edu.au/computing_services/hit/advice/voicemail

http://www.seattletimes.com (follow links to SearchArchives)

Pager Basics

NotePage	http://www.notepage.com/basics.htm
Paging demo	http://brent.dispatch.com/sw/sp

Technology Newsletters

The Gadgeteer Newletter	http://www.the-gadgeteer.com
Wireless Week	http://www.wirelessweek.com
Ziff-Davis Publishing	http://www.zdnet.com

Shareware Paging Software

PageWrite	http://www.callid.com/pagewrite.htm
Ziff-Davis Software Library	http://www.zdnet.com/downloads

CHAPTER 9

PBX Vendors

Boston Telephone Solutions	http://www.meridianphones.com
Connections	http://www.callaccounting.com

A

Equinox Systems	http://www.equinox.com
Hand Technologies	http://computerlease.com/assistant.htm
Innovative PBX Services	http://www.innovativepbx.com
JilTel Communications	http://videoteleconf.com
Lucent Technologies	http://www.lucent.com
Motorola	http://www.mot.com
Nortel	http://www.nortelnetworks.com/index.html
Siemens Information and Communications Networks	http://www.siemenscom.com

ACD Vendors

Americtech	http://www.ameritech.com
Aspect Communications	http://www.aspect.com
AVT	http://www.avtc.com
Centergistic Solutions	http://www.aaccorp.com
CenterForce Technologies	http://www.cforcetech.com
Cintech	http://cintech-cti.com
Davox (AnswerSoft)	http://www.davox.com
eOn Communications	http://www.eoncc.com
Executone Information Systems	http://www.executone.com
NexPath	http://www.nexpath.com
NICE, Dees Call Center Division	http://www.dees.com
Nova CTI	http://www.novacti.com
PakNetX	http://www.paknetx.com
Perimeter Technology	http://www.perimetertechnology.com
Rockwell Electronic Commerce	http://www.ec.rockwell.com
SoftBase Systems	http://www.softbase.com
Teloquent	http://www.teloquent.com
Telrad	http://www.telradusa.com
Teltronics	http://www.teltronics.com

CTI Software Vendors

Comverse Network Systems	http://www.comversens.com
CTiTEK	http://www.ctitek.com
Dialogic	http://www.dialogic.com

EasyRun Communication Software Systems	http://www.easyrun.com
Genesys	http://www.genesyslab.com
IBM	http://www.ibm.com
N-Soft	http://www.n-soft.com
Periphonics	http://www.peri.com

IVR Vendors

Aculab	http://www.aculab.com
Artisoft	http://www.artisoft.com
Aspect Communications	http://www.aspect.com
BICOM	http://www.bicom-inc.com
CCS TrexCom	http://www.ccsivr.com
Corepoint	http://www.corepoint.com
Crystal Group	http://www.crystalpc.com
Edify	http://www.edify.com
Envox	http://www.envox.com
GM Voices	http://www.gmvoices.com
IBM	http://www.ibm.com
Interactive Digital Systems	http://www.interactivedigital.com
InterVoice-Brite	http://www.brite.com
Lucent Technologies	http://www.lucent.com
MediaSoft Telecom	http://www.mediasoft.com
Nortel Networks	http://www.nortel.com
Periphonics	http://www.peri.com
Syntellect	http://www.syntellect.com
TALX	http://www.talx.com

Real-Time Telephone System Monitoring

Altitude Software	http://www.easyphone.com
Digisoft Computers (Telescript)	http://www.telemkt.com/digisoft
Lucent Technology	http://www.lucent.com
Pyderion Contact Technologies	http://www.pyderion.com
Switchview	http://www.switchview.com

A

Voice Recognition and Speech Synthesis Vendors

21st Century Eloquence	http://www.voicerecognition.com
Compaq Computer	http://www.compaq.com
Corepoint	http://www.corepoint.com
Dialogic	http://www.dialogic.com
Dragon Systems	http://www.dragonsys.com
Fonix	http://www.fonix.com
InterVoice-Brite	http://www.brite.com
Lernout & Hauspie	http://www.lhs.com
Nuance	http://www.nuance.com
Philips Electronics	http://www.speech.com
SpeechWorks	http://www.altech.com
T-NETIX	http://www.t-netix.com
Wildfire Communications	http://www.wildfire.com

IP Telephony Vendors

Amdocs	http://www.amdocs.com
Crystal Group	http://www.crystalpc.com
Info Directions	http://www.infodirections.com
InnoMedia	http://www.innomedia.com
Intelliswitch	http://www.intelliswitch.com
Mind CTI	http://www.mindcti.com
Nuera Communications	http://www.nuera.com
Portal Software	http://www.portal.com

Telephone Basics

Brantford	http://207.61.52.13/comdir/festivals/sesqui/bell.html
How Stuff Works	http://www.howstuffworks.com
Telestra	http://www.telstra.com

Telecommunications Terminology and Resources

Ask Jeeves	http://www.ask.com
Bigcat Systems	http://www.bigcat.net
Claremont Internet Press	http://clp.net/clp-dict.html
Computer Telephony Magazine	http://www.telecomlibrary.com

Hello Direct	http://www.hellodirect.com
Technology Guides	http://www.techguide.com
Tribute to the Telephone	http://telecom-digest.org/tribute
Whatis.com	http://whatis.com

CHAPTER 10

Ergonomic Resources

Center for Office Technology	http://www.cot.org
Combo Directory	http://www.combo.com
ErgoWorld	http://www.interface-analysis.com/ergoworld
IBM Healthy Computing	http://www.pc.ibm.com/us/healthycomputing
Office Ergonomics	http://www.office-ergo.com
Typing Injury FAQ	http://www.tifaq.org
U.S. Department of Labor Occupational Safety and Health Administration	http://www.osha.gov

Headset Vendors

ADCOM/BHS	http://www.adcombhs.com
ClearVox Communications	http://www.clearvox.com
CommuniTech	http://www.communitech.com
Headsets Direct	http://www.headsetsdirect.com
Hello Direct	http://www.hellodirect.com
KAAS Com	http://www.kaaas.com
Plantronics	http://www.plantronics.com
Progressive Ideas	http://www.progressiveideas.com
Spectrum Technologies	http://www.spectrumtec.com
Telex	http://www.computeraudio.telex.com
Tri-Tel Technical Services	http://www.tritelchicago.com

RSI Prevention Software

Niche Software	http://www.workpace.com/niche
Omniquad	http://www.omniquad.com (link to ErgoSense)
Typing Injury FAQ	http://www.tifaq.org (link to RSI shareware software)

A

CHAPTER 11

System Management Software

BMC Software	http://www.bmc.com
Cabletron Systems	http://www.cabletron.com
Cisco Systems	http://www.cisco.com
Computer Associates	http://www.cai.com
Hewlett-Packard	http://www.hp.com
IBM	http://www.ibm.com
IBM Tivoli	http://www.tivoli.com
Intel	http://www.intel.com
Microsoft	http://www.microsoft.com
Network Associates	http://www.nai.com
Seagate Technology	http://www.seagate.com
Sun Microsystems	http://www.sun.com

Network Topographies

The Atlas of Cyberspaces	http://www.geog.ucl.ac.uk (link to the Atlas of Cyberspaces)

Performance Management

Hewlett-Packard	http://www.openview.hp.com
MCI	http://www.vbns.net

Other Resources

BotSpot	http://www.botspot.com
SolarWinds	http://216.60.197.203
The Simple Times	http://www.simple-times.org
Technology Guides	http://www.techguide.com

CHAPTER 12

Optimization Software

CyberMedia, First Aid, Network Associates, PC Medic, and Nuts & Bolts	http://www.nai.com
Symantec, Norton Utilities	http://www.symantec.com

Preemptive Diagnosis Software

Aveo, Attune	http://www.aveo.com
CyberMedia, Oil Change & Repair Engine	http://www.nai.com
Support.com, Healing System	http://www.tioga.com
SystemSoft, System Wizard	http://www.systemsoft.com

Data Collection Software

Courion Corporation	http://www.courion.com
Full Circle Software	http://www.fullsoft.com/test-drive
Motive Communications, Motive Solo and Motive Duet	http://www.motive.com
NetManage, SupportNow	http://www.netmanage.com

E-mail Self-Service

Island Data	http://www.islanddata.com

Internet Self-Service

Quintus	http://www.quintus.com

Mailing Lists and Newsgroups

Computer Training Subjects	listproc@bilbo.isu.edu (enter in message body: subscribe Computer-Training your_first_name your_last_name)
Heat Call Tracking Software	http://www.heatsoftware.com/heatforum/index.html
Help Desk List (Digest—daily e-mail message with all messages sent to list that day)	LISTSERV@wvnvm.wvnet.edu (no subject and enter in message body: subscribe HDESK-L your_first_name your_last_name)
Help Desk News Group	bit.listserv.hdesk-l uwo.comp.helpdesk
Knowledge Bases	listserv@list.nih.gov (enter in message body: subscribe knowbase your_first_name your_last_name)
McAfee Help Desk (Network Associates)	subscribe-mhd@alldata.com (blank message)
McAfee's ZAC (Zero Administration Client) and Desktop Management Products	subcribe-zac@alldata.com (blank message)

A

Remedy ARS	listserv@listserv.acsu.buffalo.edu (enter in message body: subscribe arslist your_first_name your_last_name)
SupportMagic Software	listserv@cfrvm.cfr.usf.edu (enter in message body: subscribe smagic your_first_name your_last_name)
Technical Support Newsgroups	alt.management.tech-support alt.managing.techsupport
University-specific Help Desk List	listserv@vma.cc.nd.edu (enter in message body: subscribe hdi-edu your_first_name your_last_name)
University-specific list for support professionals who support computers and students in residence halls and computer clusters	listserv@vma.cc.nd.edu (enter in message body: subscribe resnet-l your_first_name your_last_name)

Other Resources

Autodesk	http://www.autodesk.com
Cisco	http://www.cisco.com

CHAPTER 13

IT Organizations and Support Associations

American Teleservices Association	http://www.ataconnect.org
Association for Women in Computing	http://www.awcncc.org
Association of Information Technology Professionals	http://www.aitp.org
Association of Support Professionals (ASP)	http://www.asponline.com
Association of Windows NT System Professionals	http://www.ntpro.org
BackOffice Professionals	http://www.bopa.org
Call Center Network Group	http://www.ccng.com
Call Centre Managers Forum	http://callcentres.com.au
CSM Group	http://www.hug.co.uk
Customer Care Institute	http://www.customercare.com
Customer Service Management	http://www.csm-us.com
Customer Support Consortium	http://www.customersupport.org

Direct Selling Association	http://www.dsa.org
Distributed Management Task Force	http://www.dmtf.org
Guide International (IBM Professionals)	http://www.share.org
Help Desk 2000	http://www.helpdesk2000.org
Help Desk Institute	http://www.helpdeskinst.com
Incoming Calls Management Institute	http://www.incoming.com
Institute for Certification of Computer Professionals	http://www.iccp.org
Interex (The International Association of Hewlett-Packard Computing Professionals)	http://www.interex.org
International Customer Service Association	http://www.icsa.com
Society of Telecommunications Consultants	http://www.stcconsultants.org
Software Support Professionals Association (SSPA)	http://www.supportgate.com
The Direct Marketing Association	http://www.the-dma.org

Software Vendors That Require Certification

Cisco Systems	http://www.cisco.com
Lotus	http://www.lotus.com
Microsoft	http://www.microsoft.com
Novell	http://www.novell.com
Oracle	http://www.oracle.com
Remedy	http://www.remedy.com
Siebel Systems	http://www.siebel.com

Market Research Companies

Datamation	http://www.datamation.com
Forrester Research	http://www.forrester.com
Frost & Sullivan	http://www.frost.com
GartnerGroup	http://gartner.com
International Data Corporation	http://www.idc.com
Ovum	http://www.ovum.com
RealMarket Research	http://www.realmarket.com
META Group	http://www.metagroup.com
The Robert Frances Group	http://www.the-rfg.com
The Yankee Group	http://www.yankeegroup.com

IT Publications

Call Center Management Review	http://www.servicelevel.com
CMP Publications (*Data Communications, Tele.com, Network Computing, Information Week*)	http://www.cmp.com
Computer World	http://www.computerworld.com
ComputerTelephony.com (*CallCenter, ComputerTelephony, Teleconnect, Network Magazine*)	http://www.telecomlibrary.com
CustomerSupport.com	http://www.customersupport.com
Help Desk Online	http://www.helpdesk-online.com
IDG (*Computerworld, InfoWorld, PC World, Network World*)	http://www.idg.net
IT Support News	http://www.servicenews.com
IT World	http://www.itworldcanada.com
Network Computing	http://www.nwc.com
Publications and Communications (*Cisco World* and *HP Chronicle*)	http://www.pcinews.com
SupportIndustry. Com	http://www.supportindustry.com
Tele.com Magazine	http://www.teledotcom.com
TeleProfessional Magazine	http://www.teleprofessional.com
The Industry Standard (Internet Economy)	http://www.thestandard.com
TMCnet (*Call CenterSolutions, Communications Solutions, Internetelephony*)	http://www.tmcnet.com
Ziff-Davis (*PCWeek* and others)	http://www.zdnet.com

Support and Help Desk Resources

Bruton Consultancy	http://www.pcug.co.uk/~bruton
Friday Funnies	http://www.mcpi.com/ff
Help Desk FAQ	http://www.philverghis.com/helpdeskfaq.html
Helpdesk.Com	http://www.helpdesk.com
Internet Resources for Help Desks	http://www.rgu.ac.uk/~sim/research/ helpdesk/hdlinks.htm
The Resource Center for Customer Support Professionals	http://www.the-resource-center.com

User Groups

Association of PC User Groups	http://www.apcug.org
DECUS A Compaq Users Group	http://www.decus.org
Microsoft Mindshare User Group	http://www.microsoft.com/mindshare
Windows Users Group Network	http://www.wugnet.com
The Forums	http://www.theforums.com

PC Support Sites

Ask-A-Tech	http://www.ask-a-tech.org
Course Technology	http://www.course.com
Experts Exchange	http://www.experts-exchange.com
Help-Site Computer Manuals	http://help-site.com
Indiana University KnowledgeBase	http://kb.iupui.edu
Information Technology Professionals Resource Center	http://www.itprc.com
Microsoft Product/Support Services	http://support.microsoft.com
NoWonder	http://www.nowonder.com
PC Mechanic	http://www.pcmech.com
Scott's Tutorial Hotlist	http://cires.colorado.edu/people/peckham.scott/tutors.html
SHARE	http://www.share.org
The Computer Information Center	http://www.compinfo-center.com
The PC Guide	http://www.pcguide.com
Tom's Hardware Guide	http://www.tomshardware.com
Tutorial Junction	http://fiat.gslis.utexas.edu/resources/lib_inf_res/tutorials.html
Ziff-Davis Help	http://www.zdnet.com/zdhelp

Other Resources

HireAbility.com	http://www.hireability.com
Technology Guides.com	http://www.techguide.com
U.S. Office of Personnel Management	http://www.opm.gov/wrkfam

GLOSSARY

24×7 support — The support group is available via telephone twenty-four hours a day, seven days a week.

abandon rate — The percentage of abandoned calls compared to the total telephone calls received.

accelerator key — *See* shortcut key.

account management — *See* customer management.

account manager — A company representative assigned to manage the interactions between a company and its customers.

accountability — Someone has the authority to correct problems when he or she defaults on commitments.

ad hoc — Designed or improvised as needed.

address — A unique identification on a computer network.

agent — A software program that collects and processes information.

alert — A special type of notification to inform selected staff or managers when there is an error condition.

application administrator — A person who defines important tables and fields used in a software application.

artificial intelligence (AI) — A software program that attempts to mimic human intelligence.

asset — Any item of value owned by an individual or corporation that could be converted to cash.

asset management — The process of collecting and maintaining a comprehensive list of items a company owns, including hardware or software components and other office equipment.

Association of Information Technology Professionals (AITP) — at http://www.aitp.org; a professional association that emphasizes training for employers, employees, managers, programmers, and computer operators.

attachment — An additional file appended to a call record that provides detailed information for troubleshooting.

auto-fill — As the user begins to type a word or phrase, the complete word or phrase that matches the typed letters is pulled in from a list of stored words.

automated attendants — CTI applications that play a recorded message based on defined criteria.

automatic call distribution (ACD) system — Special telephone equipment that manages incoming calls and handles them according to the number called and an associated database of handling instructions.

automatic number identification (ANI) — A telephone service that sends the DTMF tones along with the call to identify the telephone number that the call originates from.

automatic speech recognition (ASR) — Computer software that recognizes certain human speech and translates it to instructions that other computer programs can process.

available time — The amount of time in minutes and seconds when support staff can answer the telephone and deliver support services.

baseline — A starting point for later comparisons.

binaural — Telephone headsets that cover both ears.

bot — An abbreviation for robot. *See also* agent.

bottleneck — Occurs when a resource reaches its maximum capacity and cannot keep up with the demands placed on it.

call duration — The length of a telephone call in minutes and seconds.

call logging — The process of creating records that capture details about problems, requests, and questions as they are reported to the support group.

call priority — The order in which call records are handled, according to the business impact of the problem or request.

call summary — A concise description of the problem or request that is a few sentences in length.

caller ID — *See* automatic number identification.

caller information — Facts about the customer at the time a problem or question is reported.

canned text — *See* auto-fill.

carpal tunnel syndrome (CTS) — A common form of Repetitive Stress Injury that affects hands and wrists.

case-based reasoning (CBR) — A software program that looks for previous problem examples similar to the current problem.

category — A classification of problems or requests.

cell — The span of coverage for a mobile telephone transmitter.

cellular telephone service — A type of short-wave analog or digital transmission in which a subscriber has a wireless connection from a mobile telephone to a nearby transmitter.

change management — The process of controlling additions, modifications, and deletions of hardware or software in a computerized system.

change request — A written document that describes a technological change, the reason why the change must be made, the customers potentially affected, and the related technologies and tasks required to make the change.

charge code — A financial code used by an accounting or billing application to generate an invoice for a customer.

chargeback — The accounting activity of allocating expenses of an internal support group back to the departments that use its services, based upon the number of services they use.

column — In a database, the set of all instances of a single field from all records.

commercial software application — A program that is written or sold by a company that is in business to develop and sell software.

communication skills — Those skills that enable a person to interact effectively with others by speaking, listening, and writing.

comparison operators — Words, such as AND, OR, or NOT, that evaluate comparisons to determine if they are true or false.

computer telephony integration (CTI) — Software that links telephone-originated information—such as caller name, the telephone number the person called from, and the number the person dialed—to other computer information systems.

configuration management — *See* change management.

connectivity — Describes the connections between computers on a network.

consistent delivery — The output of a process is the same no matter who completes the procedures.

console — A workstation that can access multiple computers on multiple networks.

copy protection — Software tools that prevented people from making unauthorized copies of software.

copyright — The exclusive legal rights granted to authors, artists, composers, or programmers to distribute or sell their creations.

customer — A person who buys products and services from a company, or an employee within a company who relies upon another group for services.

customer management — The process of collecting customer information and building a relationship between a company and its customers.

customer surveys — A tool to collect feedback from customers about products or services.

customize — To add or change fields in software to match the values the company needs or wants.

daemon — A program server that runs continuously, waiting for requests for service.

data — Raw numbers or facts collected in a database.

data mining — Analysis of facts, transactions, and reports about business activities to determine relationships between actions and results.

database — A collection of data organized so that it can be easily accessed, managed, and updated.

decision tree — One of the earliest forms of expert systems, allows an interaction between the user and the knowledge through a series of yes/no or true/false questions.

demon — *See* daemon.

deployment — The rapid installation of new software or software upgrades on large numbers of desktop computers electronically.

detail report — A report that includes specific information about individual records.

dialed number identification service (DNIS) — A telephone service that identifies the source of calls that are routed to the same destination.

direct inward dialing (DID) — A telephone service that allows customers to use individual telephone numbers for each person or workstation within the company without requiring a physical line into the PBX for each possible connection.

disaster recovery — A plan for restoring critical business functions after a disaster to minimize loss of income.

discovery agents — Software tools that explore the devices on a network and collect hardware and software information in inventory files.

dispatch — To send.

dispatcher — A front-line support person who answers telephone calls but forwards problems to someone else to solve.

domain experts — People who know a lot about a specific subject.

dongle — A copy protection device that plugs into the back of the computer or attaches to a printer port that enables software to run.

drill down — The ability to take summarized information and progressively reveal more details.

dual tone multiple frequency (DTMF) — A unique signal generated as you press the telephone's touch keys.

e-mail — *See* electronic mail.

ease of use — The user friendliness of software, as defined by the combination of the user interface, required fields, auto-fill fields, pull-down lists, shortcut keys, and tab order.

eCommerce — *See* electronic commerce.

electronic commerce — Business communication and transactions that occur over networks and through computers.

electronic data interchange (EDI) — The direct computer-to-computer transfer of business information.

electronic display board — An advanced version of a whiteboard that displays information on a digitized board or television monitor.

electronic mail — The exchange of computer-stored messages by telecommunication.

enterprise management — *See* systems management.

enterprise support — Multiple support groups located in different regions of the country to allow better support coverage over different time zones.

entitlements — The number of calls a customer can make to the help desk for a set fee or the office hours when they can reach someone in customer support.

epistemology — In philosophy, the theory of knowledge and how it changes.

ergonomics — The study of the interaction between people and computer systems, programs, and other devices.

escalate — To raise an issue to the next level of support or to notify managers.

event — An action or activity that has significance to a task or programs.

executive information system (EIS) — Presents selected data graphically for quick interpretation.

expert system — Software that imitates the problem-solving procedures that human experts perform.

external support group — A support group that addresses questions, problems, or requests from customers who buy their company's products and services.

extranet — An extension of a company intranet that allows selected customers, business partners, suppliers, and mobile employees to access the company's private data and applications.

fax server — A computer with fax software.

fax-on-demand — An application that allows customers to request written product or support information from a network fax system.

field — An area in a database that contains a particular item of data.

firewall — A computer with additional security that serves as a gateway between the company intranet and the Internet.

first call resolution — The number of calls resolved while the support staff is still on the telephone with the customer.

flash report — *See* summary report.

follow the sun support — A support concept whereby problems are seamlessly handed off at the end of the workday to another support group in a different time zone.

frame — To organize and refine problem symptoms to search for a solution.

free format — A text type of field in which data is not stored in a specific structure.

free text — *See* free format.

frequently asked questions (FAQs) — Written collections of common customer queries and their answers.

front-line support — The point of first contact with the customer.

full-time equivalent (FTE) — The result of the conversion of the number of work hours possible by full- and part-time employees.

functions — Program routines that complete a series of mathematical calculations.

fuzzy logic — A way to represent values that are not completely true or false.

gateway — A network point that acts as an entrance to another network.

go-live — To begin using new software.

graphical user interface (GUI) — A picture-oriented way to interact with a computer, using a mouse or joystick to select commands instead of typing them.

groupware — Software that enables multiple people to work together electronically.

guru — A coworker who learns to use new tools quickly and who helps other employees unofficially.

handheld computer — *See* personal digital assistant.

hardware key — *See* dongle.

help desk — A single point of contact within a company for managing customer problems and requests, and providing solution-oriented support services. *See also* internal support group.

heterogeneous computing environment — A mix of different computing devices and operating systems.

hold time — The amount of time that a caller remains on hold if there is no one available to answer the telephone.

homegrown software application — A program designed and written by an employee within the company that uses it.

hotline support — A support group that doesn't usually collect information about the caller; it just counts the number of times a particular question is asked.

human-computer interaction — The study of how people interact with computers and software and the extent to which computer technologies provide successful interaction with people.

Hypertext Transfer Protocol (HTTP) — A set of rules for exchanging text, graphic images, sound, video, and other multimedia files on the World Wide Web.

inference — The creation of new knowledge from existing knowledge.

inference engine — Software that imitates human inference in creating new facts from known facts, using inference rules.

information — Data that is organized into something meaningful.

information center — A place within the company where employees could receive training and help in using personal computers.

information technology (IT) — All forms of technology used to create, store, exchange, and use information in its various forms (business data, voice conversations, images, multimedia presentations, and other forms).

Institute for Certification of Computer Professionals (ICCP) — at http://www.iccp.org; develops and maintains examinations to certify individuals as either an Associate Computing Professionals (ACP) or a Certified Computing Professionals (CCP).

integrated feature — A software feature that enables support staff to complete other support processes within the same application.

intellectual property — Elements of human intellect that are unique and original, and have value.

intelligent agent — A software program that searches Internet sites and gathers information according to user-specified criteria. *See also* agent.

Interactive Mail Access Protocol (IMAP) — A set of rules for receiving e-mail and storing it on a file server.

interactive voice response (IVR) — A combination of hardware and software that allows people to ask questions and provide answers through a telephone.

internal support group — A department within a company that responds to questions, problems, or requests from company employees.

Internet Protocol (IP) — A set of rules to send and receive messages at the Internet address level.

Internet Protocol telephony (IP telephony) — Uses the same telecommunications connections that support the Internet to exchange voice, fax, and other data that are usually carried over the public telephone network.

intranet — A network modeled on the World Wide Web, used by members of an organization and usually inaccessible to outsiders.

keywords — Search words in a text retrieval system.

knowbot — *See* intelligent agent.

knowledge — A collection of processed information that a company can use to accomplish tasks.

knowledge acquisition — The collection and organization of knowledge from human beings.

knowledge base — A centralized collection of accumulated knowledge about questions, issues, procedures, or problems that is stored electronically.

knowledge domain — A specific area of knowledge covered by a knowledge-based system.

knowledge engineer — A person who obtains knowledge from human experts and organizes it into a knowledge base.

knowledge hits — When support staff find the answers to problems in a knowledge base.

knowledge management — A relatively new business process in which a company attempts to gather, organize, analyze, and reuse its knowledge.

knowledge system — *See* expert system.

level one resolution — Level one staff either solved the problem with their own knowledge or they used a knowledge base to solve the problem.

level one support — *See* front-line support.

license agreements — Legal statements that clearly define the terms under which a person can use software.

list server — A program that handles subscription requests for a mailing list and distributes new messages, newsletters, or other postings from the list's members to the entire list of subscribers as the messages occur or are scheduled; also called a mailing list server.

listproc — A freeware mailing list processor that runs primarily on UNIX machines—similar to listserv.

listserv — An automated e-mail discussion list that processes e-mail requests for addition to or deletion from mailing lists.

logical operators — *See* comparison operators.

mailing list — A list of e-mail addresses used to distribute e-mail to a large number of recipients.

majordomo — A freeware mailing list processor, similar to listserv.

market research — To collect and analyze information about products, services, consumers, and trends.

middleware — Software that links common hardware technologies together.

mission statement — A broad, general written guideline that defines the company's vision and specific goals.

monaural — Telephone headsets that cover only one ear, which allows support staff to hear what is going on around them.

multilevel support model — Defines the role a support person plays in different support processes and the amount of interaction the support person has with a customer.

natural language — Queries that are written in the way humans ask questions.

network management software — Software that monitors the "traffic" on a network between PCs, printers, and other shared pieces of hardware.

network traffic — The transactions that pass between devices on a network.

neural net — *See* neural network.

neural network — A computer program that learns new information by simulating the way brains function when solving problems.

newsgroup — A Usenet collection of topic groups.

node — An individual device on the computer network.

noise words — Common words and numbers that don't specifically help during searches.

notifications — Updates about the support environment forwarded to customers, support staff, and managers.

number of calls by customer — The number of call records created for a specific caller.

number of calls by day of week — The total number of call records that were created on a specific day of the week.

number of calls by originator — The number of call records created by each support staff member.

number of calls by owner — The number of call records each support staff member owns.

number of calls by time of day — The number of call records created and counted for each hour of a workday.

number of calls by type — The number of call records by category.

number of calls reopened — The number of call records that moved from a closed or resolved status back to an open status.

Occupational Safety and Health Administration (OSHA) — An agency of the U.S. Department of Labor dedicated to reducing hazards in the workplace and enforcing job-safety standards for all employers.

online analytical processing (OLAP) — A method of accessing database information that enables a user to extract and view data from different points of view.

origin of call — The way a problem was reported.

outsource — To contract a service to an external support group.

owner — The support staff employee who is responsible for moving a call to a resolution and for updating the customer.

packets — Individual units of data.

pager — A small, wireless telecommunications receiver, generally used by people who are continually changing their location or who are not necessarily able to answer a telephone call immediately.

patch — A quick modification of a program, which is sometimes a temporary fix until the problem can be solved more thoroughly.

pending work — Work in progress.

Personal Communications Services (PCS) — A newer wireless telephone service that is similar to cellular and is sometimes referred to as digital cellular.

personal digital assistant (PDA) — A small, mobile handheld device that provides computing and information storage and retrieval capabilities for personal or business use.

physical inventories — A survey to confirm existing assets by locating and identifying each asset.

picklist — *See* pull-down list.

pink noise — White noise that has been filtered to reduce the volume at each octave.

pivot table — An interactive table that quickly summarizes large amounts of data.

point of sale systems — The modern versions of cash registers that print receipts, validate charge cards, record sales, transmit sales nightly to a centralized computer system, count the number of items sold, request stock replacements, and track customer demographics.

poll — To check the operational status of a piece of equipment and the connecting telephone lines.

Post Office Protocol 3 (POP3) — A set of rules for receiving e-mail and saving in a mailbox.

predefined phrases — *See* auto-fill.

private branch exchange (PBX) — A system that brings telephone signals into a company from the public telephone network and routes them to local telephone lines inside the company.

proactive mode — When the support staff uses tools to detect problems early and prevent more serious problems, rather than waiting for computer users to report problems.

problem — An event that prevents someone from completing a task.

problem history — The chronological sequence of activities that has occurred since a call record was created.

problem management — The process of collecting problem details, working on outstanding problems, assigning additional support staff as needed, and providing status updates to customers for problems that are reported to a support group.

problem resolution — The process of finding the cause of a problem, removing or preventing the cause, and correcting the disruption the problem caused.

procedure — A detailed, step-by-step set of instructions that describes who will perform the tasks in a process, along with how and when those tasks will be performed.

process — A list of the input, the interrelated work activities (or tasks), and the desired output needed to accomplish a goal.

professional services — Useful labor that does not result in a physical product, but that helps customers maximize the use of products.

programming interface — A set of program instructions that passes data between two different software applications.

protocol — A standard sets of rules to regulate the way data is transmitted between computers.

pull-down list — A predefined list of acceptable values from which only one value can be selected.

push — *See* real-time publish and subscribe.

push technology — The practice of receiving information from an agent.

query by example (QBE) — A search technique that uses queries or questions to find records that match specified conditions.

questions — Inquiries customers make about small tasks or subjects they don't understand.

queue — A line of things to be processed in sequential order.

queue time — Response time between two levels of support. *See also* response time.

reactive mode — When the support staff only respond to problems that computer users report.

reader board — *See* electronic display board

real-time publish and subscribe — A reporting technology that allows business users to subscribe to information "published" by the support center.

record — In a database, the collection of all fields with data about a single item.

reference number — A unique code that identifies a specific record in a database.

relationship management — The process of collecting and managing customer information to improve customer loyalty.

remote access control — Software that allows support staff to temporarily take "control" of the computer from the user and review or install software over the network.

remote control software — Software that enables support staff to take temporary control of a remote computer.

repetitive stress injuries (RSIs) — Symptoms of tenderness, swelling, tingling, numbness, and loss of movement in joints caused by repeating small strenuous actions with arms, wrists, and hands for long periods of time.

report writer — Software that allows users to select, manipulate, and present database information.

request — A customer order for new hardware, software, or services, or for an enhancement to a product or service a customer already uses.

request management — The process of collecting information about the customer that will be used to complete the request, identifying the tasks and resources needed to complete the request, and tracking the request until delivery.

required entry fields — Data entry fields that must be completed correctly before a record can be saved in the database.

resolution — Information on how a problem is solved or can be prevented.

resolution time — The difference in days, hours, minutes, and seconds between the time a call record is created and the time it moves to a closed status.

response time — The time it takes the support group to acknowledge a customer's problem or request and assign a resource.

return merchandise authorization (RMA) — A special code or number assigned to a product being returned that is used to record details of the problem and the desired corrective action.

return on investment (ROI) — A measurement that compares the dollar value of a support group's services and benefits to its operating costs.

role — Describes activities someone completes.

root node — The starting point in a decision tree.

rows — *See* record.

rule-based systems — *See* decision tree and expert system.

scalability — The ability of a piece of computer hardware or software to expand to meet future needs.

screen pop — Displaying records based on ANI or DNIS from a call management or marketing application.

search engine — A software program that performs text searches.

seasonal affective disorder (SAD) — A type of depression some people experience when they do not receive enough natural light.

self-healing diagnostic software — Software that can diagnose problems, determine appropriate corrections, and complete the corrections without user interaction.

self-service — The initial troubleshooting that a customer attempts using knowledge or other support tools that a support group maintains.

service level agreement (SLA) — A formal, written definition of the services a support group will deliver, when and how they will deliver those services, the customer's role in providing information about problems, and how service is measured.

shareware software application — A program written by an independent programmer and distributed free with the understanding that users may need or want to pay for it after a specified trial period.

shortcut key — A key or combination of keys that replaces several separate steps to automate a task.

Simple Mail Transfer Protocol (SMTP) — A set of rules for sending e-mail.

Simple Network Management Protocol (SNMP) — A set of standards for communication with devices connected to a TCP/IP network.

skills-based routing — An ACD feature that matches the requirements of an incoming call to the skill sets of available analysts or analyst groups.

software change management — The process computer software developers use to prioritize, manage, and control software changes, especially when many programmers are working on many computer programs.

software piracy — The act of illegally copying or using software.

speech synthesis — Translates written text to audio sounds.

status — The condition or state of a call record as it progresses through the problem management process.

stop file — A list of noise words in a text retrieval system.

structured data — Numbers and text that fit in separate fields in databases.

subject matter expert (SME) — Members of level two or level three support with a greater amount of experience or knowledge about a particular subject than level one support.

summary report — A report that contains only calculations about many records.

support environment — The collection of customers that a support group assists, the tasks customers need or want to complete, the technologies those customers and support staff use to complete tasks, and the experience and skill of the support staff.

support group — The department within a company that focuses on product support or other support services; also known as support organizations, support businesses, call centers, help desks, and contact centers.

support resources — The company employees who provide support services; also known as support staff, support employees, support analysts, and support professionals.

system availability — The comparison of the time it took to repair a failure to the time the system was accessible before the failure.

system management software — Software that monitors transactions and errors on a single piece of hardware.

systems management — The process of protecting the integrity of business applications, the company's data, and the technology assets that connect those applications and data.

tab order — The sequence in which the cursor advances from field to field when the Tab key is pressed.

technical skills — Basic computer literacy and experience with specific hardware or software.

technology — The development of new materials, equipment, and processes to improve goods and service production.

telecommuting — The practice of connecting a computer to a business's network through a modem.

Telephone Services Application Programming Interface (TSAPI) — The telephony interface used on Novell networks.

Telephony Application Programming Interface (TAPI) — A Microsoft Windows program interface between PCs and telephone-based communication.

text base — A database of text files that are indexed for rapid retrieval.

threshold — A starting boundary.

tools — The equipment, processes, or software that are necessary to perform a task or that assist someone in practicing a profession.

topology — A graphical representation of the network nodes and the links between them.

total cost of ownership (TCO) — The initial cost of hardware and software, and the cost of installation, user training and support, upgrades, and repairs.

Transmission Control Protocol (TCP) — A set of rules that controls data in the form of message units sent between computers over the Internet.

troubleshooting log — The chronological sequence of the activities the support staff performed to solve the problem.

trunk lines — Physical telephone lines.

unstructured data — Documents, presentations, or graphs that don't fit neatly into rows and columns of a database.

Usenet — A collection of notes on various subjects that are posted to servers on a worldwide network.

user interface — The portion of the software with which the user interacts.

very important person (VIP) — Someone who performs a special role in the company.

viruses — Software that produces undesirable and damaging events.

voice mail — The business term for sending, storing, and retrieving audio messages, similar to a telephone answering machine.

voice net — Another term for a telephone system.

voice over IP (VoIP) — Voice data delivered over the Internet.

warranty — A written guarantee of the integrity of a product and of the maker's responsibility for the repair or replacement of defective parts.

weight — During text retrieval, a document's importance based on the number of times keywords or combinations of keywords appear in a document.

white noise — Sound that contains every frequency within the range of human hearing.

workflow — A flowchart that describes the movement of data and the transfer of control in a business process.

workgroup — A team of people who work together on a project.

workspace — The furniture, equipment, and tools necessary for an employee to complete assigned tasks as well as the physical arrangement of these items and the space they occupy.

workstation — The computer, keyboard, mouse, processor, monitor, and all required software necessary to complete assigned tasks

INDEX